What Catholics Need to Know about Islam

WILLIAM KILPATRICK

WHAT CATHOLICS NEED TO KNOW

ABOUT

ISLAM

Manchester, New Hampshire

Crisis Publications
Box 5284, Manchester, NH 03108
1-800-888-9344

www.CrisisMagazine.com

Paperback ISBN 978-1-64413-214-2
eBook ISBN 978-1-64413-215-9
Library of Congress Control Number: 2020938852

First printing

Contents

Introduction

What You Don't Know

What you don't know won't hurt you. That's how the old saying goes. But what you don't know about Islam can hurt you quite a bit.

Not long ago, I came across an article in *Forbes* titled "Why Pakistan Should Be on Every Solo Female Traveler's Bucket List." The article was accompanied by a photo of a young woman hiking alone in a barren mountain region. Now, maybe *Forbes* knows what it's talking about when it gives financial advice, but you'd do well to ignore its travel advice.

Pakistan is a 97 percent Muslim nation, and most of the population subscribe to a strict, fundamentalist brand of Islam. Single, non-Muslim women who venture out alone are simply not safe. Every year, around one thousand women and young girls from religious minorities are kidnapped, forced to convert to Islam, and made to marry their kidnappers. Raymond Ibrahim, a historian who keeps track of Christian persecution, reports that a Christian woman was shot and killed by a Muslim man after she refused his proposal. The proposal went like this: "If you do not convert and marry me, you will die."

Even married Muslim women are not particularly safe. The same day I saw the *Forbes* piece, I ran across a story about a Pakistani man who cut off his wife's nose for not making tea. He was assisted in the deed by his brother and his cousin.

Later on in this book you can read about two young Scandinavian women who went hiking in the Atlas Mountains in Morocco in search of cultural diversity and found out too late that diversity can be deadly.

They were no doubt influenced by the heavily whitewashed picture of Islam presented in European schools and universities.

Where, then, does one turn for reliable information about Islam? You might think that the Catholic Church would be a good source of knowledge. After all, Christendom has a 1,400-year history of resisting Islamic invasions.

Unfortunately, many of today's Catholic leaders are no more reliable than *Forbes* when it comes to offering accurate information about Islam. Ever since Vatican II, a great many bishops have held to a Pollyannaish view of Islam. I call it the common ground approach. The basic ground rule of the common ground approach is to emphasize the things that Christianity and Islam have in common and to ignore all the rest.

Thus, we are told that Muslims worship one God (just like us), revere Jesus (just like us), and honor Mary (just like us). Well, if all that is true, then why worry? When filtered through the rose-colored lenses of well-meaning Catholic bishops and theologians, Islam looks just like Catholicism. If that's the case, you can turn over and go back to sleep. Everything is under control. Or so it seems.

But when you look deeper, you find that most of the supposed similarities between Islam and Christianity are quite deceptive. You don't have to search through historical and theological tomes to see it. Just look at how Islam is practiced today in most Muslim majority nations. If Muslims and Christians share the same beliefs, why has the Saudi government threatened to arrest Christian tourists if they display a Bible in public? And if Muslims and Christians share similar values, as several prominent Catholics maintain, why is failure to make tea for your husband far riskier in Pakistan than in Pennsylvania?

The story about the two young Scandinavian women who went to Morocco and came back in coffins appears later in this book in an essay about Pope Francis. What, you might wonder, does Pope Francis have to do with the two ill-fated women? Well, nothing directly. But Pope Francis has been in the forefront of recent Catholic efforts to present all religions as roughly equal, and equally good. He has, in short, encouraged the kind of naïveté about Islam that led to the deaths of the two Scandinavians.

At the same time, the pope has encouraged mass Muslim migration into Europe. This means that Europeans no longer need to go to Morocco, or Pakistan, or Somalia to encounter the Islamic value system, because Pakistan, Morocco, and Somalia are coming to them

Nothing facilitates jihad like ignorance of Islam. And since there is so much ignorance, jihad has been spreading rapidly. But we don't seem to notice. We hear scattered reports about the persecution of Christians in Nigeria, Egypt, Pakistan, and Iran. We know or should know about the daily knife and vehicle attacks in Europe. Yet we are somehow sure that such things can't happen in America. But it is precisely our naïve nonchalance that practically guarantees that it will. Meanwhile, Church leaders do nothing to dispel the ignorance. While the Vatican deludes itself with talk of common ground, Islam continues to devour ground — both geographical and cultural.

Of course, it's not just Catholics who aren't facing up to unpleasant truths about Islam's spread. After thirty-six thousand deadly jihad attacks since 2001, complacency is still the order of the day. This complacency is due in large part to the fact that we underestimate the extent of jihad. That's because we never hear about the vast majority of jihad attacks, and also because we tend to quickly forget about the ones we have heard of. The threat is real, but our memory is short.

But maybe you're still not convinced that the threat is as extensive as I've suggested. So, to make the point, let me test your memory about some large-scale Islamic terror attacks that you might have forgotten. For instance, do you remember the first attack on the World Trade Center? For many of you, that's an easy question. But younger readers may be scratching their heads: "What first attack? There was only one, wasn't there?" Many members of the "woke" generation hadn't yet been born in 1993. That's when Islamic terrorists detonated a massive truck bomb in the parking garage underneath the North Tower. It blew a hundred-foot-wide hole through four sublevels of the building, sent smoke to the

93rd floor, and resulted in six deaths and more than a thousand injuries (many from smoke inhalation).

Now, let's make the questions a little more difficult. Do you remember the bombing of four commuter trains in Madrid? It happened in 2004 and resulted in 191 deaths and 1,800 injuries. It was big news at the time, but today's fast-spinning news cycle tends to drive old events quickly out of memory to make room for new ones.

How about the massacre in Beslan, Russia? Do you recall that? In 2004, thirty Muslim terrorists took over a large elementary school in Beslan. More than 330 people — many of them children — were left dead before the army finally dispatched the terrorists. At the time, it seemed like one of those heart-wrenching stories that one never forgets. But it's a good bet that, outside Russia, many have forgotten it.

Mumbai? The attack in Mumbai by a team of Muslim terrorists was a four-day siege that left 164 dead and 300 wounded. One of the main targets of the attack was the iconic Taj Mahal Palace Hotel, large sections of which could be seen on TV news engulfed in smoke and flames. If the attack on Mumbai is still fresh in your mind, perhaps it was recalled to your memory by the release of the film *Hotel Mumbai* in February 2018.

The Bataclan Theatre attack? The London tube and bus bombings? The Brussels Airport attack? All of these were large-scale attacks with massive casualties, yet you probably have to strain your memory to bring up even a dim recollection.

Now, for the sixty-four-thousand-dinar question. Do you remember the coup attempt on the government of Trinidad? No? Well, neither did I. I came across the story only recently, and then, with a little help from *Wikipedia*, it slowly came back to me. In 1990, 115 members of a radical Muslim organization took over the Parliament and the island's only television station. After six days, they finally surrendered to the army, but not before 24 people had been killed.

I bring up the Trinidad coup attempt because it demonstrates just how widespread jihad is and how long it has been going on. At this point,

I'm tempted to launch into a discussion of the several jihad attacks on beach resorts and tourist attractions. But I don't want to spoil your next vacation, and besides, violent jihad is not even the main problem.

The main focus of this book is not on armed jihad, but on another kind of jihad that is even more threatening. I call it "cultural jihad," but it's also referred to as "stealth jihad." This kind of jihad is more dangerous because it's more widespread and because most of us are hardly aware of its existence.

Cultural jihad is a long-term campaign to spread Islamic law and culture by influencing key cultural institutions such as media, political parties, schools, and churches. Take the influence operation that Arab states have been conducting on American universities. Since 2012, tiny Qatar has donated $376 million to Carnegie Mellon University, $351 million to Georgetown, $340 million to Northwestern University, $275 million to Texas A&M, $41 million to Virginia Commonwealth University, and lesser amounts to two dozen other major universities. Saudi Arabia has donated similar sums to more than sixty universities.

Why would Islamic donors give large sums of money to already wealthy American colleges? What do they hope to get out of it? Does the emir of Qatar hope that Harvard will name a building after him? Are Saudi princes hoping to get their sons into Princeton despite low test scores? Or are they, perhaps, trying to bribe the Mideast Studies Departments, the Islamic Studies Departments, and the History Departments to present Islam in a favorable light?

Of course, the politically correct answer to the last question is: "Bribes? That's ridiculous. Who ever heard of an American university accepting bribes?"

The reality is that there are hundreds of such influence operations reaching into all our major social institutions. Some of them aren't even very stealthy, because they don't have to be. Western citizens have learned to keep their heads down and not notice things. If you notice and make a fuss, that means you're an "Islamophobe." And that could mean big trouble.

Does cultural jihad stand a chance of transforming the culture? Well, here's an analogy. Ten years ago it didn't seem as if the LGBT movement had a chance of enforcing its nuttier notions. If six years ago, you were told that libraries all over the country would someday be sponsoring drag-queen story hours for kids, you wouldn't have believed it. Likewise, you wouldn't have believed it if you were told that doctors and professors would be fired for failing to address bearded men as "Miss."

But now we're all believers. All of a sudden, the drag queens are calling the shots. This is fairly amazing when you consider that the LGBT slice of the population is only about 2 percent, and the drag queen and bearded lassies segments are smaller still.

Muslims in America are less than 2 percent of the population, but they are backed by a worldwide Muslim population of 1.7 billion. They are also backed by the same powerful forces that back drag-queen story hours and boys in girls' locker rooms—namely media, academia, courts, big business, big tech, and prominent politicians. In addition, like the LGBT lobby in America, Muslim activists in the United States use the same successful tactics. At first, they say that they're simply civil rights groups whose only desire is for equal rights. They assure you that all they want is a place at the table. Then the demands ramp up, and if you don't go along with them, you are—depending on which group you're offending—either a homophobe or an "Islamophobe."

It almost seems as though the Islamists and the leftists have been—what's the word?—"colluding." In fact, a tacit alliance has long existed between Islamists and leftists in the West. And both groups have been highly successful in their efforts to hollow out the culture from within.

Many people are unaware of this alliance. And here we come back to the knowledge-gap problem. Curiosity, they say, killed the cat, but it is lack of curiosity about Islam that is killing the West. One can't entirely fault the average citizen for his incuriosity, however, because when it comes to Islam, the press gives him little to be curious about.

Take the plot to blow up the railroad bridge over the Niagara River gorge as a New York to Toronto passenger train crossed over it. What's that? You never heard of the plot to blow up the bridge over the Niagara River? That's strange. If successful, the plot would have resulted in hundreds of deaths. Luckily, it was foiled by the Royal Canadian Mounted Police and the FBI. But don't feel bad if you didn't know. Outside of New York, the plot got very little news coverage. Apparently, the media decided it wasn't important for you to know.

Even when it's forced to pay attention to a story, the media has ways of misleading its audience. How does the deception work? Well, in the case of spectacular terror attacks, the journalists do everything they can to blur the connection between the attack and Islam. They point out that the perpetrator didn't carry an official al-Qaeda membership card, or that he was mentally ill, or that the police haven't found a motive, and so forth. You can read more about these tactics in "Groundhog Day"—an essay that appears in the "Comic Interlude" section of this book. Why comic relief? Well, because all jihad and no play can spoil an otherwise good day. And so, just to be on the safe side, there are two comic interlude sections in the pages ahead. Read them as soon as you can because, as the Ayatollah Khomeini famously said, "There are no jokes in Islam." Indeed, the day may be coming when laughing at the wrong joke may land you in hot water—and not just in the figurative sense.

As I was saying, the media covers spectacular jihad attacks by deflecting your attention away from Islam and on to something else—such as a terrorist's troubled childhood or his attention deficit disorder. But how about unspectacular, run-of-the-mill jihad attacks? Well, it's here that we need to pay attention to our own attention deficit disorder. Unless the attack takes place two blocks from the office of a major news outlet, the preferred method is not to cover it at all. Sometimes, this even happens with spectacular attacks. Later on you'll come across a piece entitled "Do Italian Lives Matter?" It's about a Muslim school-bus driver in Italy who hijacked the school bus he was driving and set it on fire with fifty children inside. In case you missed it (and you probably did), that happened on March 20, 2019. It was a story that cried out for coverage, but the American media barely touched it. Luckily, the police got there in time and the children all survived, but one wonders whether our culture will survive the massive suppression of bad news about Islam. In Europe, where the art of concealing the truth is far advanced, some observers say that an irreversible process of Islamization has already set in on large parts of the Continent.

Meanwhile, the Church hierarchy has also been doing its part in covering up for Islam. Pope Francis frequently says that we should be building bridges, not walls. But, metaphorically speaking, the Vatican has built a massive protective wall around Islam. The wall serves a dual purpose. On the one hand, it protects Islam from criticism, and, on the other, it prevents Catholics from seeing the darker aspects of the Mohammedan faith.

We are now seeing the resurrection of Islam as a great and dangerous power. But instead of taking this as a signal to prepare for spiritual and cultural war, many in the Church have taken it as an opportunity to display their tolerance, and to invite Islam ever deeper into the fabric of our culture—a culture that was shaped in large part by Christianity.

The current crop of Church leaders has shown an excessive tolerance not only toward Islam, but also toward the world, the flesh, and sometimes, it seems, even toward the devil. As a result, the Church now finds itself in a greatly weakened position. Meanwhile, Islam goes from strength to strength, and from one cultural victory to another.

That can all change, of course. The Church is still the greatest spiritual power in the world. As it did in the past, it can once again lead the resistance to Islam's totalitarian incursions. This time around, however, it won't be accomplished by raising armies and navies, but by remembering the words of Christ: "The truth shall set you free" (John 8:32, KJV). Church leaders and ordinary Catholics need to start telling the truth about Islam and its enablers in the West. That is the first step in the cultural reconquest that lies ahead of us, but it's a big first step—and one that we can't afford to delay.

1

Wake-Up Calls

We all need to educate ourselves about Islam. We also need to remember the things we have forgotten. When the alarm bells sound, we can no longer afford to hit the snooze button and go back to dreaming dreams of multicultural harmony.

Will Sri Lanka Be a Wake-up Call for the West?

I haven't yet seen *Hotel Mumbai*, but I was surprised to learn of its U.S. release in March 2019. The surprise was on two counts: first, that anyone had dared to make a movie that depicts Muslims as terrorists, and, second, that the terrorists hadn't been transformed, for politically correct reasons, into white supremacists from rural Virginia.

The story certainly merits big-screen treatment. In November 2008, ten heavily armed members of an Islamic terrorist organization laid siege for four days to the Indian city of Mumbai. Their most iconic target was the majestic Taj Mahal Palace Hotel which could be seen on televised news reports with smoke billowing from its upper floors. Altogether, 164 people were killed and 300 wounded.

I remember thinking at the time that Mumbai would be a turning point. People would finally wake up and take decisive action to counter the ideology that led to the carnage in India's largest city. But I had thought the same thing after the London tube and bus bombings (2005), the bombings of four commuter trains in Madrid (2004), and the attack on an elementary school in Beslan, Russia, which left more than 330 dead (2004).

But here we are, twelve years after Mumbai, nineteen years after 9/11, and thirty-five thousand deadly Islamic terror attacks[1] in-between, and I don't think we've made any progress in understanding the threat.

---

[1] See the website What Makes Islam So Different?, https://thereligionof-peace.com/.

And that's the optimistic assessment. The truth is, we're not simply back where we were in 2001. We've regressed. Today's average college graduate has a poorer understanding of the enemy we face than his counterpart of eighteen years ago does. The "woke" generation is alert to every variety of "microaggression," but it seems oblivious to the most macro-aggressive force on the planet. That's because the politically correct crowd have now gained a much tighter control of the narrative. In the early days of the "war on terror," it was still permissible to say that our terrorist enemies were inspired by the more radical teachings of the prophet Muhammad. The forces of obfuscation had not yet shifted into high gear, and the term "Islamophobia" had not yet been turned into a club with which to beat Islamoskeptics into submission.

Although President Bush assured us that Islam is a religion of peace, it didn't seem so to many in America at the time. Indeed, Islam looked to be an aggressive religion, and it was still possible to say so without fear of being denied a public platform or of losing one's job. Since then, the narrative has shifted nearly 180 degrees. "Islamophobia," which initially seemed nothing more than a PR ploy, is now an ironclad doctrine. The slightest criticism of Islam brings swift retribution. When a guest on Fox News began to speculate that the fire at Notre Dame Cathedral might have been purposefully set, he was immediately shut down by host Shepard Smith. Likewise, when Catholic League president Bill Donohue began to speculate in the same direction, Neil Cavuto abruptly cut him off. The religion that must not be named is now setting the parameters of public discourse.

Muslims were once suspected of being aggressors, but they are now defended as victims—of "Islamophobia," hate crimes, discrimination, and worse. This narrative was bolstered on March 15, 2019, when a deranged white supremacist killed fifty Muslims in two mosques in New Zealand. From the month-long worldwide coverage, one would have thought that this was simply the worst example of a long campaign against mosques that must now finally be brought to an end.

But that is not the case. Attacks on mosques by non-Muslims are a rarity. The New Zealand attack was essentially a one-off, not part of a pattern. Meanwhile, a very obvious pattern of attacks on Christian churches by Muslims had been unfolding for years. But, by and large, the media has refused to look at it.

The media has given only minimal attention to the hundreds of attacks on Christian churches in recent years in Nigeria, Egypt, and elsewhere.[2] Nor has it paid much attention to the hundreds of churches that have been vandalized, desecrated, and torched in France alone in 2018.[3] It wasn't until the fire at Notre Dame Cathedral that most Americans first learned of the string of attacks on French churches. And even then, they had to pay close attention. It was a brief mention of these church desecrations that caused Neil Cavuto to hang up on Bill Donohue lest viewers learn too much.

Of course, some Muslim attacks on Christians are so blatant that even the mainstream media can't ignore them. But the media can downplay them. Such was the case with the horrific attacks on three Christian churches and three luxury hotels in Sri Lanka on Easter Sunday by Muslim terrorists in 2019. As a number of columnists have observed, the mainstream media dragged a basketful of red herrings across the story in an effort to throw readers off the scent. Canadian author and commentator Mark Steyn pointed out that the lead sentence in *The Economist* was "It has been nearly ten years since the guns fell silent in Sri Lanka's civil war. But bloodshed returned with a vengeance."[4] A number of other news reports began with the same lead. If you didn't read beyond the lead, you'd think, "It's those darned Tamil Tigers again. Haven't they done enough damage?"

---

[2] William Kilpatrick, "The Mosque Attack in New Zealand and Its Consequences," *Crisis Magazine*, March 19, 2019, https://www.crisismagazine.com/2019/the-mosque-attack-in-new-zealand-and-its-consequences.

[3] Alessandra Nucci, "Notre Dame Isn't the only French Church Imperiled this Year," *Catholic World Report*, April 18, 201), https://www.catholicworldreport.com/2019/04/18/notre-dame-isnt-the-only-french-church-imperiled-this-year/.

[4] Mark Steyn, "Taqiyya for Ester," Steyn Online, April 22, 2019, https://www.steynonline.com/9317/taqiyya-for-easter.

In the meantime, several presidential candidates didn't think the story of the killing of hundreds of Christians in church was worth mentioning at all. The day after the bombings, CNN hosted a Town Hall for five Democrat candidates. Not a single one mentioned the horrific attacks.[5] Nor did the CNN anchors see fit even to raise the question. Jihad terror against Christians is, apparently, not a big issue for Democrats or for CNN.

What will it take to wake people up to the gravity and extent of the jihad threat? Will it take a more massive attack on the scale of Mumbai? Or more devastating attacks on churches and hotels like the ones that occurred in Sri Lanka?

We assume, of course, that at some point everyone will wake up, and decisive action will be taken. But that's not necessarily so. For some—in press rooms, in broadcast studios, in universities, and in government—it may well be that nothing will wake them up. In what Samuel Huntington called "the clash of civilizations,"[6] many have, in effect, already chosen sides. Their automatic defense of Islam is part of a worldview that is based on fear or dislike of Christianity and the West and on faith in diversity. They are so committed to this narrative that no evidence to the contrary will shake their faith. They may see some problems with Islam, but, like Walter Duranty, the *New York Times* correspondent who covered up Stalin's forced starvation of millions in Ukraine, they are willing to tell lies for the sake of an illusory future harmony.

If you are waiting for the mainstream media to wake up, you might be waiting for a long time. But where else shall we turn for guidance? There are some world leaders who seem to grasp the situation: Victor Orban, Sebastian Kurz, Matteo Salvini, Donald Trump, and others. But they are a minority. Many other world leaders, by contrast, seem clueless

5   Bonchi, "2020 Democrats Don't Mention Sri Lanka Islamist Attacks Once at CNN Town Hall," *Red State*, April 23, 2019, https://www.redstate.com/bonchie/2019/04/23/not-one-2020-democratic-candidate-mentioned-last-nights-cnn-town-hall/.

6   Samuel P. Huntington, *The Clash of Civilizations and the Remaking of the World Order* (New York, NY: Simon and Schuster, 1996).

about Islam. They continue to implement policies—such as increased immigration—that will lead to the deaths of their own cultures.

In times past, people could look to the Catholic Church for guidance regarding Islam. But not anymore. Amazingly, jihad terror seems to be a secondary issue for the Church. Even though the Church is one of the jihadists' main targets, the bishops' radar is focused elsewhere—on climate change, on the needs of the LGBT community, and, ironically, on "Islamophobia."

Indeed, some Church leaders are intent on portraying Islam as a beleaguered fellow faith. Many seem more interested in defending Islam from criticism than in defending Christians from violent attacks. Thus, key members of the hierarchy have consistently maintained that attacks carried out in the name of Allah have nothing to do with Islam, and Pope Francis has drawn a moral equivalence between Islam and Christianity on more than one occasion.

This policy betrays either a deep ignorance of Islam or a willingness to conceal the truth. If Church authorities are lying, they undoubtedly justify it to themselves as a "noble lie"—a lie told for the benefit of others. Perhaps they fear that the truth might provoke a "backlash" against Muslims that would set in motion a cycle of violence. Perhaps they hope to create a self-fulfilling prophecy whereby Muslims come to believe all the positive things said about their faith and strive to act accordingly. Or perhaps Church leaders fear that a frank discussion of Islam would only provoke more Islamic violence against Christians.

Whatever the reasons, the strategy of prevarication is not working. Church authorities continue to praise Islam as a religion of peace and justice, and Arab leaders applaud the pope for his defense of Islam, yet Muslim attacks on Christians keep escalating—not just in Iran, Nigeria, Egypt, Indonesia, the Philippines, and Sri Lanka but also in Europe.

Meanwhile, the odds for the backlash that secular and Church leaders fear are increasing. As it becomes more apparent that Church leaders won't tell the truth about the threat, and that the state won't protect them, more people will, unfortunately, be tempted to take matters into their own hands.

The point is, the current head-in-the-sand approach of pretending (or believing) that jihad has nothing to do with Islam serves only to fuel jihad. The repeated assurance that jihadists are a tiny minority who misunderstand their religion only guarantees that Christians will be unprepared for the next attack. They were certainly unprepared in Sri Lanka. As the archbishop of Colombo, Malcolm Ranjith, said: "It's very difficult and a very sad situation for all of us because we never expected such a thing to happen and especially on Easter Sunday."[7]

Especially not on Easter Sunday? If the archbishop had been acquainted with the activities of jihadists, he would have known that they *prefer* to attack churches on Christian holy days such as Easter, Palm Sunday, and Christmas, and he might have taken precautions. But in the current climate, simply taking precautions might be seen as an act of distrust toward one's Muslim neighbors. As Robert Spencer asks in a recent article, "Would it have been Islamophobic to have Sri Lankan churches guarded for Easter?"[8]

The doctrine of jihad—the belief that Muslims have a religious obligation to fight unbelievers—is subscribed to by a significant percentage of Muslims worldwide. It is solidly based in the Koran, the Hadith, and the Sira. Moreover, it is rooted in Islamic history. The history of Islam—a history with which today's non-Muslims are mostly unfamiliar—is largely a history of jihad. By one estimate,[9] up to eighty million people in India alone lost their lives to jihad over the centuries. Considering Sri Lanka's close proximity to India, it might be expected that the archbishop of Colombo would know some of this history. But the archbishop does not seem to be the inquiring type. Three days after the attack, he met with

---

[7] Robert Spencer, "The Sri Lanka Jihad Massacre and the Decline of the West," *FrontPage Mag*, April 22, 2019, https://www.frontpagemag.com/fpm/2019/04/sri-lanka-jihad-massacre-and-decline-west-robert-spencer/.

[8] Ibid.

[9] Mike Konrad, "The Greatest Murder Machine in History," *American Thinker*, May 31, 2014, https://www.americanthinker.com/articles/2014/05/the_greatest_murder_machine_in_history.html.

several Islamic ambassadors who assured him, he said, that the bombings had "no connection to Islam."[10]

Church leaders have rightly condemned white supremacists but seem not to have noticed that Islam is a supremacist religion that considers Muslims "the best of people" (Koran 3:110) and considers non-believers "the worst of creatures" (98:6). Unbelievers are also "unclean" (9:28), "ignorant" (6:111), "helpers of the devil" (4:76), like "cattle" (7:179), and, in the case of Jews who displeased Allah, "transformed into apes and swine" (5:60). Meanwhile, Islamic law books that are available on Amazon, and widely consulted for guidance, assert that the value of a Christian or Jew is one-third the value of a Muslim.

Since the same law books, together with the Koran, present jihad as the best deed a Muslim can perform, after believing in Allah and Muhammad, it should come as no surprise that jihad attacks are so frequent and widespread. There is even less reason to be surprised when we consider that jihadists are guaranteed immediate entrance to paradise and the company of seventy-two virgins.

Yet, like the archbishop of Colombo, people continue to be surprised. But, of course, archbishops and cardinals have less reason to be surprised than most. After all, religion is their territory.

At some future point—perhaps in as few as fifteen or twenty years—subjugated Christians in Europe and other parts of the Western world will wonder why no one had given them warning. Why, they will ask, hadn't previous generations learned the lessons provided by Mumbai, Madrid, London, Beslan, New York, Orlando, Paris, Nice, Brussels, Bali, Nigeria, Egypt, and Sri Lanka?

Catholics, especially, will wonder why their shepherds felt no obligation to inform them.

---

[10] Patrick Goodenough, "Sri Lanka Cardinal Says Muslim Envoys Assured Him Bombings Had No Connection to Islam," CNSNews, April 25, 2019, https://www.cnsnews.com/news/article/patrick-goodenough/sri-lanka-cardinal-says-muslim-envoys-assured-him-bombings-had-no.

Why You Should Worry about Virgins in Paradise

In the wake of Abdul Artan's car and knife attack at Ohio State University on November 28, 2016, which led to his own death and the injury of thirteen others, the usual questions are being asked: What was his motive? Did he have psychological problems? Will there be a backlash against the Muslim community?

But to those of us who suspect we already know the motive, the most pertinent question is the question of what can be done to defeat Islamic terrorism. The answer, according to many experts, is that you can't defeat jihad without first defeating the ideology behind it. We must, it is said, so thoroughly discredit and delegitimize that ideology that the enemy will cease to believe in it and therefore lose the will to fight.

So far, so good. That all makes sense. We should do everything we can to undermine the ideology that inspires ISIS, al-Qaeda, Hamas, Hezbollah, and the Amalgamated Brotherhood of Lone Wolves. So, what exactly is this ideology? Here, things become a bit murky. I've read a number of authors who've written about the subject, but most come up short on specifics. They seem to assume that calling the beast "radical Islamic terror" is sufficient.

The reason for the evasiveness is that the elusive ideology of the terrorists is strikingly similar to Islam itself. When terrorist leaders speak of their "ideology," they do so by citing the Koran and the commands of Allah. Here's a sampling:

> It is to this religion that we call you.... It is the religion of Jihad in the way of Allah, so that Allah's Word and religion reign Supreme. (Osama bin Laden, founder of al-Qaeda)[11]

> There is no doubt that Allah commanded us to strike the Kuffar (unbeliever), kill them and fight them by all means necessary. (Abu Musab al-Zarqawi, founder of al-Qaeda in Iraq, which later morphed into ISIS)[12]

> Support the religion of Allah through jihad in the path of Allah. Go forth, O mujahidin in the path of Allah. (Abu Bakr al-Baghdadi, founder of ISIS)[13]

Hmm. It seems that the ideology that motivates terrorists is a religious ideology. And what religion might that be? Here's where the religion-that-must-not-be-named syndrome kicks in. Say what awful things you want about al-Qaeda and ISIS; just don't say they have anything to do with Islam.

But how can you criticize the ideology of the Islamic State without also criticizing Islam? And if you can't criticize Islamic beliefs, how can you defeat the ideology of the Islamic State?

Criticize Islamic beliefs? The reason we don't want to go there is that many consider such criticism to be tantamount to declaring war on Islam. For example, intelligence expert Sebastian Gorka,[14] who makes

---

[11] "Bin Laden's Letter to America," *Guardian*, November 24, 2002, https://www.theguardian.com/world/2002/nov/24/theobserver.

[12] Robert Spencer, *The Complete Infidel's Guide to ISIS* (Washington, DC: Regnery Publishing, 2015), 28.

[13] Ibid.

[14] "Sebastian Gorka: How We Defeat the Global Jihad," *FrontPage Mag*, November 30, 2016, https://archives.frontpagemag.com/fpm/sebastian-gorka-how-we-defeat-global-jihad-frontpagemagcom/.

a very good case for waging ideological war against ISIS and other such groups, also insists that we are not at war with Islam. I understand the prudential reason for saying that. The vernacular expression of the rationale goes something like this: "Do you want to go to war with 1.6 billion Muslims?"

Still, if you can't criticize Islam, how can you defeat the ideology of the terrorists—an ideology that is inextricably bound up with Islam?

Gorka, along with others, says we should base our fight against terrorism on the Cold War model of our fight against communism. But in the Cold War, we didn't wage ideological war against "perversions" or "misunderstandings" of communism, but against mainstream communism itself. We didn't urge Russians and Eastern Europeans to practice a more moderate form of communism. We urged them to separate themselves altogether from that pernicious ideology. If we were to follow the Cold War model, we would indeed have to criticize Islam itself—or at least many aspects of it. It is faith in Islam, not faith in "violent extremism," that fuels jihad. Jihadists don't kill people for the hell of it. In fact, they do it to avoid hell, and to reap a heavenly reward.

This brings us back to the Ohio State jihadist. Last I heard, the authorities were still looking for a motive to explain why Abdul Ali Artan drove his car into a crowd of fellow students. Apparently, if you don't find an official ISIS photo ID in his wallet, there's just no way of telling. At the risk of sounding simplistic, let me advance a novel hypothesis. My guess is that a large part of Mr. Artan's motivation was the promise that several dozen virgins were anxiously awaiting his appearance in the afterlife. Oh, sure, I suppose he had other motives as well—anger over "Islamophobia," anger about all the Muslims who have been killed by American troops, and so on. But there are plenty of angry eighteen-year-olds, and the vast majority of them find ways to express their anger other than plowing their cars into pedestrians. On the other hand, the religion of Allah provides constructive things to do with your anger and frustrations. You can, as Mr. al-Zarqawi suggests, follow the command of Allah to "kill them [the unbelievers] and fight them by all means necessary." And you can be sure that you will be abundantly rewarded in a much happier life in the hereafter.

Are there other ways of claiming your reward? Yes, there are. But the only surefire method, according to Islamic tradition, is the one chosen by Artan. When Muhammad was asked by a companion if there were any deed that equaled jihad in heavenly reward, he replied "I do not find such a deed" (Bukhari 4.56.2785).

Did Artan leave any record of a desire to join the promised brides? Probably not. For some sensitive souls, some topics are just too delicate to be bandied about. Besides, as a cum laude graduate such as Artan would understand, it sounds much nobler to say you are doing this deed in "retribution"[15] for Muslim deaths than to say "I am doing this 'cause I want my seventy-two virgins."

There is, however, evidence from diaries, letters, posts, and interviews that the virgins are very much on the minds of jihadists and would-be jihadists. So, it makes sense that in order to defeat the ideology of jihad you should train your ideological weapons on that adolescent fantasy and blast it to smithereens. Take away the virgins, and you take away one of the chief incentives for jihad.

But do you really want to go there? It just so happens that this particular fantasy is shared by the vast majority of Muslim males. It's part of their religion. Here we come back to the general reluctance to criticize Islam. Part of that reluctance, as I've said, stems from the fear that criticism will precipitate World War III. The other reason for the reluctance is the (largely secular) notion that religion is a private matter between an individual and his God, and therefore it's none of our business what another person believes.

That, of course, is sheer nonsense, and especially in regard to Islam. Islam is a very public religion that aims to regulate every aspect of a

---

[15] Robert Spencer, "OSU Jihadi: 'By Allah, I Am Willing to Kill a Billion Infidels,'" *Jihad Watch*, November 28, 2016, https://www.jihadwatch.org/2016/11/osu-jihadi-by-allah-i-am-willing-to-kill-a-billion-infidels.

Muslim's life down to how he should wash his hands. Moreover, Islam is an expansionist religion that seeks dominance over all other cultures and religions—by force, if necessary. It's not exactly a private matter when a Muslim warrior takes a sex-slave in Mosul, or detonates explosives at a Boston marathon, or plows his car into a campus crowd. Islam doesn't consider itself to be a private religion, and neither should you. You have a personal stake in what Muslims believe, just as Poles, Hungarians, and East Germans had a personal stake in what communists believed.

Some say that Islam is a political ideology, some say that it is a religion, and some say that it is a mixture of both. But from one perspective, it doesn't really matter. Islam is a belief system, and since those beliefs can have dire consequences for nonbelievers, they ought to be subject to public examination and criticism. There is certainly a risk in doing so, but it's difficult to imagine anything riskier than the current policy of see-no-Islam. Ideological cold wars do not always lead to hot wars. The West's Cold War victory over the Soviet Bloc seems to have prevented one. On the other hand, our reluctance to engage the more problematic aspects of Islamic thought only ensures that more young men like Abdul Artan will be attracted to them. Jihad is accelerating, but our ideological war against it is stuck in first gear.

2

Appeasement

Despite innumerable wake-up calls over the last two decades, the Western world has responded to Islamic intimidation not with greater resolve but with abject appeasement. As history shows, that serves only to provoke further aggression.

On the Civilizational Struggle with Islam

In February 2017, female members of an official Swedish delegation to Iran[16] donned headscarves and long coats so as not to offend their Iranian counterparts. At about the same time, Marine Le Pen,[17] the leader of France's National Rally Party, canceled a meeting with Lebanon's grand mufti after he insisted that she wear a headscarf. "You can pass on my respects to the grand mufti," said Le Pen, "but I will not cover myself up."[18]

The contrast neatly captures two different responses to the ongoing Islamization of Europe. Le Pen represents resistance, and the Swedish delegation represents appeasement. So far, the party of appeasement holds the upper hand. Shortly after Le Pen's gesture of defiance, the European Parliament voted to lift her immunity from prosecution (as a member of Parliament) for tweeting images of Islamic State violence.[19]

---

[16] Andrew Stuttaford, "Iran: Sweden's 'Feminist' Government Submits," *National Review*, February 17, 2017, https://www.nationalreview.com/corner/iran-swedens-feminist-government-submits/.

[17] Soeren Kern, "A Month of Islam and Multiculturalism in France: February 2017," Gatestone Institute, March 18, 2017, https://www.gatestoneinstitute.org/10062/france-islam-multiculturalism-february.

[18] Simon Carraud, "France's Le Pen Cancels Meet with Lebanon Grand Mufti Over Headscarf," Reuters, February 21, 2017, https://www.reuters.com/article/us-france-election-lepen-idUSKBN1600R6.

[19] Robert Spencer, "EU Parliament Lifts Immunity from Prosecution for Le Pen for Tweeting Images of Islamic State Violence," *Jihad Watch*, March 3, 2017, https://www.jihadwatch.org/2017/03/eu-parliament-lifts-

Like the Swedish delegates' gesture of obeisance, this too is an act of appeasement. It signals to the Muslim world that Europeans will take it upon themselves to punish those who criticize Islam.

There may be cases in which appeasement works to placate an enemy, but it never seems to work against an implacable foe. In May 1938, while competing in Berlin, the English national football team[20] gave the Nazi salute when the German national anthem was played. They did this, reluctantly, on orders from their own foreign office. It was one of numerous futile gestures of appeasement offered to Hitler.

Some historians have suggested that Hitler could have been stopped if the Allied Powers had confronted him earlier, before he had time to build up the Wehrmacht. That's probably true. The best time to fight a war is while you still have a good chance of winning it. This applies also to the ideological struggle going on between the West and Islam. Of course, "struggle" might not be the best way to describe a conflict in which only one side is fighting. Indeed, Western authorities often join in Islam's war against the West. By passing laws against "Islamophobia" (as in Canada) and by prosecuting critics of Islam (as in Europe), the West is strengthening the hand of its foe.

Instead of appeasement, what is needed is an ideological counterattack. And the best time to launch it is now—while it is still possible to make one's case without being fined or jailed. Now is the right time from another perspective as well. The sheer volume of Islamic violence is difficult to ignore. As a result, more and more people now realize that criticism and challenge of Islam is fully justified. They realize that it should be Muslims who are put on the defensive, not the so-called Islamophobes.

Imagine if Catholics were committing violence on the same scale as Muslims, and doing it in the name of Jesus. Would the Catholic Church be afforded the kind of kid-glove treatment now given to Islam? Would

immunity-from-prosecution-for-le-pen-for-tweeting-images-of-islamic-state-violence.

20 Stuttaford, "Iran: Sweden's 'Feminist' Government Submits."

Catholic clergy be let off the hook for the crimes of tens of thousands of Catholics who cited Catholicism as their motive? Not likely. The Catholic Church would be put on the defensive—and rightly so if, indeed, the Church had a well-developed doctrine of jihad, as does Islam.

In a sane society, Islam and its representatives, not critics of Islam, would be put on the defensive. Instead of exonerating Islam of responsibility for Islamic terror, non-Muslims should pressure Muslims to justify the tenets of Islam that call for violence. Islamic authorities should be pushed back on their heels and kept there.

Just as non-Muslims can no longer deny the immensity of Islamic violence, neither can Muslims. Yet, absent any outside pressure, they can ignore it. This is a good time for Muslims to do some soul-searching about the beliefs that, in the words of Egyptian president Abdel Fattah el-Sisi, "make the entire *umma* [Muslim community] a source of concern, danger, killing and destruction for the whole world."[21] But if no one (with a few exceptions, such as Sisi) asks them to question themselves, whatever doubts Muslims may have about their faith will be brushed aside. If Western leaders persist in lauding Islam as a great religion, it will be taken as confirmation that Islam is indeed the supreme religion that the imams say it is.

Muslims won't attempt to reform Islam unless they believe there is something wrong with it. If we want to see reform, we need to drop the "great faith" pretense and confront Muslims with the troubling realities of their beliefs. Now is the time to put Islam on the defensive because the window of opportunity for doing so will soon close. It is already dangerous to question or challenge the Islamic belief system. The time is coming when it will be supremely dangerous to do so.

Right now, the West is worried about the danger of provoking Islam. But there is a greater danger. By refusing to confront and challenge

---

[21] Daniel Pipes, "Sisi and the Reform of Islam," *National Review*, January 19, 2015, https://www.nationalreview.com/2015/01/sisi-and-reform-islam-daniel-pipes/.

Islam's ideology, we allow an already confident Islam to grow stronger and more confident—two characteristics that make it all the more attractive to lukewarm Muslims and potential converts. The West's walking-on-eggshells strategy is aimed at preventing a confrontation with Islam, but it may serve only to delay a confrontation to a point when the West is too weak to stand up to Islam.

The West will continue to have the military edge for a good time to come, but possessing weapons is one thing, and possessing the will to use them is another thing altogether. The West is strong militarily but weak ideologically. It lacks civilizational confidence. It is not sure if it has anything worth defending. While Islamic countries have been busy raising a generation of devout warriors, the West has raised a generation of social justice warriors who are convinced that their own civilization deserves to be eliminated.

Conviction and confidence are potent weapons. Soldiers need them, but so do civilians. They need them all the more today because much of the campaign against the non-Muslim world is being conducted on the civilian level—through stealth jihad and lone-wolf terrorism. If that twin-pronged campaign is successful, war may not be necessary. Western citizens will simply go quietly into the long night of dhimmitude.

It's a loss of civilizational confidence that causes the West to crumple whenever Muslims press for another concession. Burqas in public? Well, OK. Muslim prayer rooms in public schools? It would be insensitive not to allow it. Laws to prevent criticism of Islam? That's only reasonable. Polygamy? If you insist. Taken one by one, these mini conquests are not decisive, but cumulatively they work to remake the culture. And one day you wake up to realize that it's too late to do anything about it.

In a way, this culture war with Islam is more difficult to fight than a battlefield war. The whole direction of our culture in recent decades presses us to yield to the multicultural other and to assume that, in any dispute, he is right and we are wrong. If Islam's cultural jihad is to be halted, that mindset must be rejected, and Islam must be put on the defensive. Apostasy laws. Blasphemy laws. Cruel and unusual punishments. Harsh discrimination against women. Child marriage. There's something very wrong here. And Muslims should be made to know it and made to feel ashamed of it. We should want Muslims to be uncomfortable with their faith—uncomfortable to the point that they begin to doubt it. As Mark Steyn put it, "There is no market for a faith that has no faith in itself."[22]

The reason that the apostasy laws and the blasphemy laws are there in the first place is because Islam is a fragile belief system. It rests on the uncorroborated testimony of one man. The system cannot stand up to questioning, and thus, questioning is not allowed. The West should take advantage of this fragility and raise the questions Muslims will not ask of themselves. Why don't we? Is it out of respect for another religion? Yes, there's some of that, but increasingly, it seems, we remain silent simply out of fear. We fear that ideological war will lead to real war. But it's worth remembering that in the 1930s a similar reluctance to challenge a similar ideology did not prevent war. On the contrary, the reluctance to face up to Nazi ideology only guaranteed that war would come.

A 2017 analysis by the Middle East Media Research Institute (MEMRI) concluded that the Trump administration's get-tough policy showed a pacifying effect on Iran. After its failed missile launch on January 29, 2017, Iran was "put on notice" by the administration. According to the MEMRI analysis, the effect on Iran was almost immediate: "a halt to long-range missile tests," "a halt to provocations against US Navy vessels," "a halt to public threats to burn and sink U.S. Navy vessels in the Persian Gulf," and "a near total moratorium on hostile anti-U.S. statements" such as the slogan "death to America."[23]

The get-tough attitude seems to have—temporarily at least—made Iran less belligerent, not more. Could a get-tough attitude improve our chances of winning the civilizational struggle with Islam? Perhaps some

---

22 Mark Steyn, *America Alone: The End of the World As We Know It* (Washington, DC: Regnery Publishing, 2006), 96.

23 P. David Hornik, "Report: Iran Already Intimidated by Trump," *Front-Page Mag*, March, 23, 2017, https://archives.frontpagemag.com/fpm/report-iran-already-intimidated-trump-p-david-hornik/.

of the slogans that apply to real war also apply to ideological war: "weakness is provocative," "if you want peace, prepare for war," and, as Osama bin Laden said, "when people see a strong horse and a weak horse, by nature they will like the strong horse."

One of the chief reasons for waging a war of ideas is to avoid real war. The Cold War was in large part an ideological war. And Western success in establishing the superiority of its ideas and beliefs did much to prevent the Cold War from turning into a hot war. The Cold War analogy, by the way, is not a stretch. The communists pursued their objective with a religious fervor worthy of today's Islamists. Indeed, the chief twentieth-century exponents of jihad, such as Sayyid Qutb (1906–1966) and Maulana Maududi (1903–1979), borrowed heavily from the Marxist-Leninist playbook. Though they rejected the atheism, they found the idea of an all-encompassing state to be very much in line with the goals of Islam. Like communism and Nazism, Islam is meant to be a system of total control. Keep that in mind the next time a priest or politician declares his solidarity with the Muslim faith. Don't let the fact that Islam is a religion keep you from realizing that it is also an ideological opponent every bit as oppressive and determined as were the Nazis and the Soviet communists.

One more thing. The point of ideological warfare is not only to cast doubts in the mind of the enemy but also to convince your own citizens that they possess a valuable heritage worth defending. To a large extent, that conviction has been lost in the West. And no amount of armaments can replace it. If it ever comes to actual war or to daily attacks by lone wolves, or to a combination of both, Western citizens had better know what they believe, why they believe it, and why it is worth defending. Islam has a mission. We must have one too.

The Corrosion of the British Spirit

If you've seen *Dunkirk* (2017), or *Darkest Hour* (2017), you got a glimpse of Britain's fighting spirit in the face of great peril. If you know a little bit more about that period, you know why Churchill could say of the British people, "This was their finest hour."

You could hardly say that now. With a few notable exceptions, Britain's spirit of resistance is at a low ebb. The middle and lower classes grudgingly submit to the dictates of the elites, and the elites willingly submit to the Islamization of their country.

Though the British people successfully stood up to Hitler's planned invasion of England, they have essentially bowed down before the Islamic invasion of the British Isles. What Hitler failed to accomplish with force of arms, Muslim migrants are accomplishing through migration. With the help of British authorities, they are gradually but inexorably imposing an alien moral code on the United Kingdom.

The most glaring example of this submissive attitude is the tepid response to the Muslim mass-rape gang attacks in towns and cities across England. Actually, "tepid" is too strong a word. "Nonresponse" is more accurate. Although authorities knew who was responsible for the rapes, they took no action. In some towns, the crimes were ignored for decades.

You may have heard of Rotherham, a town of about 250,000 where some 1,400 girls, ages eleven to fourteen, had been drugged, raped, and trafficked for years by Pakistani gangs. The authorities—city council members, the police, child protection agencies—knew about the rapes but kept silent.

The shame of Rotherham was finally brought to light in 2013.[24] The news quickly made its way around England, and if you were paying attention, you might have noted its brief appearance in American papers. But have you heard about Telford? Telford is a scenic town of about 150,000, in the Midlands of England. On March 11, 2018, the *Sunday Mirror* reported that Telford was "Britain's 'worst ever' child grooming scandal."[25] Beginning in the 1980s, as many as a thousand underage girls have been raped, beaten, sold for sex, and some even murdered. As in Rotherham, town officials covered up the abuse for decades—and for the same reason. They were afraid of being called "racist" or "Islamophobic."

Unfortunately, the rape epidemic is not confined to Rotherham and Telford. According to one reporter, it has spread to "Bristol, Derby, Rochdale, Peterborough, Newcastle, Oxfordshire, Bradford, Keighly, Banbury, Halifax, Leeds, Birmingham, Norwich, Burney, High Wycombe, Dewsbury and Middleborough."[26] That's "among other places." One of the other places is London.

In Mayor Sadiq Khan's first year in office (2016),[27] homicides in London rose by 27 percent, youth homicide jumped by 70 percent, rape increased by 18 percent to 7,600 reported cases, and child sex crimes

---

[24] Independent Inquiry into Child Sexual Exploitation in Rotherham (1997–2013), Rotherham Metropolitan Borough Council, https://www.rotherham.gov.uk/downloads/download/31/independent-inquiry-into-child-sexual-exploitation-in-rotherham-1997---2013.

[25] Nick Sommerlad and Geraldine McKelvie, "Britain's 'Worst Ever' Child Grooming Scandal Exposed: Hundreds of Young Girls Raped, Beaten, Sold for Sex And Some Even KILLED," *Mirror*, March 12, 2018, https://www.mirror.co.uk/news/uk-news/britains-worst-ever-child-grooming-12165527.

[26] Tom Quiggin, "Is the United Kingdom an Islamist Colony?" Gatestone Institute, March 22, 2018, https://www.gatestoneinstitute.org/12049/britain-islamist-colony.

[27] Raheem Kassam, "Sadiq's London: Knife Crime, Gun Crime, Theft, Burglary, Rape, Homicide all Massively Up," *Breitbart*, January 2, 2018, https://www.breitbart.com/europe/2018/01/02/sadiqs-london-knife-crime-gun-crime-theft-burglary-rape-homicide-massively/.

soared by 30 percent to 1,200 per year. London also has the most acid attacks per capita of any other city in the world.[28]

When I was younger, it was common to hear that London was one of the safest cities in the world—a place where women could walk alone at night, and police didn't have to carry guns. It was often compared favorably with crime-ridden New York City. In 2018, however, London overtook New York City as one of the most dangerous capital cities in the Western World.

What happened in London to effect such a reversal? For that matter, what happened in Yorkshire, Oxfordshire, Derbyshire, Shropshire, and all the other peaceful shires of England's green and pleasant land?

Was it the Orcs? Judging by their Herculean efforts to cover up the truth, the press and the authorities might well have preferred that you believe that. What happened, of course, was Muslim migration buttressed by high Muslim birth rates.

Still, there's more to the story than the arrival of Muslims in Britain. It's more complicated than that. Let's go back to the 1940s for a moment. Churchill was England's greatest leader, but another Englishman may well have been its greatest prophet. In 1948, George Orwell (1903–1950) wrote the classic dystopian novel *1984*.[29] It's a mistake to think of the book as simply a prediction of bad things to come, because Orwell meant it to be a commentary on bad things that were already happening (in the Soviet Bloc) or had already happened (in Nazi Germany). Orwell also saw something in the England of his day that disturbed him. Partly because of the centralization and bureaucratization required by the war effort, Britain was already on the path to socialism. Orwell favored democratic socialism but also realized that socialism had ominous potentials. After all, the totalitarian political party he describes in *1984* is called Ingsoc—short for "English Socialism."

---

[28] Hugo Gye, "NO-GO ZONE London Is the Acid Capital of the World and Has Areas Where Drivers Won't Work Because There Are So Many Attacks," *Sun*, December 20, 2017, https://www.thesun.co.uk/news/5183470/london-is-the-acid-capital-of-the-world-and-has-areas-where-drivers-wont-work-because-there-are-so-many-attacks/.

[29] George Orwell, *1984* (London: Secker & Warburg, 1949).

Modern England's governing institutions are not nearly as brutal as Ingsoc, but they do share some of its characteristics—particularly the desire to control information. For example, the Telford police didn't refer to the rape-gang members as Pakistanis or Muslims but simply as "Asians."[30] The BBC didn't report on the Telford crimes for thirty-six hours after the news broke and then offered only a short spot on BBC Radio Shropshire (the German media maintained a similar silence after the mass sex assaults in Cologne).[31] Moreover, as in *1984*, English authorities pursue thought crimes ("hate crimes" in modern parlance) as vigorously as they pursue real crimes. For example, in the midst of London's crime spree, the London police have designated nine hundred special investigators to investigate—what else?—hate crimes.[32] Ironically, the main target of these hate investigations are people on Facebook or other social media who criticize Islam and immigration. In England, child rape and acid attacks are just the price society pays for its vibrant diversity, but speaking your mind on Facebook is a hate crime. What Naz Shah, a female Labour Member of Parliament, advised the Rotherham rape victims reflects the attitude of the elites toward the rest of British society: she said the girls should "shut their mouths for the good of diversity."[33]

There is another similarity between the Britain of today and the Ingsoc of *1984*. Totalitarian societies specialize in humiliations both small and large. The humiliations are designed to demoralize citizens and break their will to resist. This seems to be happening now in Britain. Rape is an act of subjugation and humiliation, and if nothing is done about it, the humiliation turns into a corrosive demoralization. If it happens on a mass scale—as in Britain today—and if the authorities become complicit, then the whole

---

[30] Sommerlad and McKelvie, "Britain's 'Worst Ever' Child Grooming Scandal Exposed."

[31] Mark Steyn, "Of the Remenant Nedeth Nat Enquire," Steyn Online, March 19, 2018, https://www.steynonline.com/8528/of-the-remenant-nedeth-nat-enquere.

[32] Quiggin, "Is the United Kingdom an Islamist Colony?"

[33] Ibid.

society is demoralized. If, on top of that, those who complain about the outrages are silenced and even jailed, the humiliation is complete.

None of this bodes well for Britain's future. As Mark Steyn puts it, "a society that will not defend its youngest and most vulnerable girls is surely capable of rationalizing many more wicked accommodations in the years ahead."[34] One might ask, "How many more accommodations can Britain afford to make?" Thanks to the efforts of British Islamist organizations and the cowardly appeasement of British officialdom, the will to resist is being slowly crushed.

Still, we shouldn't write off Britain completely. Despite its decline, it's not beyond hope. Britons do have a proud and courageous history to draw from. All the odds are against them now, but that was also the case in 1940. At the time Churchill took office, the situation seemed so desperate that much of the government was prepared to capitulate to Hitler. Yet, against all odds, Britain prevailed.

Then, too, Britain has a Christian heritage. And historically, Christianity has been Europe's strongest bulwark against Islamization. That heritage has been squandered to the point where it is almost lost. But a revival of Christianity should not be discounted. Even atheists are beginning to recognize the vital role that Christianity plays. At a recent appearance in England, Richard Dawkins warned against celebrating the demise of Christianity "in so far as Christianity might be a bulwark against something worse."[35] Christian civilization was already in decline at the time of Churchill's speech, but he recognized that it was key to revitalizing the British spirit. Britons today would do well to go back to his speeches. Here's a sample:

> The battle of Britain is about to begin. Upon this battle depends the survival of Christian civilization. Upon it depends our own

---

[34] Steyn, "Of the Remenant Nedeth Nat Enquire."

[35] Robert Spencer, "Atheist Richard Dawkins Warns Against Celebrating Demise of 'Relatively Benign' Christianity in Europe," *Jihad Watch*, March 25, 2018, https://www.jihadwatch.org/2018/03/atheist-richard-dawkins-warns-against-celebrating-demise-of-relatively-benign-christianity-in-europe.

British life, and the long continuity of our institutions and our Empire.... Let us therefore brace ourselves to our duties, and so bear ourselves, that if the British Empire and its Commonwealth last for a thousand years, men will say, "This was their finest hour."[36]

Of course, the situation is different today. It's both better and worse. Islamists in Britain have nothing like the might of Hitler's armed forces. They must rely instead on incremental cultural warfare. That gives the British much more time than they had in 1940. On the other hand, Britain today is sorely lacking in cultural confidence. Multiculturalism and political correctness have sapped its ability to fight a culture war. Moreover, this time around, the enemy is not on the other side of the Channel. Islamist ideology is already entrenched within Britain's borders, and its proponents are aided and abetted by Britain's weak leadership and generously funded by its welfare system.

How about the United States? Americans may think that all of this has nothing to do with them. But what is happening in Britain is happening here also: the suppression of news, the accusations of "hate crimes," the cover-ups, and the shackling of free speech in the name of sensitivity and political correctness. If today's battle of Britain is lost, and along with it the battle for France, and Germany, and the rest of the European continent, America will be very much alone. And its erratic resistance to Islamization will seem all the more futile. Churchill spoke of America in his 1940 speech, and what he said then applies today:

But if we fail, then the whole world, including the United States, including all that we have known and cared for, will sink into the abyss of a new dark age made more sinister, and perhaps more protracted, by the lights of perverted science.[37]

---

[36] Winston Churchill, "Finest Hour" (speech delivered to the House of Commons, London, UK, June 18, 1940), EmersonKent.com, http://www.emersonkent.com/speeches/finest_hour.htm.

[37] Ibid.

3

Stealth Jihad

In the face of an imminent and obvious danger, many will rise to meet the challenge, as did the British when threatened by a Nazi invasion. But a threat that's difficult to detect is also difficult to resist. In the United States and in much of the Western world, the chief danger from Islam comes not in the form of armed jihad but in the form of stealth jihad—the jihad that never sleeps.

Western Self-Hatred Makes Jihad Possible

It's often said that we are engaged in an ideological struggle with radical Islam—a clash of civilizations. But what exactly does that mean?

Ideological warfare is, in its most basic sense, a war of ideas. Of course, it's not advisable to engage in pitched intellectual warfare with every group with which you disagree. As Jefferson said, "It does me no injury for my neighbor to say there are twenty gods or no god. It neither picks my pocket nor breaks my leg."[38] On the other hand, if your neighbor's religious or political beliefs do encourage him to break your leg, then it makes perfect sense to try to disabuse him of his beliefs.

The Cold War was, in part, a war of ideas. It was necessary to fight it because it was one of those cases in which the other side's ideology encouraged them to break your leg—or, as Soviet premier Nikita Khrushchev put it, "We will bury you." On top of that, communist ideology was spreading rapidly across the world. Discussion about the nature of that ideology could no longer be confined to faculty lounges in ivy-clad universities.

Today we are in the middle of a new Cold War—this time with radical Islam. Once again, we are faced with an ideology that seeks to subjugate us, and, once again, it is a fast-spreading ideology.

---

[38] "Jefferson's Religious Beliefs," *Thomas Jefferson Encyclopedia*, Monticello, https://www.monticello.org/site/research-and-collections/jeffersons-religious-beliefs.

So, it seems that ideological warfare is called for. But there is a caveat. There's no sense in engaging in a war of beliefs if you don't have any of your own, or if the ones you do have are of the wishy-washy variety. But thanks to relativism, multiculturalism, and moral equivalence, wishy-washy is the order of the day.

Many Americans—particularly younger ones—have been conditioned to believe that one belief system is as good as another. The only exception to this rule is the American-Western-Judeo-Christian tradition, which, they have been taught, is the font of all evil. So, for a significant number of Americans, the question is not "How do we defeat radical Islam?" but "Do we really have anything worth defending?" Many Americans are unequipped to fight a war of ideas because they are paralyzed by political correctness.

This brings us to Donald Trump's August 2016 Youngstown speech on defeating jihad.[39] The second half of his talk focused on home-front measures for making America more secure, but for many Americans his suggestions are nonstarters because they fly in the face of politically correct dogma.

Take Trump's proposal that we should screen Muslim immigrants for anti-American beliefs, such as adherence to sharia law. That makes sense because many elements of sharia law are opposed to constitutional law. For example, under sharia, women are not the equal of men, and non-Muslims are not the equal of Muslims. To use Cold War terminology, sharia is subversive of American values. It's a legal system that should not be allowed to gain a foothold in the United States.

Nevertheless, many Americans will respond to the idea of an ideological test that targets sharia-adhering Muslims as being somehow un-American. That's because they have come to equate the American way with relativism and moral equivalence. An ideological test would imply that our values are better than theirs, and, even worse, it would imply that there is something wrong with their values.

---

[39] Joseph Klein, "Trump Takes Aim at Jihad: 'Ideology of Death Must Be Extinguished,'" *FrontPage Mag*, August 16, 2016, https://archives.frontpagemag.com/fpm/trump-takes-aim-jihad-ideology-death-must-be-joseph-klein/.

The relativistically minded will not only oppose the idea of vetting immigrants; they will also tend to oppose the idea that immigrants should assimilate. Many Europeans, for example, believe that asking others to assimilate is an act of cultural imperialism. In some European countries, it is semi-official policy that immigrants should retain their cultural identity completely intact—an idea that happens to coincide with the radical Islamist belief that Muslims should remain apart in Muslim ghettos (now frequently referred to as "no-go zones").

Another Trump proposal from the speech calls for the reversal of the administration's 2012 purge of law-enforcement training materials.[40] That also makes sense. Our law-enforcement and investigative agencies are severely handicapped by the current policy of see-no-Islam, speak-no-Islam, and hear-no-Islam. Here again, however, our society's commitment to political correctness makes this a tough sell. It will be argued that any "profiling" of the Muslim community will be offensive and will only drive moderate Muslims into the arms of the radicals.

In fact, this was the very argument employed by the dozens of Muslim groups that requested the purge in late 2011.[41] They claimed that the training policies then in effect made a connection between Islam and terrorism and were therefore biased against the Muslim community. As a result of the purge, politically correct policing is the order of the day, and law-enforcement personnel who look too closely into Muslim activities risk demotion or job loss. For some examples of the purge's devastating effect, read Philip Haney's *See Something, Say Nothing* or Stephen Coughlin's *Catastrophic Failure: Blindfolding America in the Face of Jihad.*[42]

---

[40] Ibid.

[41] Jordan Schachtel, "Inside Mueller's PC Purge of Counter-Terror Training at the FBI," *Conservative Review*, November 27, 2017, https://www.conservativereview.com/news/inside-muellers-pc-purge-of-counter-terror-material-at-the-fbi/.

[42] Philip Haney and Art Moore, *See Something Say Nothing* (Spokane Valley, WA: Books In Motion, 2016)' Stephen Coughlin, *Catastrophic Failure:*

A further Trump proposal called for the setting up of a "Commission on Radical Islam," which would educate the American people about the core beliefs of radical Islam and help them "to identify the warning signs of radicalization, and to expose the networks in our society that support radicalization." The trouble is, the core beliefs of radical Islam are quite similar to the core beliefs of mainstream Islam, and it is the height of insensitivity to notice. Once again, Muslim advocacy groups will complain loudly that their beliefs are being attacked. And once again, the moral-equivalence crowd can be counted on to echo the complaint.

Who are the Muslim advocacy groups? They happen to be the very same groups that Trump targeted as the support networks for radicalization. These include organizations such as the Council on American-Islamic Relations (CAIR), the Islamic Society of North America (ISNA), the Islamic Circle of North America (ICNA), and the Muslim American Society (MAS). There is a good deal of evidence[43] that these groups function as subversive (there's that quaint Cold War term again) organizations that aim eventually to supplant the Constitution with sharia law. Common sense would suggest that at the very least they should be kept out of the corridors of power they now inhabit.

Trump's proposal that these support networks should be "stripped out and removed one by one"[44] will be the toughest sell of all—not only because these well-funded organizations will raise a ruckus but also because the media, academia, administration officials, and many church leaders will rush to their defense. When you go up against CAIR and company, you're going up against many of our society's elite opinion-makers. Despite the damage they do by misleading Americans about Islam, they are protected by the forces of political correctness.

Blindfolding America in the Face of Jihad (Washington, DC: Center for Security Policy, 2015).

[43] Andrew C. McCarthy, *The Grand Jihad: How Islam and the Left Sabotage America* (New York: Encounter Books, 2010).

[44] Klein, "Trump Takes aim At Jihad."

So engaging in ideological warfare will not be easy. The other side is ready for it, and we are not. Their beliefs are strong and ours are weak. They hold their ground, and we crumple up in apologies at the least suggestion that we are being offensive.

It all has to do with the will to resist. Many Americans are no doubt prepared to resist at the barricades if it comes to that, but resisting at the barricades is to resist rather late in the game. Some Europeans are now at the point of resisting at the barricades, but it's not clear whether their governments are. After being subject to decades of stealth jihad campaigns, it looks as if some European governments—Sweden comes to mind—would rather go quietly into the dark night of dhimmitude than resist. After all, why make a fuss if one set of values is as good as the next?

One reason Americans are so unprepared to resist stealth jihad is that they understand so little about it. Take the "clock boy" incident.[45] In Irving, Texas, on September 14, 2015, Ahmed Mohamed brought to school a homemade clock that teachers mistook for a bomb, leading to his detention by the police. Ahmed was hailed by the PC media as a civil rights hero for standing up to discrimination, but there is a good deal of evidence that he and his family were actually conducting a stealth jihad operation. With the assistance of Muslim "civil rights" organizations, they turned around and sued the town of Irving, and the Irving school system for fifteen million dollars.

And that's likely what they intended to do all along. It's a typical stealth jihad maneuver: create some sort of provocation, and then, when the "mark" responds in the expected manner to the provocation, sue them in the confidence that some politically correct judge will back you all the way. The intent is to create a chilling effect that will silence criticism and enable the stealth jihadists to carry on with little interference.

[45] William Kilpatrick, "Clock and Bull Story," *Crisis Magazine*, October 26, 2015, https://www.crisismagazine.com/2015/clock-and-bull-story.

Thanks to the "clock boy" and the PC media, teachers and police have fifteen million additional reasons not to look too closely into Muslim affairs.[46]

It's not just teachers who will be tempted to give Muslims wide latitude. Suppose you own a small business, or suppose you are a store manager. What will you do when an employee demands to wear a hijab at work? When a group of employees demand prayer breaks during the day? When they demand that you establish a special prayer room for them? Will you resist? Do you want to face an expensive lawsuit? Is a prayer break the hill you want to stake your career on?

Although Muslims make up only about 1 percent of the U.S. population, 40 percent of religion-based workplace complaints are Islam-related.[47] Are these just typical civil rights grievances, or are they examples of stealth jihad—efforts to expand the influence of Islam in American society and force acceptance of Islamic practices? In any event, according to one report, businesses are becoming more and more accommodative of Muslim culture out of fear of lawsuits.[48]

That's the way stealth jihad works and, as you can see, much of it is conducted under the guise of civil rights activism. Therefore, all our conditioning in relativism and multiculturalism and all our guilt over racism will persuade us to put the best possible face on each new Islamic initiative.

Understanding an enemy's core beliefs is one side of the ideological-warfare coin; the other side is understanding and valuing our own

---

[46] The lawsuit was dismissed "with prejudice" in May 2017 for lack of evidence. See Elvia Limón, " 'Clock Boy' Ahmed Mohamed's Lawsuit against Irving ISD, City Dismissed," *Dallas Morning News*, March 14, 2018, https://www. dallasnews.com/news/2018/03/15/clock-boy-ahmed-mohamed-s-lawsuit-against-irving-isd-city-dismissed/.

[47] Robert Spencer, "Muslim-Friendly Workplaces on the Rise out of Fear of Lawsuits," *Jihad Watch*, August 20, 2016, https://www.jihadwatch.org/2016/08/muslim-friendly-workplaces-on-the-rise-out-of-fear-of-lawsuits.

[48] Ibid.

beliefs. Do we believe strongly enough in them to stand up to the threat of lawsuits or job loss? To charges of hate and bigotry? The cultural confidence that is required to resist cultural jihad has been badly undermined by our allegiance to cultural relativism. Do we have enough confidence in our own values and beliefs to insist on the right to vet immigrants? To give law-enforcement agencies accurate information about Islam? To investigate possible subversive activities on the part of Islamic "civil rights" organizations? To even utter the word "subversive"?

As Mark Steyn has noted, "There is no market for a faith that has no faith in itself."[49] He was referring not only to the decline of Christianity in Europe but also to the general loss of cultural confidence in the West. Right now, Europe is having a difficult time in fighting its own ideological war with radical Islam because, as Pope Benedict observed, Europe has succumbed to a hatred of itself.[50]

Many Americans suffer from some of the same doubts. They want to defeat radical Islam, but they are reluctant to take the concrete steps necessary for its defeat. They believe that radical Islam should be opposed, but only in a politically correct and nonoffensive way. Unfortunately, that is not always possible. Ideological warfare can be a rough business. For instance, in the wake of the 2015 Paris massacres, French police conducted 2,235 raids, arrested 232 people, and shut down three mosques.[51] Vetting immigrants and investigating stealth jihad groups seems mild in comparison. Fighting stealth jihadists is likely to be a very insensitive affair, but as I wrote elsewhere, "thirty years hence,

---

[49] Steyn, *America Alone*, 96.
[50] Pope Benedict XVI, "If Europe Hates Itself," posted by Mateo el Feo, Phatmass, February 15, 2007, https://www.phatmass.com/phorum/topic/64657-if-europe-hates-itself/.
[51] "France Shuts Down Three 'Radical' Mosques in Wake of Paris Attacks," France 24, December 2, 2015, https://www.france24.com/en/20151202-france-cazeneuve-shuts-down-radical-mosques-paris-attacks.

how would you like to be the one to explain to your burqa-wearing granddaughter as she is married off to a man thrice her age that we lost the culture war against Islam because it would have been insensitive to fight back?"[52]

[52] William Kilpatrick, "Taking the Islamic Challenge Seriously," *Crisis Magazine*, May 12, 2014, https://www.crisismagazine.com/2014/taking-the-islamic-challenge-seriously.

Jihad Never Sleeps

Most Catholics in the United States are vaguely aware that Christians are being persecuted in the Middle East, Africa, and other parts of the Islamic world. Most are aware of the many terrorist attacks in Europe. And most are aware of the major jihad attacks here in America.

But if you're mainly focused on the occasional terror attack, you are probably underestimating the extent of the Islamic threat and the speed with which it is spreading. That's because people have short memories. Take the 2017 terror attacks in Spain—in Barcelona and Cambrils. You undoubtedly saw some of the news coverage of the carnage, and you probably think you won't forget the event. But memories fade. How many remember the much more deadly jihad attack on the Madrid train system in 2004?[53] The nearly simultaneous bombings aboard four commuter trains killed 191 people and injured more than 1,800. But, unless you live in Spain, the Madrid train bombings passed out of your mind years ago, and if you're under twenty-five, you likely never knew about them in the first place.

When a spectacular terror attack occurs, the average person is temporarily alarmed but then settles back into a state of complacency until the next major terror attack triggers the alarm once again. But this cycle of alarm-complacency-alarm-complacency doesn't bring us any closer to

---

[53] Michael Ray, "Madrid Train Bombings of 2004," *Encyclopedia Britannica*, https://www.britannica.com/event/Madrid-train-bombings-of-2004.

understanding the underlying problem or solving it. Indeed, it conditions us to live with a certain level of terror. We know that the jihadists will strike again, but we also know that the odds are low that we will be among the victims. And so we manage to get on with our lives. As long as bombs are not going off in nearby subways or buses, we stop thinking about jihad.

Our society's focus on acts of violent jihad makes us forget that there is another, more subtle kind of jihad that we need to worry about. Terrible as violent jihad is, cultural jihad is a greater threat. Violent jihad — Brussels, Barcelona, London Bridge — is intermittent, but cultural jihad never sleeps. It is active 24 hours a day, 365 days a year. And though your odds of being a victim of violent jihad are quite low, your odds of being a victim of cultural jihad are exceedingly high.

Cultural jihad is a long-term campaign to influence and even co-opt key social institutions such as schools, churches, media, businesses, and courts. For example, chapters of the Muslim Brotherhood–linked (and politically active) Muslim Student Association can be found on every major campus. And substantial grants from Gulf State kingdoms have persuaded American universities to adopt Islam-friendly policies and curriculums. Catholic colleges are no exception. Most of them present a whitewashed version of Islam to their students. And some Catholic institutions, such as Georgetown, have become little more than PR agents for the Islamic way of life.

In addition, Islamists have been quite successful in penetrating federal government agencies, including security agencies. As just one example among many, consider that a gentleman named Mustafa Javed Ali was appointed by then national security adviser H. R. McMaster as senior director for counterterrorism at the National Security Council in 2017.[54] The problem here is not that Javed Ali is a Muslim but that his last job was with the Council on American-Islamic Relations (CAIR) — an organization with links to terror organizations.

---

[54] William Kilpatrick, "Ali in Wonderland," *Crisis Magazine*, August 14, 2017, https://www.crisismagazine.com/2017/ali-in-wonderland.

CAIR is the quintessential cultural jihad organization. It has a small army of lawyers at its disposal, and it will sue you at the drop of a hijab if you should dare to oppose its agenda. CAIR is just one of an alphabet-soupful of Islamic organizations that work tirelessly to transform American society into a sharia-compliant society. CAIR, ISNA, ICNA, MAS, MSA, USCMO—there are about fifty major cultural jihad organizations in the United States, and hundreds of minor ones. Think of them as akin to the many leftist groups that work night and day to turn America into a utopian socialist state. The leftists will sue you if you don't bake a cake for a gay wedding, and the cultural jihadists will sue you if you don't make it with 100 percent halal ingredients.

It is largely through cultural jihad (aka "stealth jihad") that Islamic law and culture is spreading through the West. If you don't worry about it, it's because you probably don't know much about it, and if you don't know much about it, it's because you're not meant to know.

Cultural jihad never sleeps, but the cultural jihadists prefer that you remain asleep to what they're doing. In this endeavor, they receive a great deal of help from corporate America. Media giants such as PayPal, Facebook, and Google are doing their best to shut down websites that call attention to cultural jihad. Recently, for example, PayPal blocked the *Jihad Watch* website in response to a spurious claim that *Jihad Watch* was a hate group.[55] Not long before that, Google had readjusted its search engine[56] algorithms in order to make it difficult for searchers to find *Jihad Watch*. And on other occasions, Facebook has suspended the *Jihad Watch* account.

Numerous other counterjihad sites in America and Europe have been censored in a similar fashion. The aim is to choke off funding to groups

---

[55] Robert Spencer, "Overreach: PayPal Bans Jihad Watch, Then Backs Down," *FrontPage Mag.*, August 22, 2017, https://archives.frontpagemag.com/fpm/overreach-paypal-bans-jihad-watch-then-backs-down-robert-spencer/.

[56] Robert Spencer, "Video: Robert Spencer on Google Changing Its Search Results to Spike Criticism of Islam," *Jihad Watch*, August 24, 2017, https://www.jihadwatch.org/2017/08/video-robert-spencer-on-google-changing-its-search-results-to-spike-criticism-of-islam.

that are critical of Islamists or to shut them down completely. So, when the terrorists strike, the giant media monopolies strike back not against the stealth jihadists who enable the terrorists but against those who are attempting to expose the connection between cultural jihad and violent jihad. The cultural jihadists are winning the information war because the media conglomerates and the universities have sided with them and against their critics. If you try to provide accurate information about the Islamist threat, you're up against not only CAIR's lawyers but also the universities, the media, and much of corporate America.

When violent jihadists strike, we look to police and the military to protect us. But the spread of Islam is not simply a military matter; it's also a culture war. And while soldiers are trained to resist an advancing enemy, the average citizen is not trained to resist cultural warfare. On the contrary, he has been conditioned to accept all diversities—even totalitarian systems that are out to subjugate him.

That's where the Catholic Church comes in—or, more accurately, *ought* to come in. Historically, the Church was a bulwark of resistance against Islamic encroachments—and not just Islam, but other totalitarian movements as well. The Church warned about the dangers of communism decades before anyone else saw the problem. Moreover, Saint John Paul II played a major role in bringing an end to communism in Eastern Europe. Likewise, throughout the 1930s, while the smart set in Britain and America celebrated Hitler's "progressive" ideas about eugenics, the Catholic Church spoke out repeatedly against Nazi racism. In 1937, when much of Europe was still asleep, Pius XI issued the famous anti-Nazi encyclical *Mit Brennender Sorge*, and Pope Pius XII called Hitler "the greatest enemy of Christ and of the Church in modern times."[57]

Sadly, in recent years, the Church has not provided any similar guidance about the totalitarian nature of the Islamic threat. Insofar as Church leaders have offered advice on the subject, it has been bad advice: calls

---

[57] David Dalin, *The Myth of Hitler's Pope: Pope Pius XII and His Secret War Against Nazi Germany* (Washington, DC: Regnery History, 2005), 38.

for solidarity with Islam, reassurances that Islam is a close cousin to Catholicism, and repeated claims that Islamic terror has nothing to do with Islam.

Pope Francis himself has been one of the main defenders of Islam. In *Evangelii Gaudium*, he declared that "authentic Islam and a proper reading of the Koran are opposed to every form of violence."[58] On another occasion, he told Muslim migrants that they could find guidance in the Koran. And, most recently, he stated that the personal safety of immigrants should always take priority over national security. That's a high-sounding sentiment, but when you think about it, it's just another way of saying that the safety of Muslim immigrants is more important than the safety of Europeans and Americans.

"Always prioritize personal safety [of immigrants] over national security"?[59] Given the proven connection between increased Muslim immigration and increased terrorism, that seems like a rather reckless thing to say. Take the twin attacks in Barcelona and Cambrils, which left fourteen dead and over a hundred wounded. All of the twelve terrorists were immigrants or the children of immigrants. Their leader, Imam Abdelbaki Es Satty, was also an immigrant.

Before becoming an imam, Es Satty was in prison for drug smuggling. After serving his sentence, he should have been deported back to Morocco, but a Spanish judge decided that Es Satty's safety trumped the safety and security of Spanish citizens, and, thus, he was allowed to stay in Spain and plot away.[60]

---

[58] Pope Francis, Apostolic Exhortation *Evangelii Gaudium* (November 24, 2013), no. 253.

[59] Nicole Winfield, "Pope: Rights of Migrants Trump National Security Concerns," *U.S. News and World Report*, August 21, 2017, https://www.us-news.com/news/world/articles/2017-08-21/pope-rights-of-migrants-trump-national-security-concerns?int=news-rec.

[60] Martin Evans, "Imam behind Barcelona Terror Attacks Used Human Rights to Fight Deportation from Spain," *Telegraph*, August 22, 2017, https://www.telegraph.co.uk/news/2017/08/22/imam-behind-barcelona-terror-attacks-used-human-rights-fight/.

The original plot was to attack the iconic Sagrada Família Cathedral in Barcelona with vans packed with explosives.[61] When the explosives went off prematurely at the site where they were stored, the plot was shifted to smaller car and knife attacks at Cambrils and Las Ramblas in Barcelona. But suppose the original plot had succeeded. About ten thousand visitors tour the Sagrada Família Cathedral every day. Many hundreds would likely have been killed and hundreds more wounded. Would Pope Francis still say that the safety of immigrants should take priority over national security?

Unfortunately, he probably would. Francis seems constitutionally unable to connect Islam with terrorism, and he seems unaware of the threat posed by cultural jihad—the network of Muslim enclaves, mosques, and Islamist organizations that provide the enabling environment for violent jihadists to do their work.

Cultural jihad never sleeps, but many in our government, universities, and media organizations are asleep to the spread of cultural jihad. Meanwhile, the Church leadership, with Francis at the helm, is in a near comatose state. The Church was once in the vanguard of resistance to Islamic invasions. Now it is more like a sleeping giant—a powerful force for good that is asleep to the dangers posed by Islam's stealth advance. Let us pray that Church leaders will rouse themselves before it is too late.

---

[61] Iain Burns, "Spanish Terror Cell Planned to Use 'Mother of Satan' Explosive Used in 7/7 Bombings to Slaughter Hundreds in 'Spectacular' Blast at Barcelona's Famous Cathedral," *Daily Mail*, August 19, 2017, https://www.dailymail.co.uk/news/article-4804750/Spanish-terror-cell-planned-attack-Barcelona-church.html.

4

Political Correctness

Stealth jihadists understand our culture very well. Their demands for cultural capitulation take advantage of our society's subservience to the rules of political correctness. Unless you want to be branded as "insensitive," "offensive," "bigoted," and "Islamophobic," you'll go along with the demands. In return, you'll be heaped with praise for your "tolerance" and "sensitivity to diversity."

Playing Along with the Lie

As soon as Bruce Jenner announced he was a woman in 2015, the media immediately fell in line. News reports obligingly referred to him as "her," and commentators agreed that henceforth Mr. Jenner's name would be Caitlyn.

Whether it will become a hate crime to say otherwise remains to be seen. But it has already become problematic to joke about the transition. For example, Spike TV cut out a joke about Jenner made by Clint Eastwood at an award show. When introducing Dwayne "the Rock" Johnson at the 2015 Guys' Choice Awards, he compared Johnson to former athletes who had turned to acting, such as "Jim Brown and Caitlyn Somebody."[62]

That seems fairly mild as jokes go, but in our highly sensitized society it's better not to take chances, and so the Spike executives spiked the joke. As in the old Soviet Union, politically incorrect jokes are being driven underground. And, as is increasingly the case, almost any thought can be deemed to be incorrect.

The establishment understands that a joke directed at Jenner is also directed at them. The butt of the joke is not just Jenner but also the elites who laud and honor him for his "courage." So, rather than incur the wrath of the establishment, the executives at Spike, who, after all,

---

[62] "Spike TV to Cut Clint Eastwood's Caitlyn Jenner Joke, Fox News, June 8, 2015, https://www.foxnews.com/entertainment/spike-tv-to-cut-clint-eastwoods-caitlyn-jenner-joke.

are themselves part of the establishment, decided it was not nice for guys to joke around.

A common theme in the underground jokes of the Soviet era was mutual pretense. One joke that circulated widely in factories and collective farms ended with the punch line "They pretend to pay us, and we pretend to work." In societies where reality is denied, jokes are a way of reasserting reality—a way of saying, "We may pay lip service to the official deception, but we are not fooled by it."

In totalitarian societies, everyone is expected to play along with the lie. The increasingly totalitarian nature of our own society can be gauged by the number of official lies the citizenry is obliged to consent to. One of the latest and biggest whoppers is that Jenner has pole-vaulted over the gender bar. Jenner is not a woman—not physiologically and not chromosomally—but everyone is expected to collude in the pretense that he is. Looked at one way, a joke about Jenner is a measure of insensitivity. Looked at from another perspective, it's a way of holding on to reality.

In a PC society, some things are not safe to joke about—transgenders, same-sex "marriage," Muhammad. Uh, no ... better spike that last thought. One can't help but notice, however, that there is a curious connection between the Jenner affair and the establishment-mandated make-believe about Islam. As with sexual-identity groups, Muslims are considered to be victims—of oppression, bigotry, and "Islamophobia"—and thus beyond criticism or judgment. And, as with the transgender phenomenon, the establishment requires you to collude in a lie—the lie in this case being that Islam is a religion of peace, no different from any other religion.

In both cases, the lies are dangerous. That may be more obvious in regard to lies about the nature of Islam. The pretense that Islam is something it is not puts lives at risk. The strategic incoherence of the War on Terror and the resulting loss of life is due in large part to a denial of the close link between Islam and radical Islam. Western leaders never understood what was happening because they wore self-imposed blinders. Hence, they were continually caught off-guard—first by Hezbollah, then by al-Qaeda, and then, in no particular order, by al-Shabaab, Abu

Sayyaf, Boko Haram, ISIS, and numerous other groups that were simply putting the Islamic doctrine of holy war into practice.

By contrast, the Olympian efforts to normalize the transition of Bruce Jenner would appear to be a minor matter. Apart from whatever danger he may pose to his fellow motorists, in what sense can Jenner be seen as a threat to his fellow citizens? Well, if he were Bruce Jenner the supermarket clerk, there would be little cause for concern. But since he's Bruce Jenner the celebrity, the media's poster boy for gender fluidity, there is something to worry about.

It may seem quaint to say so, but the division of the sexes into male and female is still the basis of society. It's the way societies propagate themselves. And the union of male and female in marriage is the way society ensures that the propagated aren't left to fend for themselves like baby lizards.

Alternative arrangements have been tried, but no viable substitute has been found. For about the last four decades, the academic, artistic, and media elites have insisted that a flourishing society can be built out of self-actualizing individuals doing their own thing. But, apart from the world of TV sitcoms, it hasn't worked. When the experiments of the elites are tried in inner-city Baltimore, or in the rust belt, or in the no-longer-thriving mill towns of New England, the result is dysfunction on a mass scale. Prior to the 1960s, the illegitimacy rate in the United States was about 3 percent. Now it's over 40 percent and climbing. That means more fatherless children, more overtaxed mothers, more educational failure, more drug addiction, and more unsafe towns and cities. To paraphrase the ad for Chiffon Margarine, "It's not nice to fool Mother Nature."

The idea that one sex can do the work of two in raising a family will one day be seen as a suicidal notion, not unlike the Shaker belief that the best way to preserve Shaker values was to stop having children. The same goes for the idea that sexual identity is an optional lifestyle choice, because once you start tinkering with sexual identity, you are tinkering with the foundations of society.

You might be able to get away with a little such tinkering in a healthy society with a healthy birth rate and a preponderance of intact families. But after forty years of do-your-own-thing-and-let-others-pick-up-the-pieces, intact families are becoming a rarity. What makes the current fascination with gender experimentation even more suicidal is the existence of an enemy culture that uses its own population growth as a weapon to extinguish rival cultures. Europe, which gave up on *vive la différence* about half a century ago, has one of the lowest birth rates on the planet. Meanwhile, the Muslims who hope to replace them have one of the highest.

Europe is not yet in its death throes, but, given the mathematics of the situation, that day seems almost inevitable. And when it comes, "death throes" might not be the best way to describe it. At that point, old Europe won't have enough energy to throw a throe. Europe's last days will more likely be of the going-quietly-into-the-dark-night variety.

Europe's experiment with a childless society is now revealed to be about as sophisticated as Dr. Frankenstein's experiments with electricity and corpses. Sophisticated people have always thought that the Frankenstein story is a cautionary tale about scientists tinkering with forces they cannot control. But it was never intended as an allegory about scientific overreach. In fact, the character of Dr. Frankenstein was modeled on the author's husband, the poet Percy Shelley.[63] And although Shelley did conduct amateur experiments with electricity, Dr. Frankenstein's ghoulish experiments are actually a metaphor for Shelley's self-centered experiments with free love and sexual liberation. Mary Shelley's concern was not with the destructive experiments of mad scientists but with the destructive results of mad philosophies. *Frankenstein* is a reflection on her husband's proto-Nietzschean philosophy and on the damage it wrought in the lives of those close to Shelley once it was put into practice.

---

[63] E. Michael Jones, *Monsters from the Id: The Rise of Horror in Fiction and Film* (Dallas: Spence Publishing, 2000), 95.

In America, the experiments continue. And the results are predictable. The celebration of trans will not translate into healthy families or a healthy birthrate. The children of the Jenner generation will be too absorbed in questions of self-identity to do much generating—let alone to raise families. Nor are they likely to notice that a replacement population with very different ideas about self-fulfillment is on the doorstep. And when they do finally notice, it is unlikely that they will be able to resist.

Just as the anything-goes Weimar Republic was unable to resist Nazism and was, in fact, a prelude to it, our own self-obsessed society will likely pave the way for its own abolishment. What now seems to be a progress toward total freedom will someday be seen as steps on the road to total control. Whatever temporary successes its proponents may achieve, gender fluidity is not the wave of the future.

PC in Orlando and in Our Future

If the Orlando massacre at a gay night club in 2016 teaches us anything, it demonstrates the grip that political correctness has on our society.

One might call it a death grip. We now know that fears about being thought Islamophobic prevented colleagues of Major Nidal Hasan, the Fort Hood killer, from reporting his jihadist sympathies, even though they considered him to be a "ticking time bomb."[64] Likewise, a neighbor of Syed Farook and Tashfeen Malik decided not to report her suspicions about them to the police lest she be guilty of "racial profiling."[65] But for political correctness, the San Bernardino massacre might have been prevented.

Now we find that Omar Mateen, the perpetrator of the Orlando massacre, left a trail of clues in the years prior to his attack that even an Inspector Clouseau could have followed—except that our contemporary Clouseaus are hampered by politically correct policing policies. In 2013, Mateen threatened to kill a sheriff's deputy and his family.[66] He stalked

---

[64] Deroy Murdock, "See Something, Say *Nothing* Policy Kills Thousands," *National Review*, June 7, 2016, https://www.nationalreview.com/2016/06/orlando-shooting-political-correctness-islamophobia-see-something-say-nothing/.

[65] Ibid.

[66] Robert Spencer, "2013: Orlando Jihadi Threatened to Kill Sheriff and His Family, FBI Dismissed Threat," *Jihad Watch*, June 17, 2016, https://www.jihadwatch.org/2016/06/2013-orlando-jihadi-threatened-to-kill-sheriff-his-family-fbi-dismissed-threat.

one of his colleagues.[67] He told co-workers that he wanted to become a martyr, and he bragged about ties to terrorist organizations.[68] He made two trips to Mecca.[69] His father is a supporter of the Taliban. At the small mosque he attended in Fort Pierce, Florida, he associated with a man who later traveled to Syria and perpetrated a massive suicide truck bombing there.[70] A few weeks before the Orlando attack, a gun shop owner reported to the FBI that Mateen had tried to purchase body armor and bulk ammunition.[71]

The FBI did investigate Mateen in 2013 and 2014 but dropped the investigation because they believed Mateen's story that his behavior was only a reaction to his colleagues' "Islamophobia."[72] The FBI, of course,

---

[67] Robert Spencer, "Orlando Jihadi's Coworker Complained about Him, Company Did Nothing Because He Was Muslim," *Jihad Watch*, June 12, 2016, https://www.jihadwatch.org/2016/06/orlando-jihadis-coworker-complained-about-him-company-did-nothing-because-he-was-muslim.

[68] Robert Spencer, "FBI: Orlando Gay Club Jihad Mass Murderer Bragged about "Ties to Terror Organizations," *Jihad Watch*, June 12, 2016, https://www.jihadwatch.org/2016/06/fbi-orlando-gay-club-jihad-mass-murderer-bragged-about-ties-to-terror-organizations.

[69] Harry Cockburn, "Omar Mateen: Orlando Gay Nightclub Gunman Made Two Pilgrimages to Saudi Arabia," *Independent*, June 16, 2016, https://www.independent.co.uk/news/world/americas/omar-mateen-orlando-gay-nightclub-gunman-made-two-pilgrimages-to-saudi-arabia-a7085156.html.

[70] Massimo Calabresi, "Why the FBI Dropped Its Previous Orlando Shooter Investigations," *Time*, June 14, 2016, https://time.com/4368439/orlando-shooting-omar-mateen-fbi-investigation-dropped/.

[71] Leonard Greene, "Florida Gun Store Owner Says He Warned FBI about Omar Mateen after He Tried Buying Body Armor and Ammo Weeks before Orlando Massacre," *New York Daily News*, June 16, 2016, https://www.nydailynews.com/news/national/florida-gun-owner-warned-fbi-weeks-omar-mateen-article-1.2676916.

[72] Joseph Klein, "Failure to Connect the Dots Leading up to the Orlando Jihadist Massacre," *FrontPage Mag*, June 16, 2016, https://archives.frontpagemag.com/fpm/failure-connect-dots-leading-orlando-jihadist-joseph-klein/.

is completely hamstrung by the see-no-Islam policies that the Obama administration introduced into the nation's security agencies following its purge of reality-based training materials in 2011 and 2012.[73]

How many more Orlando-type atrocities will it take before America wakes up to the true nature of the threat? Probably a great many. That's because, just as political correctness prevents us from seeing obvious signs of jihadist intentions prior to a terrorist act, it also prevents us from seeing the attack for what it was after the event.

It was only a matter of time before the PC crowd began to offer alternative explanations for Orlando in an attempt to discredit the obvious one. In fact, it was only a matter of hours.

Did you think that the Orlando massacre was a jihad attack carried out in the name of Allah and reflecting traditional Islamic animosity toward homosexuals? How naïve. According to the social and media elites, the real culprits were, variously, Christians, Republicans, and the National Rifle Association. In short, all the usual suspects.

Christians? Sure. According to ESPN's Jemele Hill, it was the "legacy of Christian homophobia" that created the toxic environment that led to the murders.[74] ACLU lawyer Chase Strangio tweeted: "The Christian Right has introduced 200 anti-LGBT bills in the last six months and people blaming Islam for this. No."[75] Even a Catholic bishop concurred. According to Saint Petersburg, Florida bishop Robert Lynch, Catholicism "targets ... and also breeds contempt for gays, lesbians, and transgender people. Attacks today on LGBT men and women often plant the seeds of contempt, then hatred, which can ultimately

---

[73] Kerry Picket, "Did FBI Training Material Purge Cause Agency to Drop the Ball on Orlando Shooter?" *Daily Caller*, June 12, 2016, https://dailycaller.com/2016/06/12/did-fbi-training-material-purge-cause-agency-to-drop-the-ball-on-orlando-shooter/.

[74] Daniel J. Flynn, "The Audacity of Dopes," *American Spectator*, June 17, 2017, https://spectator.org/the-audacity-of-dopes/.

[75] Ibid.

lead to violence." Unless this attitude changes, said the bishop, "we can expect more Orlandos."[76]

So there you have it. It was the Catholics' fault. Bishop Lynch also managed to take a swipe at the Second Amendment—as did President Obama, CNN, and a host of others. According to the PC view of things, the NRA had somehow created the environment that led to the killings, as did Republicans who support the NRA and oppose gay "marriage" and gender-neutral bathrooms.

So will the Orlando massacre be the decisive wake-up call about the threat from Islamic ideology? It doesn't look that way. Instead, it's back to business as usual—that is, the business of absolving Islam and blaming everyone else in sight. If Mateen had attacked Disney World—one of the targets he had been scouting—the PC enforcers would undoubtedly have found reasons to assign blame to Christians, Republicans, and the Second Amendment.

Political correctness has acquired the status of a religious faith in Western societies. Like Islam, it's a faith that must not be questioned. And, like Islam, it brooks no opposition. Islam's ability to infiltrate and co-opt Western institutions owes a lot to its fellow faith on the left. Indeed, if anyone dares to question the tenets of Islam, the PC crowd can be relied upon to rush to Islam's defense. Thus, according to President Obama, Omar Mateen was not inspired by the clear commands of Muhammad to wage jihad and to execute homosexuals, but by "propaganda and perversions of Islam that you see generated on the Internet."[77]

---

[76] Thomas D. Williams, "Florida Bishop Blames Orlando Massacre on Catholic 'Contempt' for Homosexuality," *Breitbart*, June 14, 2016, https://www.breitbart.com/politics/2016/06/14/florida-bishop-blames-orlando-massacre-catholic-contempt-homosexuality/.

[77] Robert Spencer, "Obama: Orlando Jihad Killer Inspired by 'Propaganda and Perversions of Islam,'" *Jihad Watch*, June 13, 2016, https://www.jihad-watch.org/2016/06/obama-orlando-jihad-killer-inspired-by-propaganda-and-perversions-of-islam.

It's not just the president who enforces the PC ban on criticism of Islam. In Germany, Facebook banned the Facebook page of the gay magazine *Gaystream* after it published a series of articles critical of Islam in the wake of the massacre in Orlando.[78] It appears that in the scale of PC crimes, "Islamophobia" trumps homophobia.

How many more wake-up calls will it take? Unless Western societies can break out of the thought-world prison imposed by PC, they won't wake up in time.

---

[78] Robert Spencer, "Facebook Bans Gay Magazine Critical of Islam," *Jihad Watch*, June 18, 2018, https://www.jihadwatch.org/2016/06/facebook-bans-gay-magazine-critical-of-islam.

5

Culture Wars

You undoubtedly know about the culture war that secularists have been waging against Christians for the last fifty years. But did you know that Islamists have been waging a similar war against Christianity and Western culture? This war is being waged in the media, the schools, the universities, the courts, and the corporate boardrooms. And Christians are on the losing side. That's due in large part to the fact that Islamists have forged a tacit alliance with militant secularists and leftists.

The Cultural Capitulation Continues

Bill Clinton, along with co-author James Patterson, has written a thriller. The plot of *The President Is Missing*[79] concerns the uncovering of a cyberterrorist attack that threatens all of America. President Duncan's problems are compounded by a possible impeachment for having held a telephone conversation with "the most dangerous and prolific cyberterrorist in the world—a man named Sulliman Cindoruk, the leader of a group called 'Sons of Jihad.'"

"Ah," you may be thinking, "the Muslim connection!" But not so fast. As President Duncan informs us, "He's Turkish-born, but he's not Muslim." What's that? A Turkish jihadist who's not Muslim? According to the Turkish State, 99 percent of Turks are Muslims. What are the chances that a non-Muslim Turk would be a jihadist leader? And—seeing that jihad is an Islamic concept—how can you have a non-Islamic form of jihad?

Does Bill Clinton really believe this nonsense? Or is he just inserting the obligatory "this-has-nothing-to-do-with-Islam" clause expected of authors who write thrillers about terror? According to the description on Amazon, "this is the most authentic, terrifying novel to come along in many years." But to me, the most terrifying thing is that a former president of the United States may hold such a naïve view of Islamic

---

[79] James Patterson and Bill Clinton, *The President Is Missing: A Novel* (New York: Little, Brown, 2018).

terrorism. The novel might more accurately be titled *The President Is Missing the Point.*

The President Is Missing is yet one more example of popular culture running interference for Islam. The story reminds me of other popular thrillers that make a point of telling the reader or viewer that terrorism has nothing to do with you-know-what. A few years ago, Liam Neeson starred in *Non-Stop,*[80] a thriller about an unidentified terrorist who begins to murder one passenger every twenty minutes on board a trans-Atlantic flight. Who is the terrorist? To throw you off track, the filmmakers first cast suspicion on a Muslim doctor wearing Muslim garb and a full beard. Of course, if you're foolish enough to believe he is the culprit, it just goes to show what an unsophisticated "Islamophobe" you are. As it turns out, the doctor is one of the heroes of the story, and the real terrorist is an American combat veteran.

A similar switcheroo occurred in 2002, when Paramount released *The Sum of All Fears,*[81] a thriller based on Tom Clancy's 1991 novel of the same name. In the book, Palestinian terrorists detonate a nuclear bomb in Denver at the Super Bowl. In the movie, the terrorists are transformed into neo-Nazis. That may be because CAIR launched a two-year lobbying campaign[82] against using Muslim villains in the film version.

In Europe, they're having similar problems with fiction that comes in conflict with the politically correct fiction that Islam has nothing to do with anything bad. Michel Houellebecq, the author of *Submission,*[83] an entirely plausible novel about the Islamization of French universities,

---

[80] *Non-Stop,* directed by Jaume Collet-Serra, written by John W. Richardson, Christopher Roach et al., released February 28, 2014, https://www.imdb.com/title/tt2024469/.

[81] *The Sum of All Fears,* directed by Phil Alden Robinson, written by Tom Clancy, Paul Attanasio, and Daniel Pyne, released May 31, 2020, https://www.imdb.com/title/tt0164184/.

[82] Mark Armstrong, "Wolf Howls as NBC Yanks 'Law & Order' Episode," E! News, January 26, 2001, https://www.eonline.com/news/41074/wolf-howls-as-nbc-yanks-law-order-episode.

[83] Michel Houellebecq, *Submission: A Novel* (New York: Farrar, Straus and Giroux, 2015).

has come under fire for being racist, xenophobic, and Islamophobic. Houellebecq is currently under twenty-four-hour police protection—presumably, if you buy the party line about Islam—to keep him safe from all those angry book reviewers.

Another example—this one from the category of nonfiction—comes from Germany. In 2010, Thilo Sarrazin, a respected economist, wrote a book that took aim at his country's immigration policies, especially in regard to Muslim migrants. As a result, he came in for bitter criticism, and was pushed out of his prestigious position at the Bundesbank. However, since the book, *Germany Is Abolishing Itself*, became a bestseller, Random House again signed with Sarrazin in 2016 for a new book titled *Hostile Takeover: How Islam Hampers Progress and Threatens Society*. It was scheduled to come out in early July, but at the last moment, Random House changed its mind for fear the book would stir up "Islamophobia."[84] All of this seems to confirm the book's title: *Hostile Takeover*. Random House hasn't been taken over by Islam in the full sense of the term, but it seems willing to let Islam call the shots on what kind of books can be published about Islam.

The book titles are prescient: *Hostile Takeover*, *Submission*, and to mention another entry in the death-of-Europe book club, *The French Suicide* (*Le suicide français*) by Éric Zemmour (2014). There have been a number of suicide-of-the-West-type of books over the decades, but their authors didn't lose their jobs, require police protection, or have to dodge bullets (as in the case of Danish author Lars Hedegaard). This time, however, the suicide seems much closer at hand.

A glaring example concerns the Bataclan Theater in Paris. On November 13, 2015, three Muslim terrorists entered the theater and opened fire on the crowd, murdering 130 people and injuring 413. When the theater reopened a year later, the musician Sting sang a song called

---

[84] Bruce Bawer, "Another Day, Another Blow to Freedom," *FrontPage Mag*, July 9, 2018, https://archives.frontpagemag.com/fpm/another-day-another-blow-freedom-bruce-bawer/.

"Inshallah"—"If it be your will, it shall come to pass," or simply, "Allah willing." For the second anniversary of the attacks, smiling politicians released balloons outside the theater. For the third anniversary of the massacre, the theater management scheduled an Islamic rap concert featuring an "artist" named Médine (after Medina) whose "lyrics are filled with hatred towards non-Muslims, France, and the West." One of his most popular songs is called "Jihad."[85]

If you instinctively think of this as an outrage, you're not alone. According to Professor Guy Milliere:

> Organizations representing the families of the Bataclan victims said that an Islamic rap concert praising jihad, in a place where people were murdered and tortured by jihadists, would be an insult to the memory of the victims, and asked that the concert be cancelled.[86]

But Millière, an authority on French culture and politics thinks it unlikely that the concert will be canceled. France, he says, is already in submission mode: "Macron and the French government … speak and act as if the enemy has won and as if they want to gain some time and enjoy the moment before the final surrender."[87]

The situation is much the same in England. On June 3, London's Southwark Cathedral hosted a "Grand Iftar Service" on the anniversary of the London Bridge terror attack.[88] In that attack, Islamic terrorists

---

[85] Guy Millière, "France: A Second Jihad in the Bataclan?" Gatestone Institute, July 15, 2018), https://www.gatestoneinstitute.org/12702/france-bataclan-jihad.

[86] Ibid.

[87] Ibid. Amid widespread protests, Médine and the Bataclan announced the cancelation of the concert on September 21, 2018. "French Muslim Rapper Cancels Shows at Bataclan amid Far-Right Protests," France 24, September 24, 2018, https://www.france24.com/en/20180924-france-bataclan-rapper-medine-forced-cancel-concert-far-right-protests-paris-attacks.

[88] Robert Spencer, "UK: Cathedral Hosts Ramadan 'Grand Iftar Service' on Anniversary of Islamic State London Bridge Jihad Massacre," *Jihad Watch*,

drove a van into pedestrians on London Bridge, then began stabbing people in the nearby Borough Market area. Altogether they killed eight people and injured forty-eight others. What better way to mark the anniversary of an Islamic jihad attack than to celebrate with a "Grand Iftar Service"?

Next thing you know, Islamists and their liberal allies will want to build a large Islamic center near the site of the 9/11 attack. Oh, wait! They've already tried that. Fortunately, it didn't work out the way they had hoped. But elsewhere, cultural jihad has been a great success. Not a day goes by without a half dozen new examples of capitulation to Islamic cultural demands. Textbook publishers whitewash Islamic history. Lectures that might be offensive to Islam are canceled. A college library cautions students not to wish others a "merry Christmas." KFC stores in Australia refuse to sell sandwiches with bacon in them. Swimming pools are segregated to accommodate Muslim wishes. Santa Lucia Day celebrations in Sweden are canceled lest Muslims take offense. European Jews are advised not to wear kippahs in public. And Muslim rape-gang activities in England are covered up by the authorities for fear of seeming racist.

The escalating submission to Islam has three causes.

First and foremost is simple fear. Publishers remember what happened at the offices of *Charlie Hebdo* magazine, and they don't want it to happen to them. Theater owners saw what happened at the Bataclan Theater and the Ariana Grande concert in Manchester, and they reason that prudence is the better part of valor.

The second factor that contributes to the submission is a genuine desire to be tolerant and welcoming, combined with a genuine naïveté about Islam. Even at this late stage, there are still many people who believe that if Europeans just tried harder to be nice to Muslim migrants, everything would work out fine.

June 9, 2018, https://www.jihadwatch.org/2018/06/uk-cathedral-hosts-ramadan-grand-iftar-service-on-anniversary-of-islamic-state-london-bridge-jihad-massacre.

The third factor is cultural shame. Like others in the West, Europeans have been taught that their culture has a record of predation unmatched in history. To many, Western culture doesn't seem worth defending. They've lost faith in their culture, and in a great many cases, they've lost faith in Christianity. The only faith they have left is in relativism. And if, as relativists claim, one culture is as good as another, what difference does it make if Islam takes over? Life will still go on as usual. Won't it?

Ironically, Catholic leaders and Catholic activists are often in the forefront of those who seem to have lost faith in their culture. They decry nationalism (which, in Europe, often involves a defense of Christian culture), while promoting a utopian universalism that asserts not only that all men are equal before God but also that all cultures and belief systems are equally good.

Thus, Catholic leaders, while still affirming the wrongness of individual suicide, have become intimately involved in Europe's cultural suicide. They continue to encourage mass Muslim migration at a point when other European leaders are abandoning the idea posthaste. Street priests, nuns, and missionaries backed by bishops and heads of communities organize street protests against Italy's new, more stringent migrant policies. Others help Muslims build mosques to show their community spirit. And one Italian bishop says he is ready to "turn all the churches into mosques" if it would be useful to the cause of Muslim migration.[89]

One wonders what Church leaders would do if Saint Peter's were bombed by Islamic jihadists. Would they host a "Grand Iftar Service" at the site on the anniversary of the event as a sign of their continued solidarity with Islam? Don't dismiss the idea as preposterous and unthinkable. We live in strange times.

---

[89] Robert Spencer, "Italian Bishop Says He's Ready to 'Turn All the Churches into Mosques' to Aid the Cause of Mass Muslim Migration," *Jihad Watch*, July 10, 2018, https://www.jihadwatch.org/2018/07/italian-bishop-says-hes-ready-to-turn-all-the-churches-into-mosques-to-aid-the-cause-of-mass-muslim-migration.

The Two-Front Culture War

Islamization. Can it happen here? Will sharia someday be the law of the land in America? To most Americans that seems highly unlikely — about as improbable as a takeover by shape-shifting aliens.

But the "that'll never happen" of today often becomes the accepted reality of tomorrow. Consider that only a few years ago, the dismantling of sex-segregated bathrooms and locker rooms seemed equally improbable. But all of a sudden, the new slogan of liberation is "tear down this stall," and millionaire basketball players will boycott your state unless you agree to let the boys into the girls' room.

To understand Islamization, you first have to understand the culture war — the battles that conservative Jews and Christians have been fighting against the left over issues such as abortion, education, same-sex "marriage," transgender bathrooms, and the like.

Even conservatives concede that they've been losing that war. Perhaps the main reason is that their opponents had a head start. They began fighting the war years before proponents of family values began to fight back. It took a long time before the traditional-values people realized they were in a war.

That culture war rages on. Meanwhile, a new culture war has begun — the stealth jihad war. It bears a number of similarities to the other culture war. The leftist culture warriors accuse you of being a hateful homophobe, and the Islamic culture warriors accuse you of being a hateful "Islamophobe." Moreover, the stealth jihadists can count on the support of the same powerful forces that back the sexual revolutionaries—namely, the media, the universities, the courts, big business, and billionaire leftist donors.

As with the other culture war, defenders of Judeo-Christian values are losing this one too, and for the same reason. The stealth jihadists had a head start. They've been fighting this war for decades, and most of the rest of us don't even know that there is a war.

Whether or not you agree with the leftist-secularist agenda for transforming the culture, it's instructive to note that the jihad culture warriors follow the same game plan. They don't come out and say, "We want to dominate your culture." They say, "All we want is a little tolerance and acceptance of our way of life; we just want the same rights as other Americans." Like the leftist culture warriors, these new culture warriors operate under the banner of civil rights; and like their counterparts on the left, they make an appeal to widely shared values such as tolerance and respect for diversity.

How do they advance their agenda? By appeals to sensitivities and civil liberties. Take a recent case in Norway—one that is not difficult to imagine happening in the United States. Merete Hodne, a hairdresser and an outspoken critic of Islam, was fined for refusing to color the hair of a Muslim woman (presumably, a Norwegian convert who wished to dye her light hair black). Ms. Hodne's "Islamophobia" offended the sensibilities of Muslims and her refusal to apply hair dye was deemed a denial of civil rights. Thus, she was fined ten thousand kroner.

The Muslim woman could have gone to another hair salon but appears to have targeted Ms. Hodne's on the advice of an anti-racist center. The story is reminiscent of all those cases in the Unite States in which Christian bakers, florists, and photographers have been forced to cater to same-sex weddings. The gay customers weren't looking for cakes and flowers so much as they were looking for test cases. Islamic advocacy groups in the United States are using the same tactics. They look for people they can make an example of in order to send a message to others. As far as I know, no hairdressers have yet been targeted, but various other businesses have acceded to Muslim demands for halal menus, hijabs at work, and prayer breaks during the day.

Wearing a hijab at work may seem like a small thing. But how about a burqa? How about separate sharia courts for Muslims to settle disputes among themselves? Taken separately, each Muslim challenge appears to be no more than a civil rights complaint, but collectively they should be understood as part of a campaign to transform our culture along Islamic lines. Lawsuits about prayer breaks, for example, are not primarily about praying; they are about staking out cultural territory for Islam. Likewise, the wearing of the hijab or the burqa is not primarily a statement about freedom of expression; it's a weapon in a civilizational war.

In effect, we are facing a two-front culture war—against the left on the one hand, and against stealth jihadists on the other. In both cases, the most effective weapon of the aggressors is to convince the rest of us that there is no campaign of cultural transformation—only legitimate demands for expanded civil rights. Who wants to fight against that? Everyone understands the need to resist armed jihadists. But few understand the need to resist the culture-war jihadists. Unless we engage in that war, however, we will eventually lose our culture.

Submission

Submission. That's what the word "Islam" means. Muslims must submit to Allah, and the rest of the world must eventually submit to Islam. Submission does not necessarily require conversion, but it does require that one acknowledge the superiority of Islam, pay the jizya (the tax levied on non-Muslims by an Islamic state), and, in general, keep one's head down.

Europe is currently in the process of submitting to Islam, and America also seems destined to submit eventually. If you have young children or grandchildren, it's likely that they will have to adapt at some point to living in a Muslim-dominated society. It won't necessarily be a Muslim-majority society because, as history testifies, Muslims don't need a majority in order to take control of non-Muslim societies.

If and when Islam persuades America to submit, it probably won't be through force of arms. The civilizational struggle in which we are now engaged is primarily a culture war. America used to be good at cultural warfare because America once had cultural confidence. The Cold War was in large part a cultural war, and America won it because it didn't have qualms about demonstrating the superiority of the American way to the Soviet way.

But times change. These days, may Americans would rather shred their culture than spread it. Cultural shame rather than cultural pride rules the day. And, not surprisingly, people who are ashamed of their culture can't be counted on to defend it. Those who are eager to pull down statues of Washington, Jefferson, and Columbus are unlikely to put up much resistance to Islam's cultural aggression. Instead, they will be disposed to facilitate it.

Islam, on the other hand, is full of newfound cultural pride. After the defeat of the Russians in Afghanistan and the overthrow of the Shah in Iran, Muslims could once again believe that Allah had destined them to subjugate the world to Islam. At the same time that Americans began to doubt their own cultural heritage, Islam undertook a remarkable campaign to export its ideology to the rest of the world. Enabled by massive oil revenues, Saudi Arabia and other Gulf States funded the building of mosques and madrassas all over the world. While America was investing heavily in new weapons systems, the Gulf States were placing their bets on a weaponized religious system.

And there's the rub. Buoyed by the initial successes in Iraq and Afghanistan, Americans began to think of the war against jihad as primarily a military affair. In the process of defeating the enemy on the battlefield, we lost sight of the cultural side of the struggle. But Islamists stayed focused on the larger picture. While we were winning the armed battles in Afghanistan and Iraq, the cultural jihadists were winning battle after battle on the culture front.

Indeed, most of the Islamist victories came without a struggle. Key cultural institutions in the West simply acquiesced to whatever the Islamists wanted. Hijabs in the workplace? Diversity demands it. Prayer breaks for Muslim employees? Well, no more than five a day. Islam-friendly curriculums in kindergarten through grad school? Think of it as affirmative action for years of neglect. More Muslim immigrants? It would be against our values to say no.

A culture war can be fought only by cultural institutions — schools, churches, political and civic organizations, and so on. As things stand, however, none of our cultural institutions have shown much evidence that they are equipped to fight a culture war with cultural jihadists. The chief reason this is so is that most of these institutions are still fighting the last culture war — the civil rights struggle and the concomitant war against intolerance, racism, and bigotry. This "old-war" mentality makes it nearly impossible for our cultural and civic leaders to resist Islamization. Because so many Americans still live mentally in a time when intolerance was considered the greatest evil, they have difficulty understanding that an indiscriminate tolerance can father just as many sins.

One way of grasping the vulnerability of our society to Islamization is to ask "Who's going to stop it?" Where, exactly, are the forces of resistance?

The university? American universities are bastions of political correctness and mandatory tolerance. Most of them are already quite sympathetic to the Islamic point of view. A combination of intimidation (from both Muslim and leftist groups), Saudi money, and multicultural ideology has ensured that when push comes to shove, the universities will line up with the Islamist camp. If present trends continue, American universities will fold to Islam just as German universities once folded to the Nazis.

The media? The media refuse to make the connection between Islamic terror and Islamic belief. In general, media people see it as their duty to put the best possible face on all things Islamic. Scratch the media as a source of resistance.

The Church? As with college administrators, many Church leaders are deeply mired in multicultural ideology. They are constantly on the lookout for offenses against the "other." Accordingly, American bishops seem to think that "Islamophobia" poses a grave threat to society. Many of them seem more concerned about anti-Muslim bigotry than about the victims of Islamic terror. To prove that they themselves are not "Islamophobes," the United States Conference of Catholic Bishops (USCCB) operates one of the largest programs for resettling refugees from Muslim countries into the United States. Besides facilitating Muslim migration, American as well as European bishops have facilitated the migration of Islamic beliefs. On numerous occasions, prominent clergy have pronounced these beliefs to be benign and peaceful, and thus deserving of a warm welcome. In general, Church leaders see themselves as friends and protectors of Islam. Given their current mindset, the bishops are unlikely to recognize an Islamic cultural putsch, let alone resist it.

Big business? Corporations also qualify as cultural institutions. Much of our understanding of what is culturally acceptable and unacceptable is picked up in the workplace. This can be a good thing and often was in the past. Unfortunately, many corporations now reflect and magnify some of the worst cultural trends: arbitrary speech codes, draconian diversity policies, transgenderism, and the like. Currently, several large corporations are using their leverage to suppress speech that is critical of Islam. Giant companies such as PayPal, Google, Facebook, and Twitter are actively trying to shut down websites and individuals that provide accurate information about Islamic cultural jihad. The media monopolies are playing the role that the Ministry of Truth played in George Orwell's *1984*. All the really useful information about Islam that has been painfully accumulated in recent years is being quietly dropped down the memory hole.

Why are the counterjihad sites being shut down? Because they supposedly are intolerant and racist. Here we come back to the "old-war" mentality. The corporations, the schools, the churches, and the media are ready to do battle with racists, sexists, homophobes, "Islamophobes," and transphobes, but they lack the mindset that would allow them to resist the long march through the institutions being conducted by determined and skillful cultural jihadists. In short, their energies are focused on evils that have long been in retreat or on nonexistent evils (such as transphobia). Meanwhile, the much larger threat posed by Islam draws ever closer.

The people who might be expected to fight this new culture war are scarcely aware of its existence. They are too busy championing the cause of newly invented "civil rights." Fifty years ago, they would have been on the cutting edge; now they are on the edge of irrelevancy.

Nowadays, the cutting edge is elsewhere. And when the "cutting-edge" cultural and business elites meet the cutting edge of Islamization, they will almost inevitably submit to it. That is what they have already begun to do. And as the culture war with Islam heats up, the submission process will only accelerate.

Survival Education: Islam in the Classroom

Should schools teach about Islam, and if so, how should they teach it? There's a general consensus among educators that when dealing with controversial subjects, schools should maintain a distinction between teaching and preaching—between an objective presentation and advocacy.

But some contend that that line has already been crossed in regard to Islam in the classroom. In Chatham, New Jersey, a parent is suing the school system for forcing seventh-grade students to watch a set of videos in their world cultures and geography class that essentially proselytize for Islam.[90] One five-minute video[91] declares that:

- God gave Muhammed the noble Koran.
- The Koran is a perfect guide for humanity.
- Islam is a shining beacon against the darkness of repression, segregation, intolerance, and racism.
- The beautiful Koran is guidance for the wise and sensible.

The video ends with an invitation of sorts: "May God help us all to find the true faith, Islam."

The fact is, many American schools have blurred the line between teaching and preaching. One commonly used lesson plan requires

---

[90] "First Round Victory against Islam Course in School," Clarion Project, June 21, 2018, https://clarionproject.org/first-round-victory-against-islam-course-in-school/.

[91] Ibid.

grade-schoolers to write out the shahada — the Islamic confession of faith, which states: "There is no God but Allah, and Muhammad is the messenger of Allah."[92] This type of teaching ties in with the Deweyan precept that one learns by doing — that you have to experience something from the inside before you can understand it. Thus, teachers see no problem with the shahada lesson. But there are limits to experiential learning. If one were to propose that students learn the Apostles' Creed in order to understand Christianity better, alarm bells would start to sound.

The simple solution to the problem of preaching in the classroom is to cut out the advocacy and just stick to the facts. But that's easier said than done. Complete objectivity is nearly impossible — especially in regard to such a large and complex subject as Islam.

Take Islamic history. Even if you were able to get everyone to agree on the facts, there are so many facts spread over its 1,400-year history that it would be impossible to cover them all. So you need to be highly selective. You need to find a number of diverse groups to agree on what the essential facts are and on how they should be prioritized.

For example, is it more important to know that Muhammad was the founder of a new religion or that he was a conquering warlord? Both are essential facts, but Muslim advocacy groups might want the second fact to be de-emphasized or even omitted from the curriculum. In fact, many history texts do downplay Islamic conquests, preferring instead to talk about Islamic expansion.[93]

Which facts should be prioritized? With all due respect to the multicultural view, it seems to me that American schools, while striving to be as objective as possible, should teach those things about Islam that best serve American interests, and — more broadly — the interests of Western civilization.

---

[92] "Islamic Indoctrination in American Schools," akdart.com, http://www.akdart.com/islam4.html.

[93] Gilbert T. Sewall, "Textbook Lies about Islam," *New York Post*, August 17, 2008, https://nypost.com/2008/08/17/textbook-lies-about-islam/.

This may sound a bit ethnocentric, so let me explain. Islam has been at war with Western nations for fourteen hundred years. And, because of its perpetual-war doctrine, it still is. Iranian leaders encourage chants of "Death to America" on a regular basis, and—given their obsession with nuclear weapons—there is no reason to suppose that this is mere rhetoric. Meanwhile, the president of Turkey has warned the Austrian government that its plan to close radical mosques in Austria will lead to a war between "the cross and the crescent."[94] He has issued similar warnings to Greece and other European nations. Since President Recep Tayyip Erdogan has given many indications that he plans to restore the Caliphate to Turkey, he must be taken seriously. Another reason to take him seriously is that he commands the second-largest army in NATO (after the United States).

Though the United States is relatively secure from outside attacks, it is still vulnerable to internal subversion. Indeed, a Muslim Brotherhood document[95] written in 1991, and discovered in a search of an Annandale, Virginia, home in 2004, outlines a strategic plan to infiltrate key American institutions, such as the media, churches, and schools. There is a good deal of evidence[96] that the Brotherhood's strategy has been highly successful—or else we wouldn't need to have this discussion as to whether public school kids should be learning the shahada by heart.

Since Islam has historically been an enemy to the West, and still is, it makes sense that the subject of Islam should be taught from the perspective of national security and cultural survival, not from the perspective of multiculturalists and Islamic advocates.

---

[94] Chuck Ross, "Turkish President Erdogan Predicts Holy 'War' over Austrian Mosque Closures," *Daily Caller*, June 10, 2018, https://dailycaller.com/2018/06/10/erdogan-holy-war-austria/.

[95] "The Muslim Brotherhood's Strategic Plan for America—Court Document," Clarion Project, https://clarionproject.org/Muslim_Brotherhood_Explanatory_Memorandum/.

[96] Coughlin, *Catastrophic Failure*.

Currently, the main thing that students learn about Islam is the fairly innocuous "five pillars of Islam." The five pillars—confession of faith, prayer, fasting, almsgiving, and pilgrimage—give the reassuring impression that Islam is just like any other religion. In other words, there's nothing to worry about.

But from the perspective of cultural survival, there are a few other things that American students ought to know about Islam. They could, for example, learn five ways in which sharia law is at odds with the Constitution, five ways in which women are oppressed in Islam, and five "slay them wherever you find them"-type quotes from the Koran.

In history and "world culture" classes, students learn a lot about Islam's "golden age" and Islam's supposed invention of just about every good thing on earth. For the sake of balance, maybe they should also learn about Muhammad's massacre of between 700 and 900 Jews in Medina,[97] the estimated 1 million Europeans who were taken into slavery in North Africa,[98] and the Armenian Genocide of 1914–1923, which resulted in the deaths of 1.5 million Christians and became the model for the Nazi Holocaust.

If American students learn about all the crimes of the West, why should they be kept in the dark about the crimes of other cultures? One ought to know that these things have happened and that they can happen again.

If all this seems long-ago-and-far-away-ish, and therefore no longer "relevant" to the interests of the modern fourteen-year-old, there are plenty of current events that should raise a few "relevant" red flags. Social studies teachers love to talk about families separated at the border, police brutality, school shootings, and other things that are happening now. So why not also talk about the extermination of Christians in the

---

[97] Ibn Ishaq, *The Life of Muhammad*, trans. A. Guillaume (Oxford, UK: Oxford University Press, 2002), 464.

[98] R. Davis, *Christian Slaves, Muslim Masters: White Slavery in the Mediterranean, The Barbary Coast, and Italy, 1500–1800* (London, UK: Palgrave Macmillan, 2003), 23, 25.

name of Allah in the Middle East and parts of Africa? Why not talk about the brutalization of Europeans at the hands of Muslim migrants? For example, why not discuss the rape of thousands of English girls by Muslim "grooming" gangs? That's a topic that would certainly be of interest to American teens. Shouldn't they be given projects and assignments that will help them to better empathize with the plight of their English peers?

Numerous Islamic clerics have talked about conquering Europe through a combination of immigration and high birth rates. Various commentators familiar with the European scene predict that large parts of it will come under Islamic control within twenty to thirty years if present trends continue. It's difficult to imagine anything more "relevant" than learning that your civilization may soon be replaced by another.

Maybe you think that cultural survival is not the business of the schools. Perhaps you're of the mind that it's up to the president, Congress, and the army to take care of this. Maybe so; the army is our first line of defense. At a deeper level, however, schools are the ultimate line of defense. They form our future soldiers, police, congressmen, and presidents. We hope that schools will prepare men and women who will strive to avoid war, but if war comes, it is vital that those who are called to defend our country believe it is worth defending. This also applies to defending our culture against cultural jihad. This is certainly a frontline task, and it's one that soldiers are not equipped to handle. Teachers, on the other hand, are in the midst of this battle. Whether or not they realize it is another matter.

It's not that schools teach that nothing is worth defending, but the causes they advocate are generally leftist or liberal causes—that is, movements that tend to subvert rather than preserve culture. Many teachers are quite passionate about these cultural crusades, and they expect their students to be equally committed.

The proper response to this one-sided advocacy is not to insist that schools never take sides. They should take sides—the side of the culture to which they belong. That statement needs qualification, of course. We don't want to instill an attitude of "my country right or wrong," but we should want to encourage an informed patriotism. And to be informed, one needs to know the bad as well as the good. Students—especially in the upper grades—should be encouraged to think critically about their heritage. Just as in individual lives, so also in the lives of nations, the ability to look objectively at oneself or one's culture makes it possible to correct one's errors. As the historian Arthur Schlesinger Jr. observed, self-criticism is built into the very fabric of the West. Thus, "the crimes of the West in time generated their own antidotes."[99]

This ability to self-criticize is one of the things that separates our culture from Islamic cultures. As Islam is considered to be the perfect system, there is nothing to criticize. Thus, Muslim schools do not teach that the massacre of the Medina Jews was a shameful episode in Islamic history, and Turkish schools do not teach their students to "never forget" the horrors of the Armenian Genocide. The official Turkish position is that there was no genocide.

Unfortunately, however, the tendency to self-criticize can be taken to extremes. The problem in the West is not that students lack knowledge of the sins of the West. The problem is, that's all they know. They don't know about the great benefits that the West has conferred on mankind. They don't know the overarching narrative and the unifying ideals that hold the United States together as a society. In short, schools are failing to help students identify with their own culture. And if students don't identify with it, why should they defend it? The great folly of our contemporary schools is that they are extinguishing the instinct for self-preservation.

Traditionally, it was believed that the school's job was to transmit not only knowledge but also the cultural heritage. School was also the place where, in addition to learning the ABCs, you learned the story of your nation, your culture, and your civilization. You learned that you were part of that story and that you had a responsibility to play your part well.

---

[99] Arthur Meier Schlesinger, *The Disuniting of America: Reflections on a Multicultural Society* (New York: W.W. Norton, 1998), 132.

You learned that although there were shameful episodes in American history, there was much of which to be proud.

In their turn, teachers felt a responsibility to tell the story of American history as objectively as possible. They did not, however, feel an obligation to be neutral about every issue. There were likely very few World War II–era teachers who remained neutral regarding the Axis and the Allies.

A quip attributed to Robert Frost defines a liberal as "a man who is too broadminded to take his own side in an argument." Right now, there is an argument going on between two very different civilizations. As the contrasting claims of the two cultures butt up against each other, educational institutions can no longer afford to take the relativist view that one system or society is as good as another. They need to learn to take their own side. Like it or not, they have a dog in this fight.

Breaking the Code

In 2003, at a time when much of the world was wondering when and where al-Qaeda would strike next, a book appeared that purported to reveal a conspiracy to cover up the truth about a major world religion. According to the book, powerful people, both inside and outside this male-dominated, woman-hating religion, had conspired to represent it falsely as a religion of piety and peace.

At the time, the book and its author were widely hailed for finally breaking through the code of silence that had long protected this ancient institution from criticism.

Islam? Er, no. The repressive, misogynistic religion at the center of Dan Brown's *Da Vinci Code* (2003) is the Catholic Church. Do you really think any major publisher would dare to publish a work claiming that Islam is a fraud? That was tried in 1988 with the release of Salman Rushdie's *The Satanic Verses*. The resulting attack on two translators, one publisher, and an entire hotel-ful of people[100] convinced publishers not to make that mistake again. Yet Rushdie's criticisms of Muhammad were almost incidental to the main plot of his story and were fairly mild compared with Dan Brown's all-out assault on Catholicism. Brown has been a celebrity ever since, and Salman Rushdie, with a fatwa hanging over his head, has been under police protection.

---

[100] See "Sivas massacre," *Wikipedia*, https://en.wikipedia.org/wiki/Sivas_massacre.

What Catholics Need to Know about Islam

Looked at in perspective, the enormous popularity of *The Da Vinci Code* (both the book and the movie) presents us with a massive irony. Just at that moment when a truly misogynistic religion was spreading rapidly all over the globe, the opinion-makers decided to focus their ire on the Faith that had markedly elevated the status of women. And just when Islam's historical penchant for silencing dissenters was once again on display, the trendsetters decided to vent their spleen on an institution that for decades had given a respectful hearing to the dissenters in its midst.

The Da Vinci Code is significant not for what it says about the Catholic Church but for what it inadvertently says about the state of Western culture at the beginning of the twenty-first century. The positive reception accorded to *The Da Vinci Code* reveals a society in deep denial of reality. The book came out to its warm reception after a series of terrorist attacks. The film version came out after the Beslan school massacre, the Madrid train bombings, the London tube bombings, and three weeks of Muslim rioting in 275 French cities. The movie hit the theaters at just about the same time that news of the Mumbai train bombings (which killed 200 and injured 700) broke.

Yet such was the public mood that millions of gullible readers and moviegoers were willing to accept the thesis that the greatest threat to human happiness lay in the supposed machinations of powerful figures within the Catholic Church. Future historians will no doubt be amazed at our capacity for self-deception. That presumes, of course, that future historians won't be under the thumbs of the ayatollahs and muftis — a presumption that can no longer be safely entertained.

If the Islamization of all aspects of life — history, education, culture — is the fate of the West, *The Da Vinci Code*, along with similar fantasies, should bear some of the responsibility. By doing his best to deconstruct the religion that historically had stood as the main bulwark against Islamic fanaticism, the author has served as an enabler of Islam's spread into the West. The weakening of Christianity has done little to strengthen the cause of goddess worship, but it has done a great deal to further the cause of Islam.

Whatever future historians may say about *The Da Vinci Code*, contemporary chroniclers are already saying that the rise of Islam in the West is directly related to the decline of Christianity. As I wrote in 2015:

> As Europeans started to lose their faith, they stopped having babies. They stopped having babies because they had nothing meaningful to pass on to the next generation—and also because babies get in the way of self-gratification. The decline of Christianity in Europe created a population vacuum and a spiritual vacuum, both of which Islam soon began to fill. If Christian faith had been more robust in Europe, it is unlikely that radical Islam would have advanced so far, so fast.[101]

A number of recent surveys show that Christianity is also on the decline in America. Increasing numbers of Americans now identify as having "no religion" or as "agnostics" rather than as Christians. As in Europe, this will eventually create a population shift. Filled with faith, the Muslim population will grow, and lacking it, the indigenous population will grow older.

As in Europe, the spiritual shift will also have an effect on the will to resist Islamization. Traditionally, Christianity has been the main source of meaning in the lives of most Americans. Once deprived of that meaning, they will begin to lose the will to resist. What's the point of resisting if everything is relative? If one religion is as good as another? If you have nothing meaningful to stand for? Better in that case to submit and go along with the new order of things, distasteful as it may be.

Of course, the responsibility for the decline of Christianity in the West can hardly be pinned on Dan Brown alone. The decline was underway long before he put pen to paper. The sexual revolution, the lure of secularism, and the work of celebrity atheists had already done considerable damage to the Christian faith. Brown provided one more excuse for

---

[101] William Kilpatrick, *Christianity, Islam and Atheism: The Struggle for the Soul of the West* (San Francisco: Ignatius Press, 2015), 6.

not believing, and because his thesis was dressed up in the language of scholarship, it proved to be a potent excuse.

Brown quite obviously intended to undermine traditional Christianity and, in the process, pave the way for a nonpatriarchal, feminine-friendly type of spirituality. Ironically, one of the effects of his and similar deconstruction efforts was to strengthen the hand of the most male-dominated, anti-feminine religion on the planet. Thanks, in part, to Brown's fellow demolitionists, the institutionalized oppression of women that was once largely confined to Islamic lands has now set up shop in Europe.

There is another irony surrounding the *Da Vinci Code* phenomenon that seems to have been lost on its fans. The book's plot centers on a massive cover-up of the truth about Christianity by the Catholic Church. As any number of experts have pointed out, however, there was never anything to cover up: *The Da Vinci Code*'s version of the Christian story is an almost total fabrication.[102] On the other hand, many of its false accusations about the Catholic Church are actually true of Islam: the misogyny, the fabrication of documents, the silencing of dissenters, and the suppression of the truth about the life of Jesus. What's more, there really is a concerted, well-documented, and largely successful effort to cover up all the damaging facts about Islam.

In this case, the cover-up does not depend on forged documents, secret conclaves, or albino assassins. Social and media elites have been all too happy to cooperate in the deception—not because they deeply believe in Islam, but because they deeply believe in political correctness. By now everyone knows the PC routine by heart: "violence has nothing to do with Islam," "a handful of terrorists have hijacked a great religion," "jihadists have perverted their faith," and so on. The astonishing thing is that this false narrative about Islam has thus far prevailed. Unlike the deception described in *The Da Vinci Code*, the whole thing has been done in broad daylight. Apparently, if enough powerful people insist that black is white

---

[102] Carl E. Olson, *The Da Vinci Hoax: Exposing the Errors in* The Da Vinci Code (San Francisco: Ignatius Press, 2004).

or that violence has nothing to do with Islam, a significant portion of the populace will ignore the evidence of their eyes and go along with the lie. Here's how I described the situation in 2015:

> The cover-up is occurring at the highest levels of society: the media largely refuse to report stories damaging to Islam; presidents and prime ministers praise it as a religion of peace; and in many parts of the Western world, new laws are being proposed that would make criticism of Islam a crime. Meanwhile, school textbooks are rewritten to malign Christianity and idealize Islam; government officials in the United States are forbidden to mention the word *jihad*; and their counterparts in the United Kingdom are now required to refer to Islamic terrorism as "anti-Islamic activity."[103]

So, while millions were congratulating Dan Brown on his fictional story about the cover-up of Christianity's true meaning, they were completely oblivious to the real-life cover-up of Islam's aggressive nature.

What's more, the Islamic deception is enforced every bit as rigorously as the one described in the novel. *The Da Vinci Code* makes much of the fact that its two heroes, Robert Langdon and Sophie Neveu, are in constant danger because of their attempts to uncover the true Christian story, but in the nonfictional world, the ones who run the real risks are those who are willing to expose the violent side of Islam.

Take the case of Geert Wilders, the Dutch parliamentarian who has been highly critical of Islam. He has been under police protection since 2004, and he and his family are forced to move periodically from safe house to safe house. In addition to bodyguards, Wilders is also in need of lawyers. That's because he has been hauled before courts on a regular basis since 2008 on charges that he has defamed Islam. Currently, he is in court once again — this time on hate-speech charges.[104]

---

[103] Kilpatrick, *Christianity, Islam and Atheism*, 17.

[104] In December 2016, Wilders was found guilty of insulting Moroccan residents of the Netherlands in a 2014 campaign speech but was not fined

Wilders's sin is to warn against the threat to the West from Islam. It's a threat that anyone with common sense can now see. Even his prosecutors recognize the danger. Because of the numerous threats to his life, his trial is being conducted in a bunker under Schiphol Airport.

Wilders is not alone. For breaking the code of silence that protects Islam, numerous others have faced death threats, or trials, or both. As with *The Da Vinci Code*, you can say what you like about Christianity without fear of reprisals, but speak the truth about Islam and you will be in for a heap of trouble.

The cover-up puts us all in danger because it leaves us unprepared for the aggression that almost always follows once Muslims reach a certain percentage of the population. Europeans, for instance, were unprepared for the crime waves and sexual-assault epidemics that ensued after the admission of millions of migrants into Europe in 2015. To anyone with a knowledge of Islamic culture, religion, and history, what happened was predictable. But politically correct codes dictated that only whitewashed versions of Islamic history and beliefs could be taught in European schools. Even now, after the folly of their open-door immigration policy is blazingly evident, European elites are insistent on maintaining the cover-up. The troubles, they assert, are entirely due to the "unwelcoming" and "xenophobic" attitudes of native Europeans.

What if a massive cover-up similar to the one described in *The Da Vinci Code* was happening right now? We would be quick to spot it, wouldn't we? Or would we?

---

by the court. The public prosecutor, however, demanded a five-thousand-euro fine. Wilders and his prosecutor have appealed the ruling. See Janene Pieters, "Apology, Damage Payment Sought in Geert Wilders Hate Speech Trial," *NL Times*, June 28, 2019, https://nltimes.nl/2019/06/28/apology-damage-payment-sought-geert-wilders-hate-speech-trial.

6

Men in Skirts

One main reason that Christians are losing the culture war with Islam is that they're losing the gender war. In response to powerful social forces, boys in the Western world are becoming more feminized. Meanwhile, boys in the Muslim world are increasingly encouraged to think of themselves as warriors for Allah. In the event of a clash between these two cultures, who seems more likely to prevail?

Christianity's Masculinity Crisis

It might seem odd to classify gender theory as a national security threat. After all, if a woman feels she was meant to be a man, there seems to be no reason why her personal desires should have any impact on national policy.

But, as you're no doubt aware, gender theorists want to make it a national issue. They want to challenge all the assumptions about masculinity and femininity upon which a great many social arrangements are based. And they want your children to be indoctrinated in the latest gender fads as soon as they enter school. According to *Get Out Now*,[105] a 2019 book on public schools by Mary Rice Hasson, J.D., and Theresa Farnan, Ph.D., "most school districts across the country have embraced gender ideology." Thus, in one Minnesota kindergarten, children were introduced to the concept of gender fluidity by listening to a reading of *My Princess Boy*. Not to be outdone, a California kindergarten teacher read her students *I Am Jazz*—a book about a boy becoming a girl.

G. K. Chesterton observed that "it ought to be the oldest things that are taught to the youngest people." In other words, children should be first exposed to the time-tested ideas and facts that we're most sure of.

---

[105] Marcia Segelstein, "Get Out Now: Why You Should Pull Your Child from Public School," *National Catholic Register*, February 1, 2019, https://www.ncregister.com/blog/segelstein/get-out-now-why-you-should-pull-your-child-from-public-school.

But in today's educational wonderland, Chesterton's formula has been turned on its head. These days, educators feel they have a mandate to introduce the most novel and untested theories to the youngest people.

One of the fashionable new theories is that traditional expressions of masculinity, such as roughhousing among boys, are "toxic" and ought to be eliminated. But whatever the dangers posed to society by masculine aggression, a greater danger arises when men lack the instinct to resist aggression.

Here's where the national security threat comes in. If there ever was a time when males in Western societies needed to be unconfused about their gender, this is it. We're surrounded by enemies and potential enemies who are unapologetic about their gender identity and are quite prepared to rule over those weaker cultures that prefer appeasement to confrontation.

Islam, which is a hypermasculine religion, is the world's fastest-growing religion. Indeed, its appeal to basic masculine psychology is one of the chief reasons for its success. In military-like summer camps across the Islamic world, young boys are taught who their enemies are, and they are taught survival skills, hand-to-hand combat, and weapons use. Along with developing fighting skills, the boys also develop a sense of camaraderie and even brotherhood. And because the training includes religious study, they often acquire a sense of transcendent purpose. Because this type of life — let's call it "purpose-driven strife" — is highly appealing to many young men, the jihad doesn't have a recruitment problem.

Such an education obviously has the potential for creating a warped sense of masculinity. But it's worth recalling that, in former days, the elite English schools sought to develop masculine virtues in boys through a combination of chapel, study, and competitive sports. It was thought that by channeling natural masculine drives, boys would be better prepared for the battles of life as well as actual battles. The Battle of Waterloo was famously said to have been won on the playing fields of Eton.

The question for today is how should men in Western societies — many of whom have been taught to seek safe spaces when their ideas are challenged — respond when faced with truly toxic masculinity?

By displaying their feminine side? By wearing short skirts? Believe it or not, that's exactly how a few hundred Dutch men responded to the twelve hundred sexual assaults by Muslim migrants that took place in Cologne, Germany, on New Year's Eve 2015. To show their solidarity with the assault victims, the men marched through the streets of Amsterdam wearing short skirts.[106]

Unless you have a graduate degree in gender studies, you'll realize that the short-skirts parade is an inadequate response to what happened in Cologne. It doesn't send the message "We mean business"; instead, it sends the message "You don't need to take us seriously." Indeed, such a confused and feeble gesture serves only to embolden further those men who already think of infidel women as "easy meat."[107]

Sadly, the emasculation of much of Western society has been matched by a similar trend in the Church. In his 1999 book *The Church Impotent: The Feminization of Christianity*,[108] Leon Podles noted that women were significantly more involved in Church activities than men were. More importantly, he observed that Christian churches seemed to have lost the masculine spirit that inspired the men commissioned by Jesus to spread the gospel even in the face of persecution and martyrdom. Podles claimed that one of the chief reasons that mainline churches were losing membership is that young men considered church attendance to be unmanly.

The situation is worse today than the one Podles described twenty years ago. Some Christian schools, including Catholic schools, are submitting to parts of the LGBT agenda, and some churches now fly the rainbow flag. Although the hijab is widely understood to be a symbol of female submission, several Catholic colleges celebrate International Hijab

---

[106] "Dutch Men Put On Mini-Skirts to Support Victims of Sex Attacks," RT, January 17, 2016, https://www.rt.com/news/329221-netherlands-mini-skirts-rally/.

[107] Peter McLoughlin, *Easy Meat: Inside Britain's Grooming Gang Scandal* (Nashville: New English Review Press, 2016).

[108] Leon Podles, *The Church Impotent: The Feminization of Christianity* (Dallas: Spence Publishing, 1999).

Day to show their solidarity with Muslim women—a gesture that, in its own way, is just as misguided as Dutch men marching in skirts. We are even seeing signs of excessive deference from popes: John Paul II kissed a Koran, and Francis kissed the feet of Muslim migrants. However these gestures may have been intended, they were certainly seen as signs of submission in large parts of the Muslim world. Pope Francis's decision to allow Chinese bishops to be chosen by the Chinese government has also been seen by many as a sign of surrender.

More seriously, Church leaders have turned a blind eye to the widespread persecution of Christians. Although Christianity is the most persecuted religion in the world, and although it faces extinction in the Middle East, the Vatican has done little to respond to the crisis. Some suggest that our shepherds remain quiet in order not to provoke further aggression. Others suggest that they don't want to say anything that might jeopardize the Catholic-Muslim dialogue on which they have pinned high hopes. Whatever reluctance Church leaders show in coming to the aid of Christians, they have no hesitancy in coming to the defense of Islam. Judging by their frequent condemnation of "Islamophobia," one could conclude that they consider criticism of Islam a more serious crime than the murder of Christians.

To men of previous generations, such behavior would have seemed irresponsibly passive. And it seems so to many men and women today —particularly to parents who have families to raise and protect. They sense that the persecution of Christian communities and the abduction and enslavement of Christian girls ought to evoke a stronger response than "Hush! You might offend them."

The Church is in trouble today not because it is perceived as too masculine, but because it is perceived as too effeminate—that is, too yielding, too submissive, too absorbed in frivolous pursuits, and too concerned with appearance over substance.

It doesn't help matters that in two of the most important recent Church gatherings—the World Meeting of Families in Dublin (2018) and the Youth Synod in Rome (2018)—Church leaders showed an unusual solicitude for LGBT individuals and families[109] while paying scant attention to families of the mother-father-and-children sort.

And it certainly doesn't help that the Church is embroiled in ongoing sex-abuse scandals. The stories about wayward priests and indulgent bishops will serve only to convince many that the priesthood is not a manly vocation. Yet instead of taking decisive action to change course, many of our bishops prefer to continue down the path of therapeutic accompaniment. A number of influential prelates now seem to view the Church primarily as a nonjudgmental group-therapy institute for the working out of sexual and emotional problems. This also detracts from the sense of masculine mission that once attracted young men to the Church. Instead of urging us to get outside ourselves in order to convert the world to Christ, today's priest counselors seem to be urging us in the direction of self-absorbed navel-gazing.

In a hundred ways, Church leaders are sending out the same message as the Dutch men in skirts—namely, "You don't need to take us seriously."

Meanwhile, because men still have a religious impulse and also a need to establish their masculinity, we can expect more conversions to Islam. As I have pointed out elsewhere,[110] Islam has a serious masculinity problem of its own, but on a superficial level it seems to fit with basic masculine psychology. Islam lacks a sense of the Fatherhood of God and, as a result, it lacks the sense that masculine maturity has more to do with family and fatherhood than with conquests on the battlefield or in the bedroom. However, since many elements of Islam do mesh with a boy's or young man's immature conception of masculinity, it remains attractive to many. For one thing, young men like to be on the winning side, and, increasingly, Islam looks to be the winning side. As Osama bin

---

[109] William Kilpatrick, "The Misplaced Priorities of Youth Synod Organizers," *Crisis Magazine*, October 10, 2018, https://www.crisismagazine.com/2018/the-misplaced-priorities-of-youth-synod-organizers.

[110] Kilpatrick, *Christianity, Islam and Atheism*, chap. 12.

Laden observed, "When people see a strong horse and a weak horse, they naturally gravitate toward the strong horse."

As long as Western societies continue to sow confusion about masculinity and femininity, the gravitation toward Islam will continue, and our security will be further endangered. Our society's frivolous experimentation with gender fluidity is a very dangerous game.

Muslims for Same-Sex "Marriage"?

The German parliament voted in favor of same-sex "marriage" in June 2017, and to the wonder of all, all six Muslim members of the Bundestag also voted in favor.[111]

Well, make that to the wonder of all the "rubes." Sophisticated people wouldn't be astonished. They've always contended that Muslims will have no problem assimilating into Western culture, even with all its oddities. For example, after the vote, activist Felipe Henriques tweeted, "Most Germans and all Muslim MPs believe in equality. Who needs integration?"[112]

"Who needs integration?" The implication is that Muslims are by and large already integrated into German society. In other words, they've learned to go with the flow. And the flow, judging by the 393–226 vote in the Bundestag, is in the direction of sexual license.

So according to one sophisticate, Muslim MPs voted for same-sex "marriage" because they believe in equality. That's one way of looking at it. But is it possible that they could have had another motive?

Did the 387 non-Muslim MPs stop to think that the legalization of same-sex "marriage" is just a step on the way to the legalization of

[111] Greg Wilford, "All of Germany's Muslim MPs Voted in Favour of Same-Sex Marriage," *Independent*, July 2, 2017, https://www.independent.co.uk/news/world/europe/angela-merkel-chancellor-germany-same-sex-marriage-vote-lgbt-muslim-mps-berlin-bundestag-cdu-sdp-a7819391.html.
[112] Ibid.

polygamy? The arguments that are used to justify same-sex "marriage" can just as easily be used to justify multiple-partner marriages. If marriage is no longer to be confined to one man and one woman, why not allow one man and four women?

Italy's largest Muslim umbrella group, the Union of Islamic Communities and Organizations, has already demanded the legalization of polygamy on the grounds that Italian law permits same-sex civil unions.[113]

Could it be that the Muslim MPs in Germany who voted "for" had something else in mind besides equality for gays and lesbians? In the long run, the decision will work to the advantage of Muslims, even those Muslims who are adamantly opposed to same-sex "marriage."

Some believe the advantage is a demographic one. For instance, the founder of the aforementioned Italian Islamic union has stated that polygamy will increase the population. That's not necessarily so, because polygamy for some men acts to squeeze other men out of the marriage market altogether, thus potentially canceling out the higher birth rates of polygamous families. Whatever the case, there are other more subtle advantages that will accrue to the Muslim community if polygamy is legitimized.

It's not so much that polygamy will accelerate Muslim population growth, but that its introduction will be one more victory for the Islamic way of doing things. Although societies that allow polygamy do have higher fertility rates, it's not clear that polygamy is the reason.

What is increasingly clear, however, is that the more cultural markers Muslims are able to lay down, the more difficult it will be to prevent Islamization. Halal-only meals in public schools? Prayer services blocking public streets? The call to prayer broadcast by loudspeakers over entire neighborhoods? Burqas everywhere? Parallel sharia courts? Blasphemy trials in European courts for those who dare criticize Islam?

[113] Virginia Hale, "Muslims Demand Polygamy in Response to Same Sex Unions," *Breitbart*, August 9, 2016, https://www.breitbart.com/europe/2016/08/09/civil-union-muslims-demand-polygamy/.

This is the new normal in Europe, and the old European norms are more and more being made to submit to the new ones.

It's the Islamic version of "We're here, we're queer. Get used to it." So, when polygamy comes to Germany, it may not make a great difference population-wise, but it will be one more significant step on the way to turning Western culture into an Islamic one.

Just as the counterculture of the 1960s in America became the established culture by the end of the century, so the Islamic counterculture in Germany seems destined to become the dominant culture within a couple of decades. Polygamy may or may not increase the birth rate, but cultural confidence will.

People who have strong beliefs and a sense of mission tend to have children. People who lack strong beliefs tend to put off childbearing —sometimes indefinitely. And people who "marry" people of the same sex seem uninterested in procreation.

This brings us back to the same-sex "marriage" vote in the Bundestag. When the measure was approved, rainbow-colored confetti filled the chamber, and hundreds of MPs gave a standing ovation. But what were they celebrating? Gay "marriage" may have a future in Germany, but there is no future in gay "marriage."

By their very nature, same-sex unions don't produce future generations. That's why all societies up until recent times declined to put homosexual relationships on a par with heterosexual ones. German maternity wards are not going to be filled with the progeny of gay and lesbian couples. But it looks very much as though they will be filled with the children of those who believe not in a master race but a master religion.

The Muslim MPs who voted for same-sex "marriage" most likely don't want it for themselves or their kin. They want it for the *Gutmenschen* of Germany because they correctly perceive that marriage equality is one more way for the Germans to commit cultural suicide.

Most probably, the vote of the Muslim MPs was a tactical maneuver. The game of chess was developed in Muslim lands, and this looks very

much like a chess move: one sacrifices a pawn now so that one can cap-
ture a queen later.

If Germans and other Europeans don't wake up, all their queens,
kings, rooks, knights, and bishops will eventually end up in the hands of
another, very different culture. And same-sex "marriage" will be nothing
but a distant memory.

The Gender-Confusion Challenge
to Army Recruitment

One thing that you can say for ISIS, the Middle-East terrorist army, is that it doesn't have a recruitment problem.[114] Young men are streaming to Syria and Iraq from all over the world to join the cause. And they come not just from the Muslim world, but also from England, France, Sweden, Australia, and the United States.

Perhaps hoping to put a dent in the appeal of ISIS, some Western newspapers have made much of the expensive stolen watch visible on the wrist of ISIS leader Abu Bakr al-Baghdadi during his first public appearance at the Grand Mosque in Mosul. According to several articles, this proved that al-Baghdadi was a hypocrite because such a show of stolen worldly possessions is contrary to the spiritual nature of Islam.

As usual, the mainstream media is all wrong about Islam. As Daniel Greenfield points out, looting was a central feature of Muhammad's conquests. And it came with Allah's seal of approval. Numerous passages in the Koran and in the biography of Muhammad attest to the legitimacy of booty as the proper reward of fighting. Islam has no trouble with looting, says Greenfield, because it is "at its core a gang religion":

[114] This essay was published in 2014, when ISIS was at its greatest strength. For a summary of the rise and fall of ISIS, see "Timeline: The Rise, Spread, and Fall of the Islamic State," Wilson Center, October 28, 2019, https://www.wilsoncenter.org/article/timeline-the-rise-spread-and-fall-the-islamic-state.

The gang ... finds meaning in the ethos of the fight and in the comradeship of fellow gang members. That is why jihad is so central to Islam.... Jihad is the gang culture of Islam. Its bonding rituals are central to Islam, whose original elements derive mainly from the raids of Mohammed and his companions.[115]

Young men join gangs not just for the booty but also for the sense of brotherhood the gang confers and, perhaps primarily, for proof of masculinity. Psychologists and sociologists have known for a long time that gangs are particularly appealing to fatherless boys because boys who lack the guidance of fathers are most likely to feel insecure about their masculine identity and thus most likely to seek confirmation of it in the ultramasculine activities of gangs. Social scientists were hardly the first to discover this basic fact of male psychology. From the earliest times, almost all societies developed special rites of initiation for males to assist them in the passage from boyhood to manhood and to channel them away from antisocial activities.

When boys grow up in communities without the guidance of fathers and elders and without established rites of initiation and confirmation, they tend to create their own initiation groups and rituals of passage. This is why modern urban areas with high concentrations of fatherless boys are the places where gang formation is highest.

The epidemic of fatherless boys is a worldwide phenomenon, and it spells more recruits for the Islamic jihad. The reason the jihad doesn't have a recruitment problem is that it appeals to basic masculine psychology. It promises action, male bonding, legitimate looting, a cause to fight for, subservient females in this world, and dozens more in the next. It's the reason Muslims have been extremely successful in recruiting prisoners to Islam both in Europe and America. As I noted in *Christianity, Islam and Atheism*:

---

[115] Daniel Greenfield, "The Gang Religion of Islam," *The Jewish Press*, September 24, 2013), https://www.jewishpress.com/blogs/sultan-knish/the-gang-religion-of-islam/2013/09/24/

In the United States, roughly 80 percent of inmates who find faith during their incarceration choose Islam. Many of these men are in prison in the first place because they were attracted to the masculine world of gangs. Now they're being offered the chance to join the biggest, most powerful "gang" in the world. We're seeing the beginning of a trend in the West: fatherless boys joining gangs, then ending up in prison, then coming out of prison as converts to Islam and the jihad.[116]

There seems to be no shortage of young men willing to join up with the warrior culture of Islamic jihad. How about our own warrior culture—the U.S. military? The military still produces warriors, but the military culture is changing in ways that may make it less attractive to potential future warriors. Traditionally, the military has served, among other things, as an initiation into manhood. Past marine recruiting campaigns, for example, were built around themes such as "The Marines Make Men" and "A Few Good Men."

Exactly what today's young male recruit is being initiated into is a little more difficult to say. In 2011, Brigadier General Loretta Reynolds was put in charge of Parris Island,[117] the base where approximately half of U.S. Marines receive their basic training. By all accounts, she's a competent person. As a fellow officer put it, "Take the female part out of it, she's an outstanding officer." Take the female part out of it? But how do you do that? As General Reynolds admitted in an interview, it's confusing for some of the men who "stumble on occasion and address her as 'sir' instead of 'ma'am.'"[118] Well, yes, it can be a bit confusing when the person in charge

---

[116] Kilpatrick, *Christianity, Islam and Atheism*, 169.

[117] Craig Whitlock, "Marine Brig. Gen. L. E. Reynolds Is Parris Island's First Female Commander," *Washington Post*, August 19, 2011, https://www.washingtonpost.com/world/national-security/marine-brig-gen-le-reynolds-is-parris-islands-first-female-commander/2011/08/18/gIQA3LpqQJ_story.html.

[118] Ibid.

of manhood training is a woman. It's not a question of competency; it's a question of gender roles. Perhaps the Marine Corps can get away with putting a woman behind the top desk at Parris Island, but how would it work if the drill sergeants were women? Boot camp is a process of maturation through challenge and identification. The drill instructor is the supervisor of a male initiation rite. If he's doing his job right, he offers himself as a model of masculine excellence. But how can a woman be a model of masculinity, and how can a man identify with her as such?

Confusion about gender seems to be the order of the day in the army. When Private Bradley Manning was tried for his part in the WikiLeaks intelligence leak, his lawyers argued that the transgender soldier suffered from "gender identity confusion." The army can survive one or two gender-confused soldiers, here and there, but what happens when the top command itself is confused about matters of sex role, sexual identity, and sexual orientation? Here are some not untypical headlines:

"Pentagon Holds First-Ever Gay Pride Event"[119]

"Lesbian Couple Shares Navy's 'First Kiss' Homecoming Honors"[120]

"Soldiers Don Fake Belly, Breasts to Better Understand Pregnant Troops' Concerns"[121]

"The U.S. Could Have Its First Female Navy SEALs by 2016"[122]

---

[119] Rowan Scarborough, "Pentagon Holds First Gay Pride Event," *Washington Times*, June 26, 2012, https://www.washingtontimes.com/news/2012/jun/26/pentagon-holds-first-gay-pride-event/.

[120] Douglas Stanglin, "Lesbian Couple Share Navy's 'First Kiss' Homecoming Honors," *USA Today*, December 21, 2011, http://content.usatoday.com/communities/ondeadline/post/2011/12/lesbian-couple-share-navys-first-kiss-homecoming-honors/1#.XjPscm5FxNQ.

[121] Seth Robson, "Soldiers Don Fake Belly, Breasts to Better Understand Pregnant Troops' Concerns," *Stars and Stripes*, February 16, 2012, https://www.stripes.com/news/army/soldiers-don-fake-belly-breasts-to-better-understand-pregnant-troops-exercise-concerns-1.168786.

[122] Josh Voorhees, "The U.S. Could Have Its First Female Navy SEALs by 2016," *Slate*, June 18, 2013, https://slate.com/news-and-politics/2013/06/

The matter becomes even more complicated when you add mission confusion to gender confusion. The main mission of the army is to win wars, but it hasn't been allowed to do that in quite a long while. Moreover, at one time, it was thought a good idea to name your enemy, and for the sake of morale, you could even poke fun at him. Nowadays, enemies are identified only vaguely (as in "violent extremists"), and name-calling is not allowed. A manual for U.S. troops in Afghanistan cautions them to avoid "making derogatory comments about the Taliban." The army's mission also has something to do with instilling a sense of the values the army is fighting for. General Eisenhower spoke of the war against the Nazis as a "Crusade in Europe." Woodrow Wilson said that our participation in World War I was to "make the world safe for democracy." Now that the military has become a lifestyle laboratory, it's a bit more difficult to discern the military's mission. Here's a 2011 headline from the *Los Angeles Times*:

"Air Force Academy Adapts to Pagans, Druids, Witches, and Wiccans: Officials Say an $80,000 Stonehenge-Like Worship Center Underscores a Commitment to Embrace All Religions"[123]

We may not think very highly of ISIS soldiers, but at least they're clear about their mission — fighting for the sake of Allah and the rewards that come of it. But what's the mission of our troops? To make the world safe for wizardry? Affirmative action for transgender schoolteachers?

The Obama administration and the Pentagon may deny it, but the feminization and "gaying" of the military, together with the blurring of the army's mission, is bound to have an effect on the attractiveness of the military for young men. It's not a question of whether gays can fight or whether women make good warriors; it's a question of what kind of

---

female-navy-seals-penatagon-unveils-plan-for-women-to-train-for-elite-forces.html.

[123] Jenny Deam, "Air Force Academy Adapts To Pagans, Druids, Witches and Wiccans," *Los Angeles Times*, November 26, 2011, https://www.latimes.com/archives/la-xpm-2011-nov-26-la-na-air-force-pagans-20111127-story.html.

culture is being created. Right now, the U.S. military is in the process of creating the kind of culture that is a guaranteed turn-off for many potential enlistees. And it's not as though they have an abundance of qualified candidates from which to choose. At a time when 71 percent of American youth[124] would fail to qualify for military service because of obesity, tattoos, prescription drug use, felony convictions, and educational level, the Pentagon can ill-afford to gamble that their unprecedented social experiments will work out for the best.

By all appearances, ISIS doesn't face an obesity crisis among its pool of potential recruits. Men who, for religious reasons, are willing to fast till evening every day for the month of Ramadan are already used to the kinds of sacrifices that the warrior life requires. Moreover, ISIS and other similar groups can count on the gender-confused West to churn out even more recruits for Islam. The breakdown of the idea that men have a special role to play as protectors and providers has led to a widespread collapse of the family. And that, in turn, has resulted in an epidemic of fatherless children.

There are armies of teens in the West who are looking for an army to join. It doesn't have to be a real army. A gang will do—so long as it provides male bonding, a warrior ethos, and the "reputation" that goes along with gang membership.

A young man without a father around will naturally be looking for the biggest, toughest brotherhood on the block. Increasingly, that looks like militant Islam. It promises everything that a wannabe warrior could ask for, and it commands far more respect than the average street gang ever will.

Our own military should take note. When the armies of Islam are drawing young men from around the world to join the jihad, it might not be the best time for the U.S. Army to emphasize its feminine side.

---

[124] Miriam Jordan, "Recruits' Ineligibility Tests the Military," *Wall Street Journal*, June 27, 2014, https://www.wsj.com/articles/recruits-ineligibility-tests-the-military-1403909945.

Raising Lion Cubs for the Caliphate

There are a number of Muslim reform movements in the West and in the Muslim world that aim to make Islam a more peaceful religion by removing the more offensive parts. Some reformers, for example, want to rebuild Islam around the more peaceful verses of the Koran while discarding the violent verses.

But what if the main appeal of Islam lies precisely in those parts that the reformers wish to excise? What if the aggressiveness of Islam, its ambition to conquer the world, and its demand that others submit are its main attractions?

I recently watched a video of Syrian boys on a bus on their way to a training academy.[125] They appeared to range in age from nine to twelve, many wore camouflage uniforms, and they seemed to be enjoying themselves thoroughly. They were singing the praises of jihad. Except for the lyrics, they could have been a group of Cub Scouts or Boy Scouts going off to summer camp. The lyrics? Here's a sample:

> O Mother, don't be sad. I've chosen the land of jihad. Wipe your tears. I only went to fight the Jews.

And another:

---

[125] VICE News, "Inside the Battle: Al Nusra-Al Qaeda in Syria," YouTube video, 32:18, posted November 11, 2015, https://www.youtube.com/watch?v=7sPYOX8SrLo.

(Boy leader:) Our destiny? Our destiny?
(Chorus:) Jihad! Jihad!

A bearded man in his twenties, the leader of the group, explains to the camera: "We call this generation the cubs of a lion.... God willing these youth will establish a caliphate ... and they will carry the message of jihad." He asks one boy, "Why did you come here?" Answer: "To become a Mujahideen fighter." If you're thinking that these ISIS loyalists will be hard nuts to crack, think again. The film follows the activities of the Syrian branch of al-Nusra al-Qaeda, a group that is fighting *against* ISIS (and also against President Assad's government).

ISIS is not the only Islamic group that wants to raise up a generation of warriors. Young Palestinians, for example, receive similar paramilitary training. And along with lessons in shooting and stabbing, they are given the message that fighting and dying for Allah is life's highest calling. The warrior tradition in Islam is an ancient one, prescribed in the Koran, and, thanks to the Iranian Revolution, very much back in style.

It all seems alien to those of us who live in the West. But it shouldn't. Islamic apologists like to say that Islam is the natural religion of mankind. And, if you are speaking of the natural inclinations of males, there's a lot of truth to that assertion. Overly feminized societies have difficulty understanding that there is a natural pleasure in physical combat. I'm not talking about the bloody combat of the battlefield. Men don't take naturally to the prospect of being torn to pieces by a grenade. Soldiers need to be trained and conditioned before they're ready for actual warfare. What I'm referring to are the schoolyard and backyard tests of strength and skill that boys are naturally drawn to.

At the Catholic grammar school I attended, it was not uncommon for boys to issue friendly challenges of "combat." The most common of these involved a standing hand-wrestling contest to see who could throw the other off balance first. Sometimes the combat involved free-style wrestling contests that ended only when one party agreed to "give up" or say "uncle." The satisfaction lay not so much in hurting your opponent but in forcing him to submit. After school, we would often play at war games—using imaginary machine guns to wipe out an imaginary nest of enemies or lobbing imaginary grenades into imaginary bunkers.

Obviously, such activities have the potential for turning into something unhealthy. That's why civilized societies try to sublimate aggressive instincts into healthy channels, such as team sports (which, despite its benefits, is still a form of combat involving victory for one side and defeat for the other). It has long been recognized that one way of countering the natural tendency of young males to form tribal-like gangs is to get them off the streets and onto the basketball courts.

However, sublimation is one thing, and repression is another. If a society becomes "overcivilized," it risks losing the aggressive instinct altogether and thus the ability to defend itself. An ability and a willingness to fight is essential even in a civilized society. A healthy society doesn't try to snuff out aggressiveness and toughness; it tries to convince young men to put their strength and skills in the service of a higher cause.

But what if the higher cause *is* fighting? Or, more precisely, fighting for Allah? The appeal of Islam is that it takes the aggressive male instinct and combines it with the religious instinct. A large part of the training that the al-Nusra al-Qaeda boys receive is religious training. They sit at desks and learn their catechism—only it's a catechism of jihad. In Islam, God doesn't ask for much in the way of sublimation; he puts his seal of approval on the male's instinctual urge to fight and dominate. Religious duty and the thrill of conquest. Unfortunately, it's a combination that's hard to beat.

It seems unlikely that the Muslim reformist attempt to create an Islam-Lite is going to work. Nevertheless, non-Muslims should wish them well, because if they do succeed, Islam would quickly lose much of its appeal and energy. But it's a long shot. If you take away the fighting-and-subjugating part, and if you remove the conquest-of-the-world part, what do you have left? Not much that would interest a young man. Not much to compete with the join-the-jihad-type videos put out by ISIS and Hamas.

If, in addition, you were to take away the seventy-two-virgins-in-paradise part, you greatly increase the risk that many will lose interest in the faith. Young men like to fight, but they don't like to risk their lives for nothing. The seventy-two virgins loom very large in the calculations of young jihadists. Yes, they fight for Allah, but that, in large part, is because Allah has a rich reward in store for them.

Take away all that, and what do you have? You have a handful of scattered verses about mercy, peace, and justice, and a tradition—mostly borrowed from other religions—of prayer, almsgiving, fasting, and pilgrimage. What you have, in other words, is the kind of religion that speaks to a certain kind of soul but doesn't have much to say to the young man who is searching for a fighting faith.

In addition, the Muslim reformers are left with the problem of what to say about the main hero of Islam—Muhammad. He was the first jihadist—a warlord who ordered torture and mass beheadings, sold women and children into slavery, and pronounced sex slaves to be the rightful property of the victors. Islam minus Muhammad would be a kinder, gentler religion. But can you have an Islam without Muhammad? After all, the Islamic confession of faith requires a Muslim to testify that there is no God but God, and to testify further that Muhammad is the messenger of God. Next to Allah, Muhammad is the central figure in Islam.

Islam is a purpose-driven religion. Its purpose is to conquer the world for Allah. The boys on the bus in the video don't look mean or angry. Indeed, many of them seem sweet and affable. But they have a determined purpose, and because of that purpose, some of them will likely grow up to be killers.

Hopefully, the changes that the Muslim reformists envision can someday be accomplished. Hopefully, they will be able to convince other Muslims that subjugating the world ought not to be the purpose of their existence. In the meantime, non-Muslims can't afford to lose sight of their own higher purposes—those things in life that are worth defending.

We tend to forget how easy it is to lose sight of the essentials. As Ronald Reagan said, "Freedom is never more than one generation away from extinction." So are a number of other essential rights. Indeed, many of the core beliefs that could be taken for granted in Reagan's lifetime can no longer be assumed. Today's young people grow up in a different kind of society—one that values tolerance, diversity, and celebrity, and not much else.

If you're of a certain age, it's likely that you notice things the young don't notice—for instance, the West's pathetically passive response to repeated acts of Islamic aggression. That's not a normal state of affairs. But, as Mark Steyn recently observed:

> The young ... have no memory of when their societies were not like this. And if you have no sense that things were once other than this, you cannot mourn the loss, and you're certainly unlikely to fight to retrieve it.[126]

Even if the core virtues of Judeo-Christian, Western societies can be retrieved and reinstilled, one other thing is necessary. Even when a society knows what values are worth defending, it can't afford to lose the fighting qualities without which no effective defense can be mounted.

---

[126] Mark Steyn, "A Tale of Two Johnsons," Steyn Online, June 23, 2017, https://www.steynonline.com/7938/a-tale-of-two-johnsons.

7

Sensitizing Ourselves to Death

The sensitivity movement of the 1960s and '70s brought with it an emphasis on the subjective self that has never really gone away. In schools, the cultivation of self-esteem became more important than the acquisition of objective knowledge. And feelings became more important than facts. Many in our society had, in short, developed a mindset that was incapable of grasping dangerous realities.

The Normalization of Delusional Thinking

I sometimes wonder how so many people can be in denial about the danger posed by Islam to the rest of the world.

The textual, historical, and statistical evidence that Islam is an aggressive religion is overwhelming, but very few are willing to look at it. On the one side, you have a ton of hard evidence, and on the other side, you have ten megatons of wishful thinking: priests, prime ministers, and Hollywood celebrities assuring us that Islam is more peaceful than Christianity, more feminist than Gloria Steinem, and more caring than the Red Cross.

It's the textbook definition of a delusion: a false belief or wrong judgment held with conviction despite incontrovertible evidence to the contrary. But, as I've come to realize, this delusional thinking is not specific to the crisis posed by Islam. Rather, it's part of a larger pattern. In many ways, delusional thinking has become a main feature of the modern mind.

Take the transgender issue. All of a sudden, a significant percentage of our social and intellectual elites have succumbed to the delusion that a girl can be a boy, and a boy can be a girl, or whatever he, she, ne, ze, zir currently desires to be. This is not merely a rebellion against social convention; it's a rebellion against reality. It's a rejection of basic biology.

The most disturbing aspect of the "gender fluidity" fad is not that there are young and not-so- young (e.g., Bruce Jenner) people who are badly confused about their gender but that there are legions of professionals — doctors, psychologists, teachers — who stand ready to confirm them in their delusion and even pump them full of puberty blockers and cross-sex hormones.

More sinister still, there are other authorities who want to punish those who fail to honor the delusion. The California senate recently passed a bill to fine and even imprison nursing-home workers who fail to address patients by their preferred pronoun.[127] Meanwhile, the New York City Commission on Human Rights issued a "guidance" to business owners requiring them to use a person's preferred pronoun or face a fine of $125,000 for "misgendering."[128]

In the old South there used to be laws against miscegenation, but nowadays in sophisticated, modern Manhattan, you can be fined for "misgendering." Imagine that. If Max, the doorman, wants to be called Maxine today, you'd better go along with it, or else risk bankruptcy. And if on Thursday he decides he's Maximilian I, the emperor of Mexico, you'd be wise to address him as "your imperial majesty," just to stay on the right side of the Human Rights Commission. In short, you are at the mercy of Max and his multiple identities.

There are several parallels here to what has become the standard response to Islam. As with transgenderism, we see an official denial of reality: Islamic terror has nothing to do with Islam, the terrorists (who are only a "handful") "misunderstand" their faith, Islamic values are just the same as Christian values, and so on.

Likewise, just as you're not allowed to call Bruce Jenner "he," you're not supposed to say "radical Islamic terror" or "migration invasion" or any other words that might be offensive to Muslims. If you slip up and

---

[127] Georgi Boorman, "California Legislature Passes Bill to Punish Elder-Care Workers Who Don't Use Trans Pronouns," *Federalist*, September 15, 2017, https://thefederalist.com/2017/09/15/california-legislature-passes-bill-punish-elder-care-workers-dont-use-trans-pronouns/.

[128] Bradford Richardson, "New York Businesses Face Hefty Penalties for 'Misgendering' Customers," *Washington Times*, May 18, 2016, https://www.washingtontimes.com/news/2016/may/18/de-blasio-fine-businesses-wrong-gender-pronouns/.

use "Islamophobic" language, you can expect the same consequences that would follow if you called Maxine "Max" on the wrong day of the week—namely, ostracism, job loss, and a heavy fine. Years before the New York City Human Rights Commission started policing transgressive words, columnist Mark Steyn was hauled before three Canadian human rights commissions for defamation of religion. His crime? In an article for *Macleans*, he noted the readily verifiable fact that Muslim birthrates in Europe were outstripping those of native Europeans.

Steyn is not alone. Dozens of prominent Europeans have faced similar trials, not because they said anything false about Islam, but because they made factual statements that Muslims found offensive. That sort of treatment sends a message, and most people have no trouble understanding the message. Whether the topic is Islam, or gender ideology, it's not prudent to speak your mind. For example, although most adults realize that boys can't be girls, and vice versa, most are too cowed to say otherwise, except to trusted friends and relatives.

As Matthew Hanley observes in an incisive piece on the subject, such compelled speech is "degrading"; moreover, "making [others] agree to something they know is a lie is a hallmark of totalitarianism."[129] True enough, some people don't know it's a lie. They've been conditioned in school and college to believe that boys can be girls, that same-sex "marriage" is the equivalent of heterosexual marriage, and that Islam is responsible for most of history's great cultural and scientific breakthroughs. The fact that these lies are believed by so many is testimony to the soft totalitarian takeover of our educational system.

The totalitarian creep has been going on for quite some time. Back in the early nineties, a university colleague excitedly told me that the big new thing in educational theory was "constructivism." Actually, constructivism had already been the new thing in educational circles

---

[129] Matthew Hanley, "Gender Ideology as Abuse," *Catholic Thing*, September 20, 2017, https://www.thecatholicthing.org/2017/09/20/gender-ideology-as-abuse/print.

for at least a couple of decades prior to his personal revelation. It's the idea that there are no objective truths, and hence each individual has to construct his own reality. According to this school of thought, *Huckleberry Finn* has no objective meaning, only the meaning you read into it. If you decide that *Huckleberry Finn* is a story about a transgendered adolescent seeking his true gender (your teachers will happily encourage you in that direction), then that's the meaning of *Huckleberry Finn*. Whatever Mark Twain had in mind is irrelevant.

These as-you-like-it educational theories arose in tandem with the self-esteem movement that began to sweep through schools, colleges, and seminaries in the 1960s and '70s. The self-esteem craze came out of the work of Carl Rogers, the pioneer of nondirective, nonjudgmental therapy. Rogers taught that we should trust our inner selves, that morality is subjective, and that what's right for you isn't necessarily right for me. In his later years, as he developed an interest in Eastern thought, Rogers began to doubt the existence of objective reality. Reality, he came to believe, was something that each person created for himself.[130]

Post-Rogers, the whole direction of education shifted—from exploring the world to exploring the self; from grappling with objective realities, such as mathematics, history, and geography, to discovering every nook and cranny of the subjective self. Nondirective education was the prelude to what we have now: in the case of gender ideology, the triumph of feelings over biological facts, and, in the case of Islam, the triumph of feel-good narratives over historical realities.

Another objective reality that came under attack during the self-esteem era was the existence of God, or, more accurately, the existence of the God who reveals himself in the Old and New Testaments—the God who makes demands on the individual self. In his place, many substituted vague, New Age-ish forms of spirituality. Either that, or they began to conceive of God as a servant of their emotional needs—an

[130] William Kilpatrick, *Why Johnny Can't Tell Right from Wrong: And What We Can Do About It* (New York: Simon & Schuster, 1993), 34–37, 217–218.

all-understanding therapist in heaven who just wants everyone to feel good about himself, herself, zeself, zirself.

The famous maxim attributed to Chesterton applies here: "The first effect of not believing in God is to believe in anything."[131] Once you lose sight of the central objective reality in the universe, it's easy to lose sight of all the other realities, and you end up believing in anything—no matter how counterfactual the "anything" might be. You might believe that same-sex couples are truly married. You might believe that males can become females. You might even believe—heaven help you—that Islam is a religion of peace.

---

[131] The quotation was first attributed to G. K. Chesterton by Émile Cammaerts in *The Laughing Prophet: The Seven Virtues and G. K. Chesterton* (London: Methuen, 1937).

Revolution and Regression

"Times have changed. It's not the '90s anymore." So says a TV commercial for a brokerage firm. Presumably, the lesson is that investment strategies that worked then won't work now: the market has changed, and so should you.

Times have changed in other respects also. The assumptions that one could safely make about the world in the '90s no longer seem operative. Yet it's not at all clear that the government and the citizenry are making the necessary adjustments. To judge by our society's complacency about world events, many of us seem to assume that it still is the '90s, or, more precisely, that we can still rely on yesterday's suppositions.

But the fact is, we've entered a new era with new rules. The most obvious change is the rebirth of militant Islam. And that threat alone has several facets: the Iranian nuclear threat, the Islamic jihad threat, and the stealth jihad threat. Islam's recent history is proof that human affairs don't always move in a forward direction. Indeed, the resurgence of fundamentalist Islam marks one of the great regressions of world history. Suddenly, in historical terms, the world was thrust back not to the 1990s but to the 690s. For modern Western societies, it was not so much a case of future shock but of "past shock"—an encounter with a past that seemed almost incomprehensible.

Citizens of the early twenty-first century were no more prepared for the return of honor killings, sex slavery, and beheadings than they would have been for the arrival of robots in spaceships. So, face-to-face with the seventh century, contemporary readers of entrails explained these barbarities in the only way they knew how—that is, in terms of a twentieth-century framework. Thus, it was supposed that the jihadists were raping, beheading, and crucifying because they couldn't find jobs or because they were still chafing from past imperialism.

In addition to the resurgence of Islam, the West has been faced with a series of other massive transformations—all compressed into a short period of time. Some of these changes are also regressive in nature: nothing on the scale of Islam's great leap backward, but still disturbingly reminiscent of bad times we thought we had left behind us. Among other back-to-the-past events that we are trying to cope with are these:

- a return to the kind of racial discord and division that marred the '60s
- increasingly dangerous cities reminiscent of the worst days of the '70s and '80s, when muggers roamed city streets and movie audiences cheered on Charles Bronson's vigilante hero in *Death Wish*[132]
- the vampire-like return of the organized left, now stronger than ever after a brief period of dormancy and thirsting for blood as never before
- the beginnings of a new cold war with Russia
- the spread of diseases that were once believed to be eradicated or else thoroughly under control

Admittedly, not all of the changes we face are replays of the past. Some of the challenges confronting us are genuinely new. The dystopian societies predicted by George Orwell and Aldous Huxley (1894–1963)[133] appear to have arrived ahead of schedule. Of course, Orwell had the

---

[132] *Death Wish*, directed by Michael Winner, written by Brian Garfield and Wendell Mayes, released July 24, 1974, https://www.imdb.com/title/tt0071402/

[133] Aldous Huxley, *Brave New World* (London: Chatto & Windus, 1932).

Soviet Union in mind when he wrote *1984*. So Orwellian societies aren't entirely new. What's new is the emergence of quasi-Orwellian cultures all over the West. What we experience is not quite the total control exercised by Ingsoc in the novel, but rather a world in which traditional values and freedoms are slowly giving way to therapeutic imperatives. The thought control of the early twenty-first century is exercised in the name of "tolerance" and "sensitivity," but it is applied in a ruthlessly effective manner. You won't go to jail for saying the incorrect thing (although that time is rapidly approaching), but you might well lose your reputation and your job.

What's also new is the expanded role played by the media and entertainment industries in creating and enforcing this soft totalitarianism. One way they do this is by reinforcing the state's anti-marriage, anti-church agenda. Totalitarian societies always strive to break an individual's local loyalties and transfer them to the state. Since the main rivals to the state are church and family, absolutist governments will do their best to control and remake these institutions. The entertainment industry, which once supported church and family, now works to deconstruct them. TV networks normalized same-sex "marriage" long before the Supreme Court did. And sitcoms and talk shows have long pedaled the notion that alternative families are cool.

The attempt to remake the family is a truly revolutionary change, yet judging by various polls, the majority seem unable to grasp the radical nature of the experiment. It's difficult to comprehend because one other feature of totalitarian thought control is the erasure of the past and its replacement with ersatz history. Thus, it becomes nearly impossible to understand events in context, since the context has disappeared down the memory hole. In *1984*, it is believed that because Oceania was at war with Eurasia, "therefore Oceania had always been at war with Eurasia." In 2015, we may be approaching the point where it will be widely believed that same-sex "marriage" has always been a part of our tradition.

Occasionally, the entertainment industry manages to break out of the mold and cast a critical eye on itself. The film version of *The Hunger*

Games[134] series does a fine job of showing how entertainers can be enlisted both to support a totalitarian government and to undermine traditional notions of gender and family. The master of ceremonies of the games is a composite of Oprah, Dr. Phil, Jerry Springer, and other talk show personalities. He is a master of the tell-us-how-you-feel therapeutic style and also of the therapeutic technique of reducing all serious relationships to the level of sentimental kitsch. His sexuality is ambiguous. Is he gay? Bisexual? Transsexual? It's hard to tell. The same can be said of many of the social elites in Panemian society. They sport elaborate hairdos tinted with blues, pinks, and greens, and many of them have a drag-queenish manner about them. Quite obviously, the upper classes have little use for traditional gender roles. In one sense, they have been set free to take on whatever superficial identities they wish, yet they are all servants of the regime. They serve to put a sentimental and therapeutic gloss on a brutal system.

What has all this got to do with the threat from militant Islam? More than you'd think. Our society is not yet quite as Orwellian as the one depicted in *The Hunger Games*, but it's headed in that direction. We have already suffered a significant loss of historical context and social memory. In that environment, current events are perceived, to borrow a phrase from Elbert Hubbard, as "just one damned thing after another." Without the vantage point that a knowledge of history offers, there's no way of telling which of those things is important. Like the remaking of marriage, the advance of Islam in recent decades is a truly revolutionary movement. In fact, the chief twentieth-century architects of Islamism—people like Sayyid Qutb and Maulana A'la Maududi—envisioned the Islamist movement in exactly that way. But, as with the marriage revolution, few seem able to grasp the radical nature of this historical shift.

A revolutionary movement to take over the world? If you watch too much television, you might get the impression that the main threat to

---

[134] *The Hunger Games*, directed by Gary Ross, written by Gary Ross, Suzanne Collins, and Billy Ray, released March 23, 2012, https://www.imdb.com/title/tt1392170/.

our society is not jihad, but something called "Islamophobia"—an ir-rational fear of Islam. "Islamophobia," of course, is a therapeutic term, and like other therapeutic terms—"homophobia," for instance—it is designed to divert attention away from the main issues. "Islamophobia" is the fashionable kind of threat that media personalities are accustomed to fret over. It has nothing to do with the burning of churches or the bombing of cities and everything to do with sensitivity to feelings.

You may be tempted to laugh at this inversion of priorities, just as you may be tempted to laugh about the new gender rules. But, as Mark Steyn writes in regard to the latter, "nobody who matters, nobody who makes decisions for you and yours, nobody in the vast state apparatus is laughing."[135] For them, it's all deadly serious, and it's always full steam ahead. Meanwhile, their civilization-destroying experiments with mar-riage and family are producing individuals who are so absorbed in their own issues that they can scarcely see any larger issues. The progeny of the marriage revolution can barely recognize the Islamization process, let alone find the strength to resist it.

A few paragraphs back, I said that we are experiencing "past shock"—an encounter with brutal traditions that were long thought extinct. But that's not completely accurate. The only ones who are shocked are those members of our society who grew up in a more civilized American culture than the one we now have. Many of the younger set aren't shocked by the brutality, and some of them rather fancy it. Else why would videotaped beheadings be such a successful recruiting tool for the Islamic State?

How does one explain this lack of shock? The problem, once again, is the toxic mix of family disintegration and media manipulation. Our experiments in family deconstruction were underway long before the advent of same-sex "marriage." And the result was a multitude of single-parent households and double-worker families in which the socialization of children was largely turned over to TV, violent video games, violent

---

[135] Mark Steyn, "Boy Meets Girl," *Steyn Online*, May 30, 2015, https://www.steynonline.com/6982/boy-meets-girl.

and misogynist music, and the peer group (gangs, in some cases). I once read an article that described a group of English mothers conversing in a park while their children played nearby. The subject of pornography came up, and some of the parents wondered aloud where it could be found. Overhearing this, the children, almost in unison, volunteered the name "Porn Hub"—a British site that, according to the author, specializes in sadomasochistic pornography.

If you want to know why we are not quite as shocked as we should be by the reappearance of things such as sex slavery, consider that the socialization of our children has been handed over to organizations such as Porn Hub. Consider further that certain kinds of brutality, such as abortion, are widely accepted in our society. And, as with Panem, the brutality is most strongly endorsed by the fashionable elites. The point is, a culture that is undergoing a moral regression of its own is less likely to notice that another major historical regression is unfolding. Head-chopping is intrinsically disturbing, but not quite so disturbing if you live in a society where highly regarded organizations buy and sell baby parts.[136]

No, it's not the '90s anymore. What we are witnessing is the rebirth of something far more primitive and savage. As the TV commercial suggests, you can lose a lot of money if you don't keep up with trends in the market. If you don't keep up with historical and social trends, you can lose both your money and those more precious things that money can't buy.

[136] Tyler O'Neil, "Court Ruling: Planned Parenthood Sting Videos Were 'Not Deceptively Edited,'" PJ Media, January 29, 2019, https://pjmedia. com/trending/court-ruling-planned-parenthood-sting-videos-were-not-deceptively-edited/.

8

Catholic Confusion about Islam

The Church was not exempt from the influence of self-esteem psychology. In fact, humanistic psychology swept through the seminaries and Catholic universities in the 1960s and '70s, leaving Catholics with a diminished sense of sin and an exaggerated trust in human nature. This trust in the essential goodness of human nature and human institutions led Catholic leaders to develop some dangerous illusions about Islam—illusions that continue to hamper our ability to grasp the threat.

The Church and Islam: Nostalgia for the '60s

I recently received an e-mail from a reader who took issue with my skeptical view of Islam. Between 1963 and 1965, he worked for the Peace Corps in a Muslim area of Nigeria. He came away from the experience convinced that "all people are basically the same" and "all want the same basic things." Cultural differences, he maintained, were merely surface phenomena.

His view is common among people who came of age in the 1960s and '70s. And, since many of our society's controlling narratives were developed in that period, that optimistic view is still widespread. But times change, even if narratives don't.

For example, the reality in Nigeria today is quite different from what my correspondent experienced in the mid-1960s. It no longer seems that all want the "same basic things." In fact, many Muslims want to deny Christians some of those basics—such as the right to worship in peace and even the right to life.

Bishop Joseph Bagobiri of Kafanchan (in northwestern Nigeria) reports that, in his diocese alone, "53 villages burned down, 808 people [were] murdered and 57 wounded, 1422 houses and 16 Churches [were] destroyed."[137] Moreover, a report by the International Society for Civil

---

[137] Giulo Meotti, "Nigeria's Christians Today, Europe's Christians Tomorrow," Gatestone Institute, March 18, 2018, https://www.gatestoneinstitute. org/12042/nigeria-christians.

Liberties and the Rule of Law revealed that 16,000 Christians had been murdered in Nigeria since June 2015.

What's happening in Nigeria has been happening all over the Muslim world. Open Doors USA reports that globally some 215 million Christians face severe persecution, mostly at the hands of Muslims.[138] The question is, which is the real Islam: the peaceable Islam experienced by my correspondent in the mid-1960s or the aggressive Islam of today?

In the context of Islam's 1,400 years of aggression, the relatively peaceful interval that began with the dissolution of the Ottoman Empire in the early twentieth century seems to be the aberration. At the time my correspondent worked for the Peace Corps in Nigeria, the Muslim world was far more moderate than it is today or was in the past. The Islam he experienced was a marked departure from traditional Islam.

Some of the flavor of that period is captured in an article by Ali A. Allawi, a former Iraqi cabinet minister:

> I was born into a mildly observant Muslim family in Iraq. At that time, the 1950s, secularism was ascendant among the political, cultural, and intellectual elites of the Middle East. It appeared to be only a matter of time before Islam would lose whatever hold it still had on the Muslim world. Even that term — "Muslim world" — was unusual, as Muslims were more likely to identify themselves by their national, ethnic, or ideological affinities than by their religion.[139]

In short, Muslim societies were more moderate in those days because they were moving away from Islam. As Allawi notes: "To an impressionable child, it was clear that society was decoupling from Islam. Though

---

[138] Courtney Grogan, "Report: There Are More Than 215 Million Persecuted Christians Worldwide," *National Catholic Register*, January 16, 2018, https://www.ncregister.com/daily-news/report-there-are-more-than-215-million-persecuted-christians-worldwide.

[139] Ali A. Allawi, *Chronicle of Higher Education*, June 29, 2009, https://www.chronicle.com/article/Islamic-Civilization-in-Peril/46964.

religion was a mandatory course in school, nobody taught us the rules of prayer or expected us to fast during Ramadan. We memorized the shorter verses of the Koran, but the holy book itself was kept on the shelf or in drawers, mostly unread."

The more moderate Muslim world of the last century was the result not of deeper piety but rather of increased secularization. There are still remnants of that moderation in Muslim lands, but it should be clear to anyone who is paying attention to current events that traditional, by-the-book Islam is once again ascendant. Miniskirts are no longer worn in Tehran and Kabul as they were in the 1970s, and the hijab has made a comeback almost everywhere in the Muslim world. In other words, the process of secularization has been reversed.

The amazing thing is that much of the Western world hasn't caught up with the changes. Why? Perhaps because the return of seventh-century Islam undercuts the multicultural belief that all cultures share the same values. Hence, many prefer to think that the Muslim world is still much the same as it was in the days of King Farouk and the shah of Iran—that relatively brief moment when "secularism was ascendant."

Unfortunately, one of the important organizations that still lives in the past in regard to Islam is the Catholic Church. Many in the Church seem to think and act as though it's still 1965 and that *Nostra Aetate* (which was promulgated in 1965) is still the last word on Islam.

The section on the "Moslems" in *Nostra Aetate*[140] reflects the multicultural notion that cultural differences are unimportant, and that all people have the same basic desires. Thus, the writers of the document took pains to emphasize the similarities between Christianity and Islam, even going so far as to suggest that the two faiths share the same moral values.

Of course, it's nearly impossible to ignore the radicalization that so many Muslims have undergone since 1965. But in their anxiety to preserve the *Nostra Aetate* "narrative" about Islam, Church leaders have found a

---

[140] Second Vatican Council, Declaration on the Relation of the Church with Non-Christian Religion *Nostra Aetate* (October 28, 1965).

way to get around this inconvenient fact. Muslims who persecute and terrorize non-Muslims are said to have "distorted" or "perverted" their religion because, in the words of Pope Francis, "authentic Islam and a proper understanding of the Koran are opposed to every form of violence."[141]

Indeed, as recently as March 16, Pope Francis told the head of the Organisation of Islamic Cooperation that there is no link between Islam and terrorism.[142] On other occasions, the pope has even said that the remedy for radicalization is for Muslims to go deeper into their faith and find guidance in the Koran. That, of course, is the very opposite of Al-lawi's firsthand observation that moderation is the result not of deepened faith, but of "decoupling from Islam."

Church leaders are still clinging to a view of Islam that should have gone out with the '70s. Unless and until they acquire a longer view of Islam, they will continue to be part of the problem rather than part of the solution.

[141] Pope Francis, *Evangelii Gaudium* 253.
[142] "OIC Secretary General Discusses with Pope Francis Terrorism, Rohingya and Quds Issues," Organisation of Islamic Cooperation, March 16, 2018, https://www.oic-oci.org/topic/?t_id=17486&t_ref=9266&lan=en.

Do Christians and Muslims
Worship the Same God?

Believe it or not, there really is a religious movement called "Chrislam." It began in Nigeria in the 1980s as an attempt to foster peace between Muslims and Christians by blending elements of Islam and Christianity. Its followers stress the commonalities between the two faiths, and they recognize both the Koran and the Bible as holy texts.

Although Chrislam has supposedly spread outside Africa, it appears to be a relatively small movement. There is, however, a much larger world-wide movement that can in a sense be considered a form of Chrislam. Its adherents minimize the differences between Islam and Christianity, and they describe themselves as "people of the book" and members of the "Abrahamic faith tradition." The main ritual of the Chrislamites is the dialogue — a ceremony that will serve, they hope, to build bridges between the two faiths. People who are dubious about these bridge-building efforts are dismissed as "bigots" and "Islamophobes."

Catholics, in particular, are highly susceptible to the allure of Chrislamism. Many of them feel that a reconciliation between Islam and Catholicism is possible. They are fond of saying that "we all worship the same God," and they invariably cite the passage in the *Catechism of the Catholic Church* that says, "Together with us, they [Muslims] adore the one merciful God" (841). Catholics also point to the longer passage in *Nostra Aetate* that says much the same thing and adds that Muslims revere Jesus, honor Mary, and value the moral life (no. 3).

Though it's certainly true that Muslims and Christians can live together in peace, the hope that a bridge can be built between the two religions may be a bridge too far.

One of the most interesting commentaries on the subject was published in 1956 in, of all things, a children's book. C. S. Lewis addressed the possibility of finding common ground with Islam in *The Last Battle*, the final book in the Chronicles of Narnia. Lewis doesn't use the terms "Islam" and "Christianity" in his fictional account, but it's quite obvious to an adult reader that the Narnians are meant to represent Christians, and their enemies, the Calormenes, are meant to represent Muslims. For those in doubt on this point, the Islamic nature of Calormene society is more fully established in Lewis's earlier book *The Horse and His Boy* (1954).

The main storyline unfolds quickly. Having fallen into a state of decline and ignorance, many of the Narnians are deceived into believing that their God, Aslan, and Tash, the demonic god of the Calormenes, have much in common. "Tash" and "Aslan," they are told, are only two names for the same God:

> All that old idea of us being right and the Calormenes wrong is silly. We know better now. The Calormenes use different words but we all mean the same thing. Tash and Aslan are only two different names for you know Who. That's why there can never be any quarrel between them. Tash is Aslan: Aslan is Tash.

After a while, the hybrid God is simply referred to as "Tashlan." As time passes, however, the worship of Tashlan becomes, for all intents and purposes, the worship of Tash, and the Narnians find themselves enslaved by the Calormenes.

Lewis's story provides some much-needed perspective on the question of whether Christians and Muslims worship the same God. The quandary for Christians is that, although the Allah of Islam is different in major respects from the Christian concept of God, no one wants to deny Muslims a place among the family of believers. After all, Muslims profess to hold the faith of Abraham, and many are undeniably sincere in their desire to serve God. Saying that they don't worship the one God sounds too much like saying that their prayers are wasted. Thus, a good many Christians resolve the quandary by ignoring the theological difficulties and focusing instead on the worthy acts and prayers of Muslims.

Lewis, however, is quite clear about the theological problem, and he has no use for the Chrislam—or, as he puts it, the "Tashlan"— solution. He sees no possibility of a reconciliation between the two faiths because Tash and Aslan are of radically "different kinds." They are, in fact, "opposites."

But that doesn't mean that Calormenes can't be sincere seekers of God. One character in the story who stands out is Emeth, a young Calormene officer who has sought to serve Tash all his days and whose great desire is "to know more of him." Emeth's nobility is so evident that one of the Narnians remarks that "he is worthy of a better God than Tash."

When Emeth finally encounters the true God, Aslan, he is abashed at his former service to Tash. Here is his narration:

> But I said, "Alas Lord, I am no son of thine but the servant of Tash." He answered, "Child, all the service thou hast done to Tash, I account as service done to me.... Not because he and I are one, but because we are opposites, I take to me the services which thou hast done to him. For I and he are of such different kinds that no service which is vile can be done to me, and none which is not vile can be done to him. Therefore if any man swear by Tash and keep his oath for the oath's sake, it is by me that he has truly sworn, though he know it not, and it is I who reward him. And if any man do a cruelty in my name, then, though he says the name Aslan, it is Tash whom he serves and by Tash his deed is accepted."

This passage is somewhat reminiscent of Saint Paul's comments on discovering an altar dedicated "to an unknown god" (Acts 17:23). He tells the men of Athens that the God they seek in ignorance is the one true God. Not coincidentally, the *Catechism* alludes to the same verse almost immediately after paragraph 841 — the passage about the Muslim adoration of God:

The Catholic Church recognizes in other religions that search, among shadows and images, for the God who is unknown yet near since he gives life and breath and all things and wants all men to be saved. Thus, the Church considers all goodness and truth found in these religions as "a preparation for the Gospel and given by him who enlightens all men that they may at length have life."[143]

The statement on the Muslims (841) needs to be read in the context of this statement on the God who is yet unknown. In short, whatever "goodness and truth" there is in Islam comes not through Allah but "is given by him who enlightens all men." The theme that salvation comes through Christ and his Church is reinforced in paragraph 845, which states that the Church is prefigured by Noah's ark, "which alone saves from the flood." As in Lewis's story, however, a good deal of allowance is made for those who are ignorant of Christ. Paragraph 847 could almost be a description of Emeth's situation:

Those who, through no fault of their own, do not know the Gospel of Christ or his Church, but who nevertheless seek God with a sincere heart, and, moved by grace, try in their actions to do his will as they know it through the dictates of their conscience — those too may achieve eternal salvation.[144]

The God who is described in the Koran is different in important respects from the Christian God. The differences are so radical that it would be a mistake to call them the same God. It is still possible, however, to say that Muslims worship the one God, insofar as they "seek God with a sincere heart" and try "to do his will as they know it through the dictates of their conscience." Or, as Lewis has Aslan say, "Therefore if any man

---

[143] *Catechism of the Catholic Church* (CCC), no. 843, quoting *LG* 16; cf. *NA* 2; *EN* 53.
[144] *LG* 16; cf. *DS* 3866–3872.

swear by Tash and keep his oath for the oath's sake, it is by me that he has truly sworn, though he know it not."

It's significant that this section of the *Catechism* also contains a discussion of the doctrine that says that "outside the Church there is no salvation." Paragraph 846 asks "How are we to understand this affirmation, often repeated by the Church Fathers?[145] Re-formulated positively, it means that all salvation comes from Christ the Head through the Church which is His Body." Why does *Extra Ecclesiam nulla salus* need to be "formulated positively"? The reason, of course, is that the doctrine has often been understood in a narrow, literal way. Down through the ages, not a few Catholics have interpreted it to mean that those who attend non-Catholic Churches go to hell.

Most Catholics, I think, would now admit that *Extra Ecclesiam nulla salus* was not the most felicitous way of stating the doctrine. Is it also the case that paragraph 841 is not the best possible way of formulating "the Church's relationship with the Muslims"? A lot of confusion currently surrounds that phrase "together with us they adore the one, merciful God." Many Catholics have been left with the impression that the God of the Koran is therefore the same God that Christians believe in. Is that correct? Or are Catholics entitled to a fuller, clearer explanation?

The inadequacy of paragraph 841 of the *Catechism* is compensated for to some extent by the surrounding paragraphs. Read in its full context, paragraph 841 can hardly be considered the ringing endorsement of Islam that some have made it out to be. As with other religions, there are elements of truth and goodness in Islam, but it is a long way from the fullness of the truth offered by the Church. And just to emphasize the point that there is no equivalence between Christianity and other religions, paragraph 848 reminds the reader that although God can guide those who are ignorant of the Gospel, "the Church still has the obligation and also the sacred right to evangelize all men."[146]

---

[145] Cf. Cyprian, *Ep.* 73.21: PL 3,1169; *De unit.*: PL 4,509–536.
[146] AG 7; cf. Heb. 11:6; 1 Cor. 9:16.

Today's common-ground-at-any-cost Catholics would profit from reading all of the relevant passages on non-Christians in the *Catechism*. They would also benefit from reading Lewis's prescient tale about the dangers of succumbing to a "Tashlan" mentality.

The Church and Islam: Dangerous Illusions

When I first began writing about the Church and Islam, I devoted a lot of space to describing ways that Church leaders could resist the spread of Islam. It seemed only a matter of time until they would wake up to the need to resist. As it turned out, however, that assessment was overly optimistic.

The immediate task, as I soon learned, was not to find ways to counter Islam, but to convince the Church's hierarchy that Islam ought to be resisted. There's no use talking battle strategies to people who won't admit that they have an ideological enemy.

The enemy is not Muslims per se, but a belief system adhered to by the majority of Muslims, albeit with varying degrees of commitment. Although Islam does not easily lend itself to moderation, many Muslims manage to practice their faith in peaceful ways. Others merely give it lip service, and still others are on fire with a passionate zeal to spread it—by fire and the sword, if necessary.

The idea of opposing dangerous ideologies is not foreign to Americans, but the idea of opposing an ideology that is also a religion is more problematic. It has become increasingly problematic now that we live in an era in which merely disagreeing with another's opinions is tantamount to a hate crime. So, just for the record, critiquing Islam does not mean that one hates Muslims. Criticizing Islam is not the same as criticizing Muslims, any more than criticizing communism is equivalent to criticizing Soviet-era Russians. One can acknowledge the humanity and good intentions of others without having to endorse their ideology. And if their ideology or belief system presents a grave danger to others, it would be wrong not to criticize it. Of course, one should employ tact and prudence when offering such criticism.

The distinction between Citizen X and his beliefs is a simple one. You do not have to respect his beliefs, but you should try to respect him as a fellow human being. Many Catholic leaders, however, have difficulty making this distinction. Rather than try, they have, in the case of Islam, simply declared it to be an upstanding fellow religion with many similarities to Christianity. That way, no one's feelings are hurt. The problem of Islamic terrorists and extremists is handled in the same way: they are assumed to be a small minority who have misunderstood the peaceful nature of their religion.

By the same token, it stands to reason that critics of Islam have also misunderstood Islam and need to be set straight. If they persist in their obstinacy, they are dismissed as bigots and "Islamophobes." Likewise, Church officials assume that opponents of Muslim immigration must be poorly informed, or else racist and xenophobic. If they loved their neighbor, they would not challenge his beliefs or question his religious practices.

Under Pope Benedict XVI there were signs—such as his 2006 Regensburg address—that the Church was developing a more realistic view of Islam. But whatever ground was gained by Benedict was given up by Francis. Indeed, it seems fair to say that under Francis, the Church's understanding of Islam has regressed. Perhaps the most glaring example of this regression can be found in the pope's assertion that "authentic Islam and a proper reading of the Koran are opposed to every form of violence."[147] It's hard to imagine any of his predecessors or any of their advisers making a similar claim.

Unfortunately, very few churchmen have taken issue with Francis's profoundly flawed view of Islam. Instead, many have joined the

---

[147] *Evangelii Gaudium* 253.

chorus—some out of naïveté, some out of misplaced sensitivity, and some, perhaps, out of cowardice.

Several decades have passed since the emergence of worldwide Islamic terrorist networks, and Church leaders are still clinging to a fantasy-based view of Islam. In their defense, it must be admitted that other world leaders have also been in thrall to the cult of sensitivity, and have been equally slow in giving up their dreamy narratives. For a long time, Western leaders kept repeating the mantra that Islamic terror had nothing to do with Islam. But now their tune is beginning to change. The Austrian prime minister has threatened to close one of Vienna's largest mosques;[148] the French have shut down numerous mosques and deported several radical imams; Poland, Hungary, and the Czech Republic have effectively closed their borders to Muslim migrants; and Hungary's prime minister has unapologetically defended the Christian identity of his country.

It's strange that the Church, which, because of its history, ought to be the first to know, appears to be among the last institutions to grasp that Islam is not really a religion of peace.

Or, perhaps, Church leaders do understand the dangers of Islam and have adopted a strategy of silence to protect potential victims of Islam. That's one plausible defense of their inaction. Perhaps they fear that any criticism of Islam will bring harsh reprisals against Christians living in Muslim lands. During World War II, Catholic leaders quickly learned that denunciations of Nazism brought swift and deadly reprisals against both Jews and Christians. As Nazi power increased, the Vatican developed more covert tactics for helping Jews to escape and Catholics to resist.

One might argue that today's Catholic leaders are following a similar strategy in the hopes of mitigating the persecution of Christians and other minorities. But there's a difference. If the Church simply maintained a

---

[148] Christine Douglass-Williams, "Austrian PM threatens to close one of Vienna's largest mosques after it has children dress up as Turkish soldiers," *Jihad Watch*, April 21, 2018), https://www.jihadwatch.org/2018/04/austrian-pm-threatens-to-close-one-of-viennas-largest-mosques-after-it-has-children-dress-up-as-turkish-soldiers

prudential silence about Islamic aggressions, that argument might make sense. But Church leaders have not simply refrained from criticizing Islam. Instead, they have taken every opportunity to praise Islam, to declare their solidarity with it, and to join in various Islamic initiatives, such as the campaign against "Islamophobia." Judging by the Church's great solicitude for Islam, one would think it was the most persecuted faith on earth, rather than one of the chief persecutors.

The Church's current Islam policy does not look like the cautious approach of one who is dealing with a dangerous enemy. It looks more like the trusting innocence of one who thinks he has no enemies. Pius XII may have maintained a prudential silence about Nazi evils once it became apparent that many innocent people would pay the price, but he never praised Nazism as a force for peace, and he certainly never declared the Church's solidarity with it.

By contrast, Church leaders, and Pope Francis in particular, have become, in effect, enablers of Islam. Pope Francis has denied that Islam sanctions violence, has drawn a moral equivalence between Islam and Catholicism ("If I speak of Islamic violence, I must speak of Catholic violence"),[149] and has campaigned for the admittance of millions of Muslim migrants into Europe. Moreover, he has criticized those who oppose his open-borders policy as hard-hearted xenophobes. In return for his efforts, he has been publicly thanked by several Muslim leaders for his "defense of Islam."[150]

One might be tempted to use the word "collaborator" instead of "enabler." But "collaborator" is too strong a word. In its World War II context, it implies a knowing consent to and cooperation with an evil enterprise. It seems clear to me that the pope and others in the hierarchy

---

[149] Thomas D. Williams, "Pope Francis: 'If I Speak of Islamic Violence, I Must Speak of Catholic Violence,'" *Breitbart*, August 1, 2016, https://www.breitbart.com/europe/2016/08/01/pope-francis-speak-islamic-violence-must-speak-catholic-violence/.

[150] Robert Spencer, "The Pope of Islam," *FrontPage Mag*, September 22, 2017, https://archives.frontpagemag.com/fpm/pope-islam-robert-spencer/.

are enabling the spread of an evil ideology; it's not at all clear, however, that they understand what they're doing. Francis, for instance, seems to believe sincerely that all religions are roughly equal in goodness. Thus, for him, the spread of any religion must seem like a good thing. It's an exceedingly naïve view, but one that seems honestly held.

But one can't plead ignorance forever. Eventually, the reality of the situation will become plain to all but the most obtuse. At that point — when the threat is undeniable — we assume that the people in power will wake up and take the appropriate actions. But what if the awakening comes too late? The pope, for one, has shown little evidence that he will change his views on the subject. If anything, he has doubled down — going so far as to say that the rights of migrants trump national security.[151] We should not look to the pope to lead the way on this issue. He seems constitutionally incapable of entertaining doubts about his Islam policy. It looks like the impetus to change course will have to come from bishops, priests and Catholic laity. They had better get busy. There is no time to waste.

---

[151] Associated Press, "Pope Francis: Rights of Migrants Trump National Security Concerns," *Breitbart*, August 21, 2017, https://www.breitbart.com/faith/2017/08/21/pope-francis-rights-migrants-trump-national-security-concerns/.

Christianity and Islam: A Common Heritage?

In the summer of 2014, two prominent American bishops joined two leading Shiite Muslim scholars in Iran in issuing a statement on weapons of mass destruction. According to the statement, "Christianity and Islam cherish a common heritage that emphasizes, above all, love and respect for the life, dignity, and welfare of all members of the human community." It went on to say that "Catholicism and Shia Islam hold a common commitment to peaceful coexistence and mutual respect" and concluded with a commitment to "our mutual intention to engage in sustained dialogue based on our shared values."[152]

This emphasis on the shared heritage of Christianity and Islam is fairly representative of the USCCB's stance on Islam—namely, that Islam is a sister faith with which we have a close affinity. For example, at the National Muslim-Catholic Plenary in October 2012, keynote speaker Father Tom Michel, S.J., titled his talk "Living Our Faith Together."[153] Father Michel explained that he was uncertain whether the plenary theme was supposed to be "Living Our Faith Together" or "Living Our

---

[152] "USCCB Committee Chair, Iranian Scholars Issue Statement on Weapons of Mass Destruction," Catholic Culture, June 19, 2014, https://www.catholicculture.org/news/headlines/index.cfm?storyid=21759.

[153] Father Thomas Michel, S.J., "Muslim-Catholic National Plenary 2012/1433," United States Conference of Catholic Bishops, http://www.usccb.org/beliefs-and-teachings/ecumenical-and-interreligious/interreligious/living-our-faith-together.cfm.

Faiths Together," but he preferred the former because "we are already united."

Meanwhile, back in the real world, Christians are being butchered by the hundreds and thousands by their "partners in faith." As Islamic terrorism spreads across the globe, Church leaders might want to reconsider the common-ground-with-Islam policy that has been in place since Vatican II. It's one thing to affirm the common humanity shared by Christians and Muslims; it's another thing altogether to assert that they share a common belief system — as in "Living *Our* Faith Together."

That approach is fraught with difficulties. What's the interfaith common ground on jihad? On the equality of men and women? On amputation for theft? On the doctrine that Islam should reign supreme over all other religions? Is it wise to emphasize our "shared values" with a religion that inspires so many to maim and murder? To use an analogy, why would you want to tout your common ground with the local bully who beats his wife and intimidates his neighbors?

To ask a more basic question, why would you want to advertise your "common heritage" with a made-up religion? Even if Islam did not have a long history of depredations, in what sense does it qualify as a revealed religion — other than the fact that it claims as much for itself? Do the Catholic participants in the Muslim-Catholic dialogue believe that Muhammad actually received a revelation from God? If they don't, then they are in danger of being involved in a pretense. Why do the claims of Islam merit so much serious consideration — let alone respect and esteem — if its founder was the perpetrator of such a massive fraud?

Despite all the fashionable talk about our shared heritage, there is no organic connection between Islam and Christianity, as there is between Christianity and Judaism. Muhammad borrowed ideas and stories from the Torah and the Gospels, but the Koran can hardly be considered an outgrowth or fulfillment of either. It's more accurate to say that Muhammad hitched a ride on the Jewish and Christian traditions. He saw them, in other words, as a vehicle for his own aspiration. And that aspiration—which jumps out from almost every page of the Koran—was to be a prophet.

Initially, Muhammad seemed content to be accepted as a prophet within the Jewish tradition, but when he was rebuffed by the Jews of Medina, it became apparent that his motivation was simply to be a prophet at any cost. Muhammad began to accuse the Jews and Christians of having distorted and falsified the revelations that were given to them, and he presented the Koran as the pristine revelation that the Jews and Christians had been guilty of distorting.

And what was the revelation? Ali Sina, the author of *Understanding Muhammad*, puts it this way:

> What was his message? The message was that he had become a messenger and people had to believe in him.... Beyond that there is no other message.[154]

Sina exaggerates, but not by much. Although the Koran also emphasizes the oneness of God, the only really new element not to be found in existing revelations is that Muhammad is a prophet—and not only that, but the "seal of the prophets." The odd thing is that there is no prophecy in the Koran. Other than promising unbelievers that they will end up in hell, the Koran does not foretell anything of note. The prophet's main message, repeated over and over, is precisely that he is a prophet.

Read the Koran and test this for yourself. The most frequently repeated phrases are "Believe God and His Prophet," "Obey God and His Prophet," and variations thereof. Sometimes the words "Messenger" and "Apostle" are substituted for "Prophet," but they are all just different ways of saying "Muhammad." In short, the Koran never fails to remind its readers that Muhammad is a prophet.

---

[154] Ali Sina, *Understanding Muhammad: A Psychobiography of Allah's Prophet* (N.p.: Faith Freedom Publishing, 2008), 15.

Moreover, this prophet is on very intimate terms with the Almighty. Almost every time that Allah is mentioned in the Koran, Muhammad (under the title the "Apostle," the "Messenger," or the "Prophet") is mentioned in the same breath. This, too, is odd. In fact, it borders on the sacrilegious. The greatest sin in Islam is the sin of "shirk"—that is, the crime of associating anyone with Allah. In order to refute the doctrine of the Trinity, the Koran emphasizes that Allah has no partners. Yet Muhammad links himself with Allah on almost every page—sometimes to the point that Allah begins to seem like a junior partner. Sina puts the matter rather starkly:

> Islam is nothing but Muhammadanism. Muslims claim that they worship no one but Allah. Since Allah was only Muhammad's *alter ego*, his other alias and invisible sock-puppet, in practice, it's Muhammad whom they worship.[155]

Prince Caetani, an early-twentieth-century scholar of Islam, makes the same point in a slightly more elegant way:

> It is thus the person of Mohammed that stands out above all in the front rank, till to God is given a secondary position in His capacity as the auxiliary of the Prophet. He is no longer the Supreme Being, for whose service everything should be sacrificed, but rather the all-powerful Being who aids the Prophet in his political mission, who facilitates his victories, consoles him in defeat, assists him in unravelling all the mundane and worldly complications of a great Empire over men, and helps him smooth over the difficulties which rise up every day as he works out these new phases of his prophetic and political career.[156]

---

[155] Ibid., 7.
[156] Cited in Ibn Warraq, *Why I Am Not a Muslim* (Amherst, NY: Prometheus Books, 1995), 88.

In Caetani's view, Allah becomes little more than a *deus ex machina* who supplies Muhammad with "revelations of convenience." These were revelations that seem tailored to get Muhammad out of a jam or to resolve a dispute in his favor. Here's a sampling:

+ After the Battle of Badr, a dispute arose over the division of spoils. Muhammad promptly received a revelation that "the spoils belong to God and the Apostle" (8:1).
+ He received a revelation allowing him to marry his own daughter-in-law (33:37).
+ Another revelation allowed Muhammad to marry as many wives as he desired (33:50).
+ In another revelation, Allah freed Muhammad from his oath to one of his wives that he would stay away from his concubine, Mary (66:1-4).

After one such revelation, his young wife Aisha remarked: "Truly thy Lord makes haste to do thy bidding."

After the Swiss voted in November 2009 to ban minarets in their country, Cardinal Jean-Louis Tauran, the president of the Pontifical Council for Interreligious Dialogue, chided the voters: "I wonder," he said, "... if they have ever opened the Qur'an." One could ask the same question of the USCCB dialoguers. Because if you do read the Koran, one thing you can't miss is the centrality of Muhammad. In a large sense, it's all about him. Although Muhammad was careful not to refer to himself by name (he does so on only four occasions), see how many times "the Prophet," "the Apostle," and "the Messenger" are mentioned. The same is true of the Sira and the Hadith — the two other main sources of Islam. They are dominated by the person of Muhammad. Or consider this directive from *Reliance of the Traveller*, the definitive manual of Islamic law:

> Allah has favored him above all the other prophets and made him
> the highest of mankind, rejecting anyone's attesting to the divine
> oneness by saying "There is no god but Allah," unless they also

attest to the Prophet by saying "Muhammad is the Messenger of Allah." (v 2.1)

In short, you can't have one without the other.

Other prophets were eager to call attention to God; Muhammad seemed more eager to call attention to his own prophethood. The Koran seems to be constructed not so much to serve the needs of the people of God but to serve the needs of one individual's rather large ego. The Koran's obsession with the status of Muhammad suggests that it is an entirely human creation devised largely for the purpose of furthering the aims and ambitions of one man. After all, if Muhammad is the true author of the Koran, the words "Obey Allah and his Prophet" can just as well be translated as "Obey Allah and Me."

One can find many resemblances between the Koran and the Torah and a handful of similarities between the Koran and the Gospels, but one can also find compelling evidence within its pages that it is, in fact, the "invented tale" that its author takes great pains to deny. (For examples of these denials see 11:13; 12:112; 32:1–2; 34:43.)

This being the case, Catholic bishops ought to be careful that, in their eagerness to show respect for Islam, they do not go overboard on the matter of "common ground" and "shared heritage." What is the point of affirming your unity with a belief system that largely developed out of one man's megalomania? What does it matter if Muslims revere Jesus, if the Jesus they revere was introduced into the Koran for the purpose of denying the claims of Jesus of Nazareth while enhancing the claims of Muhammad the prophet?

Muslims refer to the Koran as the "Holy Koran." So also do numerous Western leaders, including presidents, prime ministers, and four-star U.S. generals. Bishops, however, should be more cautious about assigning sacred status to a book of such dubious origins. If the chief purpose of dialogue is to allow clerics of different faiths to congratulate each other on their shared open-mindedness, then it helps to concentrate on the mutual-heritage aspect and to avoid the obvious stumbling blocks. But "let's pretend" is not a very sound basis on which to move both parties closer to the truth.

What currently seems like the height of enlightened sensitivity on the part of bishops may eventually look like a display of simple foolishness. And considering how rapidly our illusions about Islam are being deflated by the march of events, "eventually" seems due to arrive well ahead of schedule.

9

Comic Interlude

There is nothing humorous about jihad attacks. But there is something funny about our response to them.

Groundhog Day — Jihad Version

I think I've seen this movie before. The plot goes something like this: a man drives a car into a crowd of people, gets out of his vehicle, shouts an Arabic phrase, begins to stab bystanders, and is shot by police.

You probably know the rest of the story. Ordinary people immediately understand that it's another jihad attack. But the police and the media are baffled. They spend hours and sometimes days looking into the possibility that it might be an act of terrorism. By the time they finally decide that it is terrorism, most people have moved on to the next news cycle.

Then there's the question of identity. Who did it? At first, the assailant is simply identified as a "man." Then, after a suitable interval, he's identified as a "London resident" or a "resident of Marseille," or whatever the case may be. Next, we learn that he's an "Asian man" (if the incident occurs in England) or a "North African man" (if in France). Finally, we are told that it is a Muslim man, but by this point, many have lost interest.

Next comes the matter of motive. Of course, the average citizen already knows the motive: the jihadist did it for the sake of Allah and the seventy-two virgins. But for some reason, the Kabuki ritual must be played out to the end. Very often there is no end — that is, no motive is ever found. The authorities decide that the perpetrator acted irrationally. He was mentally ill or emotionally disturbed, or other kids bullied him in school.

As Governor John Kasich said after a Muslim student at Ohio State University perpetrated a car-and-knife attack on fellow students, "we may never totally find out why this person ... snapped."[157] One sometimes gets the impression that the authorities never want to know. That would explain why the motivation behind the crime is usually left hanging.

At any rate, the mystery-motive motif is a recurring plot feature. After Khalid Masood's car-and-knife rampage, which left several dead and forty wounded in London on March 22, 2017, a senior police official said, "We must accept that there is a possibility we will never understand why he did this."[158]

One thing you can be sure of in the official version: whatever the motive, it has nothing to do with Islam. The authorities are uncertain about everything else, but they are always quite certain of that. The denial comes in several variations: "This has nothing to do with Islam," "This is a perversion of a great religion," "No religion condones terror," and even, "This is a betrayal of Islam."

The latest iteration comes from Digby Jones, a former minister of state for trade in the United Kingdom. In regard to Masood's jihadi-style attack, Jones said, "I think the fact that the man is a Muslim is utterly and completely irrelevant."[159]

Another predictable plot feature is that much time is spent determining whether the jihadist is a "lone-wolf" or a card-carrying member of ISIS. The authorities and the press seem to favor the lone-wolf scenario, perhaps because the terror threat seems less ominous when only one person is involved. Another possibility is that the authorities bear less

---

[157] Jackie Borchardt, "11 Injured, Suspect Dead after Attack on Ohio State University Campus," *Cleveland.com* updated January 11, 2019, https://www.cleveland.com/metro/2016/11/ohio_state_university_attack.html.

[158] Robert Spencer, "UK Police on London Jihadi: 'There Is a Possibility We Will Never Understand Why He Did This,'" *Jihad Watch*, March 25, 2017, https://www.jihadwatch.org/2017/03/uk-police-on-london-jihadi-there-is-a-possibility-we-will-never-understand-why-he-did-this.

[159] Robert Spencer, "UK Police on London Jihadi: 'The Fact That the Man Is a Muslim Is Utterly and Completely Irrelevant,'" *Jihad Watch*, March 24, 2017, https://www.jihadwatch.org/2017/03/uk-pol-on-london-jihadi-the-fact-that-the-man-is-a-muslim-is-utterly-and-completely-irrelevant.

blame for not preventing the attack since there's no way of predicting when and where a lone wolf will strike.

As it turns out, however, the lone wolves are often "known wolves" — known to the police, that is, for various previous crimes. Moreover, the lone wolves are not that lonely. They usually have family and friends who know what they're up to, and, not infrequently, they have made contact with terrorist-group operatives prior to the attack. In addition, they share a common belief system with jihadists everywhere. What belief system is that? Well … let's move on.

The final act of this ritual theater is a statement — by a governor, a president, or a prime minister — to the effect that we won't change who we are to suit the terrorists. As then U.K. Prime Minister Theresa May said after the Westminster Bridge attack, "Let me make it clear today … any attempt to defeat our values through violence and terror is doomed to failure."[160]

Apparently, one of those key values is tolerance. U.K Home Secretary Amber Rudd put it this way: "The British people will be united in working together to defeat those who would harm our shared values. Values of democracy, tolerance, and the rule of law."[161]

"Tolerance?" Isn't that the value that got England into this mess in the first place? Well, never mind. No one but the media pays attention to such statements of resolve.

We've been hearing that sort of thing for a dozen years, and the jihad attacks keep multiplying. On the same day as the London terror attack, a Muslim migrant in Southern Italy tried to run down police with a car.[162]

---

[160] "PM Theresa May's Statement on London Terror Attack," *Financial Times*, March 22, 2017, https://www.ft.com/content/e19a0532-0f45-11e7-b030-768954394623.

[161] Robert Spencer, "Jihadi Attack in London, UK Vows to Defend 'Tolerance,'" *FrontPage Mag*, March 23, 2017, https://archives.frontpagemag.com/fpm/jihadi-attack-london-uk-vows-defend-tolerance-robert-spencer/.

[162] Robert Spencer, "Italy: Muslim Tries to Run Down Police, Then Stabs Officer," *Jihad Watch*, March 23, 2017, https://www.jihadwatch.org/2017/03/italy-muslim-tries-to-run-down-police-then-stabs-officer.

He then attacked and injured an officer with a knife. The next day in Antwerp, a Muslim man drove a car loaded with assault rifles and knives into a crowd on a busy shopping street.[163]

I haven't seen the follow-up stories, but presumably both men were mentally ill, the incident had nothing to do with Islam, and the police will be searching for a motive for a long time to come.

That's the routine. And it seems that we are expected to get used to it. Prime Minister May said that people should just continue to act normally because that's "the best response to terrorism."[164] Meanwhile, London Mayor Sadiq Khan said that despite the attack, London would return to "business as usual." But business as usual now includes the ritual reenactment of the jihad terror cycle.

In a way, the "movie" we are in resembles the plot of *Groundhog Day* (1993). Like the main character in the movie, we seem doomed to witness the same ritual day after day, week after week. There's still hope, of course. After he finally gains some wisdom, the hero of *Groundhog Day* breaks out of the cycle.

Will we?

[163] Robert Spencer, "Belgium: Muslim Who Tried to Ram Pedestrians Had Liquid Gas, Assault Rifles and Knives in Car," *Jihad Watch*, March 23, 2017, https://www.jihadwatch.org/2017/03/belgium-muslim-who-tried-to-ram-pedestrians-had-liquid-gas-assault-rifles-and-knives-in-car.

[164] Daniel Greenfield, "A Week of Terror and Diversity in Europe," *Front-Page Mag*, March 24, 2017, https://archives.frontpagemag.com/fpm/week-terror-and-diversity-europe-daniel-greenfield/.

Ali in Wonderland

Here's a recent news item that caught my eye:

> Ayaan Hirsi Ali was scheduled to present a paper on radical Islamic
> terror at the National Security Council before being blocked by
> H. R. McMaster and his recently appointed Senior Director of
> Counter-Terrorism, Mustafa Javed Ali.[165]

Mustafa Javed Ali is now the senior director of counterterrorism?
Could that be right? Please don't accuse me of racism. After all, Islam is
not a race. For all I know, Mustafa Javed Ali could be a Caucasian convert
to Islam formerly known as Billy Bob Pickens. If I read that someone
named Vasily Vladimir Petrovich had been suddenly appointed as deputy
director of the CIA, my curiosity would be similarly piqued.

What's in a name? Usually nothing that would have a bearing on
national security. But some names make you sit up and take notice.
Take care ... er, I meant to say, "Take CAIR, for example." That's the
acronym for the Council on American-Islamic Relations. Before taking command of counterterrorism, Mr. Javed Ali was CAIR's diversity
outreach coordinator.

---

[165] Robert Spencer, "McMaster Blocked Ayaan Hirsi Ali from Speaking to
NSC and Meeting Trump: 'Islamophobic,'" *Jihad Watch*, August 5, 2017,
https://www.jihadwatch.org/2017/08/mcmaster-blocked-ayaan-hirsi-ali-
from-speaking-to-nsc-and-meeting-trump-islamophobic.

CAIR, if you don't already know, was named as an unindicted co-conspirator in the nation's largest terrorist-funding case. The organization is considered by many to be a front group for the Muslim Brotherhood. Along with its opposition to virtually every anti-terrorism initiative ever proposed, CAIR has also been at the forefront of the "Islamophobia" campaign. It's likely no coincidence that Mustafa Javed Ali's opposition to former Muslim Ayaan Hirsi Ali is that she was "Islamophobic."

The important name to remember here, however, is not M.J. Ali, but General H.R. McMaster. The H.R. stands for Herbert Raymond, which in itself should be enough to disqualify the man from the position of national security adviser. But no such luck. He's in like Flynn. Well, not like Flynn. Flynn is out. And so are a lot of other people who share Flynn's silly view that Islamic terror has something to do with Islam.

Since replacing Michael Flynn, McMaster has been firing people left and right — well, mostly on the right. The people on the left are the ones who are being hired to replace them. According to the *Washington Free Beacon*, "McMaster has been targeting long-time Trump loyalists who were clashing with career government staffers and holdovers from the Obama administration."[166] Now it looks like the Obama holdovers are holding the trump hand, and Trump is left holding the bag.

Among those fired from top positions at NSC are K.T. McFarland, Ezra Watnick-Cohen, Rich Higgins, Derek Harvey, Adam Lovinger, and Robin Townley. For the most part they are anti-Iran deal, pro-Israel, and anti-Muslim Brotherhood. Some of them also worry about the left. For example, Rich Higgins[167] was fired for a memo that warned about the

---

[166] Adam Kredo, "McMaster, On 'Warpath,' Purges Key Trump Allies From White House NSC," *Washington Free Beacon*, August 3, 2017), https://freebeacon.com/national-security/mcmaster-warpath-purges-key-trump-allies-white-house-nsc/

[167] Rosie Gray, "An NSC Staffer Is Forced Out over a Controversial Memo," *Atlantic*, August 2, 2017), https://www.theatlantic.com/politics/archive/2017/08/a-national-security-council-staffer-is-forced-out-over-a-controversial-memo/535725/

alliance between "cultural Marxists" and "Islamists." Once McMaster has completed his purge, writes Daniel Greenfield, "the NSC will be a purely Obama-Bush operation."[168]

The McMaster disaster is an example of what is meant by the "deep state," or, if you like, the "swamp." The "swamp" refers primarily to upper-level bureaucrats who seem to be permanently embedded in government agencies. They are supposed to be civil servants, but mostly they serve the man who appointed them. But if the Obama loyalists in the D.C. bureaucracy are the swamp, McMaster is more like the Creature from the Black Lagoon. The swamp waits for its victims to sink in the mud, the Creature actively seeks them out.

Of course, he has help — people like Mustafa Javed Ali. Some might question Mr. Ali's qualifications, but let's not quibble about that. His service as diversity outreach coordinator for CAIR surely qualifies him to be Senior Director of Counter-Terrorism for U.S.A. He was so qualified that McMaster catapulted him to Senior Director without even a tryout as Junior Director. Still, one could question Javed Ali's tactics. Take his cancellation of Hirsi Ali's talk. According to one source, Javed Ali said "the only way she could present her paper would be to have someone from CAIR come in to refute her work."[169]

Equal time for CAIR — an organization that, for good reason, has been dubbed the "Muslim Mafia"? It must all seem very strange to Ayaan Hirsi Ali, who has spent a good part of her life trying to escape the CAIR-ing type. She left Somalia for the Netherlands to get away from Islam's harsh treatment of women. Then she left Holland for America because of Muslim death threats against her. Now that she's in the land of the free, she must wonder why her competence to speak on Islam to the NSC

---

[168] Daniel Greenfield, "McMaster's NSC Coup Against Trump Purges Critics of Islam and Obama," *FrontPage Mag*, August 4, 2017), https://archives.frontpagemag.com/fpm/mcmasters-nsc-coup-against-trump-purges-critics-daniel-greenfield/

[169] Spencer, "McMaster Blocked Ayaan Hirsi Ali."

is being questioned by a former functionary of a Muslim Brotherhood organization.

Like Alice in Wonderland, Ali must be trying to make sense of it all. Why are the Mad Hatters and the Red Queens still in charge of Washington? Why are ex-CAIR men in the National Security Council? One could ask these questions, but perhaps it's better not to. One question leads to another, and pretty soon you're on a witch hunt or a fishing expedition and you might catch a red herring, and then where would you be?

If you're going to ask why there are Muslim Brotherhood types in the NSC, you might as well ask why the current co-chair[170] of the Democratic National Committee is a convert to Islam who spends much of his time hobnobbing with people from CAIR and ISNA. You might just as well ask why his predecessor Debbie Wasserman Schultz[171] failed to fire her top IT aide Imran Awan until after he was arrested at Dulles Airport for trying to flee the country. Imran and his two brothers, Abid and Jamal, had already been relieved of their duties[172] as information technology managers for dozens of Democrat members of the House of Representatives. The three Pakistani brothers were suspected of illegal access and data theft. Yet, over the course of several years, they worked for three members of the House Committee on Intelligence, five members of the House Committee on Foreign Affairs, and for various Democratic members of the Homeland Security Committee and the Armed Services Committee.

But who cares? Why make a mountain out of a Capitol Hill full of moles? That would be like making a fuss about the fact that John Kerry's daughter married into an Iranian family. Of course, ordinary mortals with

---

[170] Keith Elison, https://www.discoverthenetworks.org/individuals/keith-ellison/

[171] Andrew C. McCarthy, "Debbie Wasserman Schultz and the Pakistani IT Scammers," *National Review*, July 29, 2017), https://www.nationalreview.com/2017/07/debbie-wasserman-schultz-pakistani-computer-guys-bank-fraud/

[172] Daniel Greenfield, "A Muslim Brotherhood Security Breach in Congress," *FrontPage Mag*, February 8, 2017).

at-risk in-laws in Iran would be expected to recuse themselves from sensitive negotiations with the Iranian government over nuclear weapons. But John Kerry is not an ordinary person. He's a Democrat. And Democrats don't do recuse.

If you would raise a fuss about such a small thing, you're probably the kind of person who would make a big deal about Hillary Clinton appointing Huma Abedin as Deputy Chief of Staff at the State Department. Sure, Abedin's family were entangled with the Muslim Brotherhood, and sure, Abedin herself was managing editor of a Muslim Brotherhood magazine. But what of it? It's not as though the Clinton State Department ever showed any partiality to the Muslim Brotherhood—except for helping them take over Egypt, and a few other minor favors.

Why is Mustafa Javed Ali in charge of counter-terrorism at the NSC? You might as well ask why John Brennan, the head of the CIA under Obama, ordered the FBI and about 14 other security agencies to purge their training materials of any reference to "jihad" and "radical Islam." Why did he do that? It's really none of your business, but if you must know, it was because such terms are offensive to Muslims.

Speaking of purges, Obama conducted one of his own. During his eight-year tenure, he replaced several hundred generals[173] and other high-ranking officers with people who shared his own view of a more peaceful and tolerant military. As a result, the only generals left to choose from in the swam... I mean, the pool, tend to be made in the image of the ex-president. That's why every time Trump turns over a new hire card, it doesn't turn up trumps, it turns up Obamas.

While we're on the subject of cards, I want you to look at this one. It's the Queen of Diamonds. It's better that you don't trouble your mind anymore over the matters we've been discussing. Just concentrate on the

---

[173] Daniel John Sobieski, "Obama Purged Military of Those Who Sought Victory," *American Thinker*, September 10, 2016, https://www.americanthinker.com/blog/2016/09/obama_purged_military_of_those_who_sought_victory.html.

card. Empty your mind of all bothersome thoughts. These are complicated matters best left to the wise ones. The military-industrial complex is too complex for you to ever understand. When you wake you will forget everything said here.

10

Muhammad and the Koran

Why is it risky to say anything even remotely critical about Muhammad and the Koran? Perhaps because neither stands up very well to a close examination. Here are a few facts that Catholics ought to know about Muhammad and the book that Allah supposedly entrusted to him.

Time for Catholics to Reconsider Islam and the "Prophet" Muhammad?

In the fall of 2016, some prominent Catholics took pains to emphasize the supposedly special ties between Islam and Catholicism. In an editorial for *The Angelus*, the Los Angeles archdiocesan newspaper, Father Ronald Rolheiser called for greater solidarity with Islam.[174] More recently, Msgr. Stuart Swetland,[175] president of Donnelly College, appeared to suggest that Catholics are required to believe in the peaceful nature of Islam. Meanwhile, in Rome, a delegation of U.S. bishops and a delegation of Iranian religious leaders issued a joint statement that include this paragraph:

> Christianity and Islam share a commitment to love and respect for the life, dignity, and welfare of all members of the human community.... We hold a common commitment to peaceful coexistence and mutual respect.[176]

---

[174] William Kilpatrick, "Solidarity with Islam?" *Crisis Magazine*, January 26, 2016, https://www.crisismagazine.com/2016/solidarity-with-islam.

[175] William Kilpatrick, "Must Catholics Believe that Islam Is Peaceful?" *Crisis Magazine*, August 16, 2016, https://www.crisismagazine.com/2016/must-catholics-believe-islam-peaceful.

[176] Joint Declaration of U.S. and Iranian Religious Leaders, United States Conference of Catholic Bishops, August 18, 2016, http://www.usccb.org/issues-and-action/human-life-and-dignity/global-issues/middle-east/iran/joint-declaration-of-us-and-iranian-religious-leaders-2016-08-18.cfm.

Iranian religious leaders are committed to peaceful coexistence? The peaceful nature of Islam is a binding Catholic doctrine? We should be seeking greater solidarity with Islam? Such talk might have resonated with Catholics a few years ago, but now it has a dated quality about it. It flies in the face of facts with which we are now all familiar.

If nothing else, this push to put a happy face on Islam is a case of very bad timing. The American bishops' faith in their Iranian counterparts comes at a time when all the evidence suggests that the chief commitment of Iranian religious leaders is to the destruction of the "Great Satan" (America). And while Church leaders are plumping for greater solidarity with Islam, much of the rest of the world wants nothing to do with it. In Europe, for example, various polls have shown that a majority of citizens believe that Islam does not belong in Europe. Angela Merkel's party is doing badly in German elections precisely because of her Islam-friendly policy. If the Church continues to pursue solidarity with Islam, it is likely to alienate a great many non-Muslims. In Europe, for example, it will be increasingly identified with the secular elites whom many now view as traitors for having facilitated Islam's cultural putsch.

But these are pragmatic reasons for not pursuing solidarity with Islam. Are there any theological reasons?

Ironically, one reason many Catholics take an optimistic view of Islam is also the chief reason for doubting that there can be any reconciliation with Islam. Some Catholics make much of the fact that Jesus is mentioned in the Koran and is honored by Muslims as a great prophet. This respect for Jesus, they assume, is a guarantee that Islam cannot be too far away from the truth. But the fact that Jesus is included in Islamic tradition is a two-edged sword.

Saint Paul specifically warns about the misappropriation of Jesus:

For if some one comes and preaches another Jesus than the one we preached ... or if you accept a different gospel from the one you accepted, you submit to it readily enough" (2 Cor. 11:4).

Six hundred years after Paul, Muhammad came along and started preaching a different Jesus—a very different Jesus. If anything, the Muslim Jesus is an anti-Jesus; he directly contradicts the claims of the Jesus of the Gospels. In the Koran, Allah addresses the "people of the Book" (Christians) and warns them to speak the truth about God: "The Messiah, Jesus son of Mary, was no more than God's apostle.... So believe in God and His apostles and do not say 'Three' ['Trinity' in some translations].... God forbid that he should have a son!" (4:171).

That's a flat denial of the Trinity and a rejection of the Fatherhood of God and the Sonship of Jesus. In other places, Allah denies the Incarnation and the Crucifixion. It's not as though these are peripheral teachings of the Church whose denial can be overlooked for the sake of fellowship. These beliefs are the foundation of the Faith.

Muslims hold that Muhammad did not write the Koran but merely recited what Allah had told him. Thus, there are two contradictory revelations. In one, God tells us that He is a Trinity and that Jesus is the Son of the Father. In the other "revelation," Allah says he is not a Trinity and he curses those who say that Jesus is the Son of God.

Not much wiggle room there. This is not a misunderstanding that can be papered over with dialogue and happy talk about shared respect for Jesus. It's not the same Jesus. And, unless you want to dispense with the laws of logic, it's not the same God.

Islam stands apart from other non-Christian religions in its specific rejection of Christian tenets. Jesus is in the Koran not because Muhammad revered Him, but because Muhammad wanted to put Him in His place. In order to establish himself as the final prophet of God, Muhammad first had to undercut the Christian claim that Jesus is the fulfillment of all prophecy. Rather cleverly, he did not reject Jesus. Instead, he appropriated Him for his own purposes. To clear the way for his own prophethood, he reassigned Jesus as a Muslim prophet.

Although Jesus is supposedly a great prophet in Islam, He doesn't have a great deal to say or do in the Koran. By contrast, Muhammad is mentioned frequently. The phrase "God and His Apostle" recurs throughout the Koran. There are many dozens of admonitions along the order of "Believe in God and His Apostle," "Obey God and His Apostle," and "Have faith in God and His Apostle."

According to Islamic teaching, assigning a partner to God is the worst possible sin—the very sin that Christians have committed by identifying Christ as the Son of God. Yet, in effect, Muhammad assigned himself the position of partner to Allah. Read the Koran and see how many times the two are mentioned in the same breath. One gets the impression that obeying Muhammad is the equivalent of obeying Allah. In fact, verse 4:80 says just that: "He that obeys the Apostle obeys God." And verse 4:149 warns believers not to "draw a line between God and His Apostle."

As presented in the Koran and in Islamic tradition, Allah and Muhammad are a package deal. You can't have one without the other. The Islamic confession of faith declares that "there is no God but God and Muhammad is the messenger of God." As a Muslim, you are not allowed to dispense with the second half. In *Reliance of the Traveller*, one of the most authoritative guides to Islamic belief, we read:

> Allah has made him [Muhammad] the highest of mankind, rejecting anyone's attesting to the divine oneness by saying "There is no God but Allah," unless they also attest to the Prophet by saying "Muhammad is the Messenger of Allah" (v 2.1).[177]

In Islam, Muhammad is referred to simply as "the Prophet." But what kind of prophet was he? Here's a hint. In the Sermon on the Mount, Jesus warns His listeners to "beware of false prophets, who come to you in sheep's clothing but inwardly are ravenous wolves" (Matt. 7:15). Does Muhammad qualify as a false prophet? It would seem so. He proclaims that God is not a Trinity and that Jesus is neither divine nor a savior. He rejects almost all of the central Christian teachings.

---

[177] Ahmad ibn Naqib al-Misri, *Reliance of the Traveller*, trans. Nuh Ha Mim Keller (Bettsville, MD: Amana Publications, 1997), 822.

Was Muhammad a false prophet? It could be reasonably argued that he was the false prophet *par excellence*—perhaps the person whom Jesus had most in mind when he delivered his warning. There were false prophets in the days of Peter and Paul, but does anyone remember their names? Did any of them found a religion that is still alive and growing? Could any of them claim a following of 1.6 billion people?

There is a curious lack of curiosity about Muhammad on the part of Catholic leaders. He is not mentioned in *Nostra Aetate*, the document on which the current optimistic assessment of Islam is built. He is not mentioned in the *Catechism*'s statement on the Church's relationship with the Muslims. He is not, as far as I know, mentioned by Pope Francis, although Francis has spoken favorably about Islam on several occasions.

But Islam is inseparable from Muhammad. If he was a false prophet who presented a false picture of Jesus, then Islam, despite whatever truths it contains, is a false religion. For prudential reasons, you might not want to shout that from the rooftops. On the other hand, you ought not keep insisting that Catholics share much in common with Islam.

Fortunately, there are signs that the Church's Pollyannaish view of Islam may be in for a revision. The Church's Islam policy is coming under increasing scrutiny. Up until a year or two ago, Catholic journalists tended to avoid the subject of Islam except to report on terrorist attacks or on the pope's meetings with imams. As for news analysis, most writers simply echoed the Vatican's semiofficial narrative that terrorism has nothing to do with Islam. More recently, however, Catholic columnists have begun to question that narrative. More and more Catholic writers and intellectuals are taking a closer, more clear-eyed look at the Church's relationship with Islam.

A number of bishops and cardinals have also begun to question the Church's stance on Islam. American cardinal Raymond Burke,[178]

---

[178] Carl E. Olson, "Cardinal Raymond Burke on Life, Truth, Mother Teresa, Islam, and Cardinal Sarah," *Catholic World Report*, August 30, 2016,

Hungarian bishop Lázló Kiss-Rigó, Spanish cardinal Antonio Cañizares, and Iraqi archbishops Louis Sako and Amel Shamon Nona, along with others, have expressed dissatisfaction with Church policy on Islam or Vatican policy on Muslim migration.

Most importantly, the dogmatic authority of *Nostra Aetate* has come into question in higher Church circles. This is significant because the two paragraphs on the Muslims in that document are the linchpin of the argument that Christianity and Islam are similar faiths that share much in common. But according to Archbishop Guido Pozzo, formerly the secretary of the Pontifical Commission *Ecclesia Dei*, "*Nostra Aetate* does not have any dogmatic authority, and thus one cannot demand from anyone to recognize this declaration as being dogmatic."[179]

Nostra Aetate seems to have been intended primarily as a gesture of outreach to non-Christian religions. But somehow, over the years, it came to be seen by many as the Church's final and definitive statement on Islam. It became the trump card in any discussion of Islam among Catholics. Catholics who questioned the Church's pro-Islam policies were told that the Church had spoken, and that was that.

Now that *Nostra Aetate* is being put into proper perspective, the way is open for Catholics to develop a fuller, more reality-based picture of Islam. Hopefully, they will not waste any time in doing so.

---

https://www.catholicworldreport.com/2016/08/30/cardinal-raymond-burke-on-life-truth-mother-teresa-islam-and-cardinal-sarah/.

[179] Clair Chretien, "SSPX Could Be Reconciled with Rome without Accepting All of Vatican II," LifeSite News, August 10, 2016, https://www.lifesitenews.com/news/sspx-could-be-reconciled-with-rome-without-accepting-all-of-vatican-ii.

Is the Koran a Literary Masterpiece?

In a July 2018 essay for *Crisis Magazine*, I emphasized the importance of casting doubts on Islamic beliefs, just as we cast doubts on Soviet communist ideology during the Cold War.[180]

With that in mind, let's talk about the Koran. It's the fountain from which the ideology flows. It is quoted incessantly by terrorist leaders and imams alike, and it provides the motivation for both armed jihadists in combat fatigues and cultural jihadists in business suits.

So it would seem logical for those threatened by Islam to cast doubts on the Koran. If the Koran came to be seen as a man-made fabrication rather than a direct revelation from God, the prime rationale for jihad would dissolve. Since the authenticity of the Koran rests on a very fragile foundation, the case is not difficult to make.

One would think, therefore, that Western governments would have teams of experts working on the matter 'round the clock. More to the point, one would think that Christian theologians and Scripture scholars would be applying all their skills to a historical and textual critique of Islam's "holy" book. For one thing, Scripture is their area of expertise; for another, Christians are the most persecuted religious group in the world. And most of that persecution is at the hands of Muslims who claim that the Koran provides justification for their deeds.

[180] William Kilpatrick, "Losing Their Religion," *Crisis Magazine*, July 30, 2018, https://www.crisismagazine.com/2018/losing-their-religion.

Assuming that these experts are chomping at the bit, just waiting for a little direction, here is a suggestion: focus on the literary quality of the Koran. Why? Because, other than an occasional lyrical passage, the Koran doesn't have much in the way of literary quality. Yet its literary quality is the main argument for the authenticity of the Koran. "Who else but God," ask Muslim scholars, "could have written such an inimitable masterpiece?"

Certainly not Muhammad. He is traditionally (and conveniently) considered to have been illiterate. Muhammad was merely the conduit through which the divine revelation was passed—or so Muslims believe. Actually, they don't have much choice in the matter, since the Koran has already issued an I-can-beat-any-book-at-the-bar challenge. Sura 2:23 says, "If you doubt what we have revealed to Our servant [Muhammad], produce one chapter comparable to it." The challenge is repeated with slight variations in several other verses.

But to anyone who has read a literary masterpiece—say, something by Shakespeare, Tolstoy, or Dickens—it's an astonishing claim. There are many striking passages in the Koran, but for the most part, it is tedious, repetitive, and didactic. Don't take my word for it. Here are some scholarly observations:

> His characters are all alike, and they utter the same platitudes. He is fond of dramatic dialogue, but has little sense of dramatic scene or action.[181]

> The book aesthetically considered is by no means a first-rate performance ... indispensable links, both in expression and in the sequence of events, are often omitted ... and even the syntax betrays great awkwardness.[182]

---

[181] Charles Cutler Torrey, *The Jewish Foundation of Islam* (New York: Jewish Institute of Religion Press, 1933), 108.

[182] Theodor Nöldeke in *Encyclopedia Britannica*, 11th ed., vol. 15, pp. 898–906.

And here's a more recent assessment by Professor Thomas Bertonneau:

> How to describe it? The prose is unadorned, utilitarian, banal, and prone to use the imperative tense until one tires of the ceaseless exhortation.[183]

All of which is a sad commentary on God's ability to express Himself—assuming, as Muslims do, that God wrote the Koran.

But it's not just the mind-numbing repetition and the eye-glazing prose. The deeper problem is that the Koran just doesn't hang together. It's almost completely lacking in chronology, continuity, and—for want of a better word—plot.

This lack of coherence may explain why the Koran is arranged arbitrarily, with the longest chapters coming first, and the shortest coming last. Apparently, the compilers of the book gave up on trying to give it any rational order. As one of its translators notes, "Scholars are agreed that a strictly chronological arrangement is impossible."[184]

The Koran's lack of sequence and continuity extends to the stories within it. The Koran borrows heavily from stories in the Old Testament, invariably gives them a new twist, but fails to do them justice. The narrator often breaks off in the middle of a story to tell another story or to provide a lengthy commentary that is, at best, tangentially related to the story, or he interrupts the story with a description of the beauty of creation, or—more often—with a description of the fires of hell. Examples of masterful storytelling are not difficult to find. Try the Arabian Nights, the Brothers Grimm, or the short stories of Leo Tolstoy or Jack London. Just don't expect to find anything remotely comparable in the Koran. As Professor Bertonneau notes, "The compiler of the Koran lacks any talent for storytelling."[185]

---

[183] Thomas F. Bertonneau, "A Westerner Reads the Koran," Gates of Vienna, July 12, 2018, https://gatesofvienna.net/2018/07/a-westerner-reads-the-koran/#more-46164

[184] *The Koran*, trans. N. J. Dawood (London, UK: Penguin Classics, 2015), x.

[185] Bertonneau, "A Westerner Reads the Koran."

But, according to Islamic teaching, "the compiler of the Koran" is none other than God Himself. Yet hardly any of His stories are fully developed. Indeed, they are more like story fragments—a series of unconnected episodes dropped at random into the text. In addition, the characters are so poorly developed that they are practically interchangeable. Unlike the characters in the Bible stories, they lack personality.

The difference in storytelling ability between the author of the Koran and the authors of the Bible is most in evidence when we compare the Koran's story of Jesus with that found in the four Gospels. The contrast between the two Christs is startling. The story of the life of Jesus as told by Matthew, Mark, Luke, and John has been justly called "the greatest story ever told." Even those who don't accept the divinity of Jesus recognize Him as perhaps the most extraordinary man who ever lived.

And the Jesus of the Koran? Well, the most charitable thing to say is that there is simply no comparison. There is no comparison because the Gospels tell a story and the Koran doesn't. The Koran can't very well tell the story of Jesus because the main character is largely missing from the narrative. After some promising passages about his birth, Jesus puts in very few subsequent appearances. Moreover, when he does appear in the pages of the Koran, Jesus bears little resemblance to a real person. He is an entirely one-dimensional figure.

In his attempt to portray Christianity as a life-denying religion, the poet Algernon Swinburne described Jesus as the "pale Galilean."[186] But if you're looking for a real pale Galilean, look up the Jesus of the Koran. Indeed, he's so pale, and so lacking in substance, that he could be mistaken for a ghost. In a half dozen or so places in the Koran, he appears out of nowhere to utter some cryptic pronouncement or other, and then disappears again into the ether. The Jesus of the Koran is a pale creation indeed. You can't even call him a "pale Galilean," because there's no

---

[186] Algernon C. Swinburne, "Hymn to Proserpine (After the Proclamation in Rome of the Christian Faith)," The Victorian Web, http://www.victorianweb.org/authors/swinburne/hymn.html.

mention of Galilee in the Koran—and no mention of Bethlehem, Nazareth, Jerusalem, or Jericho. Peter? Pilate? Herod? Judas? Mary Magdalen? They're not there either. The wedding feast at Cana? The Sermon on the Mount? The Last Supper? Nope. The Koran's "account" of Jesus is devoid of context. There is no setting, minimal description, and very little detail. To borrow a phrase from Gertrude Stein, "There's no there, there."

As we saw earlier, The Jesus of the Gospels is a recognizable human being. The Jesus of the Koran is more like a disembodied voice, somewhat reminiscent of the phantom-like Jesus who appears in the Gnostic Gospels. Why, then, did Muhammad include Jesus in the Koran? Most probably because he saw the New Testament account of Jesus as a threat to his own self-promotion. If what the Gospels say about Jesus is true, then there is no need for another prophet or another revelation. So whenever "Jesus" is mentioned in the Koran, it is almost always for the purpose of establishing that he was just a man (e.g., 4:171; 5:17, 75; 5:116–117).

The Koran is supposedly a revelation, but the only new thing it reveals is that Muhammad is the prophet of God. The Koran doesn't add anything to our knowledge of God that is not already present in the Old Testament. It mainly serves as a vehicle for establishing Muhammad's status as a prophet. Although Muhammad is mentioned by name only four times, he is mentioned on almost every other page as "the Apostle," "the Messenger," or "the Prophet." Next to Allah, he is the main character.

All this attention to "messaging," however, is—to return to our main theme—at the expense of the Koran's literary quality. Once again, the Koran has precious little to say that hadn't already been said by other prophets. But having established himself as a prophet, Muhammad had to keep the revelations coming in order to maintain his reputation as God's final messenger. This helps to explain the constant recourse to repetition: repeated admonitions to "obey God and His Apostle," repeated curses at those "who doubt Our revelations," and repeated threats of hellfire for unbelievers—and all expressed in more or less the same boilerplate phraseology. It's as if Shakespeare had been so taken with the phrase "to be or not to be" that he repeated it on every other page of *Hamlet*.

The Koran a literary masterpiece? Here's what historian and essayist Thomas Carlyle (1795–1881) had to say about the book:

> I must say, it is as toilsome reading as I ever undertook. A wearisome confused jumble, crude, incondite; endless iterations, long-windedness, entanglement; most crude, incondite—insupportable stupidity, in short![187]

Contrary to what one might assume, Carlyle had no animus toward Muhammad. Indeed, he considered Muhammad to be one of the great men of history and included him in one of his most notable books, *On Heroes, Hero-Worship, and the Heroic in History* (1841). On the other hand, Carlyle was also an astute literary critic who had a preference for the natural over the artificial. He could not very well ignore the patchwork nature of the Koran.

"This Koran could not have been devised by any but God.... If they say: 'He invented it himself,' say: 'Bring me one chapter like it.'" Thus says sura 10:37–38 of the Koran. The first thing you notice is the defensiveness. It's exactly the type of thing that one who had invented it himself would feel compelled to say. And this is only one example. The author of the Koran never tires of reminding his audience that the Koran is a genuine revelation, not a fake one. But would the Author of Creation need to interrupt His narrative every fifteen pages in order to assure His audience that it is not an invention? To paraphrase Shakespeare, "Methinks the prophet doth protest too much."

The next thing you realize is that the claim is not true. Any fairly literate person could produce dozens, if not hundreds, of chapters from existing fiction and nonfiction that surpass any chapter in the Koran. You don't need to be a literary critic to notice the many problems with the claim that God wrote the Koran. Almost any book you pull off your

---

[187] Sherry Lewkowicz, "Carlyle's Problematic Portrayal of Mahomet and Islam," The Victorian Web, last modified April 20, 2004, http://www. victorianweb.org/authors/carlyle/heroes/lewkowicz10.html.

shelf is—from the standpoint of composition and coherence—better written than the Koran. If God wrote the Koran, why does He display so much defensiveness? Why does He endlessly repeat Himself? Why can't He get His chronology straight? Why does He lack the literary touch—the knack for storytelling, continuity, composition, and drama that we expect to find in accomplished human writers?

Did God write the Koran? The question is bound to raise anxiety levels all around. Would it make Muslims feel uncomfortable? Hopefully, yes. We should want them to feel uncomfortable—uncomfortable to the point that they are forced to entertain doubts that God had anything to do with the composition of the Koran.

Considering what's at stake, this is not a time to shy away from the question. If the Koran is the chief motivating force behind Islamic aggression, then the Koran should not be above discussion. Rather, Muslims should be encouraged to reflect critically upon the facts of their faith.

The doctrine that God wrote the Koran is untenable on many counts. Muslim scholars have painted themselves into a corner with the argument that the Koran is a literary masterpiece of unmatched perfection. Non-Muslims, if they value their survival, ought to take advantage of the weakness of this indefensible position. The fact that in recent years the Koran has been largely shielded from such an inquiry is an indication of how much cultural ground has been ceded to Islamic beliefs. Christian scholars, theologians, and apologists have much lost ground to recover. They should not let the claim of the Koran's divine authorship go unchallenged.

A "Common Word" versus Common Sense

If you've seen the movie version of *Porgy and Bess* (1959), you might recall Sammy Davis Jr.'s rendition of "It Ain't Necessarily So." At a church picnic, Sportin' Life (played by Davis), a somewhat disreputable character, tries to convince the others that "the things that you're liable to read in the Bible, it ain't necessarily so." He then proceeds to cast doubts on several Bible stories — David's defeat of Goliath, Jonah's sojourn in the whale, and Methuselah's nine-hundred-year life span ("Who calls dat livin' when no gal will give in to no man what's nine hundred years?").

The song is amusing and slightly shocking — more shocking if you're a fundamentalist Christian who believes that every word of the Bible is meant to be taken literally. Of course, such attacks on the credibility of the Bible are less of a problem for those Christians who realize that not all of Scripture is meant to be understood in the literal sense.

There is, to my knowledge, no equivalent of "It ain't necessarily so" in the Muslim world. And if there is, the lyricist is probably in hiding and living under an assumed name. That's because the Koran is understood by Muslims to be the literal word of God, written in the mind of Allah before creation and dictated by the Angel Gabriel to Muhammad in the seventh century. You may think that Muhammad composed the Koran, but Muslims do not. To their mind it was composed by Allah and is thus unchangeable and beyond criticism.

Currently, most of the "debate" over the Koran concerns its contents. Does the Koran command violence, as some say? Or does it command peace, as others, including many Catholic clergy, say? Thus, those on different sides of the Islam-means-peace debate tend to throw verses back and forth at each other.

But the question of content ought to be secondary to the question of authorship. Because if Allah didn't write the Koran, what does it matter what verse such-and-such says? If the whole thing was made up by a merchant-turned-warrior named Muhammad, why risk your neck waging jihad?

That's a question for Muslims to ponder. What Catholic leaders need to ponder is why they've allowed themselves to get roped into what might be called the "common word" approach to Christian-Islamic relations. The Common Word Initiative began in 2007 with an open letter to the Christian world signed by 138 Muslim scholars.[188] The letter was entitled "A Common Word Between Us and You," and its purpose was "to declare the common ground between Christianity and Islam." As the Common Ground website maintains, "Despite their differences, Islam and Christianity not only share the same Divine Origin and the same Abrahamic heritage, but the same two greatest commandments." If that's so, then the current Catholic approach makes sense. Instead of focusing on differences, you emphasize the common ground between the two religions. In particular, you try to convince extremist Muslims and "fundamentalist" Christians alike, that, in the words of Pope Francis in *Evangelii Gaudium*, "the proper reading of the Koran is opposed to every form of violence" (253).

The pope, along with others in the hierarchy, seem to have convinced himself that "authentic" religions are always about peace and justice. Ergo, an authentic reading of the Koran must produce peaceful results. Thus, in a talk to immigrants, Pope Francis counseled Christians to expel hatred from their hearts by reading the Bible, and Muslims to do the same

---

[188] "Introduction to A Common Word Between Us and You," *A Common Word*, https://www.acommonword.com/introduction-to-a-common-word-between-us-and-you/,

by reading the Koran. This is consistent with the Common Word thesis that both religions share much common ground and, in particular, that they share "the same Divine Origin."

But that's the main point at issue, isn't it? How can you say that both books share the same divine authorship when one of them flatly contradicts the other on numerous key points, such as the Trinity, the Incarnation, the Crucifixion, the Resurrection, and the means of salvation?

It's true that the Koran shares common material with the Bible. That's because Muhammad borrowed freely from the Bible. He included stories about Adam, Abraham, Noah, and Moses—all of them retold in ways that suited his own purposes. But that's hardly an argument for the divine origin of the Koran. If I produce a book that contains stories from the Old Testament, I can't very well claim that my book is thereby of divine origin. If I claimed that my book was the result of a direct revelation from God, you would be justified in having grave doubts. If I claimed that my book predates the Old and New Testaments, you would certainly question my veracity. If I maintained that the Old and New Testaments were deliberate distortions of the true book delivered to me by an angel … well, you get the picture.

The Common Word Initiative is very much to the advantage of Muslims, but it makes no sense for Christians to subscribe to it. Muhammad borrowed stories from the Bible that predated the Koran by hundreds and even thousands of years, added in material of his own, and then declared that his version was the authentic one. Why should Christians wax enthusiastic over that? Yet the Common Word Initiative received a warm welcome from hundreds of prominent Christian scholars and numerous Christian institutions.

Some of the warm reception may be due to the fact that there are 1.6 billion Muslims in the world, and no one wants to upset them. So let's consider the same issue in regard to a much smaller religion. The Book of Mormon also shares much in common with the Bible. Yet Catholics don't treat the Book of Mormon as though it were on a par with the Bible. Once again, authorship is crucial. Catholics don't believe the

Book of Mormon was delivered by an angel from God, as Mormons believe. Catholics believe it was written by a man named Joseph Smith circa 1830 in western New York. Hence, there is little point in trying to reconcile the Bible with the Book of Mormon. Nor is there much sense in trying to convince Mormons that if they only read their scripture in the right way, they would see that it corroborates the traditional Christian understanding of God's revelation. The whole effect of such a project would be to give the Book of Mormon a legitimacy it doesn't deserve.

For the same reason, Catholics should be cautious about the Common Word approach. The danger in accepting the "same Divine Origin" thesis is that it grants an unwarranted legitimacy to the Koran. And that, in turn, sends the wrong message to both Muslims and Christians.

You've probably seen that photo of Pope John Paul II kissing the Koran. He most certainly meant it not as an endorsement of the Koran, but as a gesture of respect for the billions of Muslims for whom the Koran is a holy book. Still, the gesture caused a good deal of concern and consternation for many Christians. And rightly so. Should he have kissed the Book of Mormon for the similar reason that it is holy scripture for Mormons? Should he have kissed *The Communist Manifesto* because it reflects the sincere belief of communists all over the world?

It makes sense for Catholics to discuss different interpretations of Scripture with Protestants, Orthodox, and Jews because all these faiths start from the same original revelation. There is much less point in trying to reconcile the Bible with the Koran, because one is a real revelation and the other is not.

Although Muhammad included stories from the Old Testament, and although the Koran recognizes Jesus as a prophet, the book has no more claim to being a revelation from God than does the Book of Mormon. Like the Koran, the Book of Mormon "honors" Jesus, but it's still a fabrication.

While it's not advisable to go around calling the Koran a fake, it's not advisable to treat it with great respect and excessive deference either. Excessive deference? Here's an example. The Southern Command guidelines for military personnel at Guantanamo Bay mandate that personnel wear clean gloves when they touch the Koran. The guidelines also require that the Koran be handled in a "manner signaling respect and reverence." "Handle the Koran," states the guidelines, "as if it were a fragile piece of delicate art."[189]

A good many scholars, theologians, and bishops also seem to have fallen into the politically correct habit of treating the Koran "as if it were a fragile piece of delicate art." That's unfortunate. Since the Koran is the main generator of Islamic violence, it warrants a critical examination. It ought to be subject to the same kind of historical and textual criticism to which the Bible has long been subjected. Muslims and Christians alike ought to be free to say that many of the claims contained in the Koran "ain't necessarily so."

By the way, the Common Word Initiative is based on a passage in the Koran—verse 3:64. Here is the Yusuf Ali translation:

> Say: O people of the Book! Come to common terms as between us and you: that we worship none but Allah; that we associate no partners with Him; that we erect not, from among ourselves, lords and patrons other than Allah.

A translation into contemporary English would read something like this:

> Listen, Christians! Agree with us that Jesus is not the Son of God, and that God is not a Trinity, and then we can talk.

That is the price of entry into the Common Word club.

---

[189] Roger Kimball, "It's Always Worse Than You Think, Koran-Handling Dept," *New Criterion*, June 11, 2005, https://newcriterion.com/blogs/dispatch/itamprsquos-always-worse-than-you-think-koran-handling-dept.

11

'Tis the Season

The spirit of Christianity and the spirit of Islam are two entirely different things. And nothing demonstrates this quite so well as the celebration of Christmas.

The Spirit of Christmas and the Spirit of Islam

The man that hath no music in himself
Nor is not moved with concord of sweet sounds
Is fit for treasons, stratagems, and spoils.

—William Shakespeare, *The Merchant of Venice*

Every year around Christmastime, Ibrahim Hooper, the spokesman for CAIR, sends out a Christmas message to Christians. The gist of the message is that Christians and Muslims have much in common because "Muslims also love and revere Jesus as one of God's greatest messengers to mankind." And to prove it, he quotes from chapter 3, verse 45 of the Koran:

> Behold! The angels said: "O Mary! God giveth thee glad tidings of a Word from Him. His name will be Jesus Christ, the son of Mary, held in honor in this world and the Hereafter and in (the company of) those nearest to God."[190]

The Catholic authors of *Nostra Aetate* probably had this verse in mind when they declared that Muslims "revere" Jesus and "honor Mary." Statements like this, along with the fact that Muslims esteem prophets and

---

[190] Robert Spencer, "Ibrahim Hooper: Muslims and Christians: More in Common Than You Think," *Jihad Watch*, December 21, 2004, https://www.jihadwatch.org/2004/12/ibrahim-hooper-muslims-and-christians-more-in-common-than-you-think.

martyrs and engage in prayer, fasting, almsgiving, and pilgrimage, are seen by many Catholics as proof that Islam and Christianity are very similar religions. Christians would do well, however, not to take too much comfort in these apparent similarities. Although Christians and Muslims share some similar texts and similar practices, the two faiths are separated by a wide gulf.

A close examination of texts will reveal the chasm, but another way of grasping the crucial differences between Islam and Christianity is to note that the two faiths have a completely different "feel." When we talk about a "gut feeling" or "getting a feeling" for a new activity, we mean that we understand something in an intuitive, experiential way. It's one thing to read an instructional manual on tennis and another thing to play it.

Christmas: A Point of Reference

One way to appreciate the different feel of the two religions is to think about Christmas. It means a lot to Christians. They decorate Christmas trees, set up mangers, exchange Christmas cards, sing carols, and celebrate solemn yet joyful liturgies. On the other hand, although Muslims celebrate a number of religious holy days, Christmas is not one of them — which, when you think about it, is a bit strange. Muslims, according to Hooper, "love and revere Jesus," but they studiously ignore His birthday.

Muslims have the Christmas story (or, at least, a truncated version of it), but they don't have Christmas. Why? Well, essentially because there's nothing to celebrate. To Muslims, Jesus is not the redeeming Savior of the world, but simply a prophet whose main job, it seems, was to announce the coming of Muhammad.

Not only does Islam lack Christmas; it lacks many of the humanizing elements that we associate with Christmas. The central image we identify with Christmas is that of the Holy Family. The fact that God became a member of a human family immeasurably elevated the importance of family, marriage, and motherhood. But there is no corresponding elevation of the family under Islam. According to Nonie Darwish, who grew up in Egypt, "Muslim weddings are more about sex and money. They do not convey the holy covenant of marriage."[191] The standard Egyptian marriage contract, she says, comes with questions about the bride's virginity, the amount of the dowry, and three spaces for the husband to record the names and addresses of wife number one, wife number two, and wife number three. And although Muslims supposedly honor Mary, this hasn't translated into a high regard for women in general. In the Koran, women are described as inferior beings, and they are treated as such in most of the Muslim world. The elevation of women was mainly a Christian achievement. It stemmed from the belief that all are equal in Christ, from the high status assigned to Mary, and from the elevation of marriage to a sacrament.

And then there's music. The wonder of Christianity is captured in the great Christian hymns and chants, but especially in the traditional carols sung at Christmastime. They seem to come from another world and, although some of them are centuries old, they seem to remain imperishable. The message they convey is joy: "joy to the world," "let nothing you dismay," "tidings of comfort and joy," "love and joy come to you," "joy, joy, joy."

Christianity is repeatedly attacked as restrictive and repressive, but these songs suggest something else, something immensely liberating. Once again, there is nothing like this in Islam. Beyond the chanted call to prayer, Islamic spirituality has little place for music. In fact, there is some debate among Islamic scholars about whether music is forbidden by Islamic tradition. But the anti-music forces seem to have the stronger case. In one of the hadith, Muhammad is quoted as saying, "Allah mighty and majestic ... commanded me to do away with musical instruments, flutes, strings, crucifixes, and the affair of the pre-Islamic era of ignorance. On the Day of Resurrection, Allah will pour molten lead into the ears of whoever sits listening to a songstress" (r 40.1).[192]

---

[191] Nonie Darwish, *Now They Call Me Infidel: Why I Renounced Jihad for America, Israel, and the War on Terror* (New York, NY: Sentinel, 2006), 80.

[192] *Reliance of the Traveller*, 774–775.

As historian Jamie Glazov points out in his book *United in Hate*,[193] there is a deep suspicion of music in Islam. Sayyid Qutb, the chief architect of modern Islamism, "reviled" music: "Like Lenin, he deemed music a distraction from the raging hatred necessary for destruction." Throughout Islamic history, says Glazov, there have been numerous attempts to ban music. In our time, "the Taliban illegalized music completely in Afghanistan, and Ayatollah Khomeini banned most music from Iranian radio and television."[194]

Khomeini's puritanism seems to have extended beyond music to a rejection of any form of good cheer. Here he is on the subject of jokes:

> Allah did not create man so that he could have fun. The aim of creation was for mankind to be put to the test through hardship and prayer. An Islamic regime must be serious in every field. There are no jokes in Islam. There is no humor in Islam. There is no fun in Islam. There can be no fun and joy in whatever is serious.[195]

No jokes? You may be tempted to laugh. Just don't do it in the wrong place. In July 2014, Turkey's deputy prime minister declared in a speech on "moral corruption" that women should not laugh in public in Turkey.[196]

For most Christians, Christmas holiday cheer also includes partaking of the good cheer provided by alcoholic drinks. With the exception of some (mostly American) denominations, Christians have lived fairly comfortably with liquor. Indeed, wine is at the heart of the Catholic liturgy, and orders of Catholic monks did much to develop the art of wine-making.

---

[193] Jamie Glazov, *United in Hate: The Left's Romance with Tyranny and Terror* (Cave Junction, OR: WND Books, 2009), 140.

[194] Ibid., 140, 141.

[195] Amir Taheri, *The Spirit of Allah* (Chevy Chase, MD: Adler & Adler, 1986), 259.

[196] Lizzie Dearden, "'Women Should Not Laugh in Public,' Says Turkey's Deputy Prime Minister in Morality Speech," *Independent*, July 29, 2014, https://www.independent.co.uk/news/world/europe/women-should-not-laugh-in-public-says-turkeys-deputy-prime-minister-in-morality-speech-9635526.html.

Although the Gospels decry drunkenness, Christian tradition does not condemn drinking in itself. Islam does. According to the Koran, wine is an abomination devised by Satan.

The difference between the Christian and Islamic views on drinking may not appear to be crucial, but it provides a clue to a crucial difference. It's not just wine versus no wine that's at issue but two entirely different ways of looking at life. You could call it balanced versus unbalanced. Islam sees one side of alcohol—the destructive, dangerous side—and comes up with a one-sided solution: ban it. Christianity sees that alcohol is both subtle and complex—just as the label on your wine bottle claims—and suggests that it be enjoyed in moderation.

Islam's suspicion of wine, just like its suspicion of music, seems overly severe. Wine, like music, is one of the great human comforts, and to suppress it, as Islam does, strikes the Western consciousness as slightly inhuman. By contrast, the Church has always followed the maxim that grace doesn't destroy nature but fulfills it. In this view, the supernatural doesn't replace the natural but completes it, raises it up, redeems it. So Jesus Christ raised bread and wine to the supernatural level and did the same for marriage by making it a sacrament. One of the beauties of Christianity is that it adds layers of meaning to ordinary human activities, giving them a specialness beyond what is ordinarily assigned to them. Despite, or perhaps because of, its call to participate in the divine life, Christianity had a humanizing influence wherever it spread.

Good Cheer versus Great Fear

Christian theologians who scour the Koran for bits and pieces of text that seem to harmonize Christianity and Islam might do well to pay attention instead to the different "feel" or "spirit" of the two faiths.

The distinctive spirit of Christianity, like the spirit of Christmas, is a spirit of good cheer. The good cheer comes from knowing that we are freed from our sins, but it also comes from the knowledge that we are sons and daughters of God. That concept—adoption as children of

God—brings with it much responsibility, but it also provides us with good reason to rejoice.

The distinctive spirit of Islam, by contrast, is a spirit of fear. The Christian idea that God is a Father who takes a personal interest in His children is alien to the tenets of Islam. The Allah of the Koran is as remote and capricious as any caliph. Humans are his slaves, not his sons and daughters. And he sends no Holy Spirit to comfort his people. Although the Koran borrows the title "Holy Spirit" from Christian Scripture, the Holy Spirit in Islam remains just that—a borrowing: a term torn from context and signifying nothing more than Muhammad's penchant for name-dropping.

Islam, with its thousand and one laws and corresponding punishments in this world and the next, is a religion of the letter rather than the spirit—the perfect illustration of what Saint Paul meant when he said "the letter killeth, but the spirit giveth life" (2 Cor. 3:6, KJV).

CAIR spokesman Ibrahim Hooper ends his Christmas message with the usual boilerplate about "shared religious heritage" and "building bridges of interfaith understanding."[197] Given CAIR's past involvement in terrorist funding and its recent designation as a terrorist organization by the United Arab Emirates, one might be justified in questioning his sincerity. Even on the assumption that he means every word, however, the deeper problem remains. Hooper concludes his message of reassurance to Christians by saying, "We have more in common than we think." Well, yes, if you think that having a common bond is just a matter of drawing up a list of shared vocabulary, then maybe that's so.

But on a deeper level, the claim is not convincing. Whatever superficial similarities there may be, the spirit of Christianity is radically different from the spirit of Islam. Like so many other Islamic PR men, Hooper knows the words, but he doesn't hear the music. Unfortunately, a good many well-meaning and eager-for-dialogue Christians suffer from a similar tone-deafness. They fail to realize that Islam marches to the beat of a decidedly different drummer.

[197] Spencer, "Ibrahim Hooper."

Life Lessons from Christmas Carols

One of the perpetual complaints against Christianity is that it is a life-denying, puritanical system. In the Victorian era, poet Algernon Swinburne referred to Christ as the "pale Galilean" from whose breath "the world has grown grey."[198] In our time, films such as *The Handmaid's Tale* (1990) portray Christians as robotic control freaks. Meanwhile, elite commentators contend that the only reason Christians oppose same-sex "marriage" and transgendered toddlers is that Christians are full of hate.

One way to rebut the charge is to point to the fact that traditional Christmas carols—the ones that retell the central Christian story—are generally full of joy and gladness. They are decidedly not "grey" or "life-denying." What, exactly, one might ask, are the life-denying elements in "Joy to the World" and "Ding Dong! Merrily on High"?

But before getting to the carols, it's instructive to note that Christianity's two main competitors for the souls of men—secularism and Islam—actually are on the grey and grim side of the continuum. That's easy enough to see in Islam. With its burqas, alcohol ban, and rigid rules for behaviors, Islam actually is a puritanical religion. But so, in its own way, is secularism. Today's universities, which are almost totally controlled by secularists, have elaborate behavior and speech codes that effectively take the spontaneity out of relationships and even out of simple conversation. You have to tread carefully in the secular world because it is seeded with

---

[198] Swinburne, "Hymn to Proserpine."

hidden booby traps. Try reciting one of Swinburne's poems to a group of fellow students and you might end up in diversity hell. You never know what will offend the new puritans until it's too late.

Christians are supposedly life-denying, but Islam and secularism are patently cultures of death. Again, this is more obvious in Islam. Jihadists like to say that they will win out over non-Muslims because "you love life, but we love death." But, in many senses, secularism is also a death cult. Although secularists aren't generally keen on martyring themselves, they don't have any principled objection to sacrificing babies (through abortion) and old people (through euthanasia) in order to make life more convenient for themselves. And this dismissive attitude toward human life has gained wide acceptance. In a photo taken when they still looked like choir boys, the Beatles posed with the dismembered parts of life-like baby dolls for the 1966 album cover *Yesterday and Today*.

For a supposedly life-affirming philosophy, secularism tends to have a distinct apathy toward new life, and toward marriage, which is the usual way of bringing new life into the world. Hollywood, which is secularism's dream weaver, is far more interested in babes than in babies.

Islam frowns on abortion, but not for the same reason as Christians. There is no well-developed theology of the value and dignity of each human life in Islam. Instead, Islam seems to have a more utilitarian view of life. One can't help forming the impression that for many Muslim leaders, raising babies is just another way of raising an army.

At first glance, Islamic attitudes toward women seem poles apart from Western secular views, but on closer inspection, the Islamic view of women is not that far removed from the Hollywood view that women are little more than sex objects. The difference is that Islam conditions Muslim men to prefer babes in paradise to babes on earth. Some are so well-conditioned in this respect that they are quite happy to exchange earthly wife and kids for heavenly maidens should the occasion present itself. In any event, the exalted view of women and motherhood that one finds in the Christian carols is largely missing from both Islam and secularism.

Degraded views of life and death, birth, and babies come from a low estimate of human value. Christmas is a celebration of that moment of enlightenment when the full value of human life became apparent. In retrospect, it was far more enlightening than the European Enlightenment, which arrived eighteen centuries later and which would have been impossible except for the light provided by the first.

The Incarnation revealed God to man, but also, as Saint John Paul II observed, it revealed man to himself. The birth of Christ revealed that the worth of men and women was far greater than anything that had hitherto been presumed. The birth of Christ also put family life in a whole new light. God entered the world not as a full-grown autonomous individual, but as a member of a family.

The birth of Christ changed everything. It added layer upon layer of meaning to the human condition. Human life was of inestimable value. Death was no longer to be feared because this Child was born to vanquish death and open the way to life everlasting. That life, moreover, was to be more than the pleasant continuation of this life envisaged by some pagan religions, and, later, by Islam. It was a new kind of life — one that transforms us into the likeness of Christ and makes us worthy of communion with God.

The wonder of all this is difficult to grasp intellectually. Indeed, the birth of any child seems miraculous. And no amount of biological science comes close to explaining it. When one considers that the particular Child who was born on Christmas day in Bethlehem set the planets in motion, the miracle is compounded beyond all understanding.

The proper response to the miracle of Christmas is a mix of wonder and joy. And few things convey that mix as effectively as the traditional Christmas carols:

> Come let us surround Him
> On this magic night
> Gather here around Him
> Wondrous Babe of Light.

That's from "Sing We Now of Christmas." Those who know the tune will agree, I think, that the words and music were made for each other. We find the same thing in almost all of the traditional Christmas carols. The harmony between heaven and earth that the birth of Jesus brought is matched by a rare harmony of music and lyrics. Indeed, the lyrics to "Pat-A-Pan" make that very point:

> God and man today become
> More in tune than fife and drum
> So be merry while you play,
> Sing and dance this Christmas Day.

Christmas carols also give us a glimpse of our heavenly destiny. Take these lyrics from "Good Christian Men, Rejoice":

> Good Christian men, rejoice
> With heart and soul and voice,
> Now ye hear of endless bliss;
> Joy! Joy!
> Jesus Christ was born for this!
> He has oped the heav'nly door
> And man is blessed evermore.

"Endless bliss"? "Blessed evermore"? But what kind of creature are we that we are meant for endless bliss? If we are honest, we think as Scrooge did (in that other *Christmas Carol*), "I don't deserve to be so happy."

Well, in our present condition, most of us don't deserve it. The good news is that we "are being changed into his likeness from one degree of glory to another" so that we become "a new creation" (2 Cor. 3:18; 5:17). In the words of "Hark! The Herald Angels Sing," Christ was

> Born to raise the sons of earth,
> Born to give them second birth.

The Savior's birth makes possible a second birth by which we become new and transformed selves. But this concept of being born again is alien to Christianity's main competitors for the souls of men. Secular man is taught to have self-esteem. He thinks he's fine just the way he is, and the suggestion that he needs a new self is highly offensive to him. Besides, his spiritual needs are already fulfilled by regular yoga and meditation. Islam is not particularly interested in spiritual transformation either. In Islam, death signifies a transformation of one's circumstances, but not a transformation of oneself. You can end up in paradise (Allah willing) and remain essentially the same person you were on earth, lustful desires and all. Indeed, the surest way to get to paradise is to commit what, from a Christian perspective, are grave and even soul-destroying sins.

In both Christianity and Islam, heaven is viewed as a better place. But for Christians it is a better place because it is filled with better people — far better than they were on earth because they have died to their sins and risen to a new sinless existence. Consider this verse from "As with Gladness, Men of Old":

> So may we with holy joy,
> Pure and free from sin's alloy,
> All our costliest treasures bring,
> Christ, to Thee, our heavenly King.

This view of man, cleansed from his sins and gloriously transformed, is remarkably different from the low estimate of man presented by secularism on the one hand, and Islam on the other. In the secular view, man's final destiny is to dissolve into the dust and take his place among the other particles on the periodic table of elements. To which the normal human response is, "Is that all?"

Islam seems to promise more, but it does not solve the problem of what C. S. Lewis called the "inconsolable longing." Suicide bombers tend to be on the young side, because it eventually dawns on even the dullest mind that endless copulation with Islam's version of the Stepford Wives will not bring infinite fulfillment.

Men and women are meant for more. The proper response both to Islam's otherworld enticements and to secularism's bleak view of human destiny is the same: "Is that all there is?" Bach's "Jesu, Joy of Man's Desiring" comes much closer to naming our deepest aspiration:

> Jesu, joy of man's desiring
> Holy wisdom, love most bright.
> Drawn by Thee, our souls aspiring,
> Soar to uncreated light.

The irony is that Christianity in the West is losing souls to secularism on the one hand, and Islam, on the other, even though both are essentially joyless belief systems. In America, increasing numbers are opting for atheism, agnosticism, or simply "no belief." Meanwhile, according to several observers, Europe may be in the process of exchanging Christianity for Islam.

Whether you trade Christianity for Islam or exchange it for secularist "no belief," it's a bad deal either way. It's as though someone offered you a quarter in exchange for the ten-dollar bill in your wallet. The uncanny thing is that so many have fallen for these bad bargains.

Just compare Islam's hymns and carols to the Christian ones. What's that you say? There are no hymns and carols in Islam? Oh, yes, I'd almost forgotten. Muhammad wasn't keen on music. "Allah," he said, "commanded me to do away with musical instruments, flutes, strings, crucifixes, and the affair of the pre-Islamic period of ignorance (r 40.1)."[199] Islam's rules for dhimmis (conquered non-Muslims), which are still in force today, also forbid Christians to ring bells or clang cymbals. Of course, there is the chanted Islamic call to prayer. Barack Obama said it was the sweetest sound he ever heard, but to most non-Muslims it seems quite a bit more ominous than sweet.

Islam's puritanism extends even to humor. As the Ayatollah Khomeini said, "There are no jokes in Islam. There is no humor in Islam."[200] Islam, in essence, is like Scrooge before his encounter with the three ghosts.

---

[199] *Reliance of the Traveller*, 774.
[200] Taheri, *The Spirit of Allah*, 259.

He chases carolers away, and he has no sense of humor. Once he catches the spirit of Christmas, however, he becomes deliriously happy, dances a jig, and is transported by the peal of church bells. Scrooge's story of redemption is aptly titled *A Christmas Carol*.

Of course, secular society does have music and jokes, but many of the jokes are not funny, and much of the music is so bad that one begins to sympathize with the idea of banning it. Islam under sharia law is a pretty grim affair, but in its attempts to take Christ out of Christmas and out of almost every other area of life, secular society has become increasingly grey. Traditional family ties have been shattered, abortions are counted in the millions, joyless promiscuity has become the norm, and tens of millions fall victim to depression, drug dependency, violence, and suicide.

Secularism doesn't offer any way out of our society's downward spiral, but Christianity does. Christ did admonish us, however, that we can't enter the kingdom of heaven unless we become as little children. Christmas carols are one way of recovering the awe and wonder that children have in the presence of the Most High:

> Come let us surround Him
> On this magic night
> Gather here around Him
> Wondrous Babe of light
>
> Sing we Noel!
> The King is born, Noel!
> Sing we now of Christmas
> Sing we here, Noel!

12

Misunderstanding Islam

The celebration of Christmas suggests that Christians and Muslims don't have as much in common as some Catholic leaders claim. The numerous attacks on Christians suggests the same thing. Church leaders are in the habit of saying that such terrorists are "misunderstanders" of Islam. But could it be that Catholic apologists for Islam are the real misunderstanders?

The Koran Is a "Sacrament"?

"The more you understand something, the less you fear it." Well, that's not exactly what the archbishop said, but the sentiment seems to be the same.

What Archbishop Michael Fitzgerald actually said in an interview on Maine Public Broadcasting Network (MPBN) was "The more you understand a religion, the better it is."[201]

The archbishop, who is billed as one of the Church's top authorities on Islam, served as the president of the Pontifical Council for Interreligious Dialogue from 2002 to 2006. Now retired, he is teaching a class on the Koran at John Carroll University, a Jesuit college in Ohio.

According to the MPBN report, "For years, Fitzgerald has been urging his fellow Christians to acquaint themselves with Islam and its holy book, the Quran." What's more, "in teaching Catholic students about Islam, he suggests they look for commonalities with their own religion."

For example, after noting the great respect shown for the Koran by Muslims, Archbishop Fitzgerald asks his class if there is "anything comparable in Catholic Christianity." And, sure enough, there is. One student mentions the Eucharist. Clearly pleased, Fitzgerald responds: "Yes. In a way the Quran is a sacrament, isn't it? It's a sign of the presence of God."[202]

---

[201] Tom Gjelten, "Learning about the Quran ... from A Catholic Archbishop", April 30, 2015, https://www.mainepublic.org/post/learning-about-quran-catholic-archbishop.

[202] Ibid.

Very reassuring—as long as you keep your eyes firmly fixed on the commonalities. That the Koran is also a manual for putting non-Muslims in their place is probably not on the archbishop's agenda. I'm all for a better understanding of the Koran, but it seems to me that the more you understand it, the more troubled you will be.

For an analogy, consider that the Jews who understood what *Mein Kampf* was all about left Germany while the going was good. Those with a fuzzier understanding of Nazism stayed on, looking for commonalities and hoping for the best. Nazis no longer threaten Jews, but it's not entirely a historical coincidence that Jews are again fleeing Europe. Muslims in Europe outnumber Jews by at least ten to one.

As attacks against them increase, Jews are beginning to realize that Muslim anti-Semitism rivals that of the Nazis. They may also remember that prominent Muslims, such as the grand mufti of Jerusalem, worked closely with Hitler and Adolf Eichmann to expedite the Holocaust.

I'm not saying that European Jews know something about Islam that Archbishop Fitzgerald doesn't know. He speaks Arabic and has studied Islam all his life, and undoubtedly, he has a vast knowledge of the subject. But knowledge alone isn't sufficient for a thorough understanding of a subject. What counts is not simply what you know but also your ability to make sense of what you know. For example, other Church specialists on Islam with even more credentials than Archbishop Fitzgerald (Jesuit Father Samir Khalil Samir[203] comes to mind) are far less sanguine about what the Koran teaches.

The applicable maxim is the old one about not being able to see the forest for the trees. Many scholars become so focused on the details of their discipline that they're unable to step back and look at the larger picture. The larger point about Islam is not that it bears some similarities

---

[203] Edward Pentin, "Paris Terror Attacks: 'What They Did Is in the Name of Islam,'" *National Catholic Register*, January 13, 2015, https://www.ncregister.com/daily-news/paris-terror-attacks-what-they-did-is-in-the-name-of-islam.

to Catholicism, but that it has historically been an enemy to Christians and other non-Muslims.

The Jews who are now fleeing Europe in droves may lack Archbishop Fitzgerald's academic background, but they seem possessed of a quality he lacks—namely, the ability to put two and two together.

There is one other thing about Archbishop Fitzgerald's approach that doesn't add up. In urging Christians to acquaint themselves with the Koran, he seems to assume that the Koran is self-explanatory. But it's not.

In the words of English historian and essayist Thomas Carlyle (who was a fan of Muhammad), the Koran is "a wearisome confused jumble." Even Islamic scholars admit that it can't be understood apart from the various supplementary texts that fill in the gaps—the *Sira*, the numerous *hadith* volumes, and the equally voluminous commentaries and law books.

Westerners who read it typically find it confusing. People I've talked with describe it as "tough sledding," "difficult," and "muddled." Some things do come through, however. Perhaps the three clearest messages in the Koran are that God is sovereign, Muhammad is the prophet of God, and unbelievers will roast in hell. Those who are looking for something deeper will be disappointed.

The kind of penetrating insights that can be found in the New Testament are few and far between in the Koran (and are mostly borrowed). Instead, it is largely a book of imprecations against unbelievers. Test this for yourself by opening a few pages at random.

One of the main takeaways from the Koran is that unbelievers are contemptible and therefore deserving of an awful fate. Thus, if you are an unbeliever (i.e., a non-Muslim), you might be reasonably worried about those who take the Koran to be the literal word of God.

One suspects, however, that the archbishop's pupils are unlikely to bother themselves with such thoughts. Their focus will be on the commonalities. What's worrisome is that Archbishop Fitzgerald's approach to teaching about Islam is essentially the same as that taken in most Catholic schools, colleges, and seminaries. And so it's likely that another generation of Catholics who can't see the forest for the trees will take the reins of the Church. Insofar as they address the topic of Islam, they will be taken up with noting the vague similarities ("in a way, the Quran is a sacrament, isn't it?") and will miss the main message to non-Muslims (convert, pay the jizya, or die).

While closely examining this or that tree in the wood ("look, here's one that's just like the birch in our backyard"), they will fail to notice that the trees are part of a large and dangerous forest. They will also fail to notice that, like Birnam Wood in Shakespeare's *Macbeth*, the forest is on the move.

Time to Tell the Truth about Islam

The important thing about a religion, said C. S. Lewis, is not whether it makes one feel good but whether it is true. This observation came to mind as I read an essay by Jesuit Father James Schall (1928–2019) titled "Speaking Honestly about Islam."[204]

Father Schall suggests that we haven't been telling the truth about Islam because to do so would violate the feel-good principle that rules Western societies. According to the feel-good principle, self-esteem is the highest value. And, therefore, every person, culture, and religion has an inalienable right to feel good about himself or itself.

People hew to the Islam-is-peace line because they don't want to give offense and also because they don't want to be accused of a hate crime. It's a well-founded fear.

In many Western societies, numerous individuals—and some of them very prominent individuals—have been put on trial for the crime of criticizing Islam: Mark Steyn and Ezra Levant in Canada, Geert Wilders in the Netherlands, Lars Hedegaard in Denmark, and Elisabeth Sabaditsch-Wolff in Austria, to name a few. In several cases, the defendants were informed that truth was no defense. The accuracy of their criticism, they were told, was beside the point (the point being that they had said hurtful things).

---

[204] Fr. James V. Schall, "Speaking Honestly About Islam," *Crisis Magazine*, July 22, 2015, https://www.crisismagazine.com/2015/speaking-honestly-about-islam.

Honesty is the best policy, according to the old maxim; but many Western governments have adopted a deliberate policy of prevarication in regard to Islam. Hardly a day goes by when some Western leader or other isn't explaining away the latest jihad attack as having nothing to do with Islam.

It's not that leaders are doing nothing about the problem of jihad. A number of European countries have belatedly launched deradicalization programs aimed at countering jihadist ideology. For example, in 2015, U.K. prime minister David Cameron announced a five-year plan to defeat Islamic extremism.

The trouble with these programs is that they can't let go of the lie. The central feature of most of these initiatives is the enlistment of moderate Muslims in a campaign to convince potential jihadists that Islam has nothing to do with jihad (or else to convince them that jihad, correctly understood, is nothing more than an interior spiritual struggle).

This puts the Muslim leaders who are willing to sign up for such campaigns in a difficult spot. They are in essence trying to defend a largely indefensible position. While it's true that Islam can be practiced peacefully (and, thank God, that's the way most Muslims practice it), that can be done only by ignoring some of Islam's fundamental teachings. As Father Schall observes, "It is senseless to pretend that a jihadist vision is not found in the Quran."

He continues:

What has to be faced by everyone is not the "violence" of Islam, but its truth. We may not "like" a jihadist view of the Quran. But we denigrate the dignity of ISIS and other violent strains in both Sunni and Shiite branches of Islam that clearly see that their interpretation of Islam has legitimate roots in the Quran, in Islamic history and in the judgment of many authoritative commentators.[205]

---

[205] Ibid.

To some extent, Father Schall is playing the devil's advocate. He does not really believe in the dignity of ISIS, but he does suggest that their beliefs are honest. What is the basic attraction that draws young men and women to Islamic movements? Father Schall replies that the main motivation is the perception that the Koran is true. Most jihadists wage jihad because they believe that is what Allah wants them to do.

A campaign based on the dubious notion that Allah does not command jihad is a hard sell. Both sides—the moderates and the radicals—can quote scripture to defend their positions, but the jihadists seem to be able to quote it much more extensively and convincingly. Many of the moderates are akin to "cafeteria Catholics." They have a family or cultural attachment to Islam, but they don't have a thorough knowledge of their faith or any great desire to follow all of its commands. They have a more Westernized and subjective understanding of Islam than their fundamentalist brethren and are inclined to say things like "That's not my Islam" when condemning jihadist violence.

In other words, for some moderate Muslims, Islam is more of a personalized construct—a religion made in the image of their own subjective inclinations. The comparison to cafeteria Catholics is useful because it helps us to understand better the relation of the moderate Muslim to his religion. The Catholic who is accepting of abortion and same-sex "marriage" is convinced that the Church will eventually come around to the same position. The truly moderate Muslim would never resort to violence, and so he convinces himself that his religion must therefore be a religion of peace. In short, the moderate Muslim adheres to what author Stephen Kirby calls "fantasy Islam."[206]

Because it's based on fantasy, the whole effort to convince jihadists and would-be jihadists that Islam is a religion of peace seems doomed to failure. Granted, many Western leaders don't really believe what they're

---

[206] Dr. Stephen M. Kirby, "The Lure of Fantasy Islam," *FrontPage Mag*, July 8, 2015, https://archives.frontpagemag.com/fpm/lure-fantasy-islam-dr-stephen-m-kirby/.

saying, and they look upon their deradicalization projects merely from a pragmatic point of view. But even looked at from a purely practical standpoint, it's doubtful that a strategy based on such a massive lie can succeed.

Muslim leaders, of course, are caught in a bind on this issue. On the one hand, they need to please their Western hosts; on the other hand, they can't afford to repudiate large parts of Islamic scripture and tradition.

But Western leaders and opinion-makers have fewer constraints. They might consider telling the truth for a change. It might prove in the long run to be a much better strategy than the current self-defeating one.

Islamic radicals have a very good case that their version of Islam is truer to the original than the moderate version. The proper way to undermine their ideology and theology is to cast doubts not on their interpretation of Islam but on the truth of Islam itself.

That may seem like an impossible undertaking, but one thing that works in favor of the truth-telling strategy is that, despite their violence, many jihadists do seem to be truth-seekers. There is abundant evidence from their letters, diaries, blogs, Facebook pages, and last-testament videos that they believe they have discovered what God truly wants them to do. For this reason, they may be more likely candidates for conversion to a higher truth than many a lukewarm Muslim.

Islam — The View from Disney Country

In April 2017, the Diocese of Orlando reprimanded a sixth-grade teacher at a Catholic school for an "unfortunate exhibit of disrespect."[207] What did he do? He provided his students with printouts of Saint John Bosco's negative assessment of Islam. Saint John Bosco called Islam a "monstrous mixture of Judaism, Paganism, and Christianity," and explained that Muhammad "propagated his religion, not through miracles or persuasive words, but by military force."

Citing *Nostra Aetate*, Jacquelyn Flanigan, an associate superintendent of the Diocese of Orlando's schools, said that "the information provided in the 6th-grade class is not consistent with the teachings of the Catholic Church."[208]

If that's so, then a lot of saints and popes expressed views on Islam that are not consistent with the teachings of the Catholic Church. Saint Thomas Aquinas, for instance, said that Muhammad "seduced the people by promises of carnal pleasure," "did not bring forth any signs produced in a supernatural way," "forced others to become his followers by the violence of his arms," and "perverts almost all the

---

[207] Anita Carey, "Catholic Teacher Scolded for Distributing Saints' Critique of Islam," *Church Militant*, April 20, 2017, https://www.churchmilitant.com/news/article/catholic-teacher-under-fire-for-writings-of-saint-john-bosco.
[208] Ibid.

testimonies of the Old and New Testament by making them into fabrications of his own."[209]

Numerous popes and saints (see Andrew Bieszad's "What Did the Saints Say about Islam?")[210] indulged in similar exhibits of "disrespect." These include Pope Calixtus III, who vowed to "exalt the true Faith and to extirpate the diabolical sect of the reprobate and faithless Mahomet in the East."[211]

The Diocese of Orlando didn't say just where the teacher deviated from Church teachings or in what way he was showing disrespect for Islam. In fact, much of what Don Bosco says is attested to by Islamic sources and Islamic historians. The claim that Muhammad "propagated his religion ... by military force" seems consistent with the testimony of Ibn Ishaq's *Life of Muhammad*, most of which is filled with accounts of raids, battles, distribution of booty, and forced conversions. Then, there's the fact that the Islamic calendar is dated not from A.D. 610, the date of Muhammad's first "revelation," but from 622, the date when he moved to Medina and commenced his career of jihad. Up until that point, Muhammad never had more than a hundred followers. After 622, Islam took off precisely because of "military force."

The handout on Bosco's views on Islam also notes that the Koran "guaranteed its followers a Paradise filled only of earthly pleasures." But the Koran really is full of depictions of paradise that portray it as a garden of earthly delights. For example:

---

[209] "St. Thomas Aquinas' Teaching against the Infidel Mohammed (Muslims)," Opus Dei Alert.com, http://www.opusdeialert.com/st-thomas-aquinas-against-mohammed.htm.

[210] Andrew Bieszad, "What Did the Saints Say about Islam?" *One Peter Five*, April 30, 2015, https://onepeterfive.com/what-did-the-saints-say-about-islam/.

[211] Quoted in Ludwig Freiherr von Pastor, *The History of the Popes, from the Close of the Middle Ages: Drawn from the Secret Archives of the Vatican and Other Original Sources* (London: K. Paul, Trench, Trubner, 1891), 346.

As for the righteous, they shall surely triumph. Theirs shall be gardens and vineyards and high-bosomed maidens for companionship: a truly overflowing cup (78:31–34).

One of the passages in the Bosco handout that a *Huffington Post* article cites disapprovingly says that Muhammad "couldn't even write."[212] But according to numerous Islamic sources, he couldn't. In fact, Muslim apologists are fond of using Muhammad's illiteracy as proof of the Koran's divine origin. How, they ask, could an illiterate man write such beautiful prose? Who else but God could have produced such a perfect book?

In other words, a case can be made that Saint John Bosco and Saint Thomas Aquinas accurately reflected Islamic doctrine in their writings. The disturbing thing is the Orlando Diocese's unwillingness even to entertain that possibility. The associate superintendent says, in effect, "You can't say that. The Church has spoken. Case closed." One assumes that, like most graduates of schools of education (including the Catholic ones), the diocese's teachers and administrators lean left of center. The curious thing is that, in most other matters, liberal Catholics spurn the argument from authority. Yet here they are wielding it like a cudgel. One is reminded of the classic Ring Lardner line: "'Shut up,' he explained."

One thing that is striking about the defenders of the new orthodoxy about Islam is their sheer lack of curiosity. Considering that the spread of Islam in recent years has been accompanied by massive violence against Christians, one would think that they would be eager to know more. Not so. Like the functionaries in the Orlando Diocese, they want the matter closed without further discussion.

Yet there are numerous questions surrounding the Church's sparse and scattered statements about Islam that beg to be answered. For example, do the Church's recent statements about Islam outweigh what it has said

---

[212] Robert Spencer, "Florida: Catholic Diocese of Orlando Reprimands Schoolteacher for Quoting Saint on Islam," *Jihad Watch*, April 22, 2017, https://www.jihadwatch.org/2017/04/florida-catholic-diocese-of-orlando-reprimands-school-teacher-for-quoting-saint-on-islam.

over the last 1,400 years? Has the Church adopted the Islamic doctrine of abrogation, whereby more recent statements cancel out earlier contradictory statements? Has the associate superintendent in Orlando ever heard of the doctrine of abrogation? Does she know that prominent Catholics have raised questions about *Nostra Aetate*, the document she cites? For instance, Pope Benedict XVI wrote about a "weakness" in *Nostra Aetate*. "It speaks of religion solely in a positive way," he said, "and it disregards the sick and distorted forms of religion."[213]

In speaking of Islam, the Council fathers stressed the commonalities between Islam and Christianity, not the differences. But this one-sidedly positive assessment needs to be understood in the context of the stated mission of *Nostra Aetate*. The first paragraph of the document states that "she [the Church] considers above all in this declaration what men have in common and what draws them to fellowship." In other words, the Council fathers were not setting out to provide a full picture of the Muslim faith but only to sketch some of its similarities with Catholicism.

This raises some oft-asked questions (though, apparently, not oft-asked in Orlando): Was *Nostra Aetate* meant to be a teaching document or a pastoral document? Was it meant to deal with matters of faith and morals in a definitive way? Or was it mainly pastoral in intent? Were the Council fathers intending to teach Catholics about the nature of Islam? Or was *Nostra Aetate* primarily meant as a gesture of outreach to non-Christians?

Several prominent bishops have suggested the latter. Vatican Cardinal Walter Brandmüller has stated that *Nostra Aetate* does "not have a binding doctrinal content."[214] And Archbishop Guido Pozzo, who served as the secretary of the Pontifical Council Ecclesia Dei, told a German newspaper, "*Nostra Aetate* does not have any dogmatic authority, and

---

[213] Samuel Gregg, "Benedict XVI and the Pathologies of Religion," *Crisis Magazine*, November 7, 2012, https://www.crisismagazine.com/2012/benedict-xvi-and-the-pathologies-of-religion.

[214] William Doino Jr., "Is Vatican II Completely Binding on Catholics?" *First Things*, May 24, 2012, https://www.firstthings.com/blogs/firstthoughts/2012/05/is-vatican-ii-completely-binding-on-catholics.

thus one cannot demand from anyone to recognize this declaration as being dogmatic."[215]

The Catholic educators in Orlando and elsewhere should take notice. They should also engage in a practice they undoubtedly encourage in their students—namely, critical thinking. When they read in *Nostra Aetate* that "they [Muslims] value the moral life," do they ever wonder if it's the same moral life that Catholics value? Do they ever wonder about the discrepancy between what Pope Francis says about the Koran ("opposed to every form of violence"), and what the Koran itself says about violence? Do they have enough intellectual curiosity to find out for themselves whether Saint John Bosco's observations about Islam are accurate? If they did want to find out, they would have to dig a lot deeper than *Nostra Aetate*.

The truth is that recent Church statements about Islam have precious little to say about Islam—certainly not enough to provide a full picture of what "authentic" Islam teaches. *Nostra Aetate, Lumen Gentium, Evangelii Gaudium*, the *Catechism of the Catholic Church*? If you add together everything these documents have to say about Islam, and subtract the repetitions, you end up with about half a page of text. The *Catechism*, which devotes six paragraphs to man's relationship with animals (2415–2418, 2456–2457), devotes only one paragraph to the Church's relationship with the Muslims (841). And that paragraph merely repeats a paragraph in *Lumen Gentium*, which was written at a time (the 1960s) when the Church's relationship with the Muslims was more or less a back-burner issue. That paragraph is forty-four words long. That's about eighty words less than the warning label on a bottle of Tylenol. And unlike the Tylenol label, it contains no warning. In short, there is room for the Church to say a lot more about Islam.

Catholics deserve a fuller picture of Islam than the rosy-hued one that prevailed among Council participants in the mid-1960s. An update is urgently needed. Otherwise, Catholics will have to learn by harsh

---

[215] Chretien, "SSPX Could Be Reconciled."

experience what their fellow Christians are learning about Islam in Nigeria, Syria, Iraq, Iran, Lebanon, Saudi Arabia, Pakistan, Indonesia, and a host of other Muslim-majority countries.

While they are waiting for the update, Catholics would be well advised to put down *Nostra Aetate* and pick up a copy of the Koran, or the *Sira* (the life of Muhammad), or *Reliance of the Traveller* (a widely consulted manual of sharia law). Then they can judge for themselves what Islam teaches.

In view of the fact that Orlando was the scene of the Islam-inspired massacre at the Pulse nightclub, you would think that the Church in Orlando might have acquired a more realistic view of Islam. But Orlando is also the home of Disney World—the place that assures us that "when you wish upon a star your dreams come true." Well, maybe that depends on which star you wish upon. If you're placing all your bets on the star with the crescent moon nearby, you are truly living in fantasyland.

13

The Next Scandal

The demonstrably false things that certain churchmen say about Islam suggest that they have only a shallow knowledge of the Muslim faith. Either that, or they are deliberately covering up the true nature of Islam. If that's the case, then the Church is facing another scandal—one that is potentially as serious as the sex-abuse scandals. Whether the cover-up is intentional or not, it is already having a devastating effect. The rosy picture of Islam painted by many in the hierarchy has left millions of Christians unprepared for the aggressive nature of the Islamic faith.

As the Church Reels, Is an Even Larger Scandal Building?

The Church has been deeply damaged by revelations in 2018 of widespread clerical sex abuse in Chile and Honduras, the further revelation that Cardinal Theodore McCarrick's predatory behavior had been hushed up, and claims by an archbishop that Pope Francis knew about sanctions imposed on McCarrick by Pope Benedict XVI but repealed them.[216]

It may seem that things couldn't get much worse for the Church, but it almost certainly will. More revelations of abuse and cover-ups at the highest levels are likely to come, and the level of distrust and discouragement among ordinary Catholics is bound to grow.

Persecution of Christians and Islamization of Europe

But there is another scandal waiting in the wings that may prove larger and more devastating than the current one. The looming scandal concerns the Church's facilitation of an Islamic takeover of much of the Western and non-Western world. If the term "Islamic takeover" seems overblown, then you may not be paying attention — to the escalating persecution of

---

[216] Edward Pentin, "Ex-Nuncio Accuses Pope Francis of Failing to Act on McCarrick's Abuse," *National Catholic Register*, August 25, 2018, https://www. ncregister.com/daily-news/ex-nuncio-accuses-pope-francis-of-failing-to-act-on-mccarricks-abuse.

Christians in Iran, Egypt, Pakistan, and Indonesia; to the genocide against Christians in Iraq, Syria, and Nigeria; and to the gradual submission of European nations to Islamic demands.

Is the Church knowingly facilitating the persecution of Christians and the Islamization of Europe? No, but the Church's semiofficial policy toward Islam, nevertheless, has that effect. Ever since Vatican II, Church policy has been one of turning a blind eye to the violent and aggressive nature of Islam while declaring "esteem" for Islam as a fellow monotheistic religion.

For years now, Catholic leaders—the pope, bishops, priests, Catholic media, and Catholic educators—have covered up the large gap that divides Islam and Christianity. Moreover, they have poured all their energies into emphasizing the similarities between the two faiths, while decrying "Islamophobia"—a term that seems to refer to any criticism of Islam.

As the gap widens between what the hierarchy says about Islam and what ordinary Catholics see in the news or encounter in their lives, many Catholics will become alienated from the Church. The priestly sex-abuse scandals that broke in 2002 had that effect. In those areas that were hardest hit by the scandals, church attendance dropped off dramatically. The same is likely to happen as the realities of Islamization put the lie to the Church's Pollyannaish view of Islam. Only this time, the disaffection will be on a greater scale.

Why? For two reasons. First because the addition of this second scandal to the sex-abuse scandals will have a compounding effect—the straw that broke the camel's back. Second, this new "straw" is potentially a good deal heavier than all the previous straws combined. The number of victims of sex abuse by priests is difficult to estimate; it could amount to tens of thousands worldwide. But the victims of worldwide Islamization will be numbered in the tens of millions.

I'm talking here not about killings and massacres but about the daily humiliations and persecutions that non-Muslims suffer in Muslim lands. If present demographic and cultural trends continue, it is quite possible that several European nations will fall under Islamic control within the next twenty years. Sweden, Belgium, and the Netherlands are prime candidates. Germany, France, and the United Kingdom are also vulnerable. As sharia law spreads through Europe, so will the abuses that accompany it. And many of these abuses are sexual or sex-related, such as honor killings, child marriages, wife beating, and female genital mutilation (FGM).

Although they are hardly identical, the two scandals resemble each other in two important respects. Both involve widespread sex abuse, and both involve cover-ups. In Europe, the abuse of vulnerable women and vulnerable minors, both Muslim and non-Muslim, is now widespread. Sweden has the second-highest incidence of rape in the world. Thousands of teenage girls in English towns such as Rotherham, Rochdale, and Telford have been victimized by Muslim rape gangs. Twelve hundred women were sexually assaulted on a single night outside the Cologne train station on New Year's Eve 2016. Meanwhile, the number of Muslim girls and women in Europe who have been subject to FGM[217] is estimated to be well over five hundred thousand.

The Silence of Church Leaders

Priests and bishops, of course, are not committing these crimes, but they are strangely silent about them. They do not speak out about them the way they do when an incident of "Islamophobia" hits the news. Perhaps they don't speak out because they are, in part, responsible for the increased presence in Europe of all those additional rapists, wife-abusers, and FGM practitioners.

It's no secret that Church leaders have been at the forefront of those calling for a more welcoming attitude toward migrants. A recent *National Post* (Canada) headline given to a syndicated *Washington Post* article

---

[217] Chris Harris, "Female Genital Mutilation: Why Do So Many Cases Go Unpunished in Europe?" Euronews.com, https://www.euronews.com/2015/02/05/how-many-cases-of-female-genital-mutilation-are-going-unpunished-in-europe.

tells the story: "The loudest opponent of Italy's new anti-migrant policy? The Catholic Church."[218] The voices of opposition range from the pope, who has said that migrant security is more important than national security, down to the village priest. The *Post* report cites one priest who said that the anti-migrant party "cannot call themselves Christians." And it quotes an archbishop who says, "The Church can't stay silent. I can't stay silent."

Yet the Church has stayed silent about the massive crime wave that has swept Europe as a result of the open-borders policies it has lobbied for. The *Post* article mentions a pro-migration statement by the Italian Bishops' Conference "illustrated on its website with the photo of a weak migrant who had been clinging to flotsam in the Mediterranean before her rescue." But where are the photos of the rape-gang victims? The victims of car and knife attacks? The bruised and bloody faces of the elderly couple attacked in their apartment by Muslim migrants? And where are the photos of the acid-scarred babies and children?[219] The city of London now has the highest per capita rate of acid attacks in the world, but such statistics seem of little interest to Church leaders.

Church's leaders have been guilty not only of encouraging mass migration of a type that would predictably result in a wave of horrific crimes but also of looking the other way when the crimes occur. And when a terror attack is too big to ignore, they assure us that such acts have nothing to do with Islam.

These daily cover-ups of Muslim criminal activity are part of a much larger cover-up — the cover-up of the full truth about Islam. As mentioned

---

[218] Chico Harlan and Stefano Pitreli, "The Loudest Opponent of Italy's New Anti-Migrant Policy? The Catholic Church," *National Post*, July 28, 2018, https://nationalpost.com/news/world/the-loudest-opponent-of-italys-new-anti-migrant-policy-the-catholic-church.

[219] Robert Spencer, "UK: Muslim Migrant Arrested for Acid Attack on His Three-Year-Old Son, Other Attackers Sought," *Jihad Watch*, July 25, 2018, https://www.jihadwatch.org/2018/07/uk-muslim-migrant-arrested-for-acid-attack-on-his-three-year-old-son-other-attackers-sought.

earlier, Church authorities and educators have presented a one-sided picture of Islam—one with all the scary parts left out. For example, in *Evangelii Gaudium*, Pope Francis asserts that "authentic Islam and a proper reading of the Koran are opposed to every form of violence." Not surprisingly, he has been thanked on several occasions by top Muslim authorities for his defense of Islam.

Like the sex-abuse scandal, this sugarcoated portrayal of Islam constitutes a betrayal of the shepherd's duty to protect. It misleads Catholics on an issue vital to their security. For example, the only threat from migrants that Pope Francis will admit to is "threats to our comfort."[220] The hierarchy's misleading assurances on Muslim migration can be summed up by a banner that "welcomers" in European countries sometimes display. It proclaims: "They're not dangerous, they're in danger." However, as more and more Europeans come to realize that a significant number of the migrants are indeed dangerous, their feelings of betrayal will increase. More and more European governments are now tightening their immigration policies. If the Church remains the last and "loudest" voice calling for the importation of cultures that are misogynistic, anti-Semitic, and anti-Christian to the core, the result may well be a final falling away from the Church on the part of those who already have their doubts.

If the Church persists in its pro-Islam policy, several consequences will likely follow. For one thing, the Church will be further discredited. As more Catholics come to realize that Church leaders have been misleading them about Islam, distrust will grow. Almost everything that Church leaders say will become suspect, and the exodus from the Church—particularly in the West—will likely accelerate.

---

[220] Robert Spencer, "Pope on Migrants: "We Must Move from Considering Others as Threats to Our Comfort to Valuing Them as Persons," *Jihad Watch*, June 14, 2018, https://www.jihadwatch.org/2018/06/pope-on-migrants-we-must-move-from-considering-others-as-threats-to-our-comfort-to-valuing-them-as-persons.

The "Evil Twin Brother" Hypothesis

Another consequence is the development of what I call the "evil twin brother" hypothesis. As Church leaders continue to emphasize their solidarity with Islam, many—both inside and outside the Church—will be prompted to ask some obvious questions. Why would anyone want to declare solidarity with a faith that considers jihad obligatory; that denies the equality of men and women; and that prescribes stoning or whipping for adultery, and death for apostasy?

Here's what I had to say about the matter in 2012:

> It was precisely by claiming that Christianity and Islam are essentially the same that atheists were able to make so much hay in the aftermath of 9/11. The atheist argument is not that Islam is a bad apple among world religions, but that it is just like all religions—irrational, cruel, and unjust. Atheists such as Hitchens and Dawkins made a particular point of portraying Islam and Christianity as evil twin brothers.... When Christian clergy identify themselves with Muslim clerics, it serves only to strengthen the atheist argument that there is little difference between the two faiths.[221]

What is especially problematic is that many Catholics—including some prominent conservative Catholics—extend the "common ground" claim to include sexual values. Some have argued that Catholics and Muslims are natural allies against immodesty, pornography, homosexuality, promiscuity, and so on.[222] But, as Nonie Darwish has demonstrated in several books (particularly in *Wholly Different*),[223] Christianity and Islam are miles apart when it comes to sexual ethics. Islam sanctions polygamy, easy divorce for men, child marriage, and, in times of war, sex slavery.

---

[221] Kilpatrick, *Christianity, Islam and Atheism*, 104.

[222] William Kilpatrick, "Are Muslims Our Natural Allies?" *Crisis Magazine*, February 20, 2014, https://www.crisismagazine.com/2014/are-muslims-our-natural-allies.

[223] Nonie Darwish, *Wholly Different: Why I Chose Biblical Values Over Islamic Values* (Washington, DC: Salem Books, 2017).

In Afghanistan, the dancing boys (*bacha bazi*) are practically a cultural institution, and in Iran it is considered perfectly legitimate for seminary students to enter into "temporary marriages"—essentially a form of prostitution. Most of these practices—especially child marriage—are strongly defended by Muslim clerics. In other words, what the West considers sexual misconduct is just business as usual in many parts of the Muslim world. As the non-Muslim world learns more about these practices, the claim by Catholics that Islam is their ally in upholding sexual morality may prove particularly damaging.

If one invites comparisons, comparisons will be made, and in one respect, transgressions by Catholic clerics suffer by comparison with similar transgressions by Muslim clerics. At first glance, both seem to be guilty of hypocrisy. But the imam with two wives, the Muslim clerics who lobby for lowering the age of marriage to twelve, and the seminary student who pays for sex are all within the letter of the law. They know better than most what Islamic law allows. They can't very well be accused of hypocrisy.

It's another matter with the Catholic cleric who violates his vow of chastity. People in the Western world are typically more outraged by hypocrisy than the actual sin committed by the hypocrite. Individuals who are forthright about their sexual activities are often celebrated in Western literature and Western media for their bravery and authenticity. The hypocrisy of Catholic clergy may lead to more defections from the Church and, ironically, to more conversions to Islam, which will be seen by some as the more honest of the two religions.

Progressive Enablers

But Christian defections to Islam is another story. Let's conclude with a very brief discussion of how both scandals—the cover-up of sexual abuse and the cover-up of the threat presented by Islam—might be dealt with. Since many others have written extensively about solutions to the first problem, let's focus on the one suggestion (other than prayer and fasting) that seems most likely to set the Church on the right path in regard to both scandals.

Many have suggested that what is needed is a thorough housecleaning at the upper levels of the Church. A clean sweep is probably not a practical goal, but a housecleaning is certainly in order. It's difficult to see how the people who allowed the sex-abuse problem to metastasize are suddenly going to turn around and solve it. There's a good deal of truth in the adage "Personnel is policy." You can create new policies on paper, but if the old personnel are in charge of implementing them, nothing will happen.

Interestingly, the people who enabled the first scandal (clerical sex abuse) are probably the same people who are facilitating the second scandal (the cover-up of Islam's aggressive nature). Those Catholic leaders who subscribe to "progressive" views on sexual morality likely subscribe to the "progressive" view that all cultures and religions are essentially the same. The relativistic and nonjudgmental thinking that Pope Saint John Paul II criticized in *Veritatis Splendor* can be used to excuse both sexual sins and cultural sins. The same false virtues of tolerance and inclusivity that allowed the first scandal to grow have now become the rationale for overlooking the many problems with Islam.

There is some anecdotal evidence that those who are "progressive" on sexual matters are also inclined to minimize the Islamic threat. Cardinal Reinhard Marx, chairman of the German Bishops' Conference,[224] who has raised the possibility of blessings for same-sex unions, has also been among the chief "welcomers" of Muslim migrants. Cardinal Theodore McCarrick, who symbolizes the current abuse crisis, may also stand as a symbol of Catholic clerics who naïvely trust in the good intentions of Islamic clergy. In 2015, after returning from an official visit to Iran, he applauded the disastrous Iran nuclear deal in an essay for the *Washington*

---

[224] Elise Ann Allen, "Cardinal Marx to Step Down as Head of German Bishops," *Crux*, February 11, 2020, https://cruxnow.com/church-in-europe/2020/02/cardinal-marx-to-step-down-as-head-of-german-bishops/.

Post and reassured his readers that they could trust the Iranians because supreme leader Ayatollah Khamenei had issued a fatwa against the possession of nuclear weapons[225] (a fatwa that proved nonexistent).

The Iran deal greatly boosted Iran's ability to sponsor terrorism worldwide, and in that sense, McCarrick could be considered an enabler of Islam. But, then, the USCCB itself was a strong supporter of the deal, and Bishop Oscar Cantu, the head of the Committee on International Justice and Peace warned Congress not to "undermine" the deal.

In any event, bishops whose sense of sin is limited to man-made climate change and the building of border walls are less likely to notice the approach of other types of evil. It is probable that clerics who saw no danger in the rise of homosexual networks in the Church will also see no danger in the spread of a supposedly "peaceful" fellow religion—even though that religion has a long history of subjugating other cultures and religion. By the time they do notice the danger, a great deal of—possibly irreversible—damage will have been done.

---

[225] Cardinal Theodore E. McCarrick, "Cardinal McCarrick: Why We Can Applaud the Iran Deal in Good Faith," *Washington Post*, July 16, 2015, https://www.washingtonpost.com/news/acts-of-faith/wp/2015/07/16/cardinal-mccarrick-why-we-can-applaud-the-iran-deal-in-good-faith/?noredirect=on.

Islam and the Church: Have Islamists Hijacked the Discussion?

Islamists have been using the hijacking strategy for decades. They've hijacked planes, oil tankers, and even a shipload of American sailors. Only nowadays they have chosen bigger targets. Why bother hijacking planes and ships when you can hijack American legislatures, media, schools, and other key institutions?

Perhaps "hijack" is too strong a word. Islamists haven't actually taken control of these institutions, but they have been able to manipulate them to their own advantage. For example, the lure of Saudi money has turned many American universities into staunch advocates for Islam. Meanwhile, Islamists have conducted highly successful influence operations on the Pentagon (see Major Stephen Coughlin's *Catastrophic Failure*), the Department of Homeland Security (see Philip Haney's *See Something, Say Nothing*), and the State Department (given the disastrous Iranian nuclear deal).

If Islamists can manipulate Homeland Security, the Defense Department, and the State Department, could they do the same to the Church? It's not unthinkable. After all, Soviet KGB agents were highly effective in infiltrating the Russian Orthodox Church during the Cold War era. Closer to home, Saul Alinsky and associates successfully manipulated liberal Catholic prelates in order to further their own leftist agenda in the 1960s and '70s.[226]

Still, Islam is an ancient enemy of the Church. Wouldn't Church officials instinctively resist Islamic inroads?

I used to think that the Catholic Church leadership would come to its senses about Islam long before secular officialdom woke up. That's because the Church possesses historical, spiritual, and theological insights that should allow it to look beyond the religion-of-peace propaganda and see clearly into the essence of Islam. Besides, I reasoned, the Vatican is located in the heart of Europe: Church leaders would soon see the destructive impact of Islam all around them and make the needed course correction.

But the course correction hasn't come. What I didn't understand was that the stealth jihad campaign for "hijacking" the Church was much further advanced than I had guessed. Nor had I realized just how thoroughly many bishops had been marinated in politically correct attitudes. Such attitudes dictated that they look upon Islam as just another friendly Abrahamic faith tradition. Political correctness also ensured that the bishops would be more eager to display their tolerance than to display any curiosity about the discrepancy between what Muslim apologists were saying about Islam and what the facts were saying.

Of course, it would be grossly inaccurate to say that Islamists have hijacked the entire Church bureaucracy, or that they're calling the shots on *Amoris Laetitia* or the appointment of cardinals. But it does seem fair to say that they have hijacked the Church's ability to discuss Islam in a critical manner. For example, it seems no exaggeration to say that the dialogue process has been co-opted by Muslims. That's the gist of an article by attorney and writer Timothy Lusch in the *New Oxford Review*.[227] In

---

[226] Lisa Bourne, "New Film Shows 'A Wolf in Sheep's Clothing' Still a Threat," LifeSite News, October 7, 2016, https://www.lifesitenews.com/news/new-film-shows-a-wolf-in-sheeps-clothing-still-a-threat.

[227] Timothy D. Lusch, "Dawah, Dislocation and the Hijacking of Catholic-Muslim Dialogue," *New Oxford Review* (May 2017), https://www.

"Dawah, Dislocation and the Hijacking of Catholic-Muslim Dialogue," Lusch suggests that the USCCB's Muslim partners are using the dialogue process to "undermine" the Church.

Who are the bishops' dialogue partners? The two main organizations are the Islamic Society of North America (ISNA) and the Islamic Circle of North America (ICNA). Both groups, says Lusch, have "ties to Hamas, the Muslim Brotherhood, and Jamaat-e-Islami."[228] And both groups were listed as unindicted co-conspirators in a major terrorist funding case.

It might be expected that the dubious associations of ISNA and ICNA would put the bishops on their guard. But this was not the case. Whatever the original intent of the dialogue, "the priority of the talks," writes Lusch, "has shifted from theological discussion (two-way 'dialogue') to advocacy in support of the Muslim community."[229] Thus, Anthony Cirelli, associate director of the USCCB's Secretariat for Ecumenical and Interreligious Affairs, told Catholic News Service that "there is an urgency to engage more in a kind of advocacy and policy in support of the Muslim community."[230] He added that U.S. bishops are "coming to stand with our Muslim colleagues … in trying to change the negative narrative surrounding Muslims in our popular media." Meanwhile, Cardinal Blase Cupich, the co-chairman of the national dialogue, expanded on the narrative by saying that Christians and Muslims must try "to replace narratives of hate and distrust with love and affection."[231]

Which means that the bishops probably have no intention of getting to the bottom of the growing Muslim genocide against Christians. That might betray distrust on their part. Most likely they will devote their

---

newoxfordreview.org/documents/dawah-dislocation-the-hijacking-of-catholic-muslim-dialogue/#.

[228] Ibid.

[229] Ibid.

[230] Timothy D. Lusch, "The Interfaith Delusion," *New Oxford Review* (April 2017), https://www.newoxfordreview.org/documents/the-interfaith-delusion/#.

[231] Lusch, "Dawah, Dislocation and the Hijacking."

energies, as they have in the recent past, to proving their "love and affection" for their Muslim dialogue partners.

How can they do that? According to Anthony Cirelli, "the bishops' priority at the moment is to listen to [Muslims'] concerns, their fears, their needs."[232] Well, if you believe ISNA, ICNA, and CAIR, a Muslim's greatest fear is "Islamophobia." So, if Christians really love their Muslim neighbors, they will join in the battle against "Islamophobia." As anyone who follows these matters knows, the bishops have done this willingly. In fact, they have made the battle against "Islamophobia" one of their chief priorities. As Bishop Robert McElroy said at the event that kicked off the latest round of dialogue, Catholics need to take an active role in fighting "the scourge of anti-Islamic prejudice."[233]

The trouble is, as I've pointed out elsewhere, there's not much evidence for the existence of this "scourge."[234] It turns out that many of the "hate crimes" against Muslims are manufactured by Muslims. In other words, the case for the rise of "anti-Islamic prejudice" relies heavily on fake news. Nevertheless, the bishops seem more interested in protecting Muslims from imaginary crimes than in protecting Christians from real crimes.

This is quite calculated on the part of Muslim activists. They know that the Catholic Church can have a powerful influence on public opinion, and so they have manipulated the bishops into using their influence to serve an Islamist agenda. The "Islamophobia" campaign is intended to deflect attention away from the victims of Islam by portraying Islam itself as a victim of prejudice. The campaign is further intended to silence criticism of Islam. It's a way of ensuring that awkward topics won't be raised—awkward topics such as persecution of Christians, apostasy and blasphemy laws, honor violence, forced marriage, child marriage, FGM,

---

[232] Lusch, "The Interfaith Delusion."

[233] Ibid.

[234] William Kilpatrick, "Bishops Ignore Laws of Probability, Chase after Red Herring," *Crisis Magazine*, January 23, 2017, https://www.crisismagazine.com/2017/bishops-ignore-laws-probability-chase-red-herring.

cruel and unusual sharia punishment, and other forms of human rights abuse.

In a sense, the bishops are being asked to observe Islam's blasphemy laws—and this includes the bishop of Rome. Sheik Ahmed al-Tayeb,[235] the grand imam of Al-Azhar University, made it known to Pope Francis that dialogue with the Vatican could be resumed only as long as a "red line" was not crossed. The red line was any criticism of Islam. The dialogue was terminated in the first place because Pope Benedict crossed the line by asking for greater protection of Christians in Egypt following a church bombing in Alexandria.

The bishops' tacit agreement not to criticize Islam seems to have had a ripple effect on other Church-related institutions. For example, Catholic media are as a rule quite careful not to cross the "red line." Thus, a February 2017 Catholic News Agency (CNA) piece on an increase in anti-Semitism manages to avoid any mention of Islam or Muslims.[236] The section on anti-Semitism in Europe does contain a brief mention of ISIS, but, of course, as everyone is expected to understand, ISIS has nothing to do with Islam. The fact that the increase in European anti-Semitism coincides with an influx of Muslims from the most anti-Semitic regions on earth doesn't seem to have stirred CNA's curiosity. Except for the one-sentence mention of ISIS, the rest of the four-page piece is devoted to making the case that increased anti-Semitism in the United States is totally due to white nationalists and the election of Trump. But, according to a recent report,[237] the "hotbed of anti-Semitism" in

---

[235] Lawrence A. Franklin, "The Pope's Pilgrimage to Al-Azhar," Gatestone Institute, April 27, 2017, https://www.gatestoneinstitute.org/10282/pope-francis-egypt-visit.

[236] Matt Hadro, "US Anti-Semitism Feared to Rise if Incidents Aren't Condemned," Catholic News Agency, February 21, 2017, https://www.catholicnewsagency.com/news/us-antisemitism-feared-to-rise-if-incidents-arent-condemned-19260.

[237] Kristine Phillips, "The 'Hotbed of Anti-Semitism' Isn't a Foreign Country. It's U.S. College Campuses, a New Report Says," *Washington Post,*

the United States is college campuses—places where white nationalists and Trump supporters tend to be in short supply. On the other hand, just about every major U.S. campus has a chapter of Students for Justice in Palestine—a virulently anti-Semitic group. But to make any connection between Muslims and anti-Semitism would quickly brand you as an "Islamophobe"—which, nowadays, is a far more serious charge than anti-Semitism. So CNA, along with most of the secular media, maintains a respectful silence. If you relied on CNA for your understanding of anti-Semitism, you would gain the impression that it has everything to do with Trump and nothing to do with Islam.

The bishops' solidarity-with-Islam policy seems also to have seeped over into Catholic schools and colleges. As mentioned earlier, in 2017, the Diocese of Orlando reprimanded a sixth-grade teacher for showing "disrespect" to Islam by giving his students a handout containing Saint John Bosco's unflattering assessment of Islam.[238] Meanwhile, Catholic students at Boston College celebrate "International Hijab Day" in order to show their solidarity with Islam, and at Georgetown's Prince Alwaleed bin Talal Center for Muslim-Christian Understanding, the main focus is on battling—you guessed it—"Islamophobia." Another stalwart foe of "Islamophobia" is Saint Louis University,[239] which in 2017 was named by the David Horowitz Freedom Center as one of the "top 10 college administrations most friendly to terrorists" for its welcoming attitude toward terrorist-supporting groups and speakers.

April 24, 2017, https://www.washingtonpost.com/news/acts-of-faith/wp/2017/04/24/the-hotbed-of-anti-semitism-isnt-a-foreign-country-but-u-s-college-campuses-report-says/.

[238] Mary Jo Anderson, "Catholic Teacher in Ocala, Florida Faces Termination over Presentation about Islam," Catholic World Report, May 8, 2017, https://www.catholicworldreport.com/2017/05/08/catholic-teacher-in-ocala-florida-faces-termination-over-presentation-about-islam/.

[239] Sara Dogan, "The Top 10 College Administrations Most Friendly to Terrorists and Hostile to the First Amendment," FrontPage Mag, May 15, 2017, https://archives.frontpagemag.com/fpm/top-10-college-administrations-most-friendly-sara-dogan/.

Catholic public-policy organizations are also doing their best to make the world safe from the "scourge of anti-Islamic prejudice." According to an article in *World Net Daily*,[240] a bill supporting American law for American courts was defeated in the Michigan Legislature when two powerful lobby groups — CAIR and the Michigan Catholic Conference — teamed up to defeat it. The 2012 bill was intended to prevent the introduction of sharia law into Michigan. The Catholic opposition to it suggests that some Catholics are now prepared to advocate for Islam on any issue — up to and including support for the anti-Constitutional and often cruel provisions of sharia law.

In the wake of the discovery that FGM was being widely practiced in Michigan, a similar anti-sharia bill was introduced last month. Will the Michigan Catholic Conference once again come down on the side of Islamic law? The *WorldNetDaily* piece doesn't venture an opinion on that, but it does predict that the Catholic Church in Michigan will support the candidacy for governor of Abdul El-Sayed, who is described as "a devout shariah-compliant guy." If elected,[241] El-Sayed, who has been compared to Barack Obama, would become the first Muslim governor in America — but probably not the last if America's Catholic leadership doesn't wake up to the ways in which they are being manipulated by their Muslim counterparts.

In his influential book *The Quranic Concept of War*,[242] Pakistani General S. K. Malik argued that the proper preparation for war is to first "dislocate" the faith of the target population. "Dislocated" is a pretty good

---

[240] Leo Hohmann, "Meet 'Next Obama' Groomed to Make Political History," *WorldNetDaily*, April, 2, 2017, https://www.wnd.com/2017/04/meet-the-next-obama-groomed-to-make-political-history/.

[241] Associated Press, "Primary Results: Progressive Michigan Muslim Falls Short as Trump Claims Ohio Victory," *Haaretz*, August 8, 2018, https://www.haaretz.com/us-news/primary-results-progressive-michigan-muslim-falls-short-as-trump-has-a-good-night-1.6359633.

[242] S. K. Malik, *The Quranic Concept of War* (New Delhi, India: Adam Publishers, 1986).

description of what has happened to many bishops and other Catholic leaders. They've been diverted from their primary teaching mission and shunted off onto a siding labeled "fight Islamophobia." There they sit, repeating the narratives that Islamists have put into their mouths and joining in Islam's fight for better PR. Meanwhile, while they sit sidetracked, the engine of Islamization is barreling down the mainline.

The Misplaced Priorities of
Youth Synod Organizers

Reading through the *Instrumentum Laboris*—the working document for the 2018 youth synod—one gets the impression that the biggest challenge young people face in life is discovering their sexuality. Fortunately, the synod fathers stand ready to "accompany" youth on their journey of self-discovery wherever it may lead. The bishops have particular solicitude for LGBT youth who "face inequality and discrimination" because of "sexual orientation" (48).

Meanwhile, quite a few young Christians in Africa and elsewhere have other things to worry about than their sexual orientation. Not only do they face "inequality and discrimination"; they also face machetes and AK-47s. The day before the synod opened, seventeen Christians in Jos, Nigeria, were slaughtered by Muslim jihadists.[243] A week before that, fourteen Christians, mostly women, were hacked to death by Islamic militants in the Central African Republic.[244]

---

[243] Stoyan Zaimov, "Nigeria: 4 Children, Grandmother among 17 Christians Slaughtered by Radicals in Mass Raid," *Christian Post*, October 2, 2018, https://www.christianpost.com/news/nigeria-4-children-grandmother-among-17-christians-slaughtered-by-radicals-raiding-homes-227704/.

[244] "Central African Republic: Dozens Feared Dead after Massacre in Bria," *World Watch Monitor*, September 17, 2018), https://www.world-watchmonitor.org/2018/09/central-african-republic-dozens-feared-dead-after-massacre-in-bria/.

They were killed not because of their sexual orientation, but because of their Faith—the Faith that many of the synod bishops seem eager to water down to make it more palatable to youth. One suspects they also hope to make it more palatable to themselves. The language of the *Instrumentum Laboris* suggests that the framers of the working document favor "dialogue" over doctrine and favor nonjudgmental flexibility over "unbending" judgment. It's not surprising that the synod organizers would prefer a less judgmental Church since, as Julia Meloni documents in a *Crisis* piece, many of the key players at the youth synod are named in Archbishop Carlo Maria Viganò's testimony as being complicit in sex-abuse cover-ups.[245]

The question is, is the watered-down form of faith that is proposed in the *Instrumentum Laboris* worth dying for when the man with the machete shows up at your door? As a number of others[246] have observed, the document suggests that the role of the Church is to listen and accompany, but not to teach. What the document authors envision is the "emergence of a new paradigm of religiosity" which is "not too institutionalized" but "increasingly liquid" (63).

"Increasingly liquid"? Isn't this just another way of saying "watered down"? It's a characteristic of youth—especially of the male variety—that they don't want to be tied down. And that's the appeal of this ever-changing liquid faith. It leaves you free to float around. The synod organizers understand this adolescent predisposition and in the *Instrumentum Laboris* they cater to it shamelessly.

One can't help but wonder if they share the same predisposition. In an intervention critiquing the *Instrumentum Laboris*, Archbishop Chaput

245 Julia Meloni, "An Open Letter to Archbishop Chaput Supporting His Call to Cancel the Youth Synod," *Crisis Magazine*, October 2, 2018, https://www.crisismagazine.com/2018/an-open-letter-to-archbishop-chaput-on-the-youth-synod.

246 Thomas R. Ascik, "The 2018 Synod: Key Themes, Deep Tensions, and Many Questions," *Catholic World Report*, October 1, 2018, https://www.catholicworldreport.com/2018/10/01/the-2018-synod-key-themes-deep-tensions-and-many-questions/.

characterized "developed" societies as being "frozen in a kind of moral adolescence; an adolescence which they've chosen for themselves and now seek to impose on others."[247] Much the same could be said of some of the prominent prelates at the youth synod. They seem overconcerned with adolescent wants, and they seem eager to legitimize whatever it is that young people (from whom we have so much to learn) want to be or do.

But religion is not a free-flowing, New Age, follow-your-bliss affair. The word "religion" is derived from the Latin *religare* — meaning "to bind fast." At some point, youth needs to grow up. And growing up in the Faith means binding yourself to a set of beliefs and behaviors and, above all, to Christ.

Even a good many nonreligious people understand that growing up means tying yourself down — to your spouse, to your children, and, often, to a thirty-year mortgage. It's not entirely clear, however, that the synod organizers understand this. A main focus of the synod is "vocational discernment," yet, as Thomas Ascik points out in a review of the *Instrumentum Laboris*, "the document has nothing to say, recommend, or advocate whatsoever about the prospects, possibilities, or 'vocational discernment' of young Catholic women concerning motherhood."[248]

The Challenge of Islamic Birth Rates

This brings us back in a roundabout way to the challenge of Islam. One of the ways Islam spreads is through high birth rates. This is well understood by Muslim leaders, and some of them are calling for even higher rates. For example, President Erdogan of Turkey has called for Turkish families living in Germany to have at least five children apiece. If you

---

[247] CWR Staff, "Abp. Chaput at Synod: Wealthy, Developed Nations Are 'Frozen in a Kind of Moral Adolescence,'" *Catholic World Report*, October 4, 2018, https://www.catholicworldreport.com/2018/10/04/abp-chaput-wealthy-developed-nations-are-frozen-in-a-kind-of-moral-adolescence/.

[248] Ascik, "The 2018 Synod."

need to ask why, you should google "Ottoman Empire" to get a better idea of Erdogan's intentions.

The obvious response to Islam's population explosion is for Church leaders to encourage Catholics to get married and bring more children into the world. But back at the synod, the bishops seem more concerned with wants and feelings than with reproduction. As Ascik observes, the working document of a synod devoted in large part to vocational discern-ment has nothing to say about motherhood. In Vienna, Birmingham, and other European cities there are already more Muslim than Christian schoolchildren. In some German daycare centers, the ratio of Muslim children to Christian children is twelve to one. As Church leaders drift further and further toward the anti-fertility LGBT camp, the birth ratio will increasingly favor Muslims.

While Catholic youth (defined as ages sixteen to twenty-nine) are encouraged to search for personal self-fulfillment in ways that will allow them to remain "liquid," Muslim youth are being taught to find meaning by aggressively spreading the message of Allah—a message that spells submission and subjugation for future generations of Christians.

In an age of Islamic resurgence, what the world needs is not more youngsters searching, 1960s-style, among a variety of lifestyles and identi-ties in order to find personal meaning. This was proven to be a dead end in the post-1960s years, and the fact that a bunch of aging bishops are willing to prescribe it again shows how out of touch they are. Someone should remind them that the most self-actualizing and meaningful thing that most human beings do in life is to get married and have children.

It also happens to be the primary way that societies ensure their con-tinued survival, especially when confronted with an aggressive foe. On the other hand, societies that are pro–personal fulfillment and anti-child can't expect much in the way of life expectancy. But, as youth are wont to say, "whatever." If you're the last in your family line, what difference does it make what happens after you're gone?

That, from a purely sociological viewpoint, is the main problem with the LGBT lifestyle. By its very nature, the LGBT relationship is not heavily invested in the future. Consequently, synod participants should be cautious about drawing a moral equivalence between same-sex unions and marriage. The odds are that many won't. As Julia Meloni[249] points out, many of Pope Francis's handpicked delegates to the synod are in sympathy with much of the LGBT agenda.

Enablers of Abuse and Enablers of Islam

There's another angle to consider. Reading through Viganò's indictment,[250] I was struck by how many on his list are also in sympathy with Islam. As it turns out, the enablers of abuse are often enablers of Islam.

Take Cardinal Theodore McCarrick.[251] At a 2015 gathering of the Islamic Society of North America (ISNA), Cardinal McCarrick told the audience, "Who you are and what you believe are very beautiful things."[252] In the face of atrocities by terrorists, ISNA must tell the world, he said, "that's not what the Quran says, that's not what the Prophet, peace be upon him, is teaching." In an article for the Center for Security Policy, Elizabeth Yore reports:

> In December 2015, Democrats Dick Durbin, Pat Leahy, Tim Kaine and Ted McCarrick collaborated with other faith leaders on a joint press release in response to the terrorist attacks in Paris and San

---

[249] Meloni, "An Open Letter to Archbishop Chaput."

[250] Archbishop Carlo Mario Viganò, "Testimony on Cover-Up of Sexual Abuse," Catholic Culture, August 25, 2018, https://www.catholicculture. org/culture/library/view.cfm?recnum=11936.

[251] Due to the scandalous revelations of sexual abuse committed by Theodore McCarrick, the former cardinal was defrocked by Pope Francis in February 2019. See Edward Pentin, "Theodore McCarrick Dismissed from the Clerical State," *National Catholic Register*, February 16, 2019, https:// www.ncregister.com/blog/edward-pentin/archbishop-mccarrick-dismissed-from-the-clerical-state.

[252] Andrew Harrod, "Disgraced Cardinal Praised ISNA and 'True Islam,'" *Jihad Watch*, September 13, 2018, https://www.jihadwatch.org/2018/09/ disgraced-cardinal-praised-isna-and-true-islam.

Bernardino. They warned against hateful and xenophobic speech … [and] cautioned that U.S. refugee policy must not be restricted or halted because of Islamic terrorist attacks.[253]

In addition, as mentioned earlier, McCarrick was one of the chief proponents of the Iran nuclear deal. He traveled to Iran on several occasions and wrote an op-ed in the *Washington Post* in which he extolled the deal and reassured his readers that they could trust the Iranians. "McCarrick," notes Yore, "could be relied upon to employ the power of the Catholic Church to minimize growing concern over Islamic radicalism."

The others cited in Viganò's letter seem almost as pro-Islam as they are pro-LGBT. In January 2017, Cardinal Blase Cupich began his tenure as the first Catholic cochair of a new National Catholic-Muslim Dialogue. "Christians and Muslims," said Cupich, should try "to replace narratives of hate and distrust with love and affection."[254] Like so many other progressive prelates, Cupich seems to think that simply changing the narrative solves the problem. The implication is that there is no real problem with Islamic teaching or sharia law; the problem lies with hateful and distrustful people who say bad things about Islam.

Bishop Robert McElroy, who is also mentioned in the Viganò statement as being aware of McCarrick's abuses, seems to be of the same mind as Cupich about hateful narratives. Speaking at the launch of the dialogue, he challenged U.S. Catholics to take an active role in combatting "the scourge of anti-Islamic prejudice."[255] After the terrorist attack on a gay nightclub in Orlando, McElroy used similar language as he called on Catholics to "combat" the "anti-gay prejudice that exists in our Catholic

---

[253] Elizabeth Yore, "The Predator and His Democrat Allies," Center for Security Policy, October 3, 2018, https://www.centerforsecuritypolicy.org/2018/10/03/the-predator-and-his-democrat-allies/.

[254] James Martone, "Catholic-Muslim Dialogue Opens to Support Islamic American Communities," Catholic News Service, January 11, 2017), https://www.catholicnews.com/services/englishnews/2017/catholic-muslim-dialogue-opens-to-support-islamic-american-communities.cfm.

[255] Ibid.

community and in our country."[256] Considering that the perpetrator of
the massacre was a Muslim, it was a bit odd that McElroy had nothing
to say about anti-gay prejudice in the Muslim community.

Cardinal Kevin Farrell, whom Viganò names as one of those who
covered up for McCarrick, also seems willing to cover up for Islam's aggressive side. When Robert Spencer, America's leading expert on jihad
terror, was invited to speak at a parish in the Diocese of Dallas, Farrell
canceled the invitation.[257]

Also mentioned in the Viganò letter is Cardinal Joseph Tobin, the
archbishop of Newark. Viganò says that the appointments of Cupich to
Chicago and Tobin to Newark "were orchestrated by McCarrick, Mara-
diaga and Wuerl."[258] A *New Jersey Monthly* article on Tobin congratulates
him for "flinging open the doors of Newark's Cathedral Basilica of the
Sacred Heart to the LGBT community."[259] Tobin also wants to fling
open the borders to Muslim refugees. As Archbishop of Indianapolis, he
famously defied Governor Mike Pence's ban on resettling Syrian refugees
in Indiana until adequate vetting could be assured.

Of course, Tobin is not alone in this. An open-borders approach to
Muslim migration now seems to be settled policy in the Church. Cardinal Parolin, the Vatican's secretary of state, who is also mentioned in
the Viganò letter, has frequently criticized critics of immigration, especially "populist leaders and movements" which "declare one's national

---

[256] Claire Chretien, "U.S. Bishop: Catechism Uses 'Very Destructive' Language on Homosexuality," LifeSite News, July 6, 2016, https://www.
lifesitenews.com/news/san-diego-bishop-supports-apology-to-gays-changing-
catechism.

[257] Robert Spencer, "The Catholic Church Is Punishing U.S. Priests for Speaking the Truth about Islam and Jihad," *Jihad Watch*, May 7, 2017, https://
www.jihadwatch.org/2017/05/the-catholic-church-is-punishing-u-s-
priests-for-speaking-the-truth-about-islam-and-jihad.

[258] Viganò, "Testimony on Cover-Up of Sexual Abuse."

[259] Tammy La Gorce, "NJ's Candid Cardinal, the Archbishop of Newark,"
New Jersey Monthly, August 13, 2018, https://njmonthly.com/articles/
jersey-living/the-candid-cardinal/.

sovereignty in terms of cultural supremacy, racial identity and ethnic nationalism."[260]

When it comes to promoting Muslim migration, however, no one can hold a candle to the one man who figures most prominently in Viganò's accusatory statement. Indeed, Pope Francis has defended Islam and Muslim migration more frequently and more forcefully than any other Catholic leader. One could fill a book with his many defenses of Islam's peaceful nature and his harsh criticism of those who resist mass migration from Muslim lands.

Although the pope and the bishops may be listening intently to youth, they seem to have no interest in listening to the concerns of ordinary people who fear the consequences of increased Muslim migration. Instead, the pope favors the listen-to-me approach. He accuses opponents of immigration of being selfish, fearful, and hard-hearted. They are guilty, he says, of "sowing violence, racial discrimination, and xenophobia."[261]

Pope Francis and numerous bishops claim that by welcoming the migrant, they are welcoming Christ. That's one way of looking at it. Another way of viewing the matter is this: while Rome burns with the fire of scandal, the prelates most responsible for enabling the abuse are demanding that a new bunch of abusers be admitted to the Continent (disclaimer for the benefit of the literal-minded: obviously, not all Muslim migrants are abusers).

In the meantime, while the Muslim population is increasing both through immigration and high birth rates, the compilers of the synod

---

[260] Cindy Wooden, "Top Vatican Official Discusses Terrorist Threat, Immigration Debate," Catholic News Service, August 28, 2017, https://www.catholicnews.com/services/englishnews/2017/top-vatican-official-discusses-terrorist-threat-immigration-debate.cfm.

[261] Pope Francis, "Migrants and Refugees: Men and Women in Search of Peace," message for the celebration of the fifty-first World Day of Peace, January 1, 2018, http://w2.vatican.va/content/francesco/en/messages/peace/documents/papa-francesco_20171113_messaggio-51giornatamondiale-pace2018.html.

document seem to be steering youth toward a life of perpetual adolescence rather than toward the vocation of marriage and parenthood.

Psychology in Seminaries

How did it happen that the bishops became so infatuated with the subject of personal self-growth that they couldn't read the Arabic writing on the wall? Possibly because this was the way they were trained. Beginning in the 1960s, an obsession with humanistic psychology swept through the seminaries. The emphasis was mainly on the self: self-esteem, self-actualization, and self-exploration. Other key themes were subjectivism, nonjudgmentalism, and fluidity (the '60s version of "liquidity").

The 1960s are long gone, but the fascination with psychology lingers. In this context, it's interesting to note that Pope Francis once taught psychology. One assumes it was of the humanistic variety because he still uses the language of the nondirective therapist: "encounter," "listening," and "accompaniment." The basic philosophy underlying humanistic psychology is a Rousseauian belief in the goodness and trustworthiness of human nature. The self, say the humanists, can always be trusted to find the right path. Thus, one can afford to experiment with different lifestyles. One can even afford, in the pope's words, "to make a mess"[262] without fear of any permanent damage.

Well, the mess has been made, and no amount of nondirective listening is going to repair the damage that has been done. Moreover, a larger "mess" is developing that could result in the submission of the Church and much of the world to Islam.

Undaunted by their failure to protect, the same cast of characters who allowed the sex-abuse crisis to metastasize are asking you to believe that they know how to handle the challenge of Islam. Still more alarmingly,

---

[262] "Pope to Youth: Shake Things Up, Bring Church to the Streets," Catholic News Agency, July 25, 2013, https://www.catholicnewsagency.com/news/pope-to-youth-shake-things-up-bring-church-to-the-streets.

they apparently plan to employ the same failed tactics—encounter, dialogue, listening, and trusting—in their dealings with Islam. For example, on numerous occasions, Pope Francis has expressed his belief that "encounters" between cultures will somehow magically solve the problems brought on by mass Muslim migration into the West.

The pope, along with his like-minded advisers, has professed an amazing faith in human nature. But the cost of this newfound faith in humanity is a diminished sense of man's fallen nature. Too often our bishops' sense of sin is limited to what the world considers sinful: plastics in the ocean, border walls, homophobia, and "Islamophobia." Not surprisingly, in their eagerness to condemn the sin *du jour*, they have failed to notice the approach of other, greater evils. It's no coincidence that bishops who saw no danger in the growth of a homosexual culture within the Church also see no danger in the advance of Islamic sharia across the globe.

Encounters are surely coming, but unless Church authorities wake up to man's sinful nature, they will not be like the encounters the pope envisions.

14

History Lessons

Philosopher George Santayana said that "those who cannot remember the past are condemned to repeat it." Those who don't want to learn the lesson of Islamic aggressiveness the hard way are well advised to consult the lessons of history. Here are two well-written books to bring you up to speed.

Was Islamic Rule in Medieval Spain
an Interfaith Eden?

No contemporary historian who wished to remain in the good graces of his colleagues would marvel about the way in which Spanish conquistadors lifted the Aztecs and Incas out of their dark ages of ignorance and superstition. Nor would any scholar rhapsodize about how the colonization of India by the British brought civilization to a backward society. Much less would any of today's historians claim that black slaves in the U.S. South lived happy and contented lives under the benevolent protection of their enlightened masters.

Yet these are the sort of things that contemporary historians routinely say about the Islamic conquest and subjugation of Spain during the medieval period. According to numerous scholars, Muslim-ruled Spain — Al-Andalus — was a beacon of enlightened tolerance in an otherwise darkened Europe. For example:

> [In the Middle Ages there emerged] two Europes — one [Muslim Europe] secure in its defenses, religiously tolerant, and maturing in cultural and scientific sophistication; the other [Christian Europe] an arena of unceasing warfare in which superstition passed for religion and the flame of knowledge sputtered weakly.[263]

---

[263] David Levering Lewis, *God's Crucible: Islam and the Making of Europe, 570–1215* (New York: W. W. Norton, 2008), 335.

Peace, harmony, tolerance, and a flowering of science and culture: that's the way academics, journalists, and politicians often portray Islamic Spain. The problem is, it's not true. In *The Myth of the Andalusian Paradise*,[264] Dario Fernandez-Morera, a professor of medieval Spanish literature, explodes this romanticized version of history and shows in great detail that the facts are otherwise.

Drawing on an abundance of primary sources, Fernandez-Morera shows that repression rather than tolerance was the norm for Islamic Spain. In addition to numerous massacres and the destruction of churches, Spain's Muslim rulers indulged in beheadings, impalings, and crucifixions. During this age of "enlightenment," inquisitions were common, and so were book burnings. The law of the land was sharia, and harsh punishments (usually death) were administered for blasphemy, apostasy, heresy, witchcraft, sodomy, and adultery. Theft, however, was dealt with more leniently. The much-vaunted Islamic philosopher Ibn-Rushd (Averroës) "approvingly observed that Malik and al-Shafi [founders of two of the most important schools of Islamic jurisprudence] agreed on the appropriateness of amputating the right hand of the thief, then the left foot in case of reincidence, then the left hand if the thief stole for a third time, and then his right foot if he stole again."[265]

And then, of course, the golden age of Islam was built on a massive slave trade:

> Al-Andalus became a center for the trade and distribution of slaves: young female sexual slaves ... male children castrated to become eunuchs in the harems; male children brought up in barracks to be slave warriors.[266]

---

[264] Dario Fernandez-Morera, *The Myth of the Andalusian Paradise: Muslims, Christians, and Jews under Islamic Rule in Medieval Spain* (Wilmington, DE: ISI Books, 2016).

[265] Ibid., 103.

[266] Ibid., 159.

The caliph Abd al-Rahman III had a harem of 6,300 women, which in plain language means that he possessed a great many sex slaves. Yet, as Fernandez-Morera observes, "some ingenious academic specialists" have argued that "sexual slavery under Islam actually promoted women's liberation."[267]

In fact, this idealized view of the harem has a long history in the West. Throughout the nineteenth and even into the early twentieth century, romanticized depictions of harem life were a favorite theme of European and American painters. Although artists have moved on to other subjects, Western scholars still have a very tolerant attitude towards Islam's "peculiar institution."

There was, of course, no equivalent institution in the "benighted" Christian world. And Christian women in Christian lands were not excluded from public life, as were Muslim women in Islamic Spain. The Visigoths who ruled Spain prior to the Muslims had female rulers; so did the Spanish Catholics who eventually forced the Muslims out. Isabella, queen of Castile and Leon, is only the most famous of a number of female rulers who governed in Spanish provinces during the long period of the *Reconquista*.

There was some flowering of Islamic civilization in Spain, but much of it, as Fernandez-Morera points out, was due to the contributions of Jews and Christians and the Greek-Roman culture they had inherited. Likewise, there was some tolerance. But Christians and Jews were tolerated mainly because their taxes (the jizya) paid for the maintenance of Islamic society. The Christian dhimmis of Spain were very low on the social scale and were subject to numerous restrictions and humiliations, but, being largely parasitical, the Islamic system depended on them. The word "dhimmi" means "protected," but, as the author points out, the dhimmi system operated like a mafia "protection" racket. In other words, "pay us and we will protect you from what we will do to you if you fail to comply."

[267] Ibid., 160.

That modern academics are able to interpret this repressive scheme as evidence of enlightened tolerance doesn't tell us much about the actual conditions in medieval Spain, but it does tell us a lot about modern academics. They are, it seems, quite willing to subordinate historical truths to their ideological agenda. Part of that agenda is to further the multicultural myth that all cultures are equally beneficent. The other part is to discredit Christianity, particularly of the Catholic variety. As the author observes, today's fantasy view of Islamic Spain is really a continuation of the Catholic-bashing school of history that emerged in the Enlightenment and led to a "tilting of the narrative against Catholic Spain."[268]

Finally, there's the money factor. Scholars who don't toe the multicultural line don't get funded. And this is particularly the case in Islamic and Middle East studies departments, where much of the funding comes from Islamic nations such as Saudi Arabia, Qatar, and the United Arab Emirates.

The Myth of the Andalusian Paradise is an important book, not only for what it says about the corruption of scholarship but also for its relevance to current affairs. The questions the author raises about Islamic Spain are not merely academic questions. They apply very much to the modern world. In 2016, it was reported that several Christians in the Syrian town of Al-Qaryatain were killed for breaking the terms of their "dhimmi contracts."[269] One of the reasons we are so unprepared for such news is that we've been deprived of crucial knowledge about Islamic history.

[268] Ibid., 4.
[269] "Syria War: IS Group Killed 21 Christians in Al-Qaryatain, Says Patriarch," BBC News, April 101, 2016, https://www.bbc.com/news/world-middle-east-36011663.

Islam's Fourteen-Hundred-Year
War on Christendom

At a time when Catholic youth are taught that "Islam" means peace, pilgrimage, and prayer, and Catholic adults are under the impression that Muslims are a misunderstood minority who only want to share their values and their baba ghanoush, it's refreshing to make contact occasionally with reality.

I mean "refreshing" here in the sense that a dive into chilly waters is refreshing. I just finished reading Raymond Ibrahim's *Sword and Scimitar*,[270] a history of fourteen centuries of war between Islam and the West, and the effect is similar to the shocked-awake effect of a plunge into cold water.

Not that I didn't have a general acquaintance with the history, but one tends to forget the details, and the devil, as they say, is in the details. Ibrahim supplies plenty of those. Moreover, the details are so shocking that one is inclined to think that the devil was intimately involved in the centuries-long jihad against Christendom.

Indeed, that's exactly what many Christians of those times did think. Muhammad and Islam were frequently referred to by popes and peasants alike as "demonic," "diabolic," and "satanic." For their part, Muslims had a particular hatred of Christians. They considered the Christian belief in Christ's divinity to be a great sin against Allah. Wherever Muslim armies

---

[270] Raymond Ibrahim, *Sword and Scimitar: Fourteen Centuries of War between Islam and the West* (Boston: Da Capo Press, 2018).

went, they desecrated and destroyed churches, broke crosses and statues, and made a particular point of violating nuns and torturing priests and monks.

In short, the violent conflicts between Muslims and Christians were primarily religious wars, not, as many modern historians suggest, wars for resources or national interests. Some historians, it seems, are less interested in the details of past events than in finding ways to fit those events into contemporary narratives. Their primary source is their own subjective "modern" outlook. By contrast, Ibrahim, who reads both Arabic and Greek, lets the Muslim and Christian witnesses to past events speak for themselves. Thus, when speaking of the Janissaries—Christian boys who were snatched from their parents and forced to become soldiers of Islam—Ibrahim, relying on centuries-old manuscripts, recounts the horror of the abductions, the abuse of the boys, and their transformation into Islamic true believers who were then turned loose against their former kin. By contrast, according to modern academics, the indoctrination of the Janissaries was "the equivalent of sending a child away for a prestigious education and training for a lucrative career."[271]

Despite the passage of more than a thousand years, the Muslim-Christian conflict was marked by certain constants. There is a remarkable continuity of belief and behavior—especially on the part of the Muslims.

One of the recurring themes is that of world conquest commanded by Allah. Muslims justified all of their wars and depredations during this immense stretch of history by referring to the Koran and to the words and deeds of Muhammad. Muslim leaders did not look upon their conquests as simply local affairs but as stepping stones to subjugating the earth. Thus, two common refrains across the centuries were "We will stable our horses in Constantinople" and "We will stable our horses in Rome"—and this from warlords who may have been more than a thousand miles distant from either Rome or Constantinople. When, in

---

[271] Diane Moczar, *Islam at the Gates: How Christendom Defeated the Ottoman Turks* (Manchester, NH: Sophia Institute Press, 2008), cited in ibid., 214.

1786, Thomas Jefferson and John Adams inquired of Tripoli's ambassador to Britain why the Barbary States preyed on American shipping, they were informed that, according to the laws of their prophet, Muslims had a "right and duty" to make war on all nations that did not acknowledge their authority.

Another constant over the centuries is what Ibrahim calls the "win-win" bargain. Whether a Muslim lived or died in battle, he was guaranteed a reward. If he survived a raid or a battle, he would be rewarded with plunder, slaves, and concubines. If he died, all his sins would be forgiven by Allah, and he would be saved from the tortures of hell. In addition, he would be rewarded in paradise with food, drink, and seventy-two "eternally young" virgins (houris). Indeed, Muslim officers and preachers would circulate among the troops before battle, reassuring them of their immortal rewards should they die in battle. Many early chronicles attributed Muslim zeal and fanaticism in battle to the "win-win" incentive.

Still another constant was slavery. One modern historian observes that "the Islamic jihad looks uncomfortably like a giant slave trade."[272] The number of the enslaved was astronomical. It was not unusual for a campaign to result in the enslavement of 100,000 people. Between 1530 and 1780, the Barbary Coast Muslims enslaved at least a million Europeans. Some three million Slavs—Poles, Lithuanians, Russians, and Ukrainians—were enslaved between 1450 and 1783. Millions more were taken captive by the Muslim conquerors of Spain. One caliph, Abd al-Rahman III, had 3,750 slaves and 6,300 concubines.

Slaving raids were also carried out in Ireland, England, Denmark, and as far away as Iceland and Scandinavia. Slaves were used for labor, as soldiers, and as concubines. White slaves were highly prized, especially blonde and red-headed girls and women. Black slaves were routinely castrated. Although few Americans are aware of the fact, the Arab and

---

[272] Hugh Kennedy, *The Great Arab Conquest* (Philadelphia: Da Capo Press, 2007), cited in Ibrahim, *Sword and Scimitar*, 37.

Ottoman slave trade lasted far longer than the Atlantic slave trade and resulted in the loss of many more lives.

Even America did not escape the reach of Islamic jihad. In its formative years, as Ibrahim points out, America was forced to make jizya payments — amounting to 16 percent of the federal budget — to Algeria for the release of captured American sailors. Indeed, America's first war as a nation was a war against Islam. Over a period of thirty-two years, the American navy fought an intermittent war to put an end to the Barbary States' attacks on American shipping. That is what is referred to by the "shores of Tripoli" in the Marine Corps hymn.

Sword and Scimitar puts to rest several important myths. One of these myths is that Christians were the aggressors in this long, bloody conflict. This is decidedly not the case. For example, the modern idea that "the crusades were unprovoked wars of conquest" is demonstrably false. As Ibrahim points out, the crusades were a very belated response to four hundred years of Muslim conquest. Two-thirds of the Christian world had already been devoured by Muslim armies before Pope Urban II made his appeal to the knights of Christendom. Many regions that are now solidly Muslim were once Christian. All of the twenty-two nations that the "Arab world" in the Middle East and North Africa now comprises were Christian. The same is true of Turkey, whose capital, formerly called Constantinople (now Istanbul), was once the center of Christendom.

Perhaps the major lesson of Ibrahim's timely book is that little has changed over the centuries. One of the misleading myths of our time is that al-Qaeda, ISIS, Boko Haram, and other major terrorist groups have perverted the meaning of Islam. They are variously described as having "hijacked," "distorted," or "misunderstood" the true message of Islam. History says otherwise. According to Ibrahim, "this book ... records a variety of Muslims across time and space behaving exactly like the Islamic State and for the same reasons." "Muslim hostility to the West," he observes, "is not an aberration but a continuation of Islamic history." Against today's wishful thinking about Islam's peaceful intentions, *Sword and Scimitar* documents "what Muslims have actually *done* to and in the West for centuries."[273]

The historical record also reveals two perennial weaknesses of the Western response to Islam. One is disunity. There were several cases of Christians' failing to come to the aid of other Christians. And there were even cases of Christians' taking the side of Islam. Protestant Queen Elizabeth I formed an alliance with the Barbary pirates against Catholic Spain, and Protestant Count Tholky of Hungary marched with the Turks against Catholic Vienna. Likewise, some Catholic rulers had more interest in fighting other Christians than in fighting the Turks. According to one historian, King Charles V "would spend more time, money, and energy fighting the French and the Protestants than he ever devoted to the war with Suleiman."[274] More shamefully, Louis XIV supported the Ottoman siege of Vienna with men, money, and engineers. When Jan Sobieski's victorious army inspected the field of battle, "a great many French" bodies were found alongside the Turks.

A second Western weakness was indifference. Many Western leaders took little notice of approaching threats until Muslim armies were on their doorsteps. As Pope Sixtus IV warned European rulers:

> Let them not think that they are protected against invasion, those who are at a distance from the theatre of war! They, too, will bow the neck beneath the yoke ... unless they come forward to meet the invader.

Even though the distance between peoples as measured by days and weeks has shrunk drastically, many in the West today still maintain an attitude of indifference toward the threat from Islam. They think that the persecution of Christians in the Middle East and Africa can't happen to

[273] Ibrahim, *Sword and Scimitar*, xv, xvii.

[274] Roger Crowley, *Empires of the Sea: The Siege of Malta, the Battle of Lepanto, and the Contest for the Center of the World* (New York: Random House, 2008), 58.

them. And many in America are unaware of the accelerating Islamiza-tion of Europe. They would do well to heed Pope Sixtus IV's words: "Let them not think that they are protected against invasion."

Can't happen in the here and now? As *Sword and Scimitar* ably dem-onstrates, what has happened over and over in the past is very likely to happen again.

15

Demography Is Destiny

Some predict that, by mid-century, several European states will have yielded power to Islam. If that's difficult to imagine, consider that Islam's culture war against the West is also a demographic war — a war of the wombs. When the birth rate falls below replacement level, it doesn't necessarily mean that there will be no replacement. Rather, in the case of Europe, it looks like one culture is about to be replaced by another.

Falling Off the Demographic Cliff

Friends who visit Europe with large families in tow tell me they soon become "tourist attractions" themselves.

Europeans are used to Muslims with large families. But Americans? People from a prosperous developed nation? How odd. Don't they know that children get in the way of self-fulfillment? that population growth is bad for the environment?

The visiting Americans with large families are almost invariably Christians—another segment of European society that, along with children, seems to be on the way out.[275] In 2016, more than 90,000 people dropped out of the Church of Sweden, and Norway's state church lost more than 25,000 members in a single month. The trend is similar in the United Kingdom, where the Archdiocese of Saint Andrews and Edinburgh will cut the number of parishes from 100 to 30. Meanwhile, the archbishop of Utrecht in the Netherlands announced that about a thousand parishes would close by 2025. The Archdiocese of Vienna is also downsizing. In the next ten years it will combine 660 parishes into just 150.

You've probably seen the dismal birth-rate figures for native Europeans. In most countries, it's below replacement level. If you're an investor, that

---

[275] Giulio Meotti, "Europe: What Happens to Christians There Will Come Here," Gatestone Institute, April 30, 2017, https://www.gatestoneinstitute. org/10230/europe-christians.

means it's time to buy funeral homes and sell dollhouse manufacturers. Actually, it's well past time for that market move. A better bet would be to invest in that new chain of hijab and burqa boutiques that is all the rage in the big cities.

According to a recent study, a quarter of European women born in the 1970s may remain childless.[276] That trend is reflected in the fact that in 2017, Europe's most important leaders were all childless. This was the case with the German chancellor, and with the British, Swedish, Dutch, Italian, Scottish, and Luxembourg prime ministers. The current president of France, Emmanuel Macron, is also childless. He is likely to remain that way since his wife and former schoolteacher is older by a quarter century.

What's the problem with leaders *sans* offspring? As every parent knows, people with children have more of a stake in the future. They worry about the kind of world that their children will have to live in. And once their children grow up, they start worrying about their grandchildren's future. On the other hand, childless individuals have less reason to worry about what comes after them. This is less of a concern when the childless couple lives in the apartment upstairs, but when they reside in the presidential palace, or the prime minister's residence, it's more worrisome.

It's not a good omen when the leader of your nation doesn't have to worry about what sort of country his or her progeny will grow up in. It's even possible that the maternal or paternal instinct can be displaced onto nonnative sons and daughters. For example, German chancellor Angela Merkel has been called "the compassionate mother"[277] of migrants, for having opened the border to millions of migrants mostly from Muslim countries. And if they don't assimilate? Well, that's a problem for other *mutters* to worry about.

---

[276] Giulio Meotti, "Europe's Childless Leaders Sleepwalking Us to Disaster," Gatestone Institute, May 6, 2017, https://www.gatestoneinstitute.org/10306/childless-europe.

[277] Ibid.

President Macron has a similar solicitude about Muslim migrants.[278] He has promised to facilitate immigration from the Arab world by preserving "an open and welcoming France," has called for the construction of more mosques in France, and has suggested that since "French culture does not exist," there is no great need for migrants to assimilate to it. French critics refer to Macron as "Peter Pan in the Elysée,"[279] but at least Peter Pan worried about the pirate problem. Macron, however, has rejected former president Hollande's assertion that "France has a problem with Islam," and he is against suspending the citizenship of jihadists.[280]

Meanwhile, as Europe's native population declines, Muslims in Europe *are* having children, and Turkey's caliph—I mean, president—wants them to have more. President Erdogan has urged Turks living in Europe to have "not three, but five children" because "you are the future of Europe."[281]

He's probably right about that. As columnist Mark Steyn likes to say, "The future belongs to those who show up for it."[282] And right now, it's the Muslim children who are showing up for Europe's future. In Vienna, Birmingham, and other European cities, there are already more Muslim than Christian children.

Just to make sure that trend continues, Turkey's interior minister, Süleyman Soylu,[283] has suggested that Turkey could send fifteen thousand

---

[278] Guy Millière, "French Elections: Emmanuel Macron, a Disaster," Gatestone Institute, May 1, 2017, https://www.gatestoneinstitute.org/10299/macron-france-disaster.

[279] Barron Bodissey, "Peter Pan in the Elysée," *Gates of Vienna*, May 10, 2017) https://gatesofvienna.net/2017/05/peter-pan-in-the-elysee/#more-42889.

[280] Meotti, "Europe's Childless Leaders."

[281] Pamela Geller, "'You Are the Future of Europe': Turkish President Urges Muslims in Europe to Have at Least 5 Kids," Geller Report, March 17, 2017, https://gellerreport.com/2017/03/you-are-the-future-of-europe.html/.

[282] Steyn, "Alone Again, Naturally," *Steyn Online*, May 6, 2014, https://www.steynonline.com/6320/alone-again-naturally.

[283] Geller, "You Are the Future of Europe."

refugees a month to Europe. Meanwhile, Turkey's foreign minister, Mevlüt Çavuşoğlu,[284] warned that "religion wars will soon begin in Europe," and he cautioned that European politicians are taking the Continent "to a cliff."[285]

Actually, Europe is not headed for a cliff; it has already gone off it—the demographic cliff, that is. It just hasn't hit bottom yet. The full effects of the demographic bust won't arrive for a decade or so. That's because the Euro Stork brings fewer babies with each passing year. The people who were never born twenty-five years ago can't very well make up the birth-rate deficit. And too many of the people who were lucky enough to be born aren't passing on the good fortune.

That doesn't apply, of course, to the European Turks, Moroccans, and Pakistanis. They're having three children per family, and if Erdogan has his way, they'll have five. A long time ago, Turkey was referred to as "the sick man of Europe." Now it looks as if the Europeans are the sick men of Europe, and the Turks look healthy by comparison. Unlike Europe's childless leaders, the Turks do seem to take an interest in the future of Europe. But what they envision is an Islamic future.

After an EU ruling allowing employers to ban headscarves, Erdogan accused the European Union of starting "a clash between crescent and cross."[286] But, as he surely realizes, no clash will be necessary. Time is on the side of the Turks, and so are the mathematics of demography. After another decade or so of demographic transformation, the aging population of Europe will be in no shape for a clash.

---

[284] Robert Spencer, "Turkish Foreign Minister: "Religion Wars Will Soon Begin in Europe," *Jihad Watch*, March 16, 2017, https://www.jihadwatch.org/2017/03/turkish-foreign-minister-religion-wars-will-soon-begin-in-europe.

[285] Geller, "You Are the Future of Europe."

[286] Christine Douglass-Williams, "Erdogan: EU Ruling on Headscarf Bans Starts Clash between Islam and Christianity," *Jihad Watch*, March 18, 2017, https://www.jihadwatch.org/2017/03/erdogan-eu-ruling-on-headscarf-bans-starts-clash-between-islam-and-christianity.

Why the Odds Favor Islam

On May 22, 2017, an Islamic suicide bomber detonated himself outside a pop concert in Manchester, England, killing and wounding dozens, many of them young children.

The terrorist was a twenty-two-year-old named Salman Abedi. A few days after the attack, I read an article about the mosque he attended—the Didsbury Mosque. "That's funny," I thought, looking at the accompanying photo. "That doesn't look like a mosque; it looks like a church."

Sure enough, as I discovered, the Didsbury Mosque was once the Albert Park Methodist Chapel. It had been bought by the local Syrian Muslim community and transformed into a Muslim place of worship.

Similar transformations have been taking place in other parts of the United Kingdom. Saint Mark's Church in London is now the New Peckham Mosque; Saint Peter's Church in Cobridge was sold to the Madina Mosque. The Brick Lane Mosque in London was originally a Methodist church. But church-to-mosque conversions are only part of a larger story.[287] There are now 423 mosques in London, and the number is expected to grow. Meanwhile, 500 London churches have

---

[287] Giulio Meotti, "Londonistan: 423 New Mosques; 500 Closed Churches," Gatestone Institute, April 2, 2017, https://www.gatestoneinstitute.org/10124/london-mosques-churches.

closed since 2001, and in all of England 10,000 churches have closed since 1960.[288]

The transformation of the Albert Park Methodist Church to the Didsbury Mosque is emblematic of one of the most significant shifts in history: the transformation of Europe from a largely Christian continent to a largely Islamic one. The transformation is far from complete, and there's an outside chance that the process can be reversed, but time and demographics favor Islam.

In several of Europe's cities, the Muslim population now hovers around the 30 percent mark. In ten years, that will be 40 percent. Of course, that doesn't mean 40 percent of highly committed Muslims facing 60 percent of deeply devout Christians. Both faiths have their share of half-hearted "nominals," for whom religion is more a cultural inheritance than a deeply held conviction. Still, the "nominal" problem is a much greater problem for European Christians than for European Muslims. In many European countries, Sunday church attendance is in the 5 to 10 percent range, whereas mosque attendance is very high in relation to the size of the Muslim population. In England, there are already more Muslims attending Friday prayers than there are Christians attending Anglican services on Sundays, even though there are many more self-identified Anglicans overall. A 2008 study by Christian Research predicted that by 2020 the number of Muslims attending prayer service in England and Wales will exceed the number of Catholics attending weekly Mass.[289]

It's also noteworthy that the expanding Muslim population in Europe is relatively young, whereas the declining "Christian" population is aging.

---

[288] Giulio Meotti, "Exposé: Europe Turns Churches into Mosques" *Arutz Sheva*, October 20, 2012, http://www.israelnationalnews.com/Articles/Article.aspx/12333.

[289] Cyril Dixon, "More Attending Mosques Than Mass by 2020," *Express*, March 26, 2008, https://www.express.co.uk/news/uk/39225/More-attending-mosques-than-Mass-by-2020.

Sixty-forty seems like good odds until you realize that the average age of the 60 percenters will be around fifty-five while the average age of the 40 percenters will be around twenty-five.

You may object that if there is any fighting to be done, most of the fighting on the "Christian" side will be done by the army, not by citizens in walkers and wheelchairs. But keep in mind that the military draws its recruits from the ranks of the young. As the population of the people that Islamists refer to as "crusaders" ages, European governments will be forced to draw more of their new recruits from the Muslim population. The same goes for the police forces. Many Muslims will serve their country or their city faithfully, but many will have divided loyalties, and some will have signed up in the first place with mutiny in mind.

Most likely, however, the transformation will be effected without major battles. It won't be a matter of numbers or of military strength but of strength of belief. Those with the strongest beliefs will prevail. Those who are not sure what to believe will submit without a fight.

Will Europe Defend Its "Values"?

That's the theme of Michel Houellebecq's *Submission* (2015), a novel about the gradual Islamization of France. The protagonist, a middle-aged professor, has a number of qualms about the Islamic takeover of the university system, but nothing sufficient to resist it. The things he values most — literature, good food, and sex — are, in the end, no impediment to accepting Islam. True, he is offered several inducements to convert — career advancement, plenty of money, and several "wives" — but one gets the impression that, even without these incentives, he would still eventually convert. At one point prior to his submission, he thinks about joining a monastic order, as his literary hero, J. K. Huysmans, had done, but he soon realizes that he lacks the necessary Christian conviction. Indeed, he has no strong convictions.

His plight is the plight of contemporary Europe in a nutshell. Many Europeans see no sense in resisting Islamization because they have nothing worth defending. To be sure, European leaders still talk about "our values," but they can't seem to specify what those values are, beyond appeals to "diversity" and "pluralism." For example, after the Manchester massacre, then British prime minister Theresa May stated, "Our values—the liberal, pluralistic values of Britain—will always prevail over the hateful ideology of the terrorists."[290]

I'm not so sure of that. In an earlier era, Brits would have connected their values to God, country, family, and honor—in other words, things worth fighting for. But "liberal, pluralistic values"? That's not very solid ground on which to take your stand. Who wants to die for diversity? Indeed, it can be argued that the worship of diversity for its own sake is what allowed terrorists to get a foothold in England in the first place. No one wanted to question all those diverse preachers spreading their diverse message about Jews, infidels, and homosexuals. The trouble is, unless there are higher values than diversity, there's no way of judging between good diversities and bad diversities—between, say, honoring your wife and honor-killing her if she displeases you.

The same is true of freedom. Freedom is a fundamental right, but what you do with your freedom is also important. There has to be some higher objective value that directs our choices to good ends rather than bad ones. Otherwise, freedom becomes a license to do anything one pleases.

An Attack on Childhood

Here we touch on a very touchy subject. I would not have liked to have been in Theresa May's shoes when, after a horrifying attack, she had to come up with just the right words. But one thing she said struck me as not quite right. She said: "We struggle to comprehend the warped and

---

[290] "Manchester Attack: Theresa May Terror Threat Speech in Full," BBC News, May 23, 2017, https://www.bbc.com/news/uk-40023457.

twisted mind that sees a room packed with young children not as a scene to cherish, but as an opportunity for carnage."[291]

It's possible to agree fully with May's sentiments while noting that there once was a time when a room full of children watching an Ariana Grande concert would not be considered "a scene to cherish." "Her dress, dancing, and song lyrics," wrote one columnist, "are deliberately decadent and immodest."[292] And, after watching some YouTube clips of her performances, I would have to agree. I'm pretty sure that most of the parents I know would not want their children to attend one of her concerts.

While the world was justly outraged at Salman Abedi's attack on innocent children, no one seems to notice the attack on childhood innocence that the typical pop concert represents. The two "attacks" should not be equated, of course. The producers of pop concerts are not the moral equivalents of a suicide bomber. Still, the fact that so many parents saw nothing wrong with dropping their children off at the Manchester concert suggests a great deal of moral confusion in the West.

Unfortunately, such moral confusion leaves people vulnerable to those who are absolutely certain about their beliefs. The moral relativism of the West is one of the chief reasons why the Islamic cultural jihad has been so successful. People who can't see that the soft-porn style of Lady Gaga, Miley Cyrus, and Ariana Grande is not good for children will have difficulty seeing the problem with polygamy, child marriage, and other aspects of sharia law. In a relativistic society, the safest default position is "Who's to judge?"

---

[291] Kate Scanlon, "Theresa May Responds to Manchester Attack: 'Our Way of Life Will Always Prevail,'" *Blaze*, May 23, 2017, https://www.the-blaze.com/news/2017/05/23/theresa-may-responds-to-manchester-attack-our-way-of-life-will-always-prevail.

[292] Fr. Mark A. Pilon (1943–2018), "A Tale of Two Atrocities," *Catholic Thing*, June 5, 2017, https://www.thecatholicthing.org/2017/06/05/a-tale-of-two-atrocities/.

Relativism Leads to Islamic Dominance

Earlier I said that Europe is being transformed from a Christian culture to an Islamic culture, but that's not quite accurate because it's actually a three-stage transformation. Much of Europe has already transitioned out of its Christian stage and into a post-Christian or secular stage. There are still many Christians in Europe, but Europe's Christian consciousness has been largely lost. The next stage is the transition from secularism to Islam. That's not inevitable, but it's likely because, without a framework of Judeo-Christian beliefs, secularism becomes relativism, and relativism can't offer much resistance to determined true believers.

In 2014, Theresa May said, "We celebrate different ways of life, we value diversity, and we cherish our freedom to lead our lives as we choose."[293] But if your culture stands for nothing more than the freedom to shop for different lifestyles, it won't last long. The contemporary Western fascination with pop culture highlights the problem. Pop culture is by its very nature a transient phenomenon. What is pop today won't be pop tomorrow. Indeed, the popular culture of tomorrow may very well favor burqas, multiple wives, and male supremacy. There may still be a place for singer-dancers like Ariana Grande and Miley Cyrus, but that place may well be as a harem dancer in a sultan's palace or as entertainment for a Saudi prince who has bought up a country estate in Oxfordshire.

It's hard to beat transcendent values with transient values. That's especially the case when the transcendent crowd are willing to die (and kill you in the process) for their values. Most Brits, on the other hand, are not willing to lay down their lives for the sake of keeping bacon on the menu or porn on the telly.

---

[293] Paul Cole, "Theresa May: Birmingham Mail 'Binds Great City of Brum Together,'" Birmingham Live, August 25, 2015, https://www.birminghammail. co.uk/news/midlands-news/theresa-may-birmingham-mail-binds-9918609.

Christianity versus Two Forms of Totalitarianism

When I use the word "transcendent," I refer only to a belief in an eternal life beyond this worldly existence. Quite obviously, as in the case of Salman Abedi, transcendent values can be twisted. The idea that God will reward you for murdering innocent young women in Manchester by furnishing you with virginal young women in paradise is a truly twisted concept. But apparently it is widely shared in the Muslim world. When, during a World Cup qualifier in Australia, a minute of silence was called to commemorate the London terror victims, the whole Saudi soccer team refused to observe it. As Sheik Mohammad Tawhidi later explained:

> In their eyes the attackers are martyrs who are going to paradise. And if they stand for a minute of silence, they are against their Muslim brothers who fought for jihad and fought the infidels.[294]

As twisted as these values may be, it's beginning to look as though secular values aren't up to the job of opposing them. The trouble with secular values when they are cut off from their Judeo-Christian roots is that they are arbitrary. Autonomy? Dignity? Equality? Says who?

"If there is no God," wrote Dostoyevsky, "everything is permitted." Secularism has no God and, therefore, no ultimate standard of judgment. The end result is that each man becomes his own god and does his own thing—even if that "thing" involves the exploitation of childhood innocence. Islam, on the other hand, does believe in God, but not the God Dostoyevsky had in mind. The God of Islam is an arbitrary despot whose commands are not rooted in reason, love, or justice.

So, we have two arbitrary systems vying for control of the West—the soft totalitarianism of secularism and the hard totalitarianism of Islam.

---

[294] April Glover and Hannah Moore, "'In Their Eyes the Attackers Are Martyrs': Islamic Sheikh Claims Saudi Arabian Team Refused Minute's Silence for London Terror Victims Because under Sharia Law 'It's Not a Sin for a Muslim to Kill a Non-Believer,'" *Daily Mail*, June 8, 2017, https://www.dailymail.co.uk/news/article-4584844/Saudi-Arabia-reason-minute-silence-refusal-lie.html#ixzz4jQvlR8QM.

Both are really forms of slavery. Muslims are slaves of a tyrannical God, and secular man becomes the slave of his own desires and addictions. It may seem unthinkable that the West will ever submit to Islam, but many Western citizens are already in submission mode. Submission to their desires has put them in a bad spot. As a result, they are looking for something bigger to submit to—something outside and above their own fragile selves. Some have already turned to Islam. Many more will unless . . .

Unless, that is, there is a recovery of the Judeo-Christian belief that God is a God of love, justice, reason, and goodness—and that we are made in His image (a concept that does not exist in Islam). In the context of that vision, belief in human dignity and the rights of man is thoroughly justified.

People who believe that they and their neighbor are made in the image of God will generally have a strong sense of their responsibility to act accordingly. Such people will be far from perfect, but they will at least realize that it is wrong to submit both to Islam's warped image of God and to secularism's degraded image of man.

In the end, the choice for the West is not between Islam and pluralistic secularism. A rootless secularism will almost certainly submit to Islam. The only real hope for the West is the recovery of the faith that once inspired Christians to build a beautiful church near Albert Park in West Didsbury, England.

Time Is Not on Europe's Side

In 2017, the Pew Research Center published a study of Europe's growing Muslim population.[295] The first thing to notice is that Pew's estimate of the current Muslim population for several countries is not much different from estimates of ten years ago. For instance, Pew says that the current size of the Muslim population in France is 8.8 percent, but ten years ago it was widely reported that the Muslim population of France was already at 10 percent. Either earlier estimates were way off, or Pew is employing rather conservative standards of measurement.

Whatever the case, the most interesting aspect of the study is not the estimate of current population, but the projection of future population. The Pew report says that the Muslim share of Europe's population will increase even with no future migration.

The study provides three scenarios — one for zero migration, one for medium migration, and one for high migration. Under the zero scenario, the Muslim percentage of France's population by 2050 would be 12.7 percent, but under the high scenario it would be 18 percent. For Germany, the low scenario would result in an 8.7 percent Muslim population, and the high scenario would translate to 19.7 percent. The high migration measure would yield 17.2 percent for the United

[295] "Europe's Growing Muslim Population," Pew Research Center, November 29, 2017, https://www.pewforum.org/2017/11/29/europes-growing-muslim-population/.

Kingdom, 18.2 percent for Belgium, 19.9 percent for Austria, and 30.6 percent for Sweden.

Since a number of observers of the European scene are predicting much higher Muslim percentages by 2050, it may be that even Pew's high estimate is on the low side.

Conversion and Emigration

Let's examine some elements that may be missing from their calculations. One missing factor is conversions. Although the Pew study briefly mentions conversion rates, it views this as a negligible factor in determining the future Muslim population. Since not much is happening on the "religious switching" scene, Pew assumes that not much will happen in the future.

But given the right conditions, conversion rates can accelerate rapidly, and a trickle can turn into a flood. For the first twelve years of his "ministry," Muhammad never had much more than a hundred followers. Then he migrated to Medina, and conversions to Islam took off. Conversions continued to accelerate after his death as Muslims swept into the Near East, North Africa, and Spain.

As the Muslim portion of the European population continues to increase, there will be increasing pressures—and incentives—to convert. In his novel *Submission*,[296] Michel Houellebecq provides a convincing description of how one man—a middle-aged professor at a French university—succumbs to the temptation to convert to Islam. Without a strong commitment to anything other than maintaining his position in life, the professor sees no reason why he shouldn't take advantage of the benefits—career advancement, money, and multiple wives—that come with being Muslim in a rapidly Islamizing France.

[296] Kenneth Colston, "A Provocative New Novel on Islam and Western Decadence," *Crisis Magazine*, December 31, 2015, https://www.crisismagazine.com/2015/a-provocative-new-novel-on-islam-and-western-decadence.

Another factor that is missing from the Pew projection is emigration. People who work for research firms aren't the only ones who make projections into the future. Ordinary people also make calculations about what will happen five or ten years down the road. And if what they see is increasing crime and violence, a good many will be tempted to leave.

In the 1960s and '70s, "white flight" from the cities to the suburbs resulted in massive and rapid population shifts in the United States. Something similar will likely occur in Europe—except that many of the suburbs are already spoken for. Of the numerous suburbs that ring cities such as Paris and Brussels, many are Muslim no-go zones, or are on their way to becoming so.

Where will non-Muslims go? Some will immigrate to Israel, some to North and South America, and some to Eastern European countries with miniscule Muslim populations, such as Poland, Hungary, Slovakia, and the Czech Republic.

The Importance of Will

Just as conversions can accelerate after a tipping point has been reached, so can emigration. But there's also a third factor that seems to have been left out of the Pew Center's calculations. It's difficult to measure, but it may be the prime factor in determining which culture predominates in Europe. The crucial factor is will. If they want their culture to survive, people must be willing to defend it, and they must be willing to bring children into the world who will carry on the culture.

You can call it "will," or "cultural confidence," or "fighting spirit," but whatever you call it, Europeans seem to be losing it. The problem begins in school. As Melanie Phillips noted in *Londonistan*,

> The British education system simply ceased transmitting either the values or the story of the nation to successive generations, delivering instead the message that truth was an illusion and that the nation and its values were whatever anyone wanted them to be.[297]

---

[297] Melanie Phillips, *Londonistan* (New York: Encounter Books, 2006), 62–63.

So, when some of the schoolyard tots grow up to be cops, it's understandable that they might be more interested in defending multicultural values than traditional ones. Consequently, crimes against multicultural ideology have gone to the head of the list. In the United Kingdom, police have turned their attention away from ordinary crimes, such as robbery and assault, and are focusing instead on thought crimes[298] against Muslims. These days, you stand a better chance of arrest if you criticize immigration policy on Facebook than if you lob a brick through a storefront window.

The new form of policing makes life more difficult for the average citizen, but somewhat easier for the police who are so busy patrolling the Internet that they don't have time to patrol the neighborhood. Of course, it's not just time they lack but also will. A survey of Swedish police reveals that 80 percent of them are thinking of finding another profession.[299] Apparently, they can't get used to the firebomb assaults on police stations, and the gang attacks against police patrols.

If the police lack the will to resist Islamization, it's understandable that ordinary people are disinclined to take chances. Outside the cinema, caped crusaders and wonder women are in short supply. When danger lurks, most people prefer to shelter in place. Thus, polls show that European women are increasingly afraid to go out after dark.[300] In

[298] Robert Spencer, "UK: New National Police Hub to Crack Down on "Hate Crime Online," *Jihad Watch*, October 9, 2017, https://www.jihadwatch. org/2017/10/uk-new-national-police-hub-to-crack-down-on-hate-crime-online.

[299] Chris Tomlinson, "80 Per Cent of Swedish Police Consider Quitting over Migrant Danger," Breitbart, September 20, 2016, https://www. breitbart.com/europe/2016/09/20/80-per-cent-swedish-police-consider-quitting-due-danger/.

[300] Oliver J.J. Lane, "Scared Sweden: Almost Half of Women 'Afraid' to Be Out after Dark in Europe's Rape Capital," Breitbart, March 4, 2016, https://www.breitbart.com/europe/2016/03/04/scared-sweden-almost-half-of-women-afraid-to-be-out-after-dark-in-europes-rape-capital/.

some parts of Sweden, when women venture outside to jog, they are now accompanied by police.[301]

In Europe, prudence rules the day. On buses, passengers look the other way when fellow passengers are harassed. In the United Kingdom, a vicar banned the hymn "Onward Christian Soldiers" for fear of offending non-Christians.[302] In Sweden, many towns have canceled the traditional Saint Lucy Day celebration in case it offends Muslims. In Belgium, the cross on the miter of Sinterklaas (Saint Nicholas) has been removed "in order not to exclude any child."[303] In France, Paris and Lyon have canceled the traditional Christmas markets.

All of the above can be explained away with one prudential excuse or another. But sometimes there is simply no excuse. As mentioned earlier, in Rotherham, England, 1,400 teenage (and younger) girls were raped by Pakistani gangs over a fifteen-year period.[304] Police knew about the crimes. So did city council members. So did social workers. Yet nothing was done about the situation for fifteen long years. Yes, there were excuses—fear of being thought racist or Islamophobic and so forth—but nothing that could possibly justify this colossal abdication of adult responsibility. The Rotherham officials seem to have been lacking in a fundamental human response.

---

[301] Chris Tomlinson, "Armed Police to Escort Joggers in Swedish City for Protection," Breitbart, November 22, 2017, https://www.breitbart.com/europe/2017/11/22/armed-police-escort-joggers-swedish-city-protection/.

[302] Robert Spencer, "UK: Vicar Bans Onward Christian Soldiers Hymn from Remembrance Sunday Service in Case It Offends Non-Christians," *Jihad Watch*, October 27, 2017, https://www.jihadwatch.org/2017/10/uk-vicar-bans-onward-christian-soldiers-hymn-from-remembrance-sunday-service-in-case-it-offends-non-christians.

[303] Robert Spencer, "Belgium: Cross Removed from St. Nicholas' Miter So as to Avoid Offending Muslims," *Jihad Watch*, December 3, 2017, https://www.jihadwatch.org/2017/12/belgium-cross-removed-from-st-nicholas-miter-so-as-to-avoid-offending-muslims.

[304] William Kilpatrick, "Islamophobia-Phobia and the Rotherham Rapes," *Crisis Magazine*, September 17, 2014, https://www.crisismagazine.com/2014/islamophobia-phobia-rotherham-rapes.

Protecting vulnerable children is a fundamental response. So is self-defense. *Killing Europe*, a 2017 documentary on the Islamization of Europe, contains footage of a teenage boy being challenged to a one-on-one fight by a Muslim youth of about the same size and age. The native European boy seems perplexed, and when the Muslim starts throwing punches, he cowers and covers, and makes no attempt to fight back. Whether the video tells the whole story of what transpired is hard to tell. But the boy's passive reaction seems indicative of a larger problem in Europe.

The Pew study tells us that Muslims currently make up 4.9 percent of Europe's population. That doesn't seem like much, but many Europeans already seem cowed. What will the situation be like in 2050, the endpoint of the study? By that time, according to the researchers, the Muslim population of Europe may be as high as 14 percent—nearly three times the current figure. As the population shift accelerates, so, in all probability, will the European descent into dhimmitude.

The Old versus the Bold

The other thing to notice is the age disparity. The median age of Muslims in Europe is thirty, but the median age for non-Muslims is forty-four. In Germany and France, the median age discrepancy is sixteen years. Or, to take another Pew statistic, 49 percent of non-Muslim Europeans are over the age of forty-five, whereas 77 percent of Muslims are forty-four or under. If there's not much fighting spirit left in Europe now, what will it be like in the future as Europe's non-Muslim population continues to age well beyond fighting age? The Pew study's high forecast for Sweden in 2050 is a 30 percent Muslim share of the population. That means that about 70 percent of the population will be non-Muslims. At first glance, that still seems like pretty good odds for the non-Muslims, until you stop and consider that a great many of those 70 percent will be living in nursing homes.

It seems almost uncivilized to put the matter in such primal terms as fighting-aged versus aged, but, then, the survival of a civilization depends on the ability and willingness of its citizens to engage in that primal activity known as reproduction. And close to half of non-Muslim women are already past childbearing age. As the native European population continues to age and as the spirit of resistance continues to decline, the Catholic Church's warnings about population control, which were once dismissed as unenlightened, may soon be seen in an entirely new light.

In *The Time Machine* (1895), H. G. Wells depicts future humanity as having evolved into two breeds — the passive, childlike Eloi and the brutal Morlocks who feed off them. Mark Steyn notes that Wells's science-fiction society is a good analogy for what's happening in Europe today: "You bomb us, run us over, decapitate us — and those who survive light candles and exchange flowers and sing songs." The only thing Wells got wrong, says Steyn, is that he was off by 800,685 years (*The Time Machine* is set in A.D. 802,701).[305]

The Pew study also seems to have a problem with timing. The tenor of their report suggests that Europe has plenty of time to sort things out. Moreover, the report contains reassuring bits of data that seem designed to quell fears. We are told, for instance, that Muslim refugees are perceived as less of a threat in countries that take in the most of them. Supposedly, this means that once you get to know your new Muslim neighbors, you'll see that they're just folks. But it could just as well mean that these are the countries where people feel least free to speak their minds to pollsters — countries where you can be arrested if you say the wrong thing about immigration.

Give it a little time, and all will be well? And then, when 2050 arrives, Pew can take the pulse of the population again to see what's up. But time has a habit of marching on a little more quickly than we anticipate. When you combine the current rate of Muslim population growth with the rapidly declining morale of non-Muslims in Europe, it may already

---

[305] Mark Steyn, "The Eloi, the Morlocks ... and Us," Steyn Online, June 9, 2017, https://www.steynonline.com/7893/the-eloi-the-morlocks-and-us.

be game over by the time 2050 rolls around. You don't need to be in the majority in order to dominate.

At one point, the Pew report hopefully points out that even though the Muslim population could triple by 2050, it would still be considerably smaller than the population of Christians and other non-Muslims in Europe. Maybe so. But if that larger population is largely made up of graying Eloi types, the numbers won't matter. Will and determination count for more than percentages.

16

Migration Invasion

The high Muslim birth rate in Europe has been compounded by an acceleration in the rate of Muslim migration into Europe. This, in turn, has led to a spike in crime and terrorism, as well as the desecration of thousands of churches throughout the Continent. The Vatican has responded to the crisis by scolding Christians for their inhospitality and by encouraging more Muslim migration.

Terrorism, Islam, and Immigration

Whenever a new terrorist attack is reported, I'm reminded of that Life-Lock commercial about a bank robbery. After a group of masked robbers smash into the bank, the uniformed officer on duty explains to frightened customers that he's not a security guard, only a security monitor. He notifies people if there's a robbery, but he doesn't do anything to stop it.

Over in Europe, people are beginning to understand that their local and federal governments aren't going to do anything about the terrorist problem. Oh, sure, the authorities will investigate the latest attack, identify the perpetrator, and, if they're lucky, break up the cell to which he belonged. But on the most basic level, nothing changes, nothing is ever done.

What are the basics that are being ignored?

Well, in the first place, it would be helpful to recognize that these acts of terror are committed by Muslims, not by Methodists or Mormons. Moreover, the higher the concentration of Muslims in a given society, the more likely it is that terrorist attacks will occur. In Hungary, Poland, and the Czech Republic, which have strict immigration laws and few Muslims, there have been no major terror attacks. In Germany, Belgium, France, and England, which have liberal immigration laws and large Muslim populations, terror attacks have become an almost weekly occurrence.

One of the primary ways to prevent terrorist attacks is to put a halt to Muslim immigration or else to curtail it sharply. But Europe's governing class is committed to open borders. They're also committed to the narrative that all cultures are created equal. So, if Muslims are acting up, it can't, by their reckoning, have anything to do with Islamic culture; it must be because of racial hatred or intolerance on the part of the natives. Like the security monitor in the LifeLock commercial, European authorities witness the invasion of their territory, but they don't do anything to stop it. Indeed, many deny that terrorism has any connection to immigration.

It can be objected here that Salman Abedi, the Manchester bomber, was not an immigrant. In fact, that objection has already been offered as proof that Muslim immigration has nothing to do with terrorism.[306] But Abedi's parents were immigrants from Libya, and the part of Manchester they lived in has been described as the world's largest Libyan enclave outside Africa. The culture in which Abedi grew up was arguably more Libyan than British. This brings us back to the all-cultures-are-equal fantasy. Libya is a violent place. So are Syria, Iraq, Afghanistan, Yemen, Somalia, and Chechnya. What's the common element that unites these diverse places? Would it be "Islamophobic" to say that Islam is the common element?

Well, yes, it would. At least, the authorities will call it "Islamophobia." And since they want to avoid any appearance of "Islamophobia" on their own part, they avoid making any connection between Islam and violence. As a result, they won't take the steps that would help to prevent terror assaults like the one in Manchester. What might those include? Answer: surveilling mosques, madrassas, and Muslim student associations; deporting radical imams; shutting down radical mosques and schools; closing sharia courts; closing radical Islamist political organizations; banning foreign funding of mosques; stopping the radicalization of Muslims in the prison system; preventing the return of foreign fighters from places such as Syria and Libya; and—the big one—calling a halt to Muslim immigration.

---

[306] Heather Mac Donald, "The Left's Unilateral Suicide Pact," *FrontPage Mag*, June 1, 2017, https://archives.frontpagemag.com/fpm/lefts-unilateral-suicide-pact-heather-mac-donald/.

Why aren't these steps being taken? Because to take them would suggest that there is a problem with Islam. As Mohammed Ullah, Muslim chaplain at the University of Manchester, said after first condemning the bombing, "But let's also be clear about this—why do we then have to stand up and say: 'we apologize'? It's not my fault. It's not the fault of the religion."[307]

But that's the question, isn't it? Is there something about this particular religion that predisposes people to commit violence against unbelievers and against fellow Muslims who don't adhere to the right brand of Islam? The terrorists themselves say there is. They leave for posterity videos and letters proclaiming their love of Allah and their desire to do his will. Terrorist organizations such as ISIS publish lengthy statements detailing the scriptural justification for their actions.

You can say that they misunderstand their religion, but that argument is hard to buy when you consider that about a half dozen major terrorist leaders have Ph.D.s either in Islamic Studies or Islamic jurisprudence. That would include Abu Bakr al-Baghdadi, the leader of ISIS who holds a Ph.D. in Islamic Studies from the University of Baghdad.

How about Abedi, the twenty-two-year-old who committed the atrocity in Manchester? Surely, he couldn't have understood much about Islam. That, at least, is the opinion of Olivier Roy, one of France's "top experts" on Islamic terrorism. Roy has a theory that the majority of jihadists have scant knowledge of Islam. Thus, "with little if any understanding of religion or Islamic culture, young people like Abedi turn to terrorism out of a 'suicidal instinct.' "[308]

---

[307] Robert Spencer, "UK: Muslim Leaders in Manchester, Site of Jihad Massacre, Claim Rise in "Islamophobia," *Jihad Watch*, May 26, 2017, https://www.jihadwatch.org/2017/05/uk-muslim-leaders-in-manchester-site-of-jihad-massacre-claim-rise-in-islamophobia.

[308] Davide Lerner, "It's Not Islam That Drives Young Europeans to Jihad, France's Top Terrorism Expert Explains," Haaretz, August 20, 2017, https://www.haaretz.com/world-news/europe/it-s-not-islam-that-drives-young-europeans-to-jihad-terrorism-expert-says-1.5477000.

This sounds like a neat theory until you dig a bit and find that Abedi was a *hafiz*—that is, a person who has committed the entire Koran to memory. Moreover, he attended mosque regularly and was described as very devout. His father was also devout, and, when he wasn't fighting for the rebels in Libya, he worked as a muezzin (the man who chants the call to prayer) at the Didsbury Mosque, which his son also attended.

Along with other "authorities," Mr. Roy is committed to the theory that terrorists must be unfamiliar with the peaceful teachings of Islam. But the short life of Salman Abedi refutes the theory. So does a recent German study based on interviews with forty-five thousand respondents. According to Nicolai Sennels, a Danish psychologist:

> The many interviews showed that Islam is distinguished by being the only religion that makes people more prone to violence the more religious one becomes.[309]

"It's not the fault of the religion," says the Muslim chaplain at the University of Manchester, but the evidence suggests otherwise. Many ordinary people are undoubtedly coming to the conclusion that there *is* something wrong with the religion founded by Muhammad. And, being common people with common sense, they realize that not much will be done to solve the problem of Islamic violence until the authorities acknowledge that it is indeed *Islamic* violence.

As I wrote this essay, reports were coming in of terror attacks on London Bridge and in nearby Borough Market. On London Bridge, a van plowed at high speed into pedestrians, and several assailants then got out and began stabbing patrons at nearby bars and restaurants. At last count, six had been killed and many more wounded. It is reported that the men shouted, "This is for Allah" as they commenced their knife attack.

---

[309] Nicolai Sennels, "The Real Cause of Islamic Terrorism: 'We Are Motivated by Our Religion, by Our Qur'an and Sunnah,'" *Jihad Watch*, May 31, 2017, https://www.jihadwatch.org/2017/05/the-real-cause-of-islamic-terrorism-we-are-motivated-by-our-religion-by-our-quran-and-sunnah.

How do you prevent incidents like this? How do you stop Islamic terror attacks on London Bridge, Westminster Bridge, a Manchester concert arena, a Paris concert hall, a Paris publishing house, a boulevard in Nice, a Christmas market in Berlin, a mall in Munich, a Brussels airport, a Brussels subway station, a Copenhagen cafe, and a shopping area in Stockholm? Do you put up concrete barricades around every square and every bridge and every major thoroughfare of every major city? Do you station troops throughout every major metropolitan area? What if the terrorists then move their operations to smaller cities and towns? Do you guard every theater, every school, every church and synagogue? And when the terrorists attack theatergoers on the way out of the theater or churchgoers on their way home from church, do you move the security perimeter further out by a couple of blocks? Do you extend airport security to the airport parking lots? To the entrance drives? To the numerous shuttle buses traveling in and out? Or, as Mark Steyn has suggested, are you better off to establish a very secure perimeter at the borders of your country?

There's a lesson to be learned here, but for Europeans the lesson comes late in the game. Once the Muslim population of a country grows beyond a certain point, it becomes very difficult to control the terror problem. Yes, of course, not every Muslim is a terrorist. But it has become something like a mathematical certainty that a certain percentage are. Thus, as the Muslim population grows, so does the number of terrorists and potential terrorists. You can belatedly close the borders, but if you wait too long, the damage will already have been done. It's not a matter of closing the barn door after the horses have escaped but of closing it after the war horses and the Trojan horses have gotten inside.

It's a different matter for the United States. In America, it's not too late to tighten up the borders, to curtail Muslim immigration, and to develop sophisticated vetting procedures. It's not too late to put Muslim communities on notice that they need to do more to purge the terrorists from their midst and to eliminate from their culture those elements that foster radicalization. None of this will happen, of course, without a radical change of mind—a realization that we are not just fighting ISIS or lone wolves but that we are also engaged in a do-or-die culture war with people who are determined, either by violence or by stealth, to replace our culture with theirs.

Across the Atlantic, the substitution of one culture for another is well under way, and the Europeans don't quite know what to do about it. It's difficult to know what to do when the enemy is already within your borders and when he is practically indistinguishable from the nonviolent practitioners of his faith. Because of years of inaction, many parts of Europe are now in a place where all the options are terrible to contemplate.

The lesson for us is that we can't afford to let the Muslim immigration problem grow to the point where—as in large parts of Europe—it is nearly impossible to deal with the consequences. Because, beyond a certain point, no amount of concrete barriers and bomb-sniffing dogs will be able to stem the terrorist tide.

Know-Nothing Catholics on Muslim Immigration

It was not surprising that Catholic bishops responded with dismay to President Trump's 2015 executive order banning immigration from seven Muslim nations. When Trump first proposed banning Muslims from entering the United States, Archbishop Joseph Kurtz, then president of the USCCB, issued a statement repudiating "the hatred and suspicion that leads to policies of discrimination."[310] At about the same time, Archbishop William Lori of Baltimore said Catholics could "not possibly countenance" restricting entry to the U.S. solely on the basis of religious affiliation.[311] It can also be expected that bishops will employ an argument they have long used against opponents of Muslim immigration—namely, that Catholic immigrants were once treated with similar suspicion.

Catholics and non-Catholics alike now laugh at the anti-Catholic prejudice of the Know-Nothings (aka, the American Party) and other groups who were opposed to immigration from Catholic countries in Europe. The anti-Catholics based their objection on the belief that Catholics owed allegiance to a foreign power (the Vatican) and, thus, Catholics could never be truly loyal to America and its Constitution. More than that, there were dark rumors about a papist plot to take over America

---

[310] Tom Roberts, "Catholic Bishops Oppose Ban on Muslim Refugees," *National Catholic Reporter*, December 14, 2015, https://www.ncronline.org/blogs/ncr-today/catholic-bishops-oppose-ban-muslim-refugees.

[311] Ibid.

and about an undersea tunnel that connected the Vatican to New York. This view—that Catholics could never assimilate to America's democratic culture—persisted in some quarters up until the election of John F. Kennedy.

The fact that some Americans once mistakenly considered Catholicism a menace is now used as an argument against critics of Muslim immigration. Just as the Know-Nothings of days gone by were wrong about Catholicism, so also will today's "Know-Nothings" be proven wrong about Islam. Or so it is claimed. The open-borders advocates in the Church assure us that Islam will turn out to be as American as apple pie: give Islam a chance, and you will discover that the local imam is just Bing Crosby's Father O'Malley with a beard—a mellow fellow whose biggest concern is to pay off the mortgage on the mosque.

But what if all the things that were once falsely charged against Catholicism are true of Islam? The nineteenth-century anti-Catholics mistakenly thought that Catholicism was a theocracy, but Islam really is a theocracy. The anti-Catholics wrongly questioned the loyalty of American Catholics, but numerous polls show that a majority of Muslims consider their primary allegiance to be to the *ummah* (the worldwide community of Muslim believers), and not to whatever nation they happen to reside in. A Pew Research survey of Muslim-Americans under thirty revealed that 60 percent of them felt more loyalty to Islam than to America.[312] The Know-Nothings worried needlessly that Catholics would be subject to foreign influence, but when you consider that 85 percent of full-time, paid imams in the U.S. are foreign-born,[313] foreign influence on American Muslims does seem a legitimate concern.

---

[312] Robert Spencer, "51% of U.S. Muslims want Sharia; 60% of Young Muslims More Loyal to Islam Than to U.S.," *Jihad Watch*, October 15, 2015, https://www.jihadwatch.org/2015/10/51-of-u-s-muslims-want-sharia-60-of-young-muslims-more-loyal-to-islam-than-to-u-s.

[313] Gillian Flaccus, "Demand for US-Born Imams Up in American Mosques," *Islamist Watch*, September 21, 2013, https://www.meforum.org/islamist-watch/42217/demand-for-us-born-imams-up-in-american-mosques.

What about the anti-Catholic fear that Catholics would be bound by canon law, not constitutional law? There was, of course, little need for worry. The scope of canon law is largely restricted to internal Church affairs, and most Catholics have only the vaguest acquaintance with its requirements. On the other hand, sharia law governs almost every aspect of daily life for Muslims. Moreover, many tenets of sharia law directly contradict the Constitution and the Bill of Rights. Sharia law permits cruel and unusual punishments; the open-ended sharia blasphemy laws make free speech highly problematic; and the apostasy and dhimmitude laws more or less cancel out religious freedom.

How seriously is sharia regarded in Muslim lands? In many Muslim nations, sharia law (or Islamic law) is the law of the land. For example, it is written into the constitutions of Saudi Arabia, Egypt, and Iraq. The Cairo Declaration on Human Rights in Islam,[314] which is the Islamic response to the United Nations' Universal Declaration of Human Rights, was ratified by all fifty-seven member nations of the Organization of the Islamic Conference. Article 24 of the declaration states, "All the rights and freedoms stipulated in this Declaration are subject to the Islamic Sharia." Article 25 states, "The Islamic Sharia is the only source of reference for the explanation or clarification of any of the articles of this Declaration." All of this sounds a bit like the fine print in a warranty that tells you that your product is completely covered for ten years except for labor and all the working parts.

But how about Muslims in America? You may think that American Muslims pay no attention to the thousand-year-old requirements of sharia law, but polls show otherwise. A nationwide survey conducted by the Polling Company for the Center for Security Policy reveals that 51 percent of Muslims agreed that "Muslims in America should have the choice of

---

[314] Islamic Conference of Foreign Ministers, Cairo Declaration on Human Rights in Islam (August 5, 1990), Refworld, https://www.refworld.org/docid/3ae6b3822c.html.

being governed according to sharia."[315] In addition, 51 percent of those polled believed that they should have the choice of American or sharia courts. Only 39 percent agreed that Muslims in the United States should be subject to American courts.

Take over the country? That's what some of the anti-Catholic nativists thought that the Catholics were planning to do. There is no evidence, however, that any Catholic groups, whether lay or clerical, ever entertained notions about subjugating America. On the other hand, numerous Islamist leaders have, in no uncertain terms, expressed a desire to conquer America. And the crazy talk is not confined to terrorist chiefs hiding out in the deserts of Libya or Iraq. "Death to America" is now the unofficial motto of one large, well-armed Islamic nation (Iran). Moreover, subjugating nations to Islam is not simply something that Muslims like to talk about. It's what they have done throughout history. The spread of Islam is the raison d'être of Islam.

How should it be spread? Not necessarily with bullets and bombs. Prominent Islamic spiritual leaders such as Yusuf al-Qaradawi have expressed confidence that Islam can conquer Europe through immigration and through higher birth rates. The 9/11 mastermind Khalid Sheikh Mohammed (KSM) has expressed similar sentiments about the defeat of the United States. Although not at all adverse to the use of violence, KSM revealed that al-Qaeda's plan to crush America was more subtle than that. According to James Mitchell, the CIA contractor who interrogated him, KSM told him:

> The "practical" way to defeat America was through immigration and by outbreeding non-Muslims. He said jihadi-minded brothers would immigrate into the United States, taking advantage of the welfare system to support themselves while they spread their

[315] "Poll of U.S. Muslims Reveals Ominous Levels of Support for Islamic Supremacists' Doctrine of Shariah, Jihad," Center for Security Policy, June 23, 2015, https://www.centerforsecuritypolicy.org/2015/06/23/nationwide-poll-of-us-muslims-shows-thousands-support-shariah-jihad/.

jihadi message. They will wrap themselves in America's rights and laws for protection, ratchet up acceptance of Sharia law, and then, only when they were strong enough, rise up and violently impose Sharia from within.[316]

It is that possibility, and not a D-Day-type invasion that worries serious critics of Islamic immigration, and it is that possibility that the new executive order is meant to forestall. More to the point, the ban on Muslim immigration is based not on bigotry but on a realistic assessment of Islam. If, as KSM and other Islamists have said, the plan is to conquer the West through immigration, then putting restrictions on Muslim immigration is the logical thing to do.

In 2016, San Diego Bishop Robert McElroy gave a speech that rehashed all the old clichés about "anti-Islamic prejudice." He reminded his audience about the anti-Catholic bigotry of the past; he cautioned them about a "new nativism"; he advised them that they should view with repugnance the "repeated falsehoods" that Islam is inherently violent or that Muslims seek to replace the Constitution with sharia law; and he told them that Catholics must speak out against "distortions of Muslim theology ... because these distortions are just as devastating in the present day as the distortions of Catholic teaching ... which were disseminated in American society in the 19th century."[317]

Except that the "distortions" of Islam that McElroy talks about are not distortions at all. They are established facts. And the fears that many in the United States have about Muslim immigration are well-founded fears. Rational discrimination against Muslim immigration in the twenty-first

---

[316] Robert Spencer, "9/11 Mastermind: Al-Qaeda Now Favors Immigration and 'Outbreeding Non-Muslims' to Destroy US," *Jihad Watch*, November 24, 2016.

[317] Dennis Grasska, "Bishop Challenges Catholics to Combat 'Ugly Tide of Anti-Islamic Bigotry,'" Catholic News Service, February 22, 2016, https://www.catholicnews.com/services/englishnews/2016/bishop-challenges-catholics-to-combat-ugly-tide-of-anti-islamic-bigotry.cfm.

century is not the same as irrational discrimination against Catholic immigration in the nineteenth century. Unless, of course, you are naïve enough
to believe that all religions are basically of the same peace-loving sort.

The term "Know-Nothings" originally referred to its members' habit
of responding to every question about its activities with the reply "I
know nothing." The moniker also captured the ignorance of its nativist
members. Their opposition to Catholic immigrants was largely based
on misinformation. Today, however, the situation is reversed. It's not
the opponents of immigration that are ill-informed, but its proponents.
Today's equivalent of the Know-Nothings are not those who have fears
about Muslim immigration. In general, their fears are based on facts about
Islamic beliefs and Islamic history—facts that are easily accessible to
anyone who bothers to look. The "Know-Nothings" of today are those
who think Muslim immigration can only be a good thing—those who
are so ignorant of Islam that they proudly proclaim their solidarity with
it. The Know-Nothings of today are all those willfully blind groups and
individuals who refuse to look at the facts about Islam, and prefer instead
to cling to the fantasy Islam of their imaginations.

Today's Know-Nothings are smug in their assurance that they hold
the moral high ground. Hence, they absolve themselves from examining
the evidence on which moral judgments should be based. They are sure
that the conventional wisdom of yesterday is adequate to understand
today's radically different situation. In their own way, they are as much of
a threat to American society as the terrorists who plan to take advantage
of their ignorance.

Is the Face of the Migrant the Face of Jesus?

In the face of increasing Muslim violence in Europe, Pope Francis has remained firm in his defense of mass migration.

In his 2017 *Urbi et Orbi* Christmas message, he compared migrants to the Holy Family forced to journey to Bethlehem and unable to find a room in the inn.[318] And in his January 1 message for the World Day of Peace, Francis denounced those who decry "the risks posed to national security" by mass migration. Such people, said the pope, are guilty of "demeaning the human dignity due to all as sons and daughters of God."[319]

As on previous occasions, Francis observed that those who fail to welcome migrants "are sowing violence, racial discrimination, and xenophobia."[320] On the other hand, those who welcome migrants are welcoming Christ. In an address to representatives of Caritas in September 2017, Pope Francis told his audience that "Christ himself asks us to welcome our brother and sister migrants and refugees with arms wide

---

[318] Staff Reporter, "Pope Francis's Urbi et Orbi 2017 Christmas Message: Full Text," *Catholic Herald*, December 25, 2017, https://catholicherald. co.uk/pope-franciss-urbi-et-orbi-2017-christmas-message-full-text/.

[319] Pope Francis, "Migrants and Refugees: Men and Women in Search of Peace."

[320] Ibid.

open."[321] On other occasions, he has said that in the face of the migrant we see the face of Jesus.[322]

One of the pope's favorite themes since his election is that those who close the borders are, in effect, closing the door on Jesus. If you're a Christian, that argument is hard to resist. Who wants to slam the door on Jesus? Who wants to be told on the Last Day, "I was a stranger and you did not welcome me"?

The pope's argument is an emotional one, but it's a powerful one, and it's based on Scripture to boot. Because of his office and because of his invocation of Jesus and the Holy Family, his appeal on behalf of migrants merits close examination—all the more so because so much is at stake.

The first thing to keep in mind is that most of Christ's admonitions are aimed at individuals, not governments. If a boat full of migrants capsizes near shore, and you are in a position to help, you have a Christian obligation to lend a hand. Governments also have a responsibility to rescue endangered migrants at sea, but they have a corresponding obligation not to encourage such a dangerous crossing in the first place. Moreover, it should be obvious that governments have no obligation to allow an unlimited flow of migrants to come across their borders. There is no duty to do what is mathematically impossible. A government's duty to its own citizens may even require the closing of its border under certain circumstances. "I was a stranger and you welcomed me," is a message directed primarily to the hearts and minds of individual Christians, not to the Swedish Migration Agency.

---

[321] Robert Spencer, "Pope Francis: 'Christ Himself Asks Us to Welcome Our Brother and Sister Migrants and Refugees with Arms Wide Open,'" *Jihad Watch*, September 27, 2017, https://www.jihadwatch.org/2017/09/pope-francis-christ-himself-asks-us-to-welcome-our-brother-and-sister-migrants-and-refugees-with-arms-wide-open.

[322] "In the faces of the hungry, the thirsty, the naked, the sick, strangers and prisoners, we are called to see the face of Christ." Message of the Holy Father Francis for the 106th World Day of Migrants and Refugees, May 15, 2020.

Still, what does an individual do when voting time rolls around? Does he vote for the welcoming party or does he vote for the close-the-borders party? And if he votes for the latter, does that mean he's shutting the door on Jesus?

The trouble with drawing an analogy between Jesus and Muslim migrants is that, like all analogies, it limps. It applies to some situations but not to others. And if it's applied too broadly, it becomes very confusing. It's easy enough to see the face of Jesus in the child who comes across the border in the arms of his mother, but how about the young man who enters with visions of jihad dancing in his head? Do you want to say to the man who has just been run over on London Bridge by a refugee jihadi that Jesus was driving the car? And while we're on the subject of London, do you want to tell the delivery man who has been the victim of an acid attack that he should strive to see the face of Jesus in the face of his assailant? According to the *Sun*, "vast areas of East, North, and South London have been declared 'no-go zones' by terrified delivery drivers because of the acid attack epidemic."[323] Members of the House of Commons were recently told that London now has more acid attacks per head than any other city in the world.

The question is, why aren't we being encouraged to see the face of Jesus in the acid-scarred face of the delivery man? Unlike many of the migrants, he truly is a victim. We know that the majority of the migrants are young men, and most of them are not fleeing war. In fact, 80 percent of migrants who claim to be fleeing the war in Syria are not really from Syria at all. Moreover, judging by the current crime wave in Europe, a significant number of these migrants are more victimizer than victim.

It's not a good idea to politicize the birth of Jesus, but that's what Pope Francis seems to have done in his 2017 *Urbi et Orbi* Christmas message. "Christmas," he said, "invites us to focus on the sign of the Child and to recognize him in the faces of little children, especially those for whom, like Jesus, 'there is no place in the inn.'" He then proceeded to

[323] Gye, "NO-GO ZONE London Is the Acid Capital of the World."

"see Jesus" in the faces of suffering children in various parts of the world, but most of them seem to be Muslim children. For example, "children of the Middle East who continue to suffer because of growing tensions between Israel and Palestinians," "Syrian children," "children I met during my recent visit to Myanmar and Bangladesh," and "children forced to leave their countries to travel alone in inhuman conditions." Pope Francis then concluded, "May our hearts not be closed as they were in the homes of Bethlehem."

The last, of course, was directed toward "selfish" and "fearful" Europeans and Americans who oppose the pope's open-borders policy. The trouble is, Francis's invocation of the Child Jesus is decidedly one-sided. As he says, we should try to see the face of Jesus in the face of suffering migrant children. But why can't we also see the face of Jesus in the face of the *victims* of Muslim migrants — those who have been beaten, raped, stabbed, and run over? How about the many child victims of the jihad truck massacre in Nice, France, in 2016; the child victims of the jihad attack on the Ariana Grande concert in Manchester, England; the 1,400 teenage victims of the Pakistani rape gangs in Rotherham, England? One could also include all those Muslim children who are victims of their own religion. For example, it's estimated that hundreds of thousands of Muslim children living in Europe have been subjected to female genital mutilation. Why is the Christ Child analogy not extended to these other child victims?

On Christmas 2017, Pope Francis also employed a related analogy — one he has often used. He drew a comparison between today's refugees and the Holy Family fleeing to Egypt to escape King Herod. Francis never specifies who today's Herods are, but it's clear that his message is aimed at those Europeans and Americans who are tempted to close their hearts to the Holy Family, who come to us today, he says, in the guise of Muslim migrants.

As with so many of the Pope's biblical references, this one can be used both ways. One can just as easily make the case that those who are opening the borders to Muslim migrants are, in effect, opening the gates to Herod's army. By importing a culture that justifies rape, honor violence, and terrorism, ecclesiastical and government elites are aiding and abetting the Herods of today. And they should not be surprised if a slaughter of the innocents ensues.

There is another analogy to consider. If Herod had succeeded in finding the Christ Child, Christianity would have been nipped in the bud. Although he failed, the attempt to exterminate Christianity is a perennial one. Today that attempt comes mainly from the Muslim world, and there can be little doubt that many Muslims hope to bring their war against Christianity to Europe. From that perspective, it is not the "welcomers" who are offering shelter to the Christ Child, but rather those courageous Europeans who are resisting today's equivalent of Herod's troops.

There is a sense in which one is justified in seeing the face of Jesus in Muslim refugees. But there is another sense in which one can quite rightly see the face of jihad.

17

More Comic Relief

Jaws — Jihad Version

Are the beaches really safe?

I watched *Jaws* the other night on TV, and it reminded me — as everything does these days — of jihad. In fact, there are some instructive parallels between the plot of *Jaws* and the official narrative about jihad.

In the 1975 film, a great white shark terrorizes the beach town of Amity Island. After the remains of the first victim are found, the police chief wants to close the beach. But he is overruled by the mayor and other town fathers, who fear that the news will ruin the island's tourist-fueled economy.

Initially, they claim that there is no shark. Their theory is that the dead swimmer was hit by a boat's propeller. When the shark claims another victim, however, they decide to offer a reward to whoever can kill it. Shortly thereafter, some local fishermen catch a large tiger shark and display the carcass on the town dock, giving the mayor the excuse he needs to proclaim the beaches safe in time for the Fourth of July weekend.

But the tiger shark is a red herring. A marine biologist insists that the killer must be a much larger shark, and this is confirmed when the great white makes its appearance on the Fourth, killing another victim and causing panic among the beachgoers.

You know the rest of the story. The police chief, the marine biologist, and a shark hunter named Quint set out on Quint's boat to find the shark. And after a harrowing ordeal, they finally manage to kill it.

Unfortunately, our own great white shark—Islamic terrorism—is still alive and gliding just offshore, and no one knows where it will strike next. We don't know how our own story will end, but otherwise the parallels to *Jaws* are worth contemplating.

Like the town fathers in Amity Island, our own town fathers—government officials, the media, and various social elites—are in denial. Their version of "there is no shark" is to deny the existence of a deeply entrenched and widely accepted doctrine of jihad warfare within Islam. Although they are willing to talk about lone wolves and extremist groups, they treat each new incident of terrorism as an isolated event that bears no relation to a larger pattern and, they assure us, has nothing to do with Islam.

The main impetus for minimizing the extent of the threat is similar to the one that motivates the town fathers of Amity Island: let's preserve the illusion that the waters are safe. The illusion that our own "town fathers" wish to maintain is that the vast majority of Muslims are peaceful moderates and that the violence is the work of a handful who have betrayed their religion.

If the illusion is not maintained, the town fathers will be revealed as having been dreadfully wrong about the biggest threat of our times. Thus, it is crucial for them that people believe that their analysis of the situation is correct, that their policies are working, and that the problem is contained.

In 2015, in an almost comical reprise of the role played by the shark-denying mayor in *Jaws*, Anne Hidalgo, the mayor of Paris, threatened to sue Fox News over a series of news segments about "no-go zones" in France. Although a French government website lists 750 of these "sensitive urban zones," the mayor claimed that there was no such thing and that Fox had dishonored the image of Paris. Paris is, of course, the most-visited city in the world, and it wouldn't help the tourist industry if word got out that the city was surrounded by shar— I mean unassimilated persons of the Islamic persuasion.

In *Jaws*, the town fathers temporarily persuade the townspeople and themselves that the marauding shark has been caught and killed. The killing of the tiger shark supposedly makes the beaches safe again. The current analogy to this is the tendency to identify the Islamic threat with particular terrorist groups. In this telling, there is no giant shark—no dogma of global Islamic conquest—but only smaller sharks such as al-Qaeda and ISIS. Once these dangers are eliminated, there will be no more threat—or so we are assured.

In another echo of the film, our government offered a bounty for the head of Osama bin Laden. The assumption seemed to be that killing him would be tantamount to killing the jihad. But jihad is bigger than any one individual. It is Allah who commands it, not bin Laden or al-Baghdadi. ISIS and al-Qaeda are like the tiger shark. Even if they are killed off, the larger problem remains.

That larger problem—our own great white shark—is the Islamic doctrine of jihad warfare against unbelievers. It's rooted in Islamic scripture, tradition, and history. Like the monster fish in *Jaws*, it won't be easily killed—and certainly not by those who deny its existence.

The Arabian Candidate

In *The Manchurian Candidate* (1962), the son of a prominent right-wing politician is captured by the Soviets and brainwashed in a secret Manchurian location. His task is to assassinate a presidential candidate, thus ensuring the election of the demagogic vice-president. Hence, the title *Manchurian Candidate*.

The film has several parallels to current events. The main difference is that in those days, Americans had to be brainwashed into serving enemy interests by psyops teams. Nowadays, they come self-brainwashed with some assist from the American educational system.

In the film, a scary lady with leftist sympathies who looks vaguely like Hillary Clinton manipulates her husband into high political office. In real life, a scary lady with leftist leanings who looks vaguely like Angela Lansbury (only scarier) manipulates herself into high political office.

In her case, teams of brainwashers are not required, since she has brainwashed herself into believing that foreign governments are dumping truckloads of cash into her family foundation because she's such a charming and intelligent woman. And also because Arab sovereigns like nothing better than to do their part to improve the lives of the poor, the hungry, the environmentally underserved, and kids who need braces — in short, the very causes for which the foundation was founded.

Another similarity is that, in the film, the Angela Lansbury character has some sort of hypnotic power over her son, the unwitting assassin. Whenever it begins to dawn on him that something funny is going on, she flashes a queen of diamonds playing card, and he falls into a catatonic state of complete obedience. In the present situation, the Angela Lansbury look-alike has merely to flash the gender card, and, presto, skeptical voters fall back into line.

There are parallels to other movies as well. Today's Queen of Diamonds has a secret server in her home so that her exchanges with foreign dono—I mean "diplomats"—can't be traced. I'm not sure if the server takes up only one room of the palatial house or a whole suite of rooms. And who knows what's in the cavern-like basement? It's all faintly reminiscent of those James Bond thrillers in which the villain's remote island estate sits atop a vast underground military-industrial complex.

At some point, the analogy breaks down. You could still convince a '60s audience that leftists were willing to sell out the country. We, on the other hand, have convinced ourselves that we live in a brave new world where such things never happen—at least, not in modern Western societies. No one would dare to pull a fast one on us because we're just too smart. We've grown up watching *CSI*, we went to schools that taught critical thinking, and our history texts were written by Howard Zinn. We've also been nurtured on relativism, so if it were discovered that Arabs controlled the White House, we would shrug our shoulders and say, "At this point, what difference does it make?"

The Clinton-Arab connection goes back to the time when Bill Clinton was governor of Arkansas and worked to secure a hefty Saudi contribution to a Middle Eastern studies program at the University of Arkansas. But let's skip all that and fast forward to relatively recent times, when Secretary of State Hillary Clinton appointed her longtime aide Huma Abedin as Deputy Chief of Staff at the State Department. When it was discovered that Abedin's family was deeply involved in the Muslim Brotherhood in Saudi Arabia, very few eyebrows were raised. After all, even then-President Obama had relatives in the Muslim Brotherhood. So it would have been silly to make something of it.

It's probably just a coincidence that while working for the Clintons, Huma herself was the assistant editor of the *Journal of Muslim Minority*

Affairs, which — you guessed it — is a Muslim Brotherhood journal. Before that, and while still interning at the White House, she was an executive board member of the Muslim Student Association (MSA) at George Washington University. The MSA was the first Muslim Brotherhood organization in the United States, and George Washington was the first Muslim president. Well, the latter hasn't yet been firmly established, but it's just a matter of time until those Saudi-funded Mideast studies professors at the University of Arkansas and the Saudi-funded professors at Georgetown (Bill's alma mater) discover the prayer rug in the attic at Mount Vernon. It's also probably a coincidence that, like her boss, Huma conducted State Department business using her personal e-mail address, connected, one supposes, to the same master server that served her master — er, mistress so well.

Abedin also worked for the Clinton Foundation. Again, this is no doubt a pure coincidence, and as the old saying goes, it has nothing to do with Islam. Although *CSI* investigators would have a field day with such coincidences, today's government officials seem curiously lacking in curiosity. In 2012, Michele Bachmann and four other House members wrote letters to the inspectors general of several government agencies, asking them to conduct an investigation into Muslim Brotherhood penetration of the government. They were particularly concerned about Huma Abedin in view of her family connections and influential position. They noted that the Clinton State Department had "taken actions recently that have been enormously favorable to the Muslim Brotherhood and its interests."[324]

The request was dismissed by numerous congressmen and senators as "offensive," "insensitive," and even "hurtful." By that time, the machinery of the "Islamophobia" industry was already in high gear and it was

---

[324] Devin Henry, "Bachmann: Investigate the Reach of the Muslim Brotherhood," *MINN POST*, July 10, 2012, https://www.minnpost.com/dc-dispatches/2012/07/bachmann-investigate-reach-muslim-brotherhood/.

deemed prudent even by Republicans to defend Abedin and to damn her accusers as McCarthyites.

Still, the case for an inquiry seemed strong. As one McCarthyite, former federal prosecutor Andy McCarthy, observed, even if Abedin was innocent of any wrongdoing, the State Department's own guidelines about foreign family connections would have disqualified her for a security clearance for such a sensitive position.[325]

But then again, a lot of people in sensitive positions don't seem to qualify for a security clearance. For example, if all your closest relatives were leftists or communists, if your chief mentors were, respectively, a member of the Communist Party and a radical left-wing preacher, and if you used to hang out with known terrorists, you probably couldn't get a job as a night watchman at an auto-parts warehouse. On the other hand, if someone with the same background throws his hat into the presidential ring, he can become commander-in-chief of the army and navy and get to set foreign policy.

He also gets to appoint secretaries of state. It shouldn't be any surprise if they turn out to be the kind of people who can't be bothered with security checks. Such people seem to live in an ethereal realm that puts them above suspicion and above conflicts of interest. Normally, when a secretary of state receives tens of millions in donations from countries that support the spread of a radical ideology, it would be a sign that something is terribly wrong. For an analogy, ask yourself if you would keep someone on at your firm if she had access to sensitive trade secrets and yet received huge gifts from rival corporations while conducting company business on her private server.

You would probably get rid of her pronto. But that's only if you apply the normal rules of logic—which apparently didn't apply to secretaries

---

[325] Andrew McCarthy, "Huma Abedin's Brotherhood Ties Are Not Just a Family Affair," PJ Media, July 27, 2012, https://pjmedia.com/andrewmccarthy/2012/07/27/huma-abedins-brotherhood-ties-are-not-just-a-family-affair/?print=1.

of state appointed by President Obama. If you applied such logic, you might also think there was something awkward about the fact that the daughter of then Secretary of State John Kerry is married to an Iranian who has extensive family ties in Iran. As Kenneth Timmerman points out, the FBI usually won't grant security clearance to "individuals who are married to nationals of an enemy nation or have family members living in that country, for fear of divided loyalties or, more simply, blackmail."[326] Of course, you would have to be some kind of conspiracy nut to think that having vulnerable in-laws in Iran would in any way have compromised Secretary Kerry's negotiations with the representatives of a country whose leaders routinely indulge in "Death to America" rhetoric.

Undoubtedly, President Obama consulted with his senior adviser, Valerie Jarrett, about the matter. Since Jarrett was born in Iran and spoke Persian as a child, she would, by current standards of expertise, be assumed to have deep insight into the Persian mind. She could have assured the president that "Great Satan" and "Death to America" are typical of the rhetorical exuberance that characterizes the rich and vibrant Iranian culture. Moreover, she could have allayed any concerns about blackmail. Anyone who has studied Cliff Notes on Islam knows that blackmail runs counter to the deeply held beliefs of the mullahs.

Jarrett's family left Iran when she was five, but apparently those five years were enough to qualify her as an expert on Iranian affairs. According to *Discover the Networks*, it was revealed in 2012 that for several months, Jarrett "had been leading secret negotiations with representatives of Iran's Supreme leader ... in an effort to normalize relations between the U.S. and Iran."[327]

---

[326] Kenneth Timmerman, "Kerry Exposes Iranian Family Tie — and Subjects Family to Blackmail," *Daily Caller*, March 25, 2013, https://dailycaller.com/2013/03/25/kerry-exposes-iranian-family-tie-and-subjects-family-to-blackmail/

[327] "Huma Abedin," Discover the Networks, last updated June 17, 2020, https://www.discoverthenetworks.org/individuals/huma-abedin/.

The mind spins at the — what's the word? — the *audacity* of it all. But the curious thing is not that there are people in high places willing to put self-interest ahead of the national interest. Such people are always with us. The curious thing is that the American people and the American press accept it with such equanimity. During the Obama-Clinton-Kerry-Jarrett-Abedin years, Russia seized the Crimea, ISIS seized large parts of Iraq and Syria, the Taliban reestablished itself in Afghanistan, allies stopped trusting us, enemies were emboldened, the Middle East was set on fire, and the army was drastically reduced. Oh, and the way was cleared for Iran to have nuclear bombs. Future generations — if there are any — will wonder what we were thinking.

What we were thinking, they may discover, goes something like this (in shorthand brain language): "Mustn't think that! Mustn't say that! Not nice! What will people think?" You'd have to go back to the Victorian era to find another society with so much concern for propriety of thought and speech. Thomas Sowell put his finger on the phenomenon in a recent editorial. When it comes to matters of survival, he observed, we have "put questions of etiquette above questions of annihilation."[328]

He's right. A sort of suicidal etiquette that chokes off common sense has grown up in our society. Under the rules of the new etiquette, we aren't allowed to say that the emperor has no clothes. We dare not even point out that the emperor and his ministers appear to be throwing open the gates to the enemy.

Let's see: the people of the United States elect as president a man they know very little about. When it becomes obvious that he has deep leftist sympathies combined with deep Islamist sympathies, they elect him again. He, in turn, appoints one secretary of state who is beholden to Arab largesse, and then, after she steps down, he replaces her with a man who practices folksong diplomacy and has close family ties with Iran.

---

[328] Thomas Sowell, "Etiquette versus Annihilation," *Townhall*, April 1, 2015, https://townhall.com/columnists/thomassowell/2015/04/01/etiquette-versus-annihilation-n1978494.

The Manchurian Candidate? On one level, the current situation is so full of farce that a serious drama like *The Manchurian Candidate* couldn't do it justice. If you were to make a movie of the current mandarin mess, it might be better to play it for laughs — an Austin Powers–type spoof or something along the lines of *Abbott and Costello Meet the Manchurian Candidate*.

On another level, the situation is so fraught with apocalyptic dangers that only a deadly serious doomsday film — something along the lines of *Fail Safe* — could bring home the enormity of our current folly. In any event, there's a title ready-made for it. If the first Obama election could be called *Death Wish I*, and his reelection, *Death Wish II*, then the election of Hillary Clinton would deservedly merit the title *Death Wish III: The Final Chapter*.

18

Islamic Family Values

Many Christians are under the illusion that Islamic family values are quite similar to Christian family values. While this may be true of some Muslim families, the Islamic view of the family differs markedly from the Christian view.

What Catholics Can Learn about
Islam from a Former Muslim

As noted earlier, many Catholics look upon Islam as an ally in the struggle against militant secularism. Since Muslims are opposed to permissiveness, pornography, same-sex "marriage," and other aspects of the secularist agenda, many Catholics assume that they must share similar values about marriage and sexuality.

But this is not the case. The Islamic emphasis on modesty and chastity shouldn't be confused with the Christian standard. Christian sexual ethics are based on respect for women, whereas Islamic sexual ethics are motivated in large part by a disparagement of women.

Islamic family values are not about honoring women, but about protecting a man's honor. And, in Islam, a man's honor is bound up with his ability to control the women in his life. If a wife, daughter, or sister does anything to jeopardize the honor of her husband, father, or brother, she risks severe punishments and even death. In the West, a disobedient Muslim daughter may have her head shaved; in the Muslim world she may be killed.

The Muslim male's control over women and girls is manifested in many ways, but one of the most disturbing is the widespread practice of female genital mutilation (FGM). According to the Population Reference Bureau, approximately half a million women and girls in the United States have undergone the procedure or are at risk of the procedure.[329] In a recent interview with Tucker Carlson, Ayaan Hirsi Ali pushed for laws that would ban the procedure, which she said is designed to "kill the sexual libido ... and ensure virginity" before marriage.[330]

Who is Ayaan Hirsi Ali?[331] Born and raised in Somalia, where genital mutilation and forced marriages are common, Ali eventually left her tribe and family and escaped to Holland. There she began a public campaign to bring attention to the mistreatment of Muslim women. In the course of time, Ali was elected to the Dutch Parliament and—partly as a result of her bad experience with Islam, and partly from her study of the Enlightenment—she became an atheist. She also became a target of radical Islamists, and, under increasing pressure from the Dutch government (which considered her to be too provocative), she left Holland for America.

The author of several books, Ali is currently a research fellow at the Hoover Institution. In addition, she heads a foundation that defends the rights of Muslim women. The AHA Foundation is dedicated to protecting girls and women from forced marriages, honor violence, genital mutilation, and oppressive sharia laws.

What might Catholics learn from Ayaan Hirsi Ali? Two important lessons come to mind. The first is that Islamic values are quite different from Catholic values. Many Catholics, including those in leadership positions, have been content to get by with a multicultural-lite view of Islam. In other words, they believe that, although Muslims may have different foods and customs, they're just like us when it comes to basics.

---

[329] Mark Mather and Charlotte Feldman-Jacobs, "Women and Girls at Risk of Female Genital Mutilation/Cutting in the United States," PRB, February 5, 2016, https://www.prb.org/us-fgmc/.

[330] Tim Hains, "Ayaan Hirsi Ali: Eliminating Female Genital Mutilation Should Be a Priority," *Real Clear Politics*, April 20, 2017, https://www.realclearpolitics.com/video/2017/04/20/ayaan_hirsi_ali_eliminating_female_genital_mutilation_should_be_a_priority.html.

[331] See Ayaan Hirsi Ali, *Infidel* (New York: Atria Books, 2008).

But as Ali and other former Muslims have pointed out, there is a world of difference. The central family value in Islam is not mutual love, but family honor. This is not to say that Muslim families are devoid of love for one another; it's to recognize that they are under enormous cultural and religious pressure to put other things first. Nonie Darwish, a Muslim convert to Christianity, makes the case that Muhammad viewed a normal family—one in which a man's first love and loyalty is to his family—as an impediment to jihad. "It is not uncommon," she observes, "for a man who is loyal to one wife and treats her with love and respect to suffer ridicule for not being man enough."[332]

Catholics seem largely unaware of the extent to which the code of honor suffuses Muslim life. Practices such as genital mutilation, forced marriage, child marriage, polygamy, wife-beating, and easy divorce (for men) are not cultural outliers; they are part of the warp and woof of Islamic societies. But the Catholic leadership has been so focused on proclaiming its respect for Islam that it has largely ignored these matters.

However intended, these proclamations of respect and even esteem for Islam are likely to be interpreted by Muslims as an endorsement of the status quo and also of Islam's all-male leadership. When Catholics declare their solidarity with Islam, what they usually mean is solidarity against "Islamophobia," or against restrictions on Muslim immigration, or similar fashionable causes. But, too often, these solidarity statements come across as blanket endorsements.

Muslim leaders can elicit these endorsements by the simple expedient of playing the victim card. They understand Catholic psychology far better than Catholics understand the psyche of Muslims, and they know that Catholic leaders reflexively side with those who claim victim status. By constantly portraying Islam as a victim of bias, bigotry, and "Islamophobia," Muslim leaders know that they can win the support of Catholics for whatever agenda they wish to pursue.

---

[332] Darwish, *Wholly Different*, 241.

Yet Islam is much more victimizer than victim. And among its chief victims are Muslim women and children. Who speaks for them? Well, Ayaan Hirsi Ali does, and so does Nonie Darwish. But I don't recall any prominent Church leaders speaking out about the oppression of Muslim women. Indeed, the Church's current policy of avoiding any criticism of Islam can easily be mistaken for an endorsement of Islam's misogynistic practices. Church authorities speak often about their concern for the most helpless and vulnerable in society, but that concern does not seem to extend to Muslim women and children, who are among the most vulnerable people in the world.

By consistently standing with institutional Islam and its representatives, the Church is, in effect, turning its back on the Muslim victims of the Islamic power structure. The Church's respect-Islam policy will, unfortunately, only increase the sense of hopelessness that many Muslims already have. Islam is an oppressive religious and social system, and many Muslims feel trapped in it. When Christian leaders won't acknowledge the oppression, it reinforces the "trapped" Muslim's belief that she has nowhere to turn.

There is a second lesson to be learned from the work of Hirsi Ali. Catholic leaders, along with many secular leaders, seem to think that the only threat from Islam comes from militant extremists. Moreover, they contend that these violent jihadists have nothing to do with Islam. According to Hirsi Ali, however, the threat is much larger, and it most assuredly does have something to do with Islam. She writes:

> In focusing only on acts of violence, we have ignored the ideology that justifies, promotes, celebrates, and encourages those acts. By not fighting a war of ideas against political Islam (or "Islamism") as an ideology and against those who spread that ideology, we have made a grave error.[333]

---

[333] Ayaan Hirsi Ali, "The Challenge of Dawa: Political Islam as Ideology and Movement and How to Counter It," *Hoover Institution*, March 21,

Ali refers to the method by which the Islamist ideology is spread as *dawa*. In its narrow sense, *dawa* means proselytizing, but in the sense that Hirsi Ali uses it, it is roughly equivalent to the term "cultural jihad." It is similar to what twentieth-century communists called the "long march through the institutions." Islamic cultural jihad is an attempt to infiltrate and influence institutions such as media, schools, courts, and government bureaucracies with the aim of advancing sharia law.

Armed jihad is one way of spreading Islamic law and doctrine, but it is not the most common way, and it is not always effective. Cultural jihad, on the other hand, is very effective because it's hard to detect and harder still to resist. Cultural jihad is difficult to counter because it takes advantage both of Constitutional protections and of the Western abhorrence of discrimination. Thus, the special rights that Muslim leaders demand are always presented as the civil rights of a victimized minority.

One of the institutions that cultural jihadists aim to influence is the Catholic Church. And, indeed, they seem to have been quite successful in their attempts to manipulate Church leaders into supporting their various agendas. European bishops have enabled the spread of Islam through their endorsement of open-borders policies. The USCCB has been one of the key players in the resettlement of Muslim refugees of the unvetted variety. Through Muslim-Catholic dialogue programs, the same bishops have lent legitimacy and respectability to Muslim Brotherhood–linked groups such as the Islamic Society of North America (ISNA) and the Islamic Circle of North America (ICNA), thereby facilitating their stealth jihad activities.

Whichever direction Islam's long march through the institutions takes, Catholic leaders seem eager to fall in line. They have joined forces with CAIR's hate-crime campaign and with its "Islamophobia" campaign — even though the latter is essentially an anti-free speech movement. Like trained seals, the bishops can be relied on to perform in the

2017), https://www.hoover.org/research/challenge-dawa-political-islam-ideology-and-movement-and-how-counter-it

expected ways. Every time non-Muslims are blown up in the name of Allah, some bishop or other is sure to voice his concern about backlash against the Muslim community and to make yet another plea for solidarity.

It's not just the bishops, of course. Catholic schools have raised a generation of students to believe that "Islam" means "peace," and that "jihad" is an "interior spiritual struggle." Catholic colleges, in the meantime, can be counted on to fight "Islamophobia" while keeping quiet about anything that puts Islam in a bad light, such as FGM and wife-beating.

Not to put too fine a point on it, Catholic leaders have been facilitating an Islamist agenda—an agenda that is inimical to the kind of family values Catholics wish for themselves. Presumably, they do so with the best of intentions. But that's small comfort to the child who is mutilated for life or to the woman whose life is held hostage to her husband's sense of honor. A large part of the problem is that Catholic leaders have been overly reliant on Muslim Brotherhood masters of *dawa* for their understanding of Islam. That's like getting your information on the Nazis from Goebbels's Ministry of Propaganda. It's time that Church leaders paid some attention to Muslims who are not part of the institutional Islamic apparatus—even if they are ex-Muslims, such as Ayaan Hirsi Ali.

I don't agree with all of Hirsi Ali's views. For instance, her hope that Muslims can be encouraged to accept a reformed—but diluted—version of Islam seems overly optimistic. Nevertheless, that view is preferable to the opinion that Islam doesn't need reform. Unfortunately, many Catholic leaders seem to think that Islam is just fine the way it is. They see no problem beyond a handful of extremists who pervert a "great faith." That assumption is built on sand, and it is being washed away daily by the tides of cultural jihad.

Islamic Family Values

Just as it's not a good idea to read too much into the cross tattooed on the bicep of the otherwise threatening biker at the bar, it's best not to read too much into the occasional concessions toward Christianity we find in Islam.

For some Catholics, it seems to be enough to hear that, as the Second Vatican Council document *Nostra Aetate* tells us, Muslims "revere" Jesus and "honor" Mary. I can't remember the number of times some hopeful Catholic has pointed out to me that there's a whole chapter named after Mary in the Koran or that Mary is mentioned more than any other woman in that book. Supposedly, that somehow compensates for all the verses in the Koran that call for crucifixions, beheadings, and amputations, and for the fact that Christians who live in Muslim lands generally lead a precarious existence.

In the grasping-for-straws department, one of the items most frequently on display is the claim that Muslims have more or less the same moral code that governs traditional Christians. For example, in *Nostra Aetate*, we read not only that Muslims honor Jesus and Mary, but that "they value the moral life." Likewise, as we have seen, numerous Catholic writers have made the case that Muslims are our natural allies in the culture wars because they oppose abortion, adultery, and pornography, and value modesty and chastity.

To be sure, many Muslim families, especially in the United States, don't seem very different from Christian families. They pray regularly, attend weekly services, give to charities, and raise polite children. As a result, it's easy to conclude that Islamic family values and Christian family values are essentially the same. But in reality, there is a world of difference between the two. To get a better picture of Islamic family values, it's advisable to look at Muslim countries or at those parts of the West that are rapidly falling under Islamic influence.

Take Great Britain. A U.K. website[334] designed to help Muslim men find second wives has more than a hundred thousand users. And it's estimated that there are already as many as twenty thousand polygamous marriages among British Muslims. In addition to polygamy, there are many other practices that one would be hard pressed to find in Christian families: tens of thousands of cases of female genital mutilation, forced marriages to first cousins, and women shrouded in burqas.

But let's focus on polygamy. It's not simply an incidental item that happens to be found in Arab cultures; rather, it's a central element in the Islamic system. The practice is completely in accord with sharia law and with the Koran. In the Koran, Muslim men are allowed up to four wives at one time. Muhammad, however, received a special revelation from Allah permitting him to have as many wives as he wanted. Since Muhammad is considered the perfect man, and the model of proper conduct, there is no theological ground for opposing polygamy. Of course, a great many Muslim men don't practice polygamy, but that's not because the practice is considered improper; it's because many men can't afford to support more than one wife. But it's always a possibility. The standard Egyptian marriage contract contains spaces for the husband to fill in the names of wife number one, two, and three, just in case.

Christianity introduced a revolution in the relationship between men and women. It erased the inequality between the sexes that practices such

---

[334] Tom Witherow, "Website That Helps Muslim Men Find a Second Wife in the UK Has 100,000 Users Despite Bigamy Carrying a Sentence of up to Seven Years in Prison," *Daily Mail*, October 23, 2017, https://www.dailymail.co.uk/news/article-5010691/Website-Muslims-second-wife-100k-users.html.

as polygamy reinforced. And it raised marriage between one man and one woman to the level of a sacrament. Under the influence of Christianity, polygamy became unlawful in the West and in many other parts of the world as well. On the other hand, the faith that Muhammad introduced retained and reinforced the practice by giving it a religious sanction. Moreover, polygamy is no mere relic of the past. With the modern-day resurgence of Islam, the practice is spreading. A Western convert to Islam can be suddenly transported back to a time when a man could rule his household much as a caliph ruled his harem.

Why did Muhammad reject the Christian vision of marriage? A theologian might trace it back to his rejection of the Trinity. Just as the Incarnation elevates our understanding of man, the doctrine of the Trinity elevates our understanding of marriage and family. The shared love between the three persons of the Trinity becomes the model for marriage and family. But there is no such heavenly model in Islam. In Muhammad's book, Allah is a solitary God and must remain so. Thus:

> Believe in God and His apostle and do not say "three." ... God is but one God. God forbid that He should have a Son! (4:171)

The Koran provides no theological basis for understanding marriage as a one-man-one-woman proposition. But theology may not have been the deciding factor. Muhammad may also have had personal motives for preferring polygamy to monogamy. It is very possible that he simply did not want to limit himself to one wife. As mentioned earlier, scholars of Islam designate a number of Muhammad's revelations as "revelations of convenience"—that is, revelations that worked to his personal advantage or helped him to resolve a family conflict. The revelation that allowed him to marry his own daughter-in-law falls into that category, and so does the revelation that permitted him to have an unlimited number of wives (and sex slaves).

But there is yet a third motive that needs to be considered. As numerous scholars have noted, totalitarian systems look upon the traditional two-parent family as a rival. The fear is that family loyalty may take precedence over the "higher" loyalty that one owes to the state. Tyrants know that the bonds of affection that develop in a family may prove stronger than one's allegiance to the ruling ideology, or to Big Brother, or to Dear Leader.

This was certainly the case with Nazism. Through organizations such as the Hitler Youth, the Nazis sought to transfer a child's loyalty from his parents to the state. Likewise, communists looked upon the traditional family as nothing more than a reactionary holdover from the days of bourgeois morality. Communists had no qualms about urging children to act as informants on their parents, and in Stalinist Russia, one such informant—thirteen-year-old Pavlik Morozov—was elevated to the status of a national hero.

As the modern secular state becomes increasingly totalitarian, it also begins to look upon the family as a rival to its aim of achieving complete control over citizens. Thus, the state seeks through various means to undermine the purpose of marriage (e.g., by promoting abortions), and to disrupt the relationship between husband and wife (e.g., by making women financially dependent on the state). Meanwhile, the media—which often acts as an agent of the state—can be counted on to extol unorthodox family arrangements. These days, sitcoms about traditional families are as verboten as cigarette commercials.

It shouldn't be surprising, then, that Islam, which is a totalitarian system par excellence, favors the polygamous family structure. Through sharia law, Islam seeks to control every aspect of an individual's life. As its advocates insist, Islam is not just a religion; it is a complete way of life. Moreover, it's a purpose-driven life. It's meant to be lived in service to the ideology of jihad for the sake of Allah. As Nonie Darwish puts it in *Wholly Different*, "In Islam, after believing in Allah, the number one priority for a Muslim believer is not family; it is jihad." Consequently, "a man who is devoted to his wife and children in a monogamous marriage is a threat to jihad."[335]

---

[335] Darwish, *Wholly Different*, 225, 233.

Darwish argues that the Christian ideal of exclusive and permanent loyalty between man and wife is at odds with the aims of Islam. Marriage so conceived is a rival to the single-minded pursuit of jihad. But a polygamous marriage is not. For one thing, the husband has no obligation to remain loyal to one wife. Just as importantly, a polygamous family by its very nature is riven with internal rivalries. It lacks the organic unity that might allow it to stand as a rival to the ideology of jihad.

According to Darwish and other former Muslims, the structure of polygamous families (combined with the knowledge that one's monogamous marriage can be suddenly transformed into a multiple one) makes for divided loyalties and dysfunctional families. It pits wife against wife, stepbrother against stepbrother, and mother-in-law against daughter-in-law.

In addition, Islamic theology creates rivalries between a husband's current wife or wives and his brides-to-be in paradise. To ensure that Muslim men will never be satisfied with their current wives, they are promised more polygamy with more desirable partners in the next world. Of course, the only surefire way of securing brides in paradise is by committing jihad for the sake of Allah. Thus, as Darwish puts it, "Islam has substituted love of jihad and martyrdom for love of family."[336]

An example of Darwish's observation is provided by Sayfullo Saipov, the jihadist who killed eight people on a New York City bike path in 2017 by running them down with a truck. Saipov is a family man but only in the most limited sense of the term. He has a wife and three children, but he also had jihad on his mind. Unlike the ordinary soldier who hopes to return from the battlefield to rejoin his wife and children, this "soldier of ISIS" was intent on joining his brides in paradise instead. The promise of perfect wives in paradise tends to weaken the ties to one's family here on earth. Moreover, as Muhammad understood, such a promise is an efficient mechanism for ensuring that there will always be an abundant supply of recruits for the jihad.

[336] Ibid., 234.

Not all Muslims are so minded, of course. They are not interested in polygamy or jihad, and they may have their doubts about the existence of the seventy-two virgins. Some Muslim marriages, as Darwish readily admits, "are happy and successful." Some Muslims manage to rise above ideology and to ignore the misogynistic teachings of Islam.

Still, on the whole, Islamic family relations are far more dysfunctional than Western citizens realize. Polygamy is not the only problem. Child marriage is common, and so are forced marriages. In Iran and other Shia Muslim societies, temporary marriage (a form of prostitution) is legal. And 91 percent of all honor violence worldwide is committed by Muslims.[337]

On that subject, Islamic law states that there is no penalty for a father or mother who kills his or her child, and no penalty for a grandfather or grandmother who kills his or her children's children (o1.4).[338] Conversely, a child may kill a parent for the sake of honor. Sons often take part in killing their mothers (or sisters) who have jeopardized family honor in some way or another. In *The Stoning of Soraya M.* (2008) — a film based on a true story — the father and the son of an accused wife and mother are the ones who throw the first stones. In the West Bank, parents deliberately raise their children to become suicide bombers. This also is for the sake of honor, because, as one might expect in a system that revolves around jihad, great honor redounds to the parents of martyrs.

If the Soviets and the Nazis encouraged children to betray their parents, the Islamic system teaches that any family member may be sacrificed by any other family member for the sake of Allah and the jihad. Child against parent, parent against child, husband against wife, brother against sister, wife against wife: it's a sinister system. And it should not be compared to the Christian family ideal.

---

[337] Phyllis Chesler, "Worldwide Trends in Honor Killings," *Middle East Forum* (Spring 2010), https://www.meforum.org/2646/worldwide-trends-in-honor-killings.

[338] *Reliance of the Traveller*, 584.

It's true, of course, that families in Western societies are often troubled and destructive. But in the Christian and post-Christian world, family dysfunction is not a function of Christian values. It's a departure from them. The troubles that afflict modern families are largely the result of acting out the anti-Christian and anti-family values of the secular society.

Christians are far from perfect. They are not immune to folly or to sin. But Christian family values are no more like Islamic values than they are like Nazi family values or Soviet family values. Catholics who draw a false equivalence between the two decidedly different visions of family life represented by Islam and Christianity ought to know better. And they ought to stop doing it.

19

Islamization

"Islamization" is the process by which Islamic values are spread throughout a society. It's happening all around you, but you won't encounter the word very often. That's because the powers that be don't want you to worry your head about it. One of the primary ways in which cultural jihad spreads is through schools — both on the K–12 level and the university level. Muslim activists don't have to be stealthy about influencing schools. Educators welcome them because they see Muslims as a victim group in need of affirmative action.

Europe Is Dying — but Don't Be Alarmed

I read an article, though I can't remember where, which referred to the "end game" in Europe. Was it one of those stories about how the Swedish police are pleading for help because they have lost control of the immigrant crime situation?[339] Or was it a story about the Italian government's plea to the EU for help because the African immigrant situation has spun out of control?[340] No matter. There are, to paraphrase the old TV series,[341] "eight million stories in the naked continent" to choose from. And they all tell a disturbing story.

If you've been following the situation in Europe, you realize that the "end game" could refer to any number of European countries faced with the prospect of Islamization. But for those who haven't been paying attention, the term "end game" must seem strange. Many people in Europe and a great many people in North America don't even know that the game has

---

[339] Nicolai Sennels, "Sweden on the Brink of CIVIL WAR, National Police Chief: 'HELP US, HELP US!'" *Jihad Watch*, June 25, 2017, https://www.jihadwatch.org/2017/06/sweden-on-the-brink-of-civil-war-national-police-chief-help-us-help-us.

[340] Jacob Bojesson, "Italy Threatens to Close Its Ports as Migrant Situation Spirals out of Control," *Daily Caller*, June 28, 2017, https://dailycaller.com/2017/06/28/italy-threatens-to-close-its-ports-as-migrant-situation-spirals-out-of-control/.

[341] *Naked City* was a television crime drama that ran on the ABC network from 1958 to 1959 and from 1960 to 1963, inspired by the 1948 motion picture of the same name.

begun—the game of Islamization, that is. A number of observers of the European scene have been predicting that large parts of Europe will be Islamic in about two decades. Although they supply acres of demographic evidence to make the point, they were until recently largely ignored. It wasn't until the immigration invasion that commenced in 2015 that people began to wake up to something that should have been obvious a decade before. Europe is being transformed into something that is European in name only.

How did a change of such immense proportions fly under the radar for so long?

One of the striking things about Douglas Murray's book *The Strange Death of Europe*[342] is how often he uses the term "no one had predicted" or words to that effect. In particular, he observes, no one had predicted the scale of Third World immigration into Europe, and thus no one was prepared for it.

A few Cassandras, he admits, did predict what would happen, but few paid attention to them. In a 1968 speech, which came to be known as the "Rivers of Blood" speech, Enoch Powell, the Conservative shadow cabinet minister, warned of dire consequences should immigration to Britain continue at its then current rate.

The speech spelled the end of Powell's political career. Yet, as Murray points out, Powell's predictions fell far short of the eventual reality. Nothing in the speech suggests that Powell had foreseen anything of the magnitude of the 1,400 rapes that occurred in the English city of Rotherham at the hands of Pakistani rape gangs over a number of years,[343] much less the 1,200 assaults by North African men that took place outside the Cologne train station in a single night in 2015.[344] Powell hadn't

---

[342] Douglas Murray, *The Strange Death of Europe: Immigration, Identity, Islam* (London: Bloomsbury Continuum, 2017).

[343] "Rotherham Child Abuse Scandal: 1,400 Children Exploited, Report Finds," BBC News, August 26, 2014, https://www.bbc.com/news/uk-england-south-yorkshire-28939089.

[344] Rick Noack, "Leaked Document Says 2,000 Men Allegedly Assaulted 1,200 German Women on New Year's Eve," *Washington Post*, July 11, 2016,

actually used the phrase "rivers of blood," but by 2017 one could speak in a figurative manner of the Mediterranean as a sea of blood. Starting in 2014, an average of 3,000 migrants were drowning each year in the crossing attempt.

Another "prophet of doom" was the French author Jean Raspail, whose 1973 novel *Camp of the Saints*[345] described a mass migration from India to the Mediterranean shores of France. Raspail not only predicted the mass Third World migration to Europe; he also correctly foresaw that a culture steeped in the doctrine of diversity would be unable to resist the invasion. What he got wrong was the magnitude of the migration. He pictured a flotilla of a hundred ships carrying a million people slowly across the Indian Ocean, around the Cape of Good Hope, and through the Straits of Gibraltar. But by 2016, almost twice that number of migrants were entering Europe every year.

Still, Powell and Raspail were far closer to the mark than the multitude of commentators who criticized them. In other words, the best predictors of Europe's future were individuals who were dismissed by their contemporaries as crackpots and alarmists. If you were a betting man, the best bet circa 1970 would have been to place all your money on Europe's biggest alarmists and then double the bet.

Unfortunately, almost fifty years later, there's still time to place your bets. There's a new wave of "alarmists" who, for the last decade or so, have been consistently right about what the spread of Islam spells for Europe. Yet they have been consistently dismissed as extremists.

The new "alarmists" would include Oriana Fallaci, Geert Wilders, Ayaan Hirsi Ali, Thilo Sarrazin, Robert Spencer, Mark Steyn, and Douglas Murray himself. Despite the dead-on accuracy of their assessments and predictions, all of them have been harshly attacked by the establishment

---

https://www.washingtonpost.com/news/worldviews/wp/2016/07/10/leaked-document-says-2000-men-allegedly-assaulted-1200-german-women-on-new-years-eve/.

[345] Jean Raspail, *The Camp of the Saints*, 4th ed. (Petoskey, MI: Social Contract Press, 1994).

media and establishment leaders—in short, by the people who have been dead wrong about almost every aspect of the Islamic problem. Fallaci, Wilders, and Steyn had to endure a series of "heresy" trials, Sarrazin lost his job, Hirsi Ali was forced to leave Holland, Spencer was denied entry to the United Kingdom, and Murray, who writes for the *Sunday Times* and the *Wall Street Journal*, has been branded as a right-wing extremist.

The attempts to silence our contemporary Cassandras help to explain why so many fail to realize that the "game" has begun, let alone that it may be approaching "game over" for some parts of Europe. The case of Robert Spencer is typical. He is one of the world's leading experts on jihad and other aspects of Islam. Yet the powers that be have gone to extreme lengths to shut him up. Catholic bishops have rescinded speaking invitations, the Southern Poverty Law Center has labeled him a "hater," the United Kingdom has denied him entry, Facebook has suspended his account, and Google has made it very difficult to find his popular site online.[346] If you google "jihad," you'll have to wade through numerous Islamic apologist sites before you finally come to Spencer's *Jihad Watch*. If a lot of people in the West don't realize how serious the Islamization problem has become, it's because the establishment elites don't want them to know.

Many in the West remain complacent about Islam's rising tide because they rely on the assurances of people who have been consistently wrong about Islam and immigration. Meanwhile, they are being denied access to the opinions of the people who have been reliably right—the so-called alarmists. It's a dangerous state of affairs because when alarming things are happening, you need someone to sound the alarm. And then you need to pay attention to what they say.

The trouble with the original Cassandra was not that her predictions were wrong. On the contrary, all of what she said came to pass. The tragedy was that no one listened to her.

---

[346] Robert Spencer, "Google Deep-Sixes Jihad Watch," *Jihad Watch*, July 1, 2017, https://www.jihadwatch.org/2017/07/google-deep-sixes-jihad-watch.

Islamization in the Schools

While jihadists across the globe are busy slitting throats, American school-children are being taught that jihad is an "inner struggle" and Islam means "peace." While Muslim rape gangs destroy the lives of teenage girls in England, American teenagers learn that Muhammad was a champion of women's rights. And although American students are taught all the gruesome details of the Atlantic slave trade, they learn little if anything about the Arab slave trade, which took many more lives.

If Islam is part of the curriculum in your child's school — and it probably is[347] — you can be almost certain that it is treated in a deferential fashion. If the prepackaged materials that your child's school uses look as though they were vetted by a committee of Muslim apologists, they probably were. And if you notice that your boy or girl is practicing Arabic calligraphy, don't worry. He or she is just writing that "there is no God but Allah, and Muhammad is his messenger."

If your child is in college, it will be more of the same — more indoctrination about Islam's peaceful nature, its many contributions to the arts and to science, and the victimization of its followers at the hands of Christian imperialists. Your child will also learn to get used to special prayer rooms for Muslims, special bathroom facilities, and sex-segregated pools and gymnasiums. If your child happens to be enrolled at Oregon

---

[347] "Islamic Indoctrination in American Schools."

State University, he or she will be asked not to eat in "shared spaces" during Ramadan to avoid offending Muslims.[348]

It doesn't matter if your child attends a Catholic school or college, as Catholic schools are as likely as their secular counterparts to run interference for Islam. Your second-grader might be reading *My Muslim Friend*[349]—a Pauline Press book that depicts Muslims as more devout than most Catholics. Your high school student, meanwhile, will learn that Islam gently "expanded" into neighboring territories, when, in fact, Islamic forces ruthlessly conquered them. What your child won't hear is anything critical of this religion of peace. Catholic teachers who question the nobility of the "Prophet" risk losing their jobs.

It's not just what's taught in the classroom that ought to concern parents. Numerous Catholic colleges have declared that they stand in solidarity with Islam, and others make a point of celebrating International Hijab Day. Some Catholic high schools and colleges even have special prayer rooms set aside for Muslim students. For example, Saint Ambrose University in Iowa recently opened a sex-segregated prayer room for Muslim students, complete with sinks for ritual foot-washing.[350]

Islamic indoctrination in public and Catholic schools is far more extensive than you might think. But don't feel bad if all this is news to you. Adults who don't have children in school don't usually keep tabs on what goes on inside school buildings. And even parents with children

---

[348] Robert Spencer, "Oregon State University: Students Asked Not to Eat in 'Shared Spaces' During Ramadan So as to Avoid Offending Muslims," *Jihad Watch*, June 5, 2018, https://www.jihadwatch.org/2018/06/oregon-state-university-students-asked-not-to-eat-in-shared-spaces-during-ramadan-so-as-to-avoid-offending-muslims.

[349] Donna Jean Kemmetmueller, *My Muslim Friend: A Young Catholic Learns about Islam* (Boston: Pauline Books & Media, 2006).

[350] Robert Spencer, "Catholic University in Iowa Opens Sex-Segregated Prayer Space for Muslim Students," *Jihad Watch*, May 10, 2018, https://www.jihadwatch.org/2018/05/catholic-university-in-iowa-opens-sex-segregated-prayer-space-for-muslim-students.

still in school generally don't know the details of the curriculum. Much of what happens in school is *terra incognita* for parents.

For proof, consider that for many decades, the vast majority of parents had no idea what was being taught under the rubric of sex education. When they did find out, it was a bit too late. The damage had already been done.

Why didn't they try harder to find out? For one thing, most couldn't imagine that what was being offered to their sons and daughters was as outrageous and obscene as it actually was. For another, they trusted the teachers. Teachers were, and still are, assumed to be caring professionals who would never put children at risk.

That's true of many teachers, but the educational establishment in America leans heavily to the left. And it's the establishment, not the teacher, that sets the curriculum. The educational leadership — the administrations, the teachers' unions, and the schools of education that train teachers — is composed in large part of left-liberal ideologues. Moreover, the people directly involved in sex education are often individuals who have a personal stake in destroying sexual norms.

Much of the sexual-revolution agenda was being pushed on middle-school students long before it was accepted by the general public. Subjective morality? Recreational sex? Gay "marriage"? Transgenderism? It was the schools, not the courts, that paved the way. Much of the left's culture war against traditional morality[351] was initially waged in the classroom — and almost always without parental knowledge or consent.

So, it shouldn't come as a surprise that the same people who sexualized American children without parental knowledge now feel no qualms about Islamizing them.

If this is difficult to believe, consider three points:

1. When it comes to controversial subjects, educators don't want you to know what they're doing. Students are sometimes told not to bring home sensitive materials.

---

[351] Kilpatrick, *Why Johnny Can't Tell Right from Wrong.*

2. In the West, Islam is spread mainly through cultural jihad, and schools—from kindergarten through college—are one of the main venues in which the cultural jihadists operate. There are, for example, about six hundred chapters of the Muslim Student Association—a Muslim Brotherhood–linked organization—spread across North American colleges.

3. A tacit, and sometimes not-so-tacit, alliance has long existed between leftists and Islamists. Leftists see Islamists as natural allies in their war to defeat Judeo-Christian values. Thus, left-leaning governments in Europe routinely arrest critics of Islam, while left-leaning media corporations routinely censor them. Meanwhile, left-leaning universities hire radical-minded Islamists while denying a platform to Islam-critical speakers. Not surprisingly, left-leaning educrats share in this pro-Islam bias.

The leftist elites don't care if Islamization spells the end of our culture. That's what they want also. So the steady incremental Islamization in schools will proceed apace with little opposition, just as did the sexualization of the students. It will proceed apace because most parents can't imagine that their local schools would cooperate in advancing the Islamic agenda while belittling the Western Christian heritage. For many parents, the first indication that something is wrong will come when, at some future point, their daughter returns from school wearing the mandatory hijab.

As I've noted, Catholic schools aren't immune to this lemming-like impulse to take the leap of faith into the wild blue multicultural yonder. Catholic teachers are trained, for the most part, in the same institutions as their secular counterparts. Moreover, what's taught in most Catholic schools of education doesn't differ a whit from what's taught at the local state teachers' college. For the most part, the Catholic universities that prepare teachers subscribe to the same theories, methods, and assumptions that prevail in secular colleges.

All of this wouldn't matter as much if bishops were doing their job of teaching and shepherding. But the bishops, who have ultimate authority over diocesan schools, are still caught up in the Vatican II–era fantasy that Catholicism and Islam are just two sides of the same coin. They can't be counted on to correct the schools because they share those same naïve assumptions about the Islamic faith. In short, the bishops look at Islam through rose-colored spectacles. When the wolf in sheep's clothing shows up at the schoolhouse door, all they see is a sheep and an opportunity to extend a warm welcome.

Schools are arguably the chief facilitators of Islamization in America. Under the guise of multicultural studies and anti-bullying curricula, students are taught a whitewashed version of Islam that will leave them unprepared to recognize or resist stealth jihad when they grow older. The classroom has already been used to indoctrinate students to accept the left's radical sexual agenda. There is good reason to believe that schools are now being turned into centers of Islamic indoctrination.

If you still find this difficult to entertain, consider that the Saudis have long been heavily invested in shaping America's perception of Islam. A 2004 report by Harvard researcher Sandra Stotsky and a 2005 four-part investigative report by the Jewish Telegraphic Agency (JTA), revealed that after 9/11 the Saudi government ramped up attempts to introduce Islam-friendly materials into K–12 schools. According to the JTA, "Saudi Arabia is paying to influence the teaching of American public-school children.... These materials praise and sometimes promote Islam, but criticize Judaism and Christianity."[352] Massive gifts to Harvard and Georgetown—used to develop the curriculum materials—gave credibility to the tendentious programs. Rudy Giuliani may have turned down Saudi money when he was was mayor of New York, but academia has been happy to accept it.

Still doubtful? Then take a look across the Atlantic, where the art of Islamizing schools is a bit further advanced. A series of investigations in 2014 by the London *Telegraph* revealed that "there is indeed an organized

---

[352] Stanley Kurtz, "Saudi in the Classroom," *National Review*, July 25, 2007, https://www.nationalreview.com/2007/07/saudi-classroom-stanley-kurtz/.

group of Muslim teachers, education consultants, school governors, and activists dedicated to furthering what one of them describes as an 'Islamizing agenda' in Birmingham schools."[353] In short, the paper had uncovered a broad-based conspiracy by Muslims to take over the schools in a major English city. The plot, to which the conspirators gave the rather obvious code name "Trojan Horse," involved removing secular head teachers and replacing them with radical Muslim staff, segregating classrooms by putting girls in the back, and introducing Islamic prayers. More than twenty-one schools were targeted in Birmingham, and similar plots were uncovered in Bradford, Manchester, and parts of east London.[354]

Most Americans would find it hard to imagine that the situation in Birmingham could ever come to our shores. But if you remember your Shakespeare, Macbeth was convinced that Birnam Wood could never come to his castle at high Dunsinane Hill. But it did, nevertheless.

That's a pretty loose analogy, but since *Macbeth* takes place in the British Isles and since Birnam and Birmingham share six letters in common, it's close enough for our purposes. As you may recall, Malcolm's conquering army comes to Dunsinane Hill by means of stealth and camouflage. And it's by stealth that Islamists plan to Islamize the United States. Unfortunately, it doesn't take too much stealth to fool people who have been taught to believe that "Islam" means "peace" and that "jihad" is "interior struggle." The left, meanwhile, is providing plenty of camouflage.

No matter how many soldiers we send to fight in the Middle East, the main battle in the clash of civilizations is being waged in America's classrooms.

---

[353] Andrew Gilligan, "Muslim Extremists, and a Worrying Lesson for Us All," *Telegraph*, March 7, 2014, https://www.telegraph.co.uk/education/10700041/Muslim-extremists-and-a-worrying-lesson-for-us-all.html.

[354] Graeme Paton and Andrew Gilligan, "Head Teachers Raise 'Serious Concerns' over Islamic School Take-Over," *Telegraph*, May 14, 2014, https://www.telegraph.co.uk/education/educationnews/10804289/Head-teachers-raise-serious-concerns-over-Islamic-school-take-over.html.

20

Can Islam Be Reformed?

Surprisingly, Islam has already undergone a reformation. By the middle of the last century, large parts of the Muslim world were becoming Westernized and secularized. Then, starting with the Iranian Revolution of 1979, Islam underwent another reform—a reform that attempted to return Islam to its original supremacist form. Is there any chance that Islam can once again become more moderate? Read on for some answers.

Are the "Vast Majority" of Muslims Moderate?

It's often said that the vast majority of Muslims are moderate. But as the newspapers like to remind us about other matters, this is asserted "without any evidence." In fact, what evidence we do have suggests that it's a dubious proposition.

Where, exactly, do all these moderate Muslims live?

Would it be in Chechnya, where authorities have set up concentration camps for gays?[355] And where eight hundred thousand Muslims rallied in 2015 to protest the *Charlie Hebdo* Muhammad cartoons?[356] Try to get that many Muslims together for an anti-ISIS rally.

Would it be in Pakistan, where one hundred thousand turned out for the funeral of an assassin?[357] The assassin had murdered an official who

---

[355] Robert Spencer, "Muslim Chechnya Opens First Concentration Camp for Homosexuals Since Hitler," *Jihad Watch*, April 10, 2017, https://www.jihadwatch.org/2017/04/muslim-chechnya-opens-first-concentration-camp-for-homosexuals-since-hitler.

[356] Robert Spencer, "Chechnya: 800,000 Muslims Protest Muhammad Cartoons; Protests Also in Iran, Pakistan, Ingushetia, Elsewhere," *Jihad Watch*, January 20, 2015, https://www.jihadwatch.org/2015/01/chechnya-800000-muslims-protest-muhammad-cartoons-protests-also-in-iran-pakistan-ingushetia-elsewhere.

[357] Terry Firma, "'I Am Qadri': 100,000 Pakistani Muslims Attend Assassin's Funeral, Admiring His Butchery," *Friendly Atheist*, March 4, 2016, https://friendlyatheist.patheos.com/2016/03/04/i-am-qadri-100000-pakistani-muslims-attend-assassins-funeral-admiring-his-butchery/.

had called for an end to the blasphemy laws. Numerous Islamist groups warned people not to attend the official's funeral or even to pray for his soul.

Would it be in Saudi Arabia, where amputations are conducted on a regular basis in public squares and where public beheadings are not uncommon? The last time something like that happened in the West was during the French Revolution.

How about the West Bank? In the West Bank, streets, parks, squares, and schools are named after "martyrs" who are honored for having killed Jewish men, women, and children. In the West Bank, it's considered cute to dress up three-year-olds in suicide bomb belts. Meanwhile, in schools and on government-run television, children are taught that killing Jews is life's highest calling.

Maybe Morocco? The home of *Casablanca* and Rick's Café? Sorry. An ADL global survey found that 80 percent of Moroccans harbor anti-Semitic views[358]—which isn't that bad when you compare it with Algeria (87 percent) and Iraq (92 percent).

Could the blessed land of moderation be Afghanistan? Only if you discount the tradition of child marriage and the popular form of entertainment called *bacha bazi*. The *bacha bazi* are teen and preteen boys who are dressed as girls, forced to dance for men, and then passed around for sexual purposes. As for the government, the hardline Taliban who once ruled Afghanistan are likely to rule it again. They can hardly be considered moderates. On the other hand, they did try to do away with the custom of *bacha bazi*.

Egypt? There must be moderates in Egypt. Well, yes, there are. Egypt's leader, President el-Sisi, has called for a reformation of Islam, and there are others of like mind. On the other hand, a 2013 Pew public opinion

---

[358] Joshua Levitt, "ADL Global Survey Finds 'Anti-Semitic Attitudes Are Persistent, Pervasive Around the World'; West Bank, Gaza Highest Scores," *Algemeiner*, May 13, 2014, https://www.algemeiner.com/2014/05/13/adl-global-survey-finds-anti-semitic-attitudes-are-persistent-pervasive-around-the-world-west-bank-gaza-highest-scores/.

poll of Egyptians found that 70 percent supported whipping and amputation for thieves, 81 percent supported stoning of adulterers, and 86 percent supported the death penalty for apostates.[359] President el-Sisi has his work cut out for him.

Turkey? For many decades, Turkey was indeed a more moderate Muslim nation. The burqa was banned, and the imams were put in their place. Turkey's current president, Recep Erdogan, however, seems determined to recreate the Ottoman caliphate in Turkey. He has, for example, built a 1,100-room palace for himself, complete with guards in Ottoman-era uniforms. Recently, he has threatened to flood Europe with hundreds of thousands of Muslim refugees.[360]

How about Iran? In Iran, large crowds led by Iranian officials regularly congregate to call for "death to Israel" and "death to America." A great many Iranians, including all of the leadership, are awaiting the return of the Twelfth Imam, who disappeared in the ninth century and is believed to exist in an occult state. It is widely believed that the "Mahdi" can be awakened from his trance only by cataclysmic events—which may be one of the reasons the Iranian leaders are so eager to acquire nuclear weapons.

Indonesia? Barack Obama has fond memories of his schooldays in once moderate Indonesia. But times change. According to a Gatestone Institute report, Indonesia is waging jihad on Christian churches.[361] Mobs of Muslims—sometimes several hundred strong—frequently attack and burn churches. In many cases, the police are complicit, and instead of arresting perpetrators, local authorities call for the demolition of more

---

[359] Pew Research Center, "The World's Muslims: Religion, Politics and Society," April 30, 2013, https://www.pewforum.org/2013/04/30/the-worlds-muslims-religion-politics-society-beliefs-about-sharia/.

[360] Laura Pitel and Arthur Beesley, "Erdogan Threatens to Let 3m Refugees into Europe," *Financial Times*, November 25, 2016, https://www.ft.com/content/c5197e60-b2fc-11e6-9c37-5787335499a0.

[361] Raymond Ibrahim, "The Indonesian Jihad on Christian Churches," Gatestone Institute, November 11, 2015, https://www.gatestoneinstitute.org/6860/indonesian-christian-churches.

churches. Meanwhile, Islamic leaders issue text messages saying: "We will not stop hunting Christians and burning churches. Christians are Allah's enemies!"[362]

Iran? Syria? Libya? Somalia? Yemen? Where do the supposedly vast majority of moderate Muslims reside? Or do they reside only in the imaginations of hopeful Westerners?

Perhaps what people really mean when they say that the vast majority of Muslims are moderate is that the vast majority are nonviolent. Like most people everywhere, most Muslims, one supposes, would prefer to go about their daily business rather than get involved in the bloody business of attacking and killing people and possibly being killed in the process. But this natural human propensity to avoid risky behavior should not be confused with moderation.

Moreover, the general inclination toward extremist beliefs and practices in Muslim societies makes it more likely that Muslims will turn violent when the time and circumstances are right. It's a good bet that the individuals who make up the mobs of church burners in Indonesia spend the majority of their lives in nonviolent pursuits. They are peaceful until they are not.

It's worth remembering that there have been numerous instances in which once-friendly Muslims turned against their Christian neighbors in Indonesia, Syria, and Iraq once it became safe to do so.

The notion that the vast majority of Muslims are moderate needs to be taken with a grain of salt. It's not based on any evidence, and it creates a host of unrealistic expectations. Most of all, it leaves us unprepared for those times when, in obedience to their faith, once "moderate" Muslims turn immoderate.

[362] Ibid.

Losing Their Religion

From time to time, readers of my articles will ask: "What do you want to do — go to war with 1.7 billion Muslims?" The question implies that any criticism of Islam will force the members of this "peaceful religion" to respond with massive violence.

More or less the same argument was used during the Cold War. A great many people, including some of my relatives, took the view that we (the United States) shouldn't say or do anything to upset the Soviets; otherwise all hell would break loose. Yet when one president challenged the Soviets over Cuba, and another challenged them to tear down the Berlin Wall, the end result was not the end of the world but the end of the Soviet Union.

For the record, I have never advocated going to war with 1.7 billion Muslims, although I have from time to time stressed the importance of having a strong military and being willing to use it if necessary, and — of equal importance — conveying that willingness to potential enemies.

For the most part, however, my emphasis has been on winning the culture war with Islam using cultural rather than military weapons. If Islam wins the culture war — and currently it is winning — it won't need AK-47s, mortars, and nuclear warheads. There aren't any Islamic armies in Europe, but many parts of Europe are slowly submitting to Islam precisely because postmodern Europeans lack cultural confidence. Lacking it, they lack the will to resist.

How do you fight a culture war? Well, primarily with the conviction that you're right and they're wrong. This doesn't require chest-thumping and flag-waving, but it does require firmness, resolution, and willpower. It also requires a willingness to undermine your opponent's convictions. The Cold War victory came about in large part because communists lost faith in their own ideology. They also lost it, in part, because of various economic and diplomatic pressures applied by the West.

In a similar way, the West and its non-Western allies should aim to weaken the faith of Muslims. This may sound like a cruel thing to do, and if, as some say, Islam is the moral equivalent of Christianity and Judaism, then it would be a cruel thing. However, if Islam is a cruel and oppressive system, then a weakening of the system would benefit many, if not most, Muslims.

Inducing a loss of faith in Islam? This might seem to belong in the "impossible dream" category. It may seem impossible, but consider that it has already happened—and not that long ago.

Historian Raymond Ibrahim provides a lucid account of the Muslim world's loss of faith in *Crucified Again*. It was never a complete loss, but due to the influence of European colonial powers, many Muslims lost their confidence in the Islamic way. It began, writes Ibrahim, with the invasion and subjugation of Egypt by Napoleon in 1798. Subsequent conquests and colonization by European powers convinced many Muslims that Islam was no match for the West. The obvious military, technological, economical, educational, and political superiority of the West created doubts about Islam's claim to be the supreme way of life. Thus,

> Muslims ... began to emulate the West in everything from politics and government to everyday dress and etiquette. The Islamic way, the Sharia, was the old, failed way. Thus during the colonial era and into the mid-twentieth century, all things distinctly Islamic—from Islam's clerics to the woman's "hijab," or headscarf—were increasingly seen by Muslims as relics of a

backward age, to be shunned. Most "Muslims" were Muslim in name only.[363]

Yet, just when it appeared that Muslims were finally breaking free of Islam, Islam came back with a vengeance. As Gandalf was drawn into the Balrog's realm by the last lash of the monster's whip, Muslims were drawn back into fundamentalist sharia Islam.

However, that's another story for another time. Let's focus instead on the earlier lapse of faith, when Islam was losing its hold on the Muslim world. Are there any lessons for us? Can Islam be defanged again? The essential point to keep in mind is that the Islamic world has already suffered a loss of faith. It's not far-fetched to think that it can happen again. On the other hand, those who think it impossible to induce a loss of faith among Muslims will never try. This also holds for those who think such a strategy is too dangerous or too politically incorrect. They will gain nothing because they will venture nothing.

Let's address the objection that it's futile to hope for such a profound transformation in belief. Many people believe that deeply rooted beliefs are nearly impossible to change, but, in fact, history is full of examples to the contrary. For instance, in a relatively short time, the civil rights movement managed to overturn what were thought to be deeply held racial prejudices. Although prejudices still linger in America, practically no American today would accept the legitimacy of segregated buses, water fountains, and lunch counters, which was once taken for granted in the Jim Crow South.

Another example? Forty years ago, Ireland was often cited as one of the most Catholic countries on the planet. The Faith seemed as deeply rooted in Ireland as a faith could be. Yet, in recent years, the Irish have decisively voted against the Church on the issues of homosexual "marriage" and abortion. In short, a great many Irish appear to have jettisoned their "deeply rooted" faith.

---

[363] Raymond Ibrahim, *Crucified Again: Exposing Islam's New War on Christians* (Washington, DC: Regnery Publishing, 2013), 10.

Therefore, it's not inevitable that the Muslim world must remain deeply committed to Islam. As the history of the past century demonstrates, Turks, Egyptians, and Iraqis are just as capable as the Irish of watering down their deeply held beliefs.

Having established that it can be done, the next question is, should it be done? Do we have any right to attempt to undermine deeply held beliefs? This is probably the key question for many in the West. After decades of immersion in relativism, multiculturalism, and moral equivalence, many adults are afraid to challenge the shallowly held beliefs of their three-year-olds, let alone the deeply held beliefs of the "sacred" other. If the only value you admire is tolerance, it will be practically impossible to challenge and resist Islamic beliefs and practices that run counter to Western values. Yet, at the present moment, "challenge and resist" is exactly what we must do.

Why can't we just take a live-and-let-live attitude toward other religions? Well, in the case of most religions, this is probably best. The trouble is, Islam is not a live-and-let-live type of religion. It's more of a convert-or-die type (or, to be completely accurate, convert, pay the jizya, or die).

The reason we can't take a relaxed view of Islam is that Islam is an aggressive religion. However James Bondish it may sound, the mission of Islam is to conquer the world for Allah, but—to reiterate a point that is often missed—not necessarily by force. I can't remember the exact figure, but the Saudi government has spent a staggering sum over the last few decades on the building of mosques and madrassas all over the world, and on the preparation of imams and teachers to staff them.

Islamic mosques, schools, activist organizations, websites, and governments (Turkey, Iran, Qatar, and Saudi Arabia are the best examples) are working 24/7 to spread Islam. As a simple matter of self-defense, non-Muslim societies ought to work to counter this forward momentum—if not by calling Islamic beliefs into question, at least by making the case for their own.

Fortunately, almost no one is a complete relativist. Most people could see the importance of undermining Nazi ideology during World War II.

Likewise, most of us feel that it's legitimate to challenge the deeply held beliefs of racists. During the Cold War, our government, in collaboration with other governments, sought to discredit communist ideology, and the Vatican at various times has challenged both Nazi and communist ideology.

How to Undermine Belief in Islam

Assuming that one is willing to sow the seeds of doubt in the minds of one's opponents, the next question is, how does one do it? Although fundamental changes can sometimes occur as a result of slow "evolutionary" processes, it's usually the case that someone is working hard to create the changes. The rapid erosion of faith in Ireland was not the result of random mutations and natural selection. It was the result of a deliberate campaign to undercut the influence of the Catholic Church (aided, admittedly, by a series of scandals within the Church in Ireland). Likewise, the secularization and Westernization of Muslim countries in the last century was not a matter of chance. For example, Mustafa Ataturk in Turkey and the Shah in Iran launched highly successful campaigns for minimizing the influence of Islam on the populace.

Obviously, the West has no direct control over any Muslim nation as did Ataturk and the Shah. On the other hand, the West had no direct control over the Soviet Union or its Eastern European satellite countries, yet it managed to wage a successful campaign to discredit Soviet communism.

Embarking on such a campaign requires planning, and planning requires thinking. During the later stages of the Cold War, President Ronald Reagan and Pope Saint John Paul II worked together to undermine communism.[364] Both men had thought long and hard about communism so

---

[364] See Paul Kengor, *A Pope and a President: John Paul II, Ronald Reagan, and the Extraordinary Untold Story of the 20th Century* (Wilmington, DE: ISI Books, 2017).

both had a clear sense of their opponents' weakness and a clear sense of what had to be done and how far they could go.

That clarity was missing during the Obama administration in regard to Islam, but there are signs that it is now returning. On July 22, 2018, Secretary of State Mike Pompeo delivered a positively Reaganesque speech on Iran policy at—where else?—the Reagan Library.[365] Speaking to an audience that included many members of the Iranian-American community, he outlined a plan to "deny the Iranian leadership the resources, the wealth, the funds, the capacity to continue to foment terrorism around the world and to deny the people inside of Iran the freedom they so richly deserve."

Significantly, he used the word "campaign" six times—twice to describe the Iranian regime's "campaign of ideologically motivated violence," and four times to describe the administration's "diplomatic and financial pressure campaign to cut off the funds that the regime uses to enrich itself and support death and destruction."

Again, significantly, he also indicated that the desired changes need not take forever: "I always remind those who think it's not possible or think the time horizon will be measured in centuries not hours, I always remind them that things change." Moreover, he pointed out that people with a plan will know how to take advantage of "disjunctive moments ... when things happen that are unexpected, unanticipated."

Pompeo's address shows a thorough understanding of Muslim and Middle Eastern respect for strength, but it goes beyond that. Although the campaign he outlined is mostly diplomatic and financial in nature, he also paid attention to ideology. His talk has a cultural and religious component—one that takes particular advantage of Iranian dissatisfaction with the mullahs and ayatollahs. During the recent mass protests in Iran, a number of slogans were aimed at religious leaders—for example, "The people are paupers, while the mullahs live like gods." In his speech,

---

[365] Mike Pompeo, "Supporting Iranian Voices," U.S. Department of State, July 22, 2018, https://www.state.gov/supporting-iranian-voices/.

Pompeo referred to "intolerant, black-robed enforcers." He also revealed that a number of ayatollahs (who "seem more concerned with riches than religion") have become fabulously wealthy. For example, Supreme Leader Ayatollah Khamenei "has his own personal off-the-books hedge fund … worth $95 billion, with a B."

This is not a direct criticism of Islam, but it does serve to weaken trust in the guardians of the religion, which, in turn, often leads to a weakening of faith in the religion itself. Catholics have some experience of this phenomenon. Studies have shown that the fall-off in church attendance following the revelation of the priestly sex-abuse scandals was greatest in those areas hardest hit by the scandals (e.g., Massachusetts).[366] But if one cared to make an issue of it, anecdotal evidence suggests that imams and mullahs are far more prone to abusive behavior than Catholic priests.

Our Responsibility to Criticize Islam

A commonplace has emerged among media and political elites that criticism of Islam or even of radical Islam will serve only to drive moderate Muslims into the radical camp.

That argument should be questioned because it can just as easily be that lack of criticism has led to the rebirth of militant Islam. Far from being critical of Islam, Western governments, media, academia, and even churches have bent over backwards to claim that all the atrocities committed in the name of Islam have nothing to do with Islam. Indeed, the Western media have adopted a rigid system of self-censorship that keeps them from admitting that these atrocities are, in fact, committed in the name of Islam.

The latest example is the reporting on the assassination of a Russian ambassador by a Turkish policeman. Almost the first words out of the

---

[366] Mark Silk, "Explaining Religious Decline in the Northeast," Religious News Service, January 5, 2015, https://religionnews.com/2015/01/05/explaining-religious-decline-northeast/.

assassin's mouth after the shooting were: "We are those who have given a pledge of allegiance to Muhammad that we will carry on jihad."[367] If you don't remember him saying that, it's because that part of the statement was omitted from almost all news and television reports. Apparently, our betters in the media were afraid that if we were aware of the man's devotion to Muhammad, we might say something provocative that would turn untold numbers of peaceful Muslims into bomb-throwing jihadists.

Perhaps the prime example of the wages of silence is the current crisis in Europe. Islamic terrorists have declared war on Europe, and the result has been a series of deadly attacks—at airports, subways, cafés, concert halls, and, most recently, Christmas markets. All this mayhem is the indirect result of ignorance about Islam—an ignorance that, in turn, is the result of an almost complete blackout of news unfavorable to Islam.

Anyone with a thorough understanding of Islamic culture and religion could have predicted that, even without the 2015–2016 flood of Muslim migrants, the steady flow of Muslim immigrants over the years would create a combustible situation. The amazing thing is that the consequences of this massive migration were never discussed—except in glowing terms. Just about the only thing allowed to be said about the migrants was that they would solve labor shortages, refill welfare coffers, and bring cultural enrichment to Europe.

That was the official line. Anyone who deviated from it could expect censure, possible job loss, or even a criminal trial. Say something negative about Muslim immigration on your Facebook page, and you would be visited by police. Say it in public, and you would receive a court summons. It didn't matter if you were a famous writer (Oriana Fallaci),[368] the president of the Danish Free Press Society (Lars Hedegaard), or a popular

---

[367] Robert Spencer, "Killer of Ambassador: 'We Are Those Who Have Given a Pledge of Allegiance to Muhammad That We Will Carry on Jihad,'" *Jihad Watch*, December 20, 2016.

[368] Associated Press, "Trial of Author Oriani Fallaci, Charged with Defaming Islam, Open in Italy," *USA Today*, June 12, 2006), http://usatoday30.usatoday.com/life/books/news/2006-06-12-fallaci-trial_x.htm.

member of the Dutch parliament (Geert Wilders).[369] If you couldn't say something nice about Islam, you shouldn't say anything at all.

In the European case, the idea that criticizing Islam will create an army of radicals doesn't hold up. Criticism of Islam is essentially a crime in many parts of Europe and has been for a long time. In Europe, few dared criticize Islam, but the radicals came anyway. More than anything else, it was silence that allowed Islamization and radicalization to spread through France, Germany, Belgium, the Netherlands, and Sweden.

Practically no one spoke up about no-go zones, sharia courts, polygamy, and forced marriages, refusal to integrate, crime waves, and the rape epidemic. Now that many are finally beginning to speak out, it may be too late to avoid capitulation (Sweden's likely fate) or bloody conflict (more likely in France).

The very argument that criticism of Islam will drive moderates into the radical camp suggests that criticism is needed. If Islam is such a hair-trigger religion that the slightest offense might radicalize adherents, there is something radically wrong with the religion itself. We don't worry that criticizing Catholicism is going to produce angry Catholic mobs rampaging through the streets. We don't fear that one wrong word is going to cause a young Southern Baptist to strap on a suicide belt.

Islam invites criticism. Given its bloody past and present, it would be highly irresponsible not to subject it to a searching analysis and critique. Such a critique would aim not at alienating Muslims (although some will inevitably be alienated) but at alerting likely victims of jihad.

One of the basics that non-Muslims need to know is that Islam divides the world in two—the House of Islam, and the House of War (all non-Islamic societies). And every Muslim is expected to do his part to make the House of War submit to the House of Islam. Europeans are now experiencing a don't-know-what-hit-me sense of bewilderment because they never learned this basic fact about Islam.

---

[369] Mark Steyn, "The Absurd Trial of Geert Wilders," *Maclean's*, February 18, 2010, https://www.macleans.ca/general/the-absurd-trial-of-geert-wilders/.

One reason for our reluctance to analyze and criticize Islam (an idea) is that such criticism seems tantamount to criticizing Muslims (a people). Unfortunately, even if that is not the intention, it is often the result. A person can't separate himself entirely from his beliefs, and, consequently, we take criticism of our religion personally. That's a good reason for presenting the critique as tactfully as possible. But it's not a good reason for offering no critique at all.

If you can't criticize a belief system because it would hurt the feelings of people who subscribe to that system, then we were wrong to criticize Nazism, communism, and Japanese imperialism. Ordinarily, we refrain from criticizing other religions. Such a live-and-let-live approach is generally sensible, but when the other religion takes the attitude that you must either convert, submit, or die, then live-and-let-live is no longer an option. That is the position that we are in with regard to Islam. And it is suicidal to pretend that things are otherwise.

21

Free Speech and Media Bias

As I suggested in the previous section, we have a responsibility to criticize Islam. But others think differently. A great many in government, in the media, in big tech, and even in the Church believe we should never criticize Islam. But that gives the Islamic world no incentive to change, and it leaves the rest of us in the dark. In the following pages I explore the various ways in which the media massages the news about Islam.

The Francis-Friendly Media

When the first sex-abuse scandal broke in 2002, the secular media carried a lot of anti-Catholic commentary. Popular columnists such as Maureen Dowd and Christopher Hitchens savaged the Church with gusto.

By contrast, media coverage of the current abuse crisis in the Church has been rather restrained. Take the treatment of the February 2019 Vatican summit on sex abuse. The reporting was not all sunshine and roses, but it could have been much harsher.

For example, there was relatively little coverage of Pope Francis's role in ignoring or covering up for abuse. A recent allegation that Francis knew about the abuse of students at Catholic schools for the deaf in Italy and Argentina, but apparently took no action, was not widely reported.[370]

Had it been so minded, the media also could have exploited the case of Bishop Gustavo Zanchetta, who was protected and promoted by Francis despite repeated allegations that Zanchetta had abused seminarians in Argentina. A Fox News headline proclaimed: "Argentine Bishop Case Overshadows Pope's Sex Summit."[371] But other media outlets seemed

---

[370] Associated Press, "Argentina Probes Sex Abuse at Deaf School, What Vatican Knew," *Crux*, December 24, 2016, https://cruxnow.com/global-church/2016/12/argentina-probes-sex-abuse-deaf-school-vatican-knew/.

[371] Nicole Winfield, "Argentine Bishop's Case Overshadows Pope's Sex Abuse Summit," Fox News, February 24, 2019, https://www.foxnews.com/world/argentine-bishops-case-overshadows-popes-sex-abuse-summit.print.

less interested in the story than Fox. If they were truly determined to put Francis on the spot, the Zanchetta story provided the perfect occasion. Yet the coverage was either minimal or restrained.

The truth is that the media prefers not to put Francis in an awkward position. Although the largely liberal media is no more a friend of the Catholic Church than it was in 2002, it sees Francis as a fellow liberal who will champion the "right" causes and who will nudge the Church in a more "progressive" direction.

Another opportunity to "bash" Francis came in the form of the controversial 2019 book titled *In the Closet of the Vatican: Power, Homosexuality, Hypocrisy* by Frederic Martel, a gay French sociologist. But once again, the secular media decided to forgo the pleasure of going after the pope. To the extent that columnists discussed the book, they tended to adopt the author's own ideological view—namely, that the problem in the Vatican was not homosexuality per se, but rather a virulent homophobia among conservative clergy that forces gay priests into leading unhealthy double lives. According to Martel, Pope Francis is really the hero of the story because he fights the "rigidity" behind which, in the pope's words, "there is always something hidden, in many cases a double life."[372]

In his review of Martel's book, columnist Andrew Sullivan, who is also gay, adopts the same line of reasoning. He writes:

> The only tiny consolation of the book is the knowledge that we now have a pope—with all his flaws—who knows what he's dealing with, and has acted, quite ruthlessly at times, to demote, defrock, or reassign the most egregious cases to places where they have close to nothing to do.[373]

---

[372] Frederic Martel, *In the Closet of the Vatican: Power, Homosexuality, Hypocrisy* (London: Bloomsbury Continuum, 2019).

[373] Andrew Sullivan, "The Corruption of the Vatican's Gay Elite Has Been Exposed," *Intelligencer*, February 22, 2019, https://nymag.com/intelligencer/2019/02/andrew-sullivan-the-vaticans-corruption-has-been-exposed.html.

Donald Cozzens followed suit in the *National Catholic Reporter* by observing:

> What puts these prelates [rigid, orthodox homophobic prelates who are actually closet homosexuals] at considerable dis-ease, however, is the realization that Francis is on to their games — that the carnival may soon be over.[374]

The Francis-to-the-rescue theme is also present in several media treatments of the pope's defrocking of Cardinal McCarrick in February 2019, just before the summit. A typical account[375] informs us that McCarrick was elevated to cardinal by Pope John Paul II in 2001, and then goes on to leave the reader with the impression that nothing was done about McCarrick until Francis came along many years later and lowered the boom. What these accounts conveniently leave out is the fact that Benedict XVI imposed on McCarrick sanctions and restrictions that were later lifted by Francis. It was Francis who put McCarrick back in circulation, making him a trusted adviser and unofficial global envoy. So the portrait of Francis as the man who will finally clean house doesn't quite fit the facts. And it is further belied by his appointment of McCarrick protégés such as Cardinals Cupich and Farrell to key positions.

How much longer the media will cover for Francis is difficult to say. If he should deviate from the liberal party line, he will come in for some rough treatment. If, for example, he speaks out too strongly against the normalization of homosexuality or if he reverses his position on mass migration, he will probably fall out of favor with the press.

---

[374] Donald Cozzens, "Duplicity, Hypocrisy of the Prelates Exposed in Martel's 'Closet' Book," *National Catholic Reporter*, February 21, 2019, https://www.ncronline.org/print/news/opinion/duplicity-hypocrisy-prelates-exposed-martels-closet-book.

[375] Hada Messia, Rob Picheta, and Daniel Burke, "Vatican Defrocks Ex-US Cardinal McCarrick over Sexual Abuse Allegations," CNN, February 26, 2019, https://www.cnn.com/2019/02/16/us/theodore-mccarrick-defrocked-intl/index.html.

Likewise, if it turns out that there are other skeletons in Francis's closet besides Bishop Gustavo Zanchetta, Monsignor Battista Ricca, Cardinal Theodore McCarrick, Father Julio César Grassi, and other embarrassing friends,[376] the media may begin to look on him as more of a liability than an asset. In that case, they will drop him like the proverbial hot potato, and the media's wait for a more progressive pontiff who is also more prudent will begin.

[376] Marco Tosatti, "Pope Francis's Parade of Embarrassing Friendships," *One Peter Five*, January 22, 2019, https://onepeterfive.com/francis-embarrassing-friendships/.

Do Italian Lives Matter?

On March 15, 2019, an anti-immigrant white man who wanted to send a message to the world killed fifty people in a mosque in New Zealand. Five days later, a pro-immigrant black man, who also wanted to send a message, kidnapped and tried to immolate fifty children on a school bus near Milan, Italy.

If you missed the first story, you must be a hermit living in the Idaho backwoods in a cabin with no TV, radio, or Internet access. If you missed the second story, you can be forgiven because, outside Europe, it didn't receive much coverage.

According to the European media,[377] the bus driver, an "Italian citizen" who migrated from Senegal several years ago, hijacked his bus full of middle-school children, forced the three school chaperones to handcuff the children with plastic ties, then took off on the highway, ramming into cars along the way. When he was stopped by a police barricade, he set fire to the bus, which he had previously doused with fuel. Luckily, the police were able to break the bus windows and free the students. No one was seriously injured, but several children suffered shock, bruises, and smoke inhalation. The bus driver, Ousseynou Sy, told the panicked children that what he was doing was revenge for his own three children

[377] "Driver Sets Italian School Bus on Fire with 51 Children Inside," *The Local*/AFP, March 20, 2019, https://www.thelocal.it/20190320/driver-sets-bus-on-fire-to-avenge-deaths-at-sea-none-seriously-harmed.

who had died while crossing the Mediterranean in an attempt to get to Italy. He told police that he was retaliating for the thousands of migrants who had drowned in the sea crossing in recent years.

I first became aware of the bus hijack while browsing the *Jihad Watch*[378] website around 2:00 p.m. on the day of the incident. Robert Spencer's piece contained a long excerpt from a *Telegraph* article[379] published hours earlier. I wondered when the American media would pick up the story.

At 4:30 p.m. I checked Google News. There were plenty of articles about the New Zealand mosque massacre, but nothing about the near massacre in Italy. I checked again at 6:00 p.m. Still nothing, but there were six headline stories about the New Zealand shooting with a "click for more stories" link that brought up dozens more stories about the mosque attack. I thought that Google News was a bit slow on the uptake. I assumed that they were trying to decide how to minimize the story.

At around 7:30 p.m., Fox News carried a brief account of the hijacked children and the blazing bus. I tried Google News again. There was nothing about Italy, but one could have spent most of the evening reading all the stories about New Zealand. In addition, there was a Snopes piece entitled, "Did 'Muslim militants' kill 120 Christians in Nigeria in February/March 2019?" To put the New Zealand attack in perspective, a number of Christian and conservative sites had run stories about the almost daily attacks on Christians by Muslims in Nigeria. The Snopes piece was an obvious attempt to undercut that narrative. It emphasized that the Muslim-Christian troubles in Nigeria should be understood as a range war—conflicts and clashes between farmers and cow herders

---

[378] Robert Spencer, "Italy: Muslim Migrant Bus Driver Rams Bus Full of Children into Cars on Highway, Sets It on Fire," *Jihad Watch*, March 20, 2019, https://www.jihadwatch.org/2019/03/italy-muslim-migrant-bus-driver-rams-bus-full-of-children-into-cars-on-highway-sets-it-on-fire.

[379] Nick Squires, "Italy Bus Fire: Driver Hijacks and Sets Fire to School Coach Full of Children 'In Retaliation' for Migrant Drownings," *Telegraph*, March 21, 2019, https://www.telegraph.co.uk/news/2019/03/20/bus-full-children-set-alight-angry-driver-retaliation-migrant/.

over land. As Snopes presented it, the Nigerian massacres were just like the stories of farmers and cowboys fighting over grazing lands in the Old West. And shame on you for thinking it has anything to do with Islam.

I checked Google News again at midnight and at various times the next day and found nothing about a bus hijacking in Italy; but, again, there were numerous stories, new and old, about the New Zealand tragedy.

Those of a certain age will remember a story from 1976 about a school bus full of children that went missing for thirty-six hours near the town of Chowchilla, California.[380] Along with their driver, the children had been kidnapped by three men who, after an eleven-hour drive, hid the bus and transferred the children to two vans that had been hidden underground in a rock quarry. Happily, the children, aided by their driver, managed to escape.

Another school bus full of children went missing in Italy. Only it didn't go missing from sight. It went missing from the news. Not entirely, of course, but for such a big story, the coverage seemed minimal; and, as of this writing, Google News hasn't covered it at all. That's strange. It's a great big look-at-me story full of drama and human interest. Most parents, especially those with school-age children who take buses to school, would want to know about a story like this. Grandparents would also want to know. Wouldn't you? Don't the people at Google News have children? Don't they care? Or is something else at work? The Chowchilla school bus story was nationwide news for several days, but that was in a time before the news became highly politicized.

Google News didn't run the story because it undercut the narratives that they had been pushing for days. One of those narratives is about widespread anti-Muslim bigotry, or "Islamophobia" for short. But the story out of Italy didn't fit that narrative. The revengeful bus driver wasn't

---

[380] Snejana Farberov, "Heroic School Bus Driver Who Rescued 26 Children BURIED ALIVE in 1976 Kidnapping Dies Aged 91," *Daily Mail*, May 18, 2012, https://www.dailymail.co.uk/news/article-2146583/Heroic-school-bus-driver-rescued-26-children-BURIED-ALIVE-1976-kidnapping-dies-aged-91.html.

bigoted against Muslims. In fact, seeing that he comes from Senegal, a country that is 92 percent Muslim, he most probably is a Muslim.

Another narrative that Google favors is that opposition to immigration creates a climate that leads to violence. After all, the New Zealand shooter had pronounced anti-immigrant views. But the Italian bus driver was very much the opposite. He was pro-immigration—so much so that he was willing to kill fifty children in order to protest Italy's new restrictive policy on immigration.

If you don't think that Google is biased and is deliberately trying to manage what we are allowed to know, imagine that the children on the bus were Muslim, and their driver was a white nationalist anti-immigrant. Would Google have given the story the silent treatment?

The other reason Google and other media don't want to dwell on the story is that the bus driver's views on immigration are uncomfortably close to their own, and it wouldn't do for people to think too much about that fact. Like Ousseynou Sy, the media elites tend to think that borders should be open and that all migrants deserve to be safely escorted across the sea (the kidnapper's views on immigration also happen to coincide closely with those of Pope Francis, a majority of European bishops, and the USCCB). Sy railed against interior minister Matteo Salvini's immigration policies, but as Ned May observes in *Gates of Vienna*, "[he should] have realized that his actions were an affirmation of Mr. Salvini's argument against allowing third-world immigrants into Italy."[381]

Of course, the people who write the news do realize that. They are smart enough to know that Mr. Sy's behavior is not a good advertisement for their own open-borders position. And so, they have given him short shrift. The story came and went in the blink of an eye. The *New York Times*

[381] Baron Bodissey, "Bus Full of Schoolchildren Hijacked and Torched by a Culture-Enricher," Gates of Vienna, March 20, 2019, https://gatesofvienna.net/2019/03/bus-full-of-schoolchildren-hijacked-and-torched-by-a-culture-enricher/#more-47902.

claims it carries "all the news that's fit to print," but Google News, along with numerous other news outlets, has a different agenda—something along the line of "all the news that fits our narrative."

It's bad enough that Google won't cover stories that challenge its view of the world. What's worse is that it's been trying to silence those who will. As I mentioned earlier in this piece, I came across the bus hijack story in Robert Spencer's *Jihad Watch*. For a long time, Spencer has complained that Google's search-engine division has been targeting *Jihad Watch* by adjusting its algorithms to make it difficult to find his site. Other media companies and financial giants—Facebook, Patreon, Mastercard, and Visa—have also attempted to silence Spencer in various and sundry ways. Spencer fears that in the wake of the New Zealand massacre, leftist and Islamic groups will soon succeed in their attempts "to silence all criticism of jihad terror and Sharia oppression of women and others."[382] This won't happen by means of legislation, he says, but through "a complete deplatforming." "We will be able to speak," says Spencer, "but no one will be able to hear us, as we won't be allowed on Facebook, Twitter, YouTube, and the rest."

Does it really matter that much if Spencer's site is taken down? Aren't there plenty of other sources to bring us the needed information? The answers are, "Yes, it really does matter" and "No, there aren't plenty of other sources." Moreover, the alternative sources that do exist can also be charged with "Islamophobia" and quickly find themselves without a platform and without funding.

You're reading about the aborted bus massacre here because I first read about it on Spencer's site. It's true that I would most likely have come across the story even if *Jihad Watch* were no longer in business. It was, after all, a sensational story complete with a wild bus chase, brave

---

[382] Robert Spencer, "Robert Spencer: So Long, Everybody," *FrontPage Mag*, March 18, 2019, https://www.frontpagemag.com/fpm/2019/03/robert-spencer-so-long-everybody-robert-spencer/.

students, heroic police, and photos of the bus engulfed in flames and children reuniting with loved ones.

But how about all the smaller stories that, taken together, give us a picture of how cultural jihad and violent jihad are changing the face of the globe?

Had there been no *Jihad Watch*, I would have missed many of these. I don't subscribe to dozens of international newspapers, and I don't have far-flung correspondents who will alert me of the latest jihad outrages in France, Germany, India, Nigeria, and elsewhere.

Here, from the last ten days, is a sampling of news stories that I might have missed had *Jihad Watch* been canceled by the censorship zealots:

Canada: University cites New Zealand massacre as reason for canceling Islamocritical talk by ex-Muslim.[383]

London's Muslim mayor defends arrest of Christian preacher: "There's not an unlimited right to free speech."[384]

MI5: Number of "far right" terrorism cases "absolutely dwarfed" by the number of jihad terror cases.[385]

---

[383] Christine Douglass-Williams, "Canada: University Cites New Zealand Massacre as Reason for Canceling Islamocritical Talk by Ex-Muslim," *Jihad Watch*, March 22, 2019, https://www.jihadwatch.org/2019/03/canada-university-cites-new-zealand-massacre-as-reason-for-canceling-islamocritical-talk-by-ex-muslim.

[384] Robert Spencer, "London's Muslim Mayor Defends Arrest of Christian Preacher: 'There's Not an Unlimited Right to Free Speech,'" *Jihad Watch*, March 22, 2019, https://www.jihadwatch.org/2019/03/londons-muslim-mayor-defends-arrest-of-christian-preacher-theres-not-an-unlimited-right-to-free-speech.

[385] Christine Douglass-Williams, "MI5: Number of 'Far Right' Terrorism Cases 'Absolutely Dwarfed' by the Number of Jihad Terror Cases," *Jihad Watch*, March 22, 2019, https://www.jihadwatch.org/2019/03/m15-number-of-far-right-terrorism-cases-absolutely-dwarfed-by-the-number-of-jihad-terror-cases.

Germany: Two hundred cops arrest ten Muslims who were "plotting ... to kill as many people as possible."[386]

Germany: Muslim migrant crimes concealed to prevent "prejudice."[387]

Netherlands: Utrecht jihad mass murderer left a note saying he acted in the name of Allah.[388]

Netherlands: Muslim migrant who was "reading the Qur'an a lot" stabs Jewish father and son.[389]

Australia: Muslims plotted jihad massacres to "defeat all the infidels."[390]

Well, you get the picture. Jihad is now a normal event in the Western world, and the Islamization of Europe is well underway. But, if the

---

[386] Robert Spencer, "Germany: 200 Cops Arrest 10 Muslims Who Were 'Plotting to Use a Car and Guns to Kill as Many People as Possible,'" *Jihad Watch*, March 22, 2019, https://www.jihadwatch.org/2019/03/germany-200-cops-arrest-10-muslims-who-were-plotting-to-use-a-car-and-guns-to-kill-as-many-people-as-possible.

[387] Christine Douglass-Williams, "Germany: Muslim Migrant Crimes Concealed to Prevent 'Prejudice,'" *Jihad Watch*, March 14, 2019, https://www.jihadwatch.org/2019/03/germany-muslim-migrant-crimes-concealed-to-prevent-prejudice.

[388] Robert Spencer, "Netherlands: Utrecht Jihad Mass Murderer Left Note Saying He Acted in the Name of Allah," *Jihad Watch*, March 20, 2019, https://www.jihadwatch.org/2019/03/netherlands-utrecht-jihad-mass-murderer-left-note-saying-he-acted-in-the-name-of-allah.

[389] Robert Spencer, "Netherlands: Muslim Migrant Who Was 'Reading the Qur'an a Lot' Stabs Jewish Father and Son," *Jihad Watch*, March 22, 2019, https://www.jihadwatch.org/2019/03/netherlands-muslim-migrant-who-was-reading-the-quran-a-lot-stabs-jewish-father-and-son.

[390] Robert Spencer, "Australia: Muslims Plotted Jihad Massacres to 'Defeat All the Infidels,' Prosecutor Says 'Islam Not on Trial Here,'" *Jihad Watch*, March 19, 2019, https://www.jihadwatch.org/2019/03/australia-muslims-plotted-jihad-massacres-to-defeat-all-the-infidels-prosecutor-says-islam-not-on-trial-here.

anti-"Islamophobia" zealots have their way, don't expect to have that clear picture for much longer. They want you to see only what they want you to see. And they want you to look at it only through the rose-colored lenses that they provide.

The Left's War on Free Speech

Whatever your views on Donald Trump, it is wrong to put the burden of responsibility on him for the violence at his Chicago campaign rally in 2016 when Black Lives Matter and other leftist groups harassed and attacked the rally-goers.

According to the mainstream media's explanation, the clashes inside and outside the rally venue were entirely due to Trump's abrasive manner and provocative comments. But leftists don't need excuses to intimidate and riot. They do it all the time. If Ted Cruz or Marco Rubio or John Kasich were the frontrunner in the campaign, he would just as surely be targeted by well-organized leftist mobs. That's because, for the left, it's not about tone or manners; it's about the revolution.

The left is even quick to turn on its own if its ever-shifting tests of ideological purity are not met. It was not too long ago that two Black Lives Matter protesters forcibly took over the mic during one of Bernie Sanders's rallies.[391] Sanders is hard left, but on that particular day, he was apparently insufficiently attentive to the concerns of Black Lives Matter. The leftist vanguard had moved on, and good soldier Sanders silently accepted his chastisement for not keeping up.

[391] Tim Hains, "'Black Lives Matter' Protesters Disrupt Sanders Event in Seattle, Sanders Gives Up the Mic to Them," RealClearPolitics, August 9, 2015, https://www.realclearpolitics.com/video/2015/08/09/black_lives_ matter_protesters_disrupt_bernie_sanders_event_in_seattle_sanders_ gives_up_mic_to_them.html.

So Republicans are not the only targets of the revolutionaries. After all, the mother of all convention riots occurred during the 1968 Democratic Convention in Chicago, when the establishment Democrats failed to march to the tune of leftist, anti-war demonstrators.

Trump can hardly be blamed for that. Neither can he be blamed for the recent spate of attempts to outlaw free speech on college campuses. It's well known that conservative speakers at universities are regularly shouted down, but now student activists have turned on the colleges themselves for their failure to provide "safe spaces" and prevent "microaggressions" (so called, presumably, because they are invisible to any normal person). By almost anyone's standards, the administration and the faculty at most colleges lean to the left but, as it turns out, not far enough left to satisfy the ever-expanding grievances of young utopians.

Likewise, the mayors of most major cities tend to be left-leaning Democrats, and their police commissioners are usually models of political correctness. But that hasn't prevented leftists from staging numerous anti-police protests in cities across the country. Chicago witnessed weeks of such protests in December 2015.

Viewed from a wider perspective, the violent protest at the Trump rally in Chicago was not a one-time reaction to one particular candidate's supposedly divisive rhetoric. It was, instead, part of a long-standing pattern. Violence, intimidation, and unreasonable demands are the modus operandi of the left.

And not just in America. In Europe, violent leftist attacks[392] on "conservative" rallies are more the rule than the exception. I put "conservative" in quotes because the European media refer to patriotic Europeans as "far-right," "extremists," and "xenophobes." By American standards, however, many of them would qualify as liberals due to their support of

---

[392] William Kilpatrick, "Bishops in Brussels: A Rear-View Mirror Vision of the World," *Catholic World Report*, March 10, 2015, https://www.catholicworldreport.com/2015/03/10/bishops-in-brussels-a-rear-view-mirror-vision-of-the-world/.

the social welfare state. In any event, what brings these nationalist groups in conflict with the leftist media and the leftist mob is their opposition to immigration—particularly of the Muslim variety. For that sin, the media hammers them in print and the mob hammers them literally—with bottles, stones, and iron rods.

The generic name for the well-organized leftist gangs is "antifas," short for "anti-fascists"—an Orwellian irony if ever there was one, seeing that the antifas' tactics are thoroughly fascist. When anti-Islamization groups such as PEGIDA (Patriotic Europeans against the Islamization of the West) hold peaceful rallies or candlelit "evening strolls," they are often met by much larger gangs of antifa thugs intent on shutting them down and shutting them up. If they're lucky, the peaceful protesters are protected by the police, and, if they're not lucky, they get beaten up.

It's no coincidence that the leftist media in Europe, along with the leftist gangs, so often work in the service of Islamic interests. The tacit alliance[393] between leftists and Islamists has been in effect for a long time. In Europe, it manifests itself in the elite's embrace of mass Muslim immigration. In America, it was evident in Obama's embrace of the Muslim Brotherhood during his presidency.

How does one explain this affinity? The short answer is that both Islamism and leftism are fascist totalitarian movements (for a thorough explication of the left's fascist tendencies, see Jonah Goldberg's book *Liberal Fascism*).[394] Leftists get along with Islamists because they are fellow fascists and also because the left is a quasi-religious movement. Its devotees are true believers who find meaning in life by spreading the leftist gospel. As with Islam, it's best not to question the belief system of the left, because it is protected by strict blasphemy laws. If you disagree

[393] William Kilpatrick, "Double Trouble: The Leftist Threat and the Islamist Threat," *Crisis Magazine*, March 20, 2014, https://www.crisismagazine.com/2014/double-trouble-the-leftist-threat-and-the-islamist-threat.

[394] Jonah Goldberg, *Liberal Fascism: The Secret History of the American Left, from Mussolini to the Politics of Change* (New York, NY: Crown Forum, 2009).

with the tenets of leftists, you are not, from their perspective, entitled to your opinion; you are committing blasphemy. And you deserve to be punished.

Rather than debate their opponents, the faithful prefer to silence them. Leftists are far more passionate about their ideology than they are about free speech. They have no use for free speech unless they can use it to further their interests. For them, it is not a first principle but a tool or a weapon. Thus, they have no qualms about suppressing the free speech of others.

The media, which should be one of the chief guardians of free speech, often plays the same game. In browsing through a couple of dozen news articles on the Chicago protest, I noticed that all of them put the blame for the Friday night shutdown almost entirely on Trump. Yet all the evidence shows that it was student activist groups along with Black Lives Matter, MoveOn.Org, and various other leftist groups that deliberately planned to shut down the event. According to the *Los Angeles Times*:

> Planning for the [Friday] event started Monday night when leaders from a range of groups gathered in a campus lecture hall. They included the Black Student Union, the Muslim Student Association, and the Fearless Undocumented Association, which advocates for immigrants in the country illegally.[395]

The point is, this is not a civility issue; it's a free speech issue. Leftist groups want veto power over what others say. As Robert Spencer put it in a recent essay:

> In that scenario, you see, it becomes incumbent upon Trump not to say anything that leftist thugs might dislike, or he will have partial responsibility for what they do. Cruz, Rubio, and Kasich, of

---

[395] Kate Linthicum, Kurtis Lee, "How Black, Latino and Muslim College Students Organized to Stop Trump's Rally in Chicago," *Los Angeles Times*, March 12, 2016, https://www.latimes.com/politics/la-na-trump-protesters-20160312-story.html.

course, will also have to be careful not to "create an environment" that might force the left-fascists to shut them down as well.[396]

In short, if you say the wrong thing, the left-fascists will riot. But who determines which words are permissible and which words are not? Why, the leftists, of course. And if they attack you, you have no one to blame but yourself. You should have known better.

In this regard, the media tend to treat leftist mobs in the same way they treat Muslim mobs—as groups of individuals who bear no responsibility for what they do if they are offended. What's more, the media seems to accept as legitimate the right of the mob to be the sole arbiter of what is offensive. The operative assumption is that if they are offended, we have done something wrong, and we'd better be more careful about what we say in the future. This, of course, is a formula for narrowing the boundaries of free speech until only politically correct platitudes can be uttered.

In assessing the debate over campaign rhetoric and tone, it's important not to lose sight of the big picture. The big picture is that there are many powerful forces in the United States and abroad that want to cancel free speech. In response to the shutdown of Trump's rally, Hillary Clinton said, "If you play with matches, you're going to start a fire you can't control."[397] Clinton seems to subscribe to the notion that people aren't free to control themselves when they are offended. Rather, they are assumed to be like forest fires: once the fire gets started, it has no control over itself. Therefore, speech has to be tightly controlled, and it's up to the political fire marshals such as Clinton to decide which speech is incendiary and which is not. It's no coincidence that one of Clinton's

---

[396] Robert Spencer, "Violent Left-Fascists Shut Down Trump Rally; Cruz, Rubio, Kasich Blame Trump," *Jihad Watch*, March 12, 2016, https://www.jihadwatch.org/2016/03/violent-left-fascists-shut-down-trump-rally-cruz-rubio-kasich-blame-trump.

[397] Mark Z. Barabak and Michael Finnegan, "As Republican Rivals Take Aim, Donald Trump Deflects Blame for Near-Riot in Chicago," *Los Angeles Times*, March 13, 2016, https://www.latimes.com/nation/politics/la-na-trump-ohio-20160313-story.html.

chief agendas while secretary of state was to work closely with the Organisation of Islamic Cooperation (OIC) to promote anti-blasphemy laws[398] and other restrictions on free speech. That should come as no surprise. Clinton is a woman of the left, and that's what leftists do.

What's worrisome is that some conservatives have yielded to the temptation to follow suit. Several Republicans have gone along with the idea that Trump bears much of the responsibility for the Chicago violence because of the "toxic environment" he has created. But the left created its own toxic environment long before Trump ever appeared on the scene. Republicans should be careful that they don't end up aiding and abetting the foes of free speech. By letting leftist agitators set the ground rules for debate, conservatives are putting in jeopardy the First Amendment as well as their own chances of success.

And that caution applies to Trump as well. Trump himself is hardly a stalwart friend of free speech. He strongly criticized Pamela Geller's[399] cartoon exhibit and free speech event in Garland, Texas, in May 2015, on the grounds that it was offensive to Muslims. He has also called for expanded libel laws, which would make it easier to sue newspapers for criticizing public figures such as Donald Trump. The irony is that such laws could conceivably make his own criticisms of Islam an actionable offense.

Those who love Trump and those who loathe him should think more carefully about the importance of free speech and whether they are willing to submit what they say to the self-appointed guardians of political correctness and their thug enforcers on the left.

---

[398] Michael Curtis, "The State Department Should Leave the Istanbul Process," *American Thinker*, November 10, 2013, https://www.americanthinker.com/articles/2013/11/the_state_department_should_leave_the_istanbul_process.html.

[399] Spencer, "Violent Left-Fascists Shut Down Trump Rally."

Time for Some Trust-Busting?

Which organizations are most likely to advance the cause of Islamic dominance? ISIS? Al-Qaeda? Hezbollah? The Muslim Brotherhood?

If you've been keeping track of world events, these are the names that will most likely come to mind.

There are, however, other names to consider — organizations that at first glance seem entirely nonthreatening yet are capable of clearing the path for the spread of Islam more efficiently than al-Qaeda and ISIS could ever hope to do.

I'm referring to companies such as Mastercard, Discover, PayPal, Twitter, Facebook, and Google. We're all aware of how much easier life has become because of these companies. But, because they're so big, they also have the capacity to make life miserable.

Recently, they've been making life miserable for critics of Islam. By "critics" I don't mean those who have nothing good to say about the faith of Muslims. I mean that anyone who simply "critiques" or discusses the doctrines, practices, and laws of Islam in ways that Muslims don't approve can run afoul of the big tech companies.

Sometimes this is done in a heavy-handed way, as when Facebook simply shuts down the Facebook page of a counterjihad site, and sometimes it is done in more subtle ways. For example, there's "the search engine manipulation effect" described by former *Psychology Today* editor

Robert Epstein.[400] By manipulating algorithms, says Epstein, Google can determine which information goes to the top of your search list. Since we tend to assume that items appearing at the top of a list are the most relevant and valuable, we tend to discount or ignore items that come further down on the list. For example, if you google Islamic terms, you're more likely, thanks to Google, to land on Islamic-friendly sites than on Islamic-critical sites. As a result, the information you gather on Islam will come with a positive slant.

Just as the media giants can control the flow of information, the financial giants control the flow of cash. And when the media giants work in cooperation with the financial giants, the two become an almost irresistible force.

For years now, both the financial companies and the media companies have been trying to shut down Robert Spencer's site *Jihad Watch*. Facebook has suspended him.[401] PayPal has refused to process his payments.[402] And Google's search-engine algorithms seem to discriminate against his site.[403] In 2019, when Spencer attempted to join Patreon—a crowdfunding platform—he was denied service because Mastercard pressured Patreon to deplatform him.[404]

---

[400] Ruthie Blum, "Peter Schweizer's 'The Creepy Line' Takes Tech Giants to Task," Gatestone Institute, January 10, 2019, https://www.gatestoneinstitute.org/13491/the-creepy-line.

[401] Robert Spencer, "CAIR Calling Shots on Who Gets Banned from Facebook and Twitter," *FrontPage Mag*, January 14, 2019, https://www.frontpagemag.com/fpm/2019/01/cair-calling-shots-who-gets-banned-facebook-and-robert-spencer/.

[402] Pamela Geller, "PAYPAL Suspends Jihad Watch after ProPublica Hit Piece against Anti-Jihad News Sites #BoycottPaypal," *Geller Report*, August 19, 2017, https://gellerreport.com/2017/08/boycott-paypal.html/.

[403] Robert Spencer, "Google's New 'Hate Speech' Algorithm Is Anti-Semitic and Pro-Jihad," *Jihad Watch*, July 30, 2017, https://www.jihadwatch.org/2017/07/googles-new-hate-speech-algorithm-is-anti-semitic-and-pro-jihad.

[404] Allum Bokhari, "Bokhari: The Terrifying Rise of Financial Blacklisting," *Breitbart*, January 2, 2019, https://www.breitbart.com/tech/2019/01/02/bokhari-the-terrifying-rise-of-financial-blacklisting/.

Mastercard and Visa have also refused to process payments to the David Horowitz Freedom Center[405]—a conservative site that features articles on political, cultural, and Islamic issues. Although fee-processing service has been restored to the center, conservative and counterjihad sites now live in constant fear of losing one of their main sources of funding.

One might think that the simple solution to the deplatforming strategy is to create alternative platforms: alternative Patreons, alternative Twitters, Facebooks, and so forth. But, as you can imagine, that's a tall order. And even if you succeed in setting up a platform, the problem of funding remains. As technology correspondent Allum Bokhari points out in a *Breitbart* piece:

> That's also why so many free-speech alternatives to Patreon have failed: FreeStartr, Hatreon, MakerSupport, and SubscribeStar all tried to offer a more open platform, and were promptly dumped by the credit card companies. All are unable to do business.[406]

Bokhari continues:

> Those who oppose Silicon Valley censorship aren't allowed to just build their own alternative platforms. They must build their own global payment processing infrastructure to have any hope of restoring free speech online.

I don't pretend to be able to interpret the Apocalypse, but that almost sounds like a fulfillment of Revelation 13:17—the passage that tells us that no one can buy or sell unless he has the mark of the beast.

Whether or not the Mastercard logo turns out to be the mark of the beast, critics of Islam—along with social and political conservatives, orthodox Christians, and other mavericks—are in for tough sledding. The business of buying and selling has suddenly become quite problematic for them. Technically, they still have free speech, but without a platform

[405] Ibid.
[406] Ibid.

their audience will be small, and without funding many will be forced to find other ways to earn a living.

Meanwhile, the rest of us will be left in the dark regarding Islam. The media will still carry puff pieces about Muslim doctors and model Muslim families in order to assure us that the face of Islam is friendly and familiar. But you won't hear much about those things that seem to hold no interest for the mainstream media: the daily jihad attacks reported in *Jihad Watch*; the increasing incidence of honor killings, child marriages, gang rapes, and attacks on Jews recorded by Gatestone Institute, Gates of Vienna, and *FrontPage Magazine*; and the accelerating persecution of Christians by Muslims in the Muslim world, which Raymond Ibrahim tracks in detail on his website.

Perhaps you don't need to know about such things. Perhaps the threat has been overblown by "alarmists." But should it be left up to the corporate thought police to decide what you need to know and what you don't need to know? Should Google and Facebook and Discover[407] decide which sites are safe for you to visit?

And should Twitter be enforcing Pakistan's blasphemy laws? Not long ago, *FrontPage* editor Jamie Glazov received a notice from "Twitter Legal" informing him that content on his account was "in violation of Pakistan law: Section37 of PECA-2016, Section 295B and Section 295C of the Pakistan penal code."[408] Section295 B criminalizes "defiling the Holy Quran" and carries a life sentence. Section 295C mandates that anyone who "defiles the sacred name of the Holy Prophet Muhammad (PBUH) shall be punished with death or imprisonment for life."

---

[407] Robert Spencer, "MasterCard and Discover Banned Me. Are You Next?" PJ Media, September 24, 2018, https://pjmedia.com/homeland-security/mastercard-and-discover-banned-me-are-you-next/.

[408] Jamie Glazov, "Twitter Warns Me My New Book Violates Pakistan's Blasphemy Law," *Jihad Watch*, December 24, 2018, https://www.jihad-watch.org/2018/12/jamie-glazov-twitter-warns-me-my-new-book-violates-pakistans-blasphemy-law.

One reason this ought to be of concern to Catholics is that many basic expressions of Christian faith are considered provocative by Muslims, and some are considered blasphemous. Ringing church bells, singing loudly in church, and conducting outdoor liturgical processions are considered provocative by many Muslims. And several Christian doctrines—the Trinity, the divinity of Christ, and the Crucifixion—are held to be blasphemous. Recently, the *Washington Times* reported that in Uganda—a majority-Christian country—a Muslim group attacked Christian preachers for "mocking Islam by publicly saying Jesus was the Son of God."[409]

Will Muslim groups one day complain to Facebook and Twitter that Catholic writers and websites are in violation of their blasphemy laws? And, if they do loudly complain, what will the media corporations do? While you're thinking that over, consider that in 2019 Facebook blocked an ad for a pro-life movie that tells the story behind the Supreme Court's *Roe v. Wade* decision.[410] The year before, Facebook also blocked access to the film's crowdfunding site.

The decision to offend pro-lifers rather than pro-choicers was probably not a difficult one for Facebook to make. Likewise, it's not difficult to guess whose side the media and financial giants would take if given a choice between offending Muslims and offending Christians. Evidence continues to accumulate that they have already chosen sides. In July 2017, Facebook vice president Joel Kaplan visited Pakistan to assure the government that it would remove "anti-Islam" material from its pages.[411]

---

[409] Tonny Onyulo, "Ugandan Christians Live in Fear of Minority Muslims on Quest for Conversions," *Washington Times*, December 24, 2018, https://www.washingtontimes.com/news/2018/dec/24/uganda-christians-face-muslim-persecution-record-l/.

[410] Doug Mainwaring, "Facebook Blocks Ad for Pro-Life Movie Telling the True Story about Roe v Wade," LifeSite News, January 14, 2019, https://www.lifesitenews.com/news/facebook-blocks-ad-for-pro-life-movie-telling-the-true-story-about-roe-v-wa.

[411] Robert Spencer, "Blasphemy? Google Has an App for That," *FrontPage Mag*, December 11, 2018, https://archives.frontpagemag.com/fpm/blasphemy-google-has-app-robert-spencer/.

In November 2018, at the request of the Indonesian government, Google launched a new app that will allow "Muslims to report individuals who commit blasphemy, or insult Islam."[412]

So curb your tongue, and if you can't say anything nice about Islam, don't say anything at all. Islamic radicals won't necessarily come after you, but Facebook and Google—the self-appointed foes of "hate"—just might.

What we have here is not a communication problem, but a monopoly problem. The game that is being run by the tech companies and the credit-card monopolies is just about the only game in town. The old joke was that the only people who had freedom of the press were the ones who owned the printing presses. The new, not-so-funny joke is that the only people with freedom of expression are the ones who own social media companies or major credit-card companies.

It's beginning to look as if the only solutions to corporate suppression of speech are tighter regulations and antitrust legislation. In the distant past, progressives thought of trust-busting as a noble cause. Now that they've become proficient at the game of monopoly, however, they don't want any competition.

[412] Ibid.

22

Pope Francis and Islam

Although the mainstream media display a good deal of favoritism toward Islam, they are, in comparison with Pope Francis, models of impartiality. Seemingly oblivious to the dangers involved, Francis has become an outright advocate for Islam. What explains his behavior? Could it be that Francis subscribes to indifferentism — the belief that all religions are of equal value?

Pope Francis, Indifferentism, and Islamization

Two young Scandinavian women who were hiking in the Atlas Mountains in Morocco were found dead in mid-December 2018 in their tent. The ISIS terrorists later posted a video of themselves decapitating one of the victims.

The mother of one of the women told reporters, "Her priority was safety. The girls had taken all precautionary measures before embarking on this trip."[413]

"Except," as Robert Spencer commented in *Jihad Watch*, "that it no doubt didn't even occur to them that what they thought they knew about Morocco's religion and culture might be inaccurate and designed to whitewash Islam, leaving them ill-informed about a threat that they actually did end up facing."[414]

If one depended on the European media and European schools for one's knowledge of Islam, one would indeed come away with a misleading picture of Islam. But the same could be said of Catholics who rely on Church pronouncements about Islam. Ever since the Second Vatican Council, Church leaders have presented a smiley-faced version of Islam

---

[413] Robert Spencer, "Morocco: Muslims Who Murdered Scandinavian Girls Say Killings Were 'Allah's Will,' Victims Were 'Enemies of Allah,'" *Jihad Watch*, December 201, 2018, https://www.jihadwatch.org/2018/12/morocco-muslims-who-murdered-scandinavian-girls-say-killings-were-allahs-will-victims-were-enemies-of-allah.

[414] Ibid.

that emphasizes its commonalities with Catholicism and leaves out its alarming elements.

Currently, the chief proponent of this bowdlerized view of Islam is Pope Francis. He has reassured Christians that Islam is opposed to violence, has advised Muslim migrants to find comfort in the Koran, and has portrayed terrorists as betrayers of true Islam.

More significantly, he has become perhaps the world's foremost spokesman for an open-borders, let-everyone-in policy toward immigration. Seemingly indifferent to the increasingly dangerous situation created by jihad-minded Muslims in Europe, Francis has encouraged a welcoming attitude toward all while scolding opponents of mass migration as fearful and xenophobic.

In short, Pope Francis has acted as an advocate for Islam. He has portrayed it as a religion of peace, the moral equivalent of Catholicism, and a force for good. A number of people, however, now feel that the pope has seriously misled Christians about the nature and goals of Islam and Islamic immigration. Like the teachers and other cultural elites who left the two Scandinavian women "ill-informed about a threat that they actually did end up facing," Pope Francis, by whitewashing Islam, has left millions of Christians unprepared for the escalating threat that is now facing them.

The analogy between the misinformed Scandinavian friends and misinformed Europeans breaks down in one respect: No one forced the young women to travel to Morocco. They went there of their own accord. It's one thing to invite yourself into the high mountains of Morocco and take your chances, but it's quite another thing altogether to invite Morocco into Europe and let ordinary Europeans bear the consequences. This is what the European elites—with much encouragement from Francis—have done.

The combination of high Muslim birth rates, mass Muslim migration, and European concessions to Islam's blasphemy laws has set Europe on a course toward Islamization. Islamization, in turn, will spell *dhimmitude* for Christians. As the Islamic influence grows, Christians will be subject to increasing restrictions on the practice of their faith, perhaps even to the point of persecution. It's possible that Christianity in Europe will be exterminated.

Is Francis Naïve about Islam?

The pope has done much to promote the cause of Islam—so much so that he has been praised by Islamic leaders for his defense of their faith. The questions that then arise are these: Is Francis aware of the possibility that Islam will become dominant in Europe? Is he aware that this may spell the end of European Christianity? And if he is aware, does he care?

For a long time, I thought that Francis was simply naïve regarding Islam. His counterfactual statements about Islam and his Pollyannaish view of mass Muslim migration must, I thought, be the result either of blissful ignorance or of bad advice from "experts," or a combination of both.

Now, however, I have my doubts. The catalyst for these doubts is Francis's approach to the current sex-abuse crisis. I originally supposed that he was naïve about this, too: perhaps he didn't realize the full extent of the problem or the full extent of the cover-ups, or perhaps he wasn't aware of the numerous lavender networks in seminaries, in dioceses, and in the Vatican itself. But in light of recent revelations, it no longer seems possible to give him the benefit of the doubt. In several cases, he not only knew of the crimes and cover-ups, but he took steps to protect or promote those involved. Francis seems determined to push through a revolution in doctrine and morals—what he calls "a radical paradigm shift"[415]—and it doesn't seem to matter that the men he has chosen to help him achieve his goals are the ones most deeply implicated in the scandals. By all accounts, Pope Francis is a "hands-on" pope who knows exactly what he wants, carefully calculates his moves, and leaves little to chance.

---

[415] Bree A. Dail, "New Book Exposes Dangers of Pope's 'Paradigm Shift,'" LifeSite News, December 13, 2018, https://www.lifesitenews.com/news/new-book-exposes-dangers-of-popes-paradigm-shift.

Why, then, should we suppose Francis is completely naïve about the extent of the threat from Islam and from Islamic immigration? It's difficult to imagine that he isn't fully aware of the widespread persecution of Christians in Muslim lands. And it's just as difficult to think that he's ignorant of the Islamic crime wave on his own doorstep—the escalating incidence of rape, riots, and terrorist attacks in Europe. Does he really believe that such things have nothing to do with Islam?

Unless one assumes that Francis is ignorant of history and out of touch with current events, one must entertain the possibility that—to repeat a favorite slogan of his—he wants to "make a mess" in Europe.

But why? Why risk the damage to the Church that would surely follow on the Islamization of Europe? Doesn't Francis care about the Church? Increasingly, it seems that he does not. This is to say that he doesn't have much use for the "old" Church—the one that was handed down by the apostles and has now become too narrow and tradition-bound to suit his liberal tastes.

The Fluid Church of the Future

What he does care about is the new Church of the future—a Church of openness, inclusiveness, and fluidity. Led by the Spirit and free of bothersome dogma, this liberated Church would be able to adjust to the changing needs of the times. If one reads between the lines, this is what Francis and those around him seem to desire.

Indeed, one needn't bother to read between the lines. In the words of Father Thomas Rosica, a media adviser to the Vatican: "Pope Francis breaks Catholic traditions whenever he wants because he is free of disordered attachments." Moreover, "Our Church has indeed entered a new phase. With the advent of this first Jesuit pope, it is openly ruled by an individual rather than by the authority of Scripture alone or even its own dictates of tradition plus Scripture."[416]

[416] Matthew Cullinan Hoffman, "'Pope Francis Breaks Catholic traditions Whenever He Wants': Vatican Advisor Fr. Rosica," LifeSite News, August

And this is from Francis himself speaking at a conference on church closings:

> The observation that many churches, which until a few years ago were necessary, are now no longer thus, due to a lack of faithful and clergy ... should be welcomed in the Church not with anxiety, but as a sign of the times that invites us to reflection and requires us to adapt.[417]

Translation: Francis is not particularly concerned about church closings. Perhaps he even thinks of them as a blessing, i.e., a necessary end to the old order of things that will clear the way for the construction of the new order.

What is this new order? In many respects, it resembles the new world order envisioned by politicians and academics on the left. Like them, Francis has a dim view of national borders and national sovereignty, and, like them, he has an almost unquestioning belief in the benefits of international institutions. One gets the impression that Francis would be quite content to let the U.N. run the world, despite the fact that the U.N. is increasingly run by leftists and Islamists. For example, Francis has praised the U.N.'s global compact for migration because he believes that immigration should be governed globally rather than by individual nations.[418]

How does this relate to Christianity and Islam? Just as Francis seems to favor a one-world government, he also seems to be drawn by the

---

14, 2018, https://www.lifesitenews.com/news/fr.-tom-rosica-praises-pope-francis-reign-he-breaks-catholic-traditions-whe.

417 Terry Mattingly, "Amid Church Closings, Pope Says Not to Be 'Anxious,'" *UExpress*, December 5, 2018, https://www.uexpress.com/on-religion/2018/12/5/amid-church-closings-pope-says-not.

418 Thomas D. Williams, "Pope Francis Lauds U.N. 'Global Compact' for Immigration," *Breitbart*, December 17, 2017, https://www.breitbart.com/immigration/2018/12/17/pope-francis-lauds-u-n-global-compact-for-immigration/.

vision of a one-world religion. He hasn't said so in so many words, but he has given several indications that he envisions an eventual blending of religions. This would not be the "one flock, one shepherd" Church that Christ spoke of but something a bit more diverse.

One way to achieve this unity in diversity is by deemphasizing doctrine. Doctrinal differences are, after all, the main dividing line between different faiths. Thus, by downplaying the importance of doctrine—something he has done fairly consistently throughout his papacy—it's probable that Francis hopes to smooth the path to interreligious harmony. Just as Francis disapproves of borders between nations, it's quite likely that he looks upon borders between religions as artificial and unnecessarily divisive.

Indifferentism

This is speculation, of course, but it's not sheer speculation. As George Neumayr points out in *The Political Pope*,[419] Francis frequently shows signs of indifferentism—i.e., the belief that all religions are of equal value. For example, when speaking of the murder of Father Jacques Hamel by two jihadists, he drew a moral equivalence between Islam and Christianity, saying "If I speak of Islamic violence, I must speak of Catholic violence."[420]

Other signs of his indifferentism are not difficult to find.[421] In 2014, he told a group of Protestants, "I'm not interested in converting Evangelicals to Catholicism. I want people to find Jesus in their own community." On another occasion, he criticized Pope Benedict's "ordinate" for Anglicans interested in becoming Catholics by saying that they should remain "as Anglicans." On still other occasions, he has waxed enthusiastic about Martin Luther and the Protestant Reformation.

---

[419] George Neumayr, *The Political Pope: How Pope Francis Is Delighting the Liberal Left and Abandoning Conservatives* (New York: Center Street, 2017).

[420] Thomas D. Williams, "Pope Francis: 'If I Speak of Islamic Violence, I Must Speak of Catholic Violence,'" *Breitbart*, August 1, 2016.

[421] Neumayr, *The Political Pope*, 154, 155–157.

Ironically, several examples of his indifferentism can be found in *Evangelii Gaudium*—ostensibly an exhortation to evangelize. Although the document urges us to spread the joy of the gospel, it provides a number of reasons why we shouldn't bother. The main reason given is that we already share so many ethical and spiritual values with other faiths that there's no point in converting non-Catholics.

Thus, *Evangelii Gaudium* leaves the impression that Jews shouldn't be evangelized (an impression that was later explicitly confirmed by the Vatican). Moreover, Francis also seems to exempt Muslims from any need to convert. As I wrote in *Crisis*:

> After reading *Evangelii Gaudium*'s positive assessment of Islam, one could be forgiven for concluding that the conversion of Muslims is not an urgent matter. And, indeed, there is no suggestion in the document that Muslims should be evangelized. At the most, Christians should dialogue with Muslims about their "shared beliefs."[422]

Rather than converting others, Francis seems more interested in learning from them. In *Evangelii Gaudium* and in numerous talks, he frequently extols the "richness" and "wisdom" of other cultures. Whereas Christ commanded His apostles, "Go therefore and make disciples of all nations," Francis's message is more along the lines of: "Go therefore and learn the wisdom of other cultures." Francis's attitude toward evangelization can perhaps be summed up in something he said to atheist journalist Eugenio Scalfari: "Proselytism is solemn nonsense."[423]

If this is the case, Pope Francis probably has no desire to convert the Muslims streaming into Europe. After all, like Evangelicals, Muslims can also "find Jesus in their community." Of course, it's not the same Jesus, but perhaps the resemblance is close enough for someone with scant interest in doctrinal differences. Exactly what, then, does Pope Francis have in

---

[422] William Kilpatrick, "Do Muslims Need the Gospel?" *Crisis Magazine*, May 17, 2018, https://www.crisismagazine.com/2018/muslims-need-gospel.

[423] Neumayr, *The Political Pope*, 152.

mind by encouraging mass migration into Europe? One possibility, as I suggested earlier, is that he envisions a kind of multicultural blending of religions. But for this to happen, it would be necessary for the respective faiths to dilute their doctrinal positions. Pope Francis seems quite willing to do this on the Catholic side. He has already made substantial concessions to the Chinese communist government on the appointment of bishops. He seems willing to alter Church teachings in order to build bridges with the LGBT "community" and other sexual revolutionaries. And, in general, he prefers to be guided by the prompting of the Spirit rather than by the teachings of the Church.

Moreover, he seems more concerned with political and humanitarian goals than with the goal of getting to heaven. As George Neumayr has noted in *The Political Pope*, when awarded the Charlemagne Prize, Francis "used his acceptance speech not to call for the restoration of Christianity, but for the spread of a 'new European humanism.'" And, as Francis sees it, the main obstacle to achieving these humanitarian goals is the fundamentalist Christians who refuse to integrate with Muslim migrants and, in general, fail to adapt to changing times. Perhaps he thinks that a flood of migrants will force fundamentalists to encounter the "other" and come to terms with their "otherness."

But what about fundamentalist Muslims? A harmonious world religion dedicated to humanitarian ends would require not only a watering-down of Christianity but also a considerable moderation of Islam. Both in terms of percentages and in absolute numbers, there are far more fundamentalist Muslims in the world than fundamentalist Christians. Francis has acknowledged the existence of fundamentalist Muslims, but he claims that they do not represent "authentic" Islam, and he seems to believe, contrary to much polling data, that they are only a small minority. "All religions have these little groups," he has said.[424]

---

[424] Reuters, "Pope Blasts Christian, Muslim Fundamentalists While Leaving Turkey," *Jerusalem Post*, December 2, 2014, https://www.jpost.com/printarticle.aspx?id=383405.

A Self-fulfilling Prophecy?

Whether or not he believes that fundamentalists are a small minority, he seems to have a rough strategy for facilitating the emergence of a more moderate Islam. This strategy is to claim that Islam is already—and always has been—a moderate and peaceful faith. Most notably, he asserted in *Evangelii Gaudium* that "authentic Islam and the proper reading of the Koran are opposed to every form of violence."

The strategy Francis seems to be employing is referred to by sociologists as a self-fulfilling prophecy. The idea is that if you express high expectations for others, they will endeavor to live up to the expectations and thus fulfill your "prophecy." But, according to Robert K. Merton, the sociologist who coined the term, "the self-fulfilling prophecy is, in the beginning, a *false* definition of the situation." But the false definition or assumption can evoke "a new behavior which makes the original false conception come *true.*"[425]

Sometimes self-fulfilling prophecies work, and sometimes they don't. A lot depends on the awareness of the subject. Young children are more susceptible to such influence, and adults who understand what is being attempted are less so. I recall reading an article on a radical Islamic website that accused Pope Francis of using just such a strategy. I don't remember if the author used the term "self-fulfilling prophecy," but he did complain that the pope was deliberately painting a false but pleasing picture of Islam in order to win Muslims over to a moderate view.

In any event, the self-fulfilling prophecy strategy seems an awfully slender reed upon which to stake the future of the world. For decades now, global leaders have been assuring us that "Islam" means "peace," that violence has nothing to do with Islam, and that the vast majority of Muslims are moderate. Yet most of the evidence suggests that the Western "prophecy" about Islam's pacific nature is not working. With

---

[425] Robert Merton, "The Self-Fulfilling Prophecy," *Antioch Review* (Summer 1948), https://www.jstor.org/stable/4609267?seq=1.

some notable exceptions, moderates have been losing ground, while fundamentalists are in the ascendancy.

Just as he has little anxiety about the wave of church closings, Francis seems to have little anxiety about the Islamization of Europe. Indeed, as evidenced by his encouragement of mass migration, he seems to have no objection to Islamization.

Either because he truly believes the false narrative that Islam is a religion of peace, or because he believes that the self-fulfilling prophecy strategy will create a more moderate Islam, Francis seems to be at peace with the fact that Islam is spreading rapidly.

Whatever he has in mind, it seems that Pope Francis is betting against the odds. Those two young Scandinavian women mentioned earlier took a similar gamble when they embarked on a camping trip in Morocco. They were betting their lives on the assumption that the whitewashed narrative of Islam that they had no doubt learned in school and university was the correct one. They lost the "bet." They had—to borrow a line from *Casablanca*—been "misinformed" about the situation in Morocco.

Whether Francis has been misinformed about Islam or whether he has adopted a strategy of misinformation, he is taking a huge gamble—not only with his own life, but with the lives of millions. When the religion of Muhammad meets the religion of indifferentism, which seems more likely to prevail?

Pope Francis and the Devil:
Misreading the Signs of the Times

Despite his penchant for theological innovation, Pope Francis seems to hold some fairly traditional beliefs about the devil. Here's an example from *Gaudete et Exsultate*:

> It is precisely the conviction that this malign power is present in our midst that enables us to understand how evil can at times have so much destructive force.... Hence, we should not think of the devil as a myth, a representation, a symbol, a figure of speech or an idea. This mistake would lead us to let down our guard, to grow careless and end up more vulnerable.[426]

It has been said that one of the devil's greatest achievements is to convince people he doesn't exist. Pope Francis hasn't fallen for that deception. He realizes that the devil is no myth. "When we let down our guard," says Francis, "he takes advantage of it to destroy our lives, our families and our communities."

But when it comes to the question of how the devil is most likely to take advantage of us, Pope Francis seems to deviate from the path of tradition. Indeed, he seems to think that the devil does much of his work by making use of traditional pieties. Thus, the pope has frequently rebuked

[426] Pope Francis, Apostolic Exhortation *Gaudete et Exsultate* (April 9, 2018), nos. 160, 161.

conservative critics of his silence over the sex-abuse scandals as being in league with Satan, the "Great Accuser."[427] On different occasions he has implied that they are "a pack of wild dogs," scandal-mongers, and even collaborators in crucifixion.

So, in the pope's estimation, traditional Catholics—i.e., those who are more likely to be shocked and outraged by drug-fueled sex orgies in the Vatican and the like—are doing the devil's work by exposing and criticizing such things. If they were good Christians, he seems to say, they would keep quiet and not add fuel to the scandals.

Who is most guilty of sowing division in the Church? Pope Francis seems to suggest that the greater blame lies not with the worldly bishop who takes the Sixth Commandment as a suggestion, but rather with the conscientious Catholic who takes it seriously and wants the hierarchy to take it seriously as well.

One can see a similar pattern in Pope Francis's response to the migration invasion of Europe and the resulting crime wave. He extends every consideration to those who are directly responsible for the trouble—namely, criminal migrants and their European enablers—while excoriating those Europeans who oppose the migration. For example, he once observed that those who fail to welcome migrants "are sowing violence, racial discrimination, and xenophobia."[428]

Thus, as in the sex-abuse cover-ups, we see the pope circling the wagons to protect those most to blame for the crisis, while taking aim at those who are trying to call attention to the crisis. It's a classic case of shooting the messenger.

---

[427] Dorothy Cummings McLean, "Pope Makes Yet Another Cryptic Reference to 'Great Accuser' amid Viganò Allegations," LifeSite News, September 18, 2018, https://www.lifesitenews.com/news/pope-shares-fourth-installment-of-his-great-accuser-homily-series.

[428] Pope Francis, "Migrants and Refugees: Men and Women in Search of Peace."

The Great Accuser and the Great Migration

We don't know what role the Great Accuser is playing in the matter of Muslim migration, but it's worth speculating on the question because Pope Francis has probably already speculated, and he has quite possibly reached the wrong conclusion.

If he thinks that the devil's strategy in regard to the sex-abuse scandal is to stir up "fundamentalist" Catholics into a frenzy of overreaction, what role does he assign the devil concerning the spread of Islam? Does Francis assume that Satan seeks to disrupt the harmony that would otherwise exist between Christians and the followers of Muhammad by hardening the hearts of fundamentalist Christians and other types of "fundamentalists," such as nationalists and xenophobes?

We know from his various statements over the years that Francis does worry about the activities of Satan. Indeed, the whole final section of *Gaudete et Exsultate* is concerned with "Spiritual Combat, Vigilance and Discernment." He speaks of the "constant battle" against the "temptations of the devil" and the "wiles of the devil," and he speaks also of the need for discernment so that we can know "if something comes from the Holy Spirit or if it stems from the spirit of the world or the spirit of the devil."[429]

But just how good is Francis (and his key advisers) when it comes to discernment? The record suggests that they are not particularly gifted in this respect. The trouble is, it's quite easy to confuse the Holy Spirit with the spirit of the times, and therefore one can be forgiven for thinking that the pope and his inner circle regularly fall into this trap. The spirit of the times declares that climate change should be our most urgent priority, and Francis and company second the motion. The spirit of the times requests that we take a more relaxed view of sex between consenting adults, and key Vatican advisers seem to be of the same mind. The spirit of the times tells us that the transgender agenda is as normal as apple pie, and leading bishops find themselves in accord. A few years ago, the spirit of the times dictated that the Iranians could be trusted 100 percent

[429] *Gaudete et Exsultate*, nos. 158, 162, 166.

not to violate the nuclear deal, and lo and behold, that also became the opinion of the Vatican.

So, when Pope Francis tells us that the Holy Spirit is prompting us to welcome millions of migrants from Islamic lands, Catholics are justified in wondering whether he hasn't once again confused the Holy Spirit with the spirit of the times. The fact that the Church's stance on Muslim immigration coincides so closely with that of so many secular leaders is cause for suspicion. So is the fact that both European leaders and Vatican leaders are agreed—contrary to a mountain of evidence—that Islam is a religion of peace. It sometimes seems that the Vatican's discernment meter is broken, for it always points in the direction of the prevailing winds.

To his credit, Francis tries to discern the devil's machinations—"the wiles of the devil"—but on the debit side, he seems to assume that the devil tends to strike from the "right"—by manipulating "fundamentalists" and "rigid" traditionalists. The idea that the devil might strike from the left by manipulating liberals such as Francis himself seems not to have occurred to him. Yet that is what seems to be happening. The policies Francis pursues in regard to Islam and immigration—policies that assume a benign interpretation of Islam and its aims—would seem to mesh nicely with the devil's plans.

A Devil's-Eye View

Granted that this business of discerning the devil's motives is a tricky one, let's nevertheless try to look at the matter from the devil's point of view.

To begin with, let's suppose that his main goal is to destroy Christ's Church. If that is so, then a migration invasion of Europe would suit his purposes very well. Since Islam has been a perennial enemy of Christianity, its implantation in Europe—once the heart of Christendom—would be a great victory for him. Islam has already had considerable success in exterminating Christianity in the Middle East and North Africa. The subjugation of Europe would do much to strengthen the claim that the religion of Allah is the true religion. And it would set the stage for the collapse of Christianity in other parts of the world.

Yet Francis's policies seem to play into the devil's hands. Against all the best interests of the faith he is supposed to protect, Francis has energetically promoted the migration of Muslims and, thus, of the Islamic faith into Europe. The only scenario in which this would make sense would be if Europe were a vibrantly Christian continent capable of assimilating masses of Muslims and even converting them. But that is not the case. Christianity has been dying in Europe for decades, and it has been further weakened and discredited by the recent sex-abuse scandals. If anyone is to be converted, it seems likely that it will be the few remaining Christians in Europe (along with a great many secularists).

Naturally, the devil's plan of action would have to be somewhat subtle since a direct invasion by Islamic armies would be unlikely to succeed. A gradual, slowly-boiled-frog approach would have a much better chance of success. It would encounter little resistance, and it would appeal to the sense of self-satisfaction that European elites take in displays of tolerance. On the other hand, it's difficult to see why Satan would want to stir up the "xenophobic" alarmists and thus risk Europeans' being prematurely alerted to the dangers. Continued complacency would better serve his purposes.

From a Satanic point of view, it would also help immensely if the campaign for the Islamization of Europe could be painted in a noble light. If the devil could somehow prompt European elites to promise that immigration would be beneficial in solving both the labor shortage problem and the welfare shortage problem, people would be more willing to adjust themselves to the new situation. If, on top of that, the pope could be induced to give his imprimatur to the project, so much the better. Of course, in ordinary times the devil wouldn't set his hopes so high, but—*mirabile dictu*—this is exactly what Pope Francis has, in effect, done.

In *Gaudete et Exsultate,* Pope Francis says we must "be attentive" and be mindful of scriptural cautions to keep "our lamps lit" and "keep awake." He also reminds us that "even Satan disguises himself as an angel of light."[430] All very good advice. But is the pope following it?

There is, of course, no way of knowing for certain if Satan has taken a hand in the spread of Islam into Europe. But if he has, he has been very successful in disguising it as an "angel of light" project. In fact, most of the work of sanctifying the migration has been done for him by numerous clerics, both Catholic and Protestant. Pope Francis, in particular, has drawn a halo around the immigration project— suggesting not only that migrants will enrich European society but also that the welcomers would be acting in a Christlike way. More than "angels of light," the pope has consistently portrayed migrants as representatives of Christ.

The devil, as Francis points out, is a master of disguise. He can appear as an angel of light. He can quote Scripture. And he is certainly not above taking advantage of a Christian's best instincts—particularly the impulse to charity. But, as I have noted elsewhere:

> One has to wonder about charitable impulses that facilitate the takeover of Europe by a decidedly anti-Christian religious ideology. How charitable is it to consign Europeans, their children, and their grandchildren to a life of bloodshed and civil war, or else to a life of subservient dhimmitude such as Christians now experience in many parts of the Muslim world?[431]

It would be a great triumph for Satan if he could convince Christians that they are doing the will of God when, in fact, they are carrying out his own agenda.

---

[430] Ibid., nos. 164, 165.

[431] William Kilpatrick, "A Dark-Forces Assault on the Church?" *Crisis Magazine,* October 2, 2017, https://www.crisismagazine.com/2017/dark-forces-assault-church.

The Holy Spirit or the Spirit of the Devil?

In speaking against opponents of mass migration, Pope Francis said, "The Holy Spirit will help us to keep an attitude of trusting openness that will allow us to overcome every barrier and scale every wall."[432] It seems, however, that Francis should give consideration to the possibility that it is not the Holy Spirit who wants to open the floodgates of migration into Europe, but the "spirit of the devil." After all, the way the immigration issue is currently being framed by Catholic leaders is exactly how one would expect a supremely intelligent but "malign power" to frame it. He would present the "welcoming" response as a good and noble act of Christian charity, he would quote the words of Christ, and he would label opponents of immigration as unchristian. As I wrote previously:

> The Church's welcoming response to Islam and Islamic migration can be looked upon as a shining example of Christian charity, or it can be looked upon as an example of stubborn foolishness and presumption in the face of a fast-spreading evil. It's a devilishly complicated situation. And that should make us wonder if the devil himself isn't intimately involved in it.[433]

Rather than let down our guard, Pope Francis suggests that we need to practice discernment:

> We must remember that prayerful discernment must be born of a readiness to listen: to the Lord and to others, and to reality itself, which always challenges us in new ways.

This, too, is good advice, but once again we need to ask if Francis is following it. Does he manifest a "readiness to listen"? It's becoming obvious

---

[432] Thomas D. Williams, "Pope Francis Says Concern for 'Cultural Identity' Doesn't Justify Opposition to Mass Migration," *Breitbart*, September 22, 2017, https://www.breitbart.com/europe/2017/09/22/pope-francis-says-concern-for-cultural-identity-doesnt-justify-opposition-to-mass-migration/.

[433] Kilpatrick, "A Dark-Forces Assault on the Church?"

that Francis does not listen to his critics. He ignores them, fails to respond to their sincere concerns, demotes them, and, in some cases, criticizes them harshly. Does he listen to "reality itself"? Well, that's a matter of judgment. But as I and others have argued, he does seem to be ignoring the reality of the worsening situation in Europe. Just as important, Francis seems to be engaging in wishful thinking about the history and nature of Islam. His declaration in *Evangelii Gaudium* that "authentic Islam and the proper reading of the Koran are opposed to every form of violence" is about as far removed from reality as one can get. Instead of allowing himself to be challenged by realities, he seems content to be guided by pleasant but unexamined narratives.

In *Gaudete et Exsultate*, Pope Francis says: "[Christ] asks us to examine what is within us ... and what takes place all around us—'the signs of the times'" (168). But what exactly are the signs of the times that might lead us to believe that Islam has reformed itself and is now interested not in conquest but only in harmonious encounter and dialogue? Every day, in Europe, Egypt, Nigeria, Somalia, Syria, Gaza, Pakistan, the Philippines, Iran, Turkey, the Central African Republic, and elsewhere, the signs of the times are saying quite the opposite. Figuratively speaking, they are billboard-size signs lit up in neon. Yet they don't seem to figure at all into the pope's process of discernment. Instead, he studiously ignores them.

Pope Francis has not been very discerning about the men he has elevated to key positions in the Church. Why should we suppose that he has correctly discerned the promptings of the Holy Spirit in other vital matters?

23

Last Chance

Pope Francis has often spoken of the importance of paying attention to the signs of the times. But the signs being displayed by Islam are much the same as the signs it has displayed throughout its 1,400 years of aggression; and now they are flashing red alert.

Many in our society are standing on the sidelines perhaps waiting for some more definitive sign. It's very possible, of course, that the sign they are looking for has already appeared. And that is the subject of these final essays.

A Turning Point in History

I dare say that most people who have read history would like to think that if they had been present at some pivotal point in history, they would have chosen the right side — with the Allies and against the Axis, with Wilberforce and against the slave traders, with the Romans and against the child-sacrificing Carthaginians.

If I had lived back then, we tell ourselves, I would have fought with the right side, no matter the odds.

Well, now's your chance. Because it looks very much as though we are at one of those pivotal moments — possibly at one of the major turning points in history, and probably one of the most dangerous. We tend to think that historical turning points generally involve a breakthrough to a higher plane — a turn for the better rather than for the worse. But that's not always the case. Sometimes, the pendulum of history swings backward and slices off centuries of progress. The turning point at which we now stand threatens to cast us back more than a thousand years to some of history's darkest days. We may soon be fighting for things we thought had been secured for all time — basics such as freedom of religion, freedom of speech, and even freedom from enslavement.

The turning point I refer to is the civilizational struggle between Islam and the West (acknowledging, of course, that much of the Western tradition has been adopted by people who live outside the traditional geographic boundaries of the West). On a larger view, the struggle can more accurately be described as a conflict between Christianity and Islam, because if the West loses its Christian soul, it will also lose the ability and the will to defend its freedoms.

Of course, some people deny that there is any "clash of civilizations." All religions and all cultures want the same thing, they say, and they assure us that the tiny handful of troublemakers in the Muslim world do not represent the vast majority.

But time and again, polls have shown that at least a majority of Muslims want to be ruled by sharia law—a throwback to the harsh legal system that developed in seventh-century Arabia. Contrary to "enlightened" expectations, it turns out that a great many Muslims in a great many places favor cruel and unusual punishments for theft, adultery, blasphemy, and apostasy.

That's what they want for fellow Muslims who go astray. But if you're a non-Muslim, you don't have to go astray in order to be punished. The mere existence of Jews, Christians, and other minorities is considered an affront by many Muslims. As a result, discrimination against non-Muslims is endemic in the Muslim world. It can't be blamed on a tiny minority of bigots, because just about everyone—including police, government officials, employers, and next-door neighbors—expects unbelievers to know their place.

Jews and Christians got the message a long time ago. That's why there are so few of them left in places that used to be their homelands—in the Middle East, North Africa, and Turkey. For those who don't leave voluntarily, the daily low-level persecution sometimes breaks out into organized violence. That was the case in the 1914–1923 genocide against Armenian, Assyrian, and Greek Christians living in the Ottoman Empire, in the 1933 massacre of Assyrian Christians in Simele, Iraq, and in the 1941 Farhud (pogrom) against the Jewish population of Baghdad. In more recent years we've witnessed the slaughter of Christians and Yazidis by ISIS in Syria and Northern Iraq, the numerous massacres of Christians carried out by Boko Haram in Northern Nigeria and by al-Shabaab in Somalia and Kenya, and the frequent attacks on Coptic Christian churches in Egypt.

"Witnessed" may be too strong a word. Many in the West simply noted these atrocities and then continued to go about their business as though nothing had happened. But, to paraphrase Trotsky, "You may not be interested in the clash of civilizations, but the clash of civilizations is interested in you." For a long time, people in the United States and in Europe were able to ignore the barbarities in Africa, Iraq, and elsewhere. But then the clash of civilization moved north and into Europe. When the "clash" made its appearance in the streets of Paris, in Christmas markets in Germany, and in a concert hall in Manchester, only the willfully blind could fail to notice.

But, apparently, there are a lot of those. In Europe, America, and Canada, the elites in government, media, academia, and even the Church continue to insist that there is no clash. That's true in a sense. You can't have a clash if only one side is fighting. And thus far, the pushback against jihad—both of the armed variety and the stealth variety—has been feeble. The elites won't even contemplate the obvious first step—tight restrictions on Muslim immigration.

Moreover, they do everything they can to cover up the clash. Police aren't allowed to report on the extent of immigrant crime; news media won't carry stories about the crimes unless they are exceptionally violent, outspoken critics of Islam or immigration are brought before magistrates; and ordinary citizens who post "Islamophobic" remarks on Facebook are visited by police.

The West's self-imposed blindness to what is happening forces us to another observation about the historical turning point that is now developing. The battle is not simply a civilizational struggle between Islam and the West; it also involves a war within Western civilization itself. Many of our Western institutions now reject the Western heritage, and many of them have effectively taken the side of Islam.

On almost any issue involving a conflict between Islam and traditional Western values, the schools, the media, the courts, and many of the churches stand with Islam. They may not look at it that way. They may rationalize their actions as nothing more than a defense of the civil rights of Muslims. Many of them are likely unfamiliar with the concept of stealth jihad. But they are facilitating it just the same. The main form this facilitation takes is the suppression of any bad news about Islam. Thus, in 2012, Congress refused to investigate Muslim Brotherhood penetration of government agencies,[434] and in the same year, the FBI, the Pentagon, and other security agencies bowed to Muslim pressure and purged their training materials of any suggestion that Islamic terrorists were motivated by Islamic ideology.[435] More recently, media giants such as Google, Facebook,[436] and Twitter have taken to stifling the voices of those who speak out against Islamic oppression.

One could cite numerous other instances of this near-suicidal impulse to side with our ideological enemies: the judges who block restrictions on Muslim immigration, the bishops who sign up with the deceptive anti-"Islamophobia" campaign, and the Obama administration's gift of billions of dollars to Iran.[437]

With a few exceptions, such as the bishops, these enablers of cultural jihad are secular progressives. Despite their moniker, however, progressives can be decidedly regressive. They champion abortion at every stage of pregnancy—a practice that suggests that the distance between us and the child-sacrificing Carthaginians is not as great as we may think.

---

[434] "Congressional Leaders Call for Investigations of Muslim Brotherhood Penetration of the Obama Administration," Center for Security Policy, June 15, 2012, https://www.centerforsecuritypolicy.org/2012/06/15/congressional-leaders-call-for-investigations-of-muslim-brotherhood-penetration-of-the-obama-administration-2/.

[435] Jordan Schachtel, "Inside Mueller's PC purge of Counter-Terror Training at the FBI," *Conservative Review*, November 27, 2017, https://www.conservativereview.com/news/inside-muellers-pc-purge-of-counter-terror-material-at-the-fbi/.

[436] Robert Spencer, "Facebook Censors, Suspends and Threatens Voice of Europe for Criticizing Migration," *Jihad Watch*, April 9, 2018, https://www.jihadwatch.org/2018/04/facebook-censors-suspends-and-threatens-voice-of-europe-for-criticizing-migration.

[437] David Harsanyi, "Yes, Obama Helped Fund the Iranian Regime," *National Review*, January 8, 2020, https://www.nationalreview.com/corner/yes-obama-helped-fund-the-iranian-regime/.

Progressives promise to pull us into the future, yet they often act to drag us into the past. Several progressive voices now want severe restrictions on freedom of speech. This has already happened on college campuses where hate speech codes effectively stifle free expression. The average college student today has no more freedom of speech than a serving woman in the court of Cleopatra. The "enlightened" progressives who run Google, YouTube, and Facebook don't have much use for freedom of expression either. Critics of Islam are particularly liable to be restricted, suspended, or banned by these Internet monopolies.

Here is the situation in brief. We stand at one of the major turning points of history. Two powerful forces for regression threaten to drag us into a dark past. On the one hand, Islamists want to bring back the subjugation of women, female genital mutilation, sex slavery, beheadings, and dhimmitude for nonbelievers. On the other hand, their high-tech progressive enablers are decimating non-Muslim populations by promoting contraception and abortion, while controlling the flow of information about Islam using speech-suppressing strategies that no absolute monarch could have imagined.

If you've ever wished that you could have been around at one of history's decisive moments, your wish has been granted. And if you've ever wished to be on the side of the beleaguered underdog, that wish also has been granted. The forces of regression are in the ascendancy, and Christian civilization is in retreat.

Now is a time for choosing. I won't say the choice is clear. Much has been done to muddy the waters—to make sure that we remain confused and complacent. Moreover, few things are ever completely clear when you're caught in the middle of events. For many Jews in the early 1940s, their situation became completely clear only when they were hauled off to concentration camps. For many Americans in 1941, the world situation became clear only with the attack on Pearl Harbor. Those who wait for absolute clarity often find that they have waited too long.

Although the means of obfuscating the truth are far more sophisticated now than they were in the 1940s, we still have a marked advantage over our counterparts in that era. We have far more historical perspective than was available to them. For example, when the Nazis were building up their military machine in the 1930s, there was no thousand-year history of Nazi aggression to serve as a warning. The Nazi party was little more than a decade old, and Hitler had not come to power until 1933. There was some excuse for those who naïvely gave the Nazis the benefit of the doubt.

We, on the other hand, have very little excuse for ignoring the signs of the time. For those who study history, they are very familiar signs. That's because Islam has a 1,400-year history of aggression. And the battle plan has been remarkably consistent over time—even including migration as a means of invasion. The latest installment of that 1,400-year-old plan for world conquest in the name of Allah has already begun. We are witnessing a remarkable expansion of Islam into every corner of the world—Africa, Australia, the Philippines, China, Russia, Europe, and North and South America.

Only this time the forces of Islam are being aided and abetted by the very powerful forces of leftist progressivism. Earlier, I mentioned some of the ways leftists defend Islam. Here's another. In 2017, after delivering a lecture in Iceland on the jihad threat, author Robert Spencer was poisoned by a leftist,[438] then denied proper testing and treatment by an emergency room doctor (also a leftist ideologue). After more than a year has passed, police had still taken no action against the suspected poisoner, and the Icelandic Medical Ethics Committee has taken no action against the derelict doctor.

Committed leftists and committed Islamists: it's a hard combination to beat. Both believe very firmly in what they believe. Unless Christians believe very firmly that they must be stopped, both will continue to expand. We stand at a decisive point in history. Choosing to stay on the sidelines will serve only to increase the odds that these regressive forces will triumph.

---

[438] Robert Spencer, "Leftist Privilege: Poisoned in Iceland A Year Ago, No One Arrested," *FrontPage Mag*, May 31, 2018, https://archives.frontpagemag.com/fpm/leftist-privilege-poisoned-iceland-year-ago-no-one-robert-spencer/.

Our Lady of Victory

In 1952, Bishop Fulton Sheen wrote that Mary, Our Lady of Fatima, was the key to converting Muslims.[439] Bishop Sheen believed that the devotion Muslims already had toward Mary would eventually lead them to her divine Son. Moreover, Our Lady of Fatima would have a special appeal to Muslims because she appeared in a town that was named after the daughter of Muhammad, who according to her father, "has the highest place in heaven after the Virgin Mary."

Judging by subsequent events, Bishop Sheen may have been overly optimistic, but those subsequent events also seem to suggest that nothing short of a heavenly intervention will turn Islam away from its goal of conquering the planet. Fulton Sheen may have underestimated the difficulty of converting Muslims, but the strategies for moderating Islam proposed by current world leaders border on the delusional. All the efforts of secular leaders to appease Islam have only made Islam stronger and the West weaker. Many Christian leaders seem to suffer from the same delusions about Islam. Despite all their efforts to "dialogue" with Islam, to declare "solidarity" with Islam, and to join the fight against "Islamophobia," persecution of Christians by Muslims has accelerated dramatically. The position of Christians vis-à-vis Islam has deteriorated

---

[439] Fulton J. Sheen, *The World's First Love* (New York: Image Books, 1956), chap. 17.

so badly since 1952 that it may well require a miraculous intervention to set things right.

With that in mind, let's take a closer look at Bishop Sheen's thesis. The first question that comes to mind was raised by Msgr. Charles Pope in a 2012 article.[440] He asked, "Do Muslims today still manifest the reverence to Mary that Sheen described in 1952?" The answer is "probably not." Although it's difficult to come by statistics, there are reasons to believe that the Islam of Sheen's era is no longer with us. Sheen lived at a time when the militant side of Islam was kept firmly in check by secular rulers. Islam's forward momentum had come to a halt, and the power of the imams was greatly reduced. According to Ali Allawi, a former Iraqi cabinet minister:

> At that time, the 1950s, secularism was ascendant among the political, cultural, and intellectual elites of the Middle East. It appeared to be only a matter of time before Islam would lose whatever hold it still had on the Muslim world.[441]

If the upper classes were free to embrace secularism, the common people were freer to explore other religions. Under the circumstances, it's likely that many Muslims may have cultivated a devotion to Mary. In many parts of the Muslim world, folk-religion forms of Islam flourished—syncretic blends of Islam and other faiths. This was particularly true in Africa and India—the two regions cited by Sheen as evidence of Muslim devotion to Our Lady.

But times change. The situation that prevailed in Sheen's time is rapidly disappearing. It now appears that the Islam that Sheen was familiar with was an aberration—a brief departure from the path laid down by Muhammad: an interregnum followed by a revival of militant,

---

[440] Msgr. Charles Pope, "Our Lady of Fatima and the 'Muslim Connection,'" Community in Mission, May 15, 2013, http://blog.adw.org/2013/05/our-lady-of-fatima-and-the-muslim-connection/.

[441] Ali A. Allawi, "Islamic Civilization in Peril," Chronicle Review, June 29, 2009, https://www.chronicle.com/article/Islamic-Civilization-in-Peril/46964.

supremacist, intolerant Islam. Judging by the harsh treatment accorded to Christians in the Muslim world today, Muslims who display a devotion to Mary might well be putting themselves in danger.

But isn't Mary held in high esteem in the Koran? As Bishop Sheen pointed out, there are more references to Mary in the Koran than to any other woman. In sura 3:42 of the Koran, the angels say "O Mary! Allah hath chosen thee and purified thee—chosen thee above the women of all nations."

The Koran's respectful treatment of Mary seems promising. But there are a few difficulties to take note of. From the Islamic point of view, Mary, like Jesus, was a Muslim, not a Jew or a Christian. She is important because she is the mother of a Muslim prophet. Most significantly, she is not the Mother of God. In fact, the suggestion that she is, is, from an Islamic perspective, a blasphemy of the highest order. Tellingly, the Koranic description of the Annunciation and the birth of Jesus is followed by an admonition: "Such was Jesus son of Mary. That is the whole truth, which they [Christians] still doubt. God forbid that He Himself should beget a Son!" (19:34–35).

So, the tribute to Mary is capped with a slap-down of Christian beliefs about Mary and Jesus. Why, then, is Mary in the Koran? As I've suggested elsewhere,[442] it's probable that she is there for the same reason that Jesus is in the Koran—namely, to deny the divinity of Jesus. Muhammad included stories from the New Testament and the Old Testament in the Koran because he wanted to attract Christians and Jews living in Arabia to his new religion. But it was also necessary for him to discredit the Christian claim that Jesus is divine. Why? Because if Jesus is who Christians say He is, then there is no need for a new revelation and a new prophet. In short, there is no need for Muhammad. Thus, when Jesus speaks in the Koran or is spoken of, it is often for the purpose of establishing that He was just a man.

In the Koran, Jesus is almost always referred to as "Jesus son of Mary." This is done not to elevate Mary but to demote Jesus. It is a reminder that

[442] Kilpatrick, *Christianity, Islam and Atheism.*

Jesus is not the Son of God, but simply another prophet. Here's a typical passage: "Christ, the Son of Mary, was no more than a Messenger; many were the messengers that passed away before him" (5:75). This passage is followed by another dig at Christians: "See how Allah doth make his Signs clear to them [Christians]; yet see in what ways they are deluded away from the truth!" (5:75). Many Catholics see the similarities between Christianity and Islam as a sign of hope for peace between the two faiths. Yet the similarities are there because Muhammad had no qualms about borrowing stories from the Gospels and then claiming them as part of the revelation he received from Allah. It seems that Muhammad's main motive for including Jesus and Mary in his religion was to co-opt them for his own purposes.

Does this mean that Mary is to play no role in the conversion of Muslims? No. In fact, it appears that Mary has already been active in the battle to resist the advance of Islam. In 1571, in one of the great naval battles of history, Catholic forces decisively defeated a larger Muslim fleet and thus prevented an Islamic invasion of Europe. The victory at Lepanto is often attributed to Mary's intercession. Prior to the battle, Pope Saint Pius V asked all Europeans to pray the Rosary for victory. And on board the Christian ships, every fighter was given a rosary. The flagship of Don Juan of Austria carried a banner with an image of Christ crucified; Gianandrea Doria, one of the admirals, carried an image of Our Lady of Guadalupe.[443] October 7, the date of the Christian victory, was thereafter declared the Feast of "Mary, Queen of Victory."

The image of Our Lady of Guadalupe entrusted to Admiral Doria was one of five copies that were touched to the original tilma. The image itself recalls a verse from Revelation: "And a great portent appeared in heaven, a woman clothed with the sun, with the moon under her feet" (Rev. 12:1).

---

[443] Fr. George W. Rutler, "The Banners of Lepanto," *Crisis Magazine*, October 7, 2016, https://www.crisismagazine.com/2016/the-banners-of-lepanto.

The moon in the image is a crescent moon—the symbol of the serpent god Quetzalcoatl that was worshipped by the Aztecs. Mary's foot resting on the moon is a symbol of her victory over the pagan god. Up until the revelation of the image to Juan Diego, the Aztecs had been highly resistant to conversion. In the ten years following, some nine million converted to Christianity.

The crescent moon is also, of course, the chief symbol of Islam. When Admiral Doria carried the image of Our Lady of Guadalupe into battle, he undoubtedly understood that the image could also be interpreted as a symbol of victory over Islam.

"Our Lady of Victory." The title reminds us that spiritual battles can have a physical component. The victory at Lepanto can, in a sense, be considered part of a larger spiritual battle, yet it came at great physical cost. More than forty thousand men lost their lives—more than in any other battle in history (it should be added that fifteen thousand Christians—galley slaves of the Ottoman Turks—were freed).

I bring up the Battle of Lepanto because in reading Fulton Sheen and others with a similar outlook, one can get the impression that the conversion of Muslims will be a gradual, almost painless process. Consider this excerpt from *The World's First Love*:

> Missionaries in the future will, more and more, see that their apostolate among the Moslems will be successful in the measure that they preach Our Lady of Fatima. . . . Because the Moslems have devotion to Mary, our missionaries should be satisfied merely to expand and develop that devotion, with the full realization that Our Blessed Lady will carry the Moslems the rest of the way to her Divine Son.[444]

Living as he did in the sleepy-time-Islam era of King Farouk and the Shah of Iran, Sheen might understandably have underestimated the difficulty of the task. What is less understandable is that many of our contemporary

---

[444] Sheen, *The World's First Love*, 174.

sleepyhead prelates still live mentally in that bygone era when Islam and Christianity seemed so much closer to each other than they really are. These clerics seem to think that Muslims can be made to see the light through a painless process of interreligious dialogue. Some seem to think that Muslims already have the light and are therefore not in need of conversion.

But the message of Our Lady of Fatima is all about the necessity of conversion. And, unfortunately, Muslims seem almost as resistant to conversion as the Aztecs were prior to the appearance of Our Lady of Guadalupe. When asked her name by Juan Diego, the Lady included in her response in the Aztec language the words *te coatlaxopeuh*, which is variously interpreted to mean "one who crushes the head of the stone serpent,"[445] or "she who has dominion over serpents."[446]

The words remind us of God's words to the serpent in the Garden of Eden:

> I will put enmity between you and the woman,
> and between your seed and her seed;
> he shall bruise your head
> and you shall bruise his heel. (Gen. 3:15)

In the image, the head of the stone serpent is symbolically crushed by Our Lady of Guadalupe. She is in the business of crushing serpents and releasing people from religions of blood sacrifice. Mary's work is still cut out for her. The fastest-growing religion in the world today is a religion that demands blood sacrifice, and its symbol is a crescent moon. We can comfort ourselves with the thought that Muslims practice a religion similar in some respects to Christianity, or we can concern ourselves that they are caught up in the coils of a dangerous belief system. I suspect that the view from heaven is closer to the latter perspective.

---

[445] "Our Lady and Islam: Heaven's Peace Plan," University of Dayton Blogs, https://udayton.edu/blogs/imri/_resources/weekly-features/2015-01-19/ Our%20Lady%20and%20Islam%20Heavens%20Peace%20Plan.pdf.

[446] Gloria Anzaldua, *Borderlands / La Frontera: The New Mestiza* (San Francisco, CA: Aunt Lute Books, 2012), 27.

Mary will need some help, of course. Catholics ought to pray for the conversion of Islam just as they once prayed for the conversion of Russia. Catholics also need to inform themselves. If Muslims are ever to be converted away from Islam in large numbers, Catholics will need to gain a more realistic perspective on Islam. I have suggested that Bishop Sheen was overly optimistic about the prospects for Muslim conversions, but he was also a realist—far more realistic about Islam than many of today's bishops. Consider this passage from his chapter on "Mary and the Moslems":

> At the present time, the hatred of the Moslem countries against the West is becoming a hatred against Christianity itself.... There is still grave danger that the temporal power of Islam may return and, with it, the menace that it may shake off a West which has ceased to be Christian, and affirm itself as a great anti-Christian world power.[447]

"Hatred against Christianity," "menace," "anti-Christian world power." Very few bishops today would dare to use that kind of language about Islam. Yet, today there is a much greater warrant for that view than there was in Sheen's day. Sheen was optimistic about the chances for Muslim conversion, but he also had fears about Islam's return as an anti-Christian power. At this time, it looks as though his fears are being realized. Some of the blame for that rests on the shoulders of Catholic leaders who have adopted an attitude of wishful thinking about Islam. If Sheen's hopes are ever to be realized, they need to discard their gauzy view of Islam and replace it with a realistic perspective.

They could start by focusing less on the supposed similarities between Islam and Christianity, and more on the differences. They might, for instance, concentrate on the fact that, for a growing number of young Muslim men, the only virgins they are devoted to are the seventy-two that Allah has reserved for them in paradise.

---

[447] Sheen, *The World's First Love*, 172.

Acknowledgments

The essays in this book were previously published in the following publications.

1. Wake-Up Calls

   Will Sri Lanka Be a Wake-up Call for the West?: *Catholic World Report*, April 28, 2019

   Why You Should Worry about Virgins in Paradise: *FrontPage*, December 6, 2016

2. Appeasement

   On the Civilizational Struggle with Islam: *Crisis Magazine*, April 4, 2017

   The Corrosion of the British Spirit: *Crisis Magazine*, March 27, 2018

3. Stealth Jihad

   Western Self-Hatred Makes Jihad Possible: *Crisis Magazine*, August 29, 2016

   Jihad Never Sleeps: *Crisis Magazine*, August 29, 2017

4. Political Correctness

   Playing Along with the Lie: *Catholic World Report*, July 1, 2015

   PC in Orlando and in Our Future: *Crisis Magazine*, June 20, 2016

9. Comic Interlude

Groundhog Day—Jihad Version: *The Catholic Thing*, April 14, 2017

Ali in Wonderland: *Crisis Magazine*, August 14, 2017

10. Muhammad And The Koran

Time for Catholics to Reconsider Islam and the "Prophet" Muhammad?: *Catholic World Report*, September 8, 2016

Is the Koran a Literary Masterpiece?: *Crisis*, August 10, 2018

A "Common Word" Versus Common Sense: *Crisis Magazine*, January 29, 2018

11. 'Tis the Season

The Spirit of Christmas and the Spirit of Islam: *Catholic World Report*, December 21, 2014

Life Lessons from Christmas Carols: *Crisis Magazine*, December 22, 2017

12. Misunderstanding Islam

The Quran Is a "Sacrament"?: *National Catholic Register*, May 22, 2015

Time to Tell the Truth about Islam: *National Catholic Register*, August 30, 2015

Islam—The View from Disney Country: *Crisis Magazine*, May 4, 2017

13. The Next Scandal

As the Church Reels, Is an Even Larger Scandal Building?: *Catholic World Report*, August 29, 2018

Islam and the Church: Have Islamists Hijacked the Discussion?: *Catholic World Report*, June 14, 2017

The Misplaced Priorities of Youth Synod Organizers: *Crisis Magazine*, October 10, 2018

About the Author

William Kilpatrick is the author of several books about cultural and religious issues, including *Christianity, Islam, and Atheism: The Struggle for the Soul of the West*; *The Politically Incorrect Guide to Jihad*; and the best-selling *Why Johnny Can't Tell Right from Wrong*. Professor Kilpatrick's articles on cultural and educational topics have appeared in *First Things*, *Policy Review*, *FrontPage*, and various scholarly journals. His articles on Islam have appeared in *Crisis Magazine*, *Catholic World Report*, *The Catholic Thing*, *National Catholic Register*, and other publications. His weekly commentary on current issues can be found on his website, turningpointproject.com.

CRISIS Publications

Sophia Institute Press awards the privileged title "CRISIS Publications" to a select few of our books that address contemporary issues at the intersection of politics, culture, and the Church with clarity, cogency, and force and that are also destined to become all-time classics.

CRISIS Publications are *direct*, explaining their principles briefly, simply, and clearly to Catholics in the pews, on whom the future of the Church depends. The time for ambiguity or confusion is long past.

CRISIS Publications are *contemporary*, born of our own time and circumstances and intended to become significant statements in current debates, statements that serious Catholics cannot ignore, regardless of their prior views.

CRISIS Publications are *classical*, addressing themes and enunciating principles that are valid for all ages and cultures. Readers will turn to them time and again for guidance in other days and different circumstances.

CRISIS Publications are *spirited*, entering contemporary debates with gusto to clarify issues and demonstrate how those issues can be resolved in a way that enlivens souls and the Church.

We welcome engagement with our readers on current and future CRISIS Publications. Please pray that this imprint may help to resolve the crises embroiling our Church and society today.